MAFIA REPUBLIC

Italy's Criminal Curse: Cosa Nostra,
Camorra and 'Ndrangheta from
1946 to the present

John Dickie

SCEPTRE

...Great Britain in 2013 by Sceptre
...print of Hodder & Stoughton
An Hachette UK company

First published in paperback in 2014

5

Maps by Clifford Webb

A CIP catalogue record for this title is available from the British Library

ISBN 978 1 444 72641 1

Printed and bound by CPI Group (UK) Ltd, Croydon, CR0 4YY

Hodder & Stoughton policy is to use papers that are natural, renewable and
recyclable products and made from wood grown in sustainable forests. The logging
and manufacturing processes are expected to conform to the environmental
regulations of the country of origin.

Hodder & Stoughton Ltd
338 Euston Road
London NW1 3BH

www.hodder.co.uk

Dedicated to the memory of Gilbert Dickie (1922–2011)

Contents

Mondragone

Casal di Principe

San Cipriano d'Aversa

Aversa

Giugliano

Marano

Pianura

NAPLES

Torre Annunziata

Castellammare di Stabia

Sorrento

Terra di Lavoro

Caserta

Nola

Acerra

Pomigliano

Cercola

Vesuvius

Pompeii

Scafati

Sarno

Avellino

Montevergine

Salerno

Tyrrhenian
Sea

ITALY

CAMPANIA

CAMPANIA

0   20km

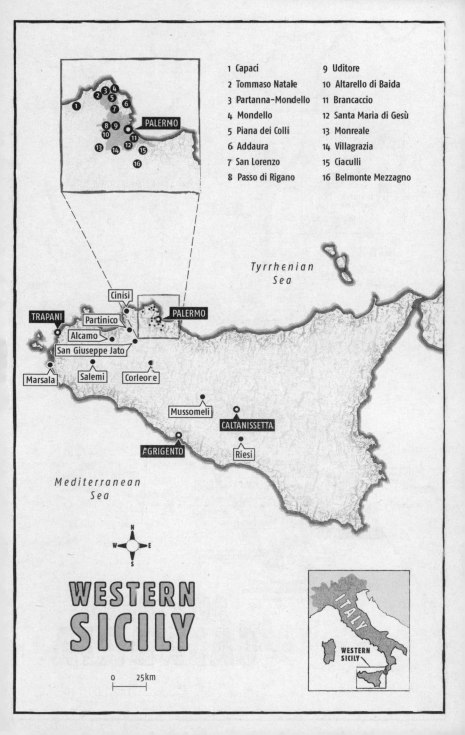

1 Capaci
2 Tommaso Natale
3 Partanna-Mondello
4 Mondello
5 Piana dei Colli
6 Addaura
7 San Lorenzo
8 Passo di Rigano

9 Uditore
10 Altarello di Baida
11 Brancaccio
12 Santa Maria di Gesù
13 Monreale
14 Villagrazia
15 Ciaculli
16 Belmonte Mezzagno

PALERMO

Tyrrhenian Sea

Cinisi
TRAPANI
Partinico
Alcamo
San Giuseppe Jato
PALERMO
Marsala
Salemi
Corleone
Mussomeli
CALTANISSETTA
AGRIGENTO
Riesi

Mediterranean Sea

N
W E
S

WESTERN SICILY

0   25km

ITALY
WESTERN SICILY

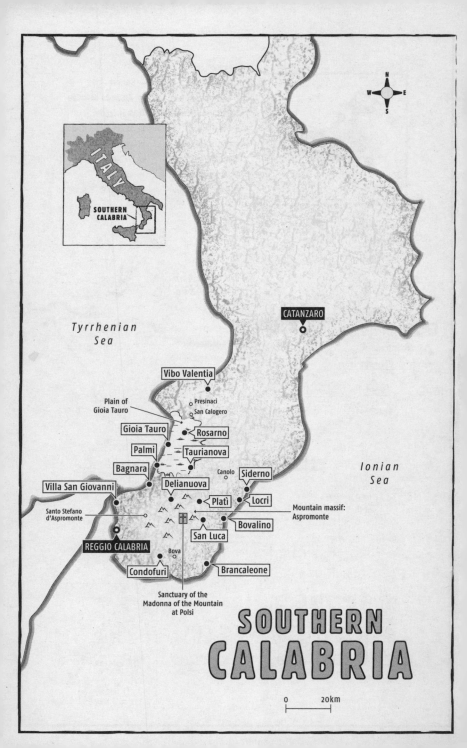

ITALY

SOUTHERN
CALABRIA

N
W — E
S

*Tyrrhenian
Sea*

CATANZARO

Vibo Valentia

Plain of
Gioia Tauro

Presinaci
San Calogero

Gioia Tauro   Rosarno

Palmi   Taurianova

Bagnara   Canolo   Siderno

Villa San Giovanni   Delianuova

Santo Stefano   Platì   Locri
d'Aspromonte
Mountain massif:
Aspromonte

REGGIO CALABRIA   Bovalino

San Luca

Bova

Condofuri   Brancaleone

Sanctuary of the
Madonna of the Mountain
at Polsi

*Ionian
Sea*

SOUTHERN
CALABRIA

0   20km

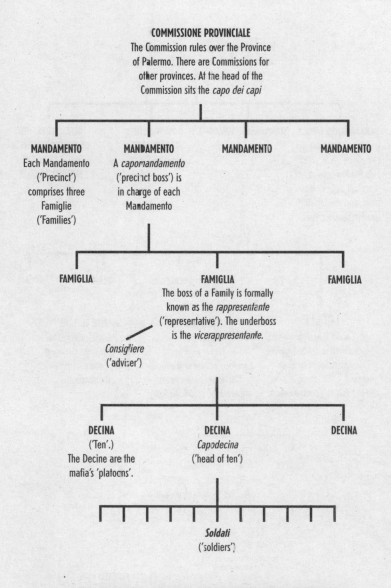

COMMISSIONE PROVINCIALE
The Commission rules over the Province
of Palermo. There are Commissions for
other provinces. At the head of the
Commission sits the *capo dei capi*

MANDAMENTO
Each Mandamento
('Precinct')
comprises three
Famiglie
('Families')

MANDAMENTO
A *capomandamento*
('precinct boss') is
in charge of each
Mandamento

MANDAMENTO

MANDAMENTO

FAMIGLIA

FAMIGLIA
The boss of a Family is formally
known as the *rappresentante*
('representative'). The underboss
is the *vicerappresentante*.

FAMIGLIA

Consigliere
('adviser')

DECINA
('Ten'.)
The Decine are the
mafia's 'platoons'.

DECINA
Capodecina
('head of ten')

DECINA

Soldati
('soldiers')

THE STRUCTURE OF COSA NOSTRA
As first described by Tommaso Buscetta in 1984

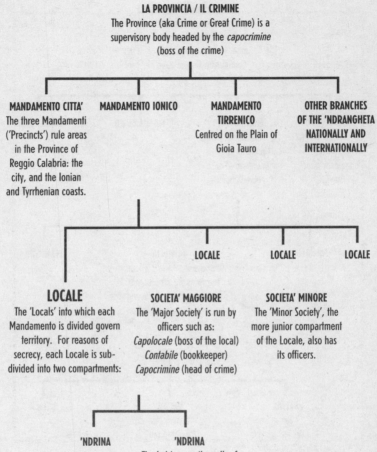

LA PROVINCIA / IL CRIMINE
The Province (aka Crime or Great Crime) is a
supervisory body headed by the *capocrimine*
(boss of the crime)

MANDAMENTO CITTA'
The three Mandamenti
('Precincts') rule areas
in the Province of
Reggio Calabria: the
city, and the Ionian
and Tyrrhenian coasts.

MANDAMENTO IONICO

**MANDAMENTO
TIRRENICO**
Centred on the Plain of
Gioia Tauro

**OTHER BRANCHES
OF THE 'NDRANGHETA
NATIONALLY AND
INTERNATIONALLY**

LOCALE

LOCALE

LOCALE

LOCALE
The 'Locals' into which each
Mandamento is divided govern
territory. For reasons of
secrecy, each Locale is sub-
divided into two compartments:

SOCIETA' MAGGIORE
The 'Major Society' is run by
officers such as:
Capolocale (boss of the local)
Contabile (bookkeeper)
Capocrimine (head of crime)

SOCIETA' MINORE
The 'Minor Society', the
more junior compartment
of the Locale, also has
its officers.

'NDRINA

'NDRINA
The 'ndrine are the cells of
the 'ndrangheta organization.

THE STRUCTURE OF THE 'NDRANGHETA

(Source: 'Operazione Crimine', summer 2010.)

DOTI	Padrino ('godfather')	Members of the 'ndrangheta have to attain these 'flowers' to be eligible for the most senior positions.
The 'gifts' (i.e. ranks) that mark the status of an 'ndranghetista. They are also known as FIORI ('flowers').	Quartino	
	Trequartino	
	Vangelista ('gospelist')	'Ndranghetisti have to reach these doti to become officials in the Major Society
	Santista ('saintist')	
	Camorrista di sgarro ('camorrista who is up for a fight', a.k.a. sgarrista)	'Ndranghetisti with these ranks belong to the Minor Society
	Camorrista	
	Picciotto ('lad')	
	Giovane d'onore ('honoured youth')	Giovani d'onore are being prepared to enter the organisation.

RANKS IN THE 'NDRANGHETA

Preface

Graziella Campagna was a petite, baby-faced, dark-haired girl of seventeen. Her hobby was embroidery. She was last seen on 12 December 1985, waiting for the bus she always took home from her job at the dry cleaner's. She was dressed in a red jacket and black trousers.

Like many young people in Sicily, Graziella was paid an under-the-counter pittance for long hours of menial work. And, like many young people in Sicily, she would not be able to get married unless her family saved for years. So her disappearance was probably a fuitina (an elopement): she had run off with her boyfriend to save her parents the expense of a full-scale wedding. Or at least that was what the police told her worried father.

Graziella's brother Pietro was a Carabiniere – a military policeman. He did not buy the fuitina story and searched the whole area for his sister on a borrowed motorbike. After two days, up in the mountains above town, he stopped at a sandwich stall to show Graziella's picture. Just then, a man in a BMW pulled up and, breathless with emotion, said that he had just found the body of a girl dressed in a red jacket and black trousers near an abandoned fort.

Pietro rushed to where the girl lay, and to a sight that outstripped his nightmares. 'I saw what I saw,' was all he could later bring himself to say.

It would take many years of campaigning for Graziella's family to confirm the truth about her murder. The laundry where she worked was in the little town of

Villafranca, in the Sicilian province of Messina. Among the regular clients was an affable, balding civil engineer in his mid-forties who went by the name of Eugenio Cannata. Cannata was always accompanied on his visits to the laundry by a younger, much quieter friend. One day, while sorting through a bundle of Cannata's laundry, Graziella found a transparent plastic wallet in the breast pocket of a shirt; it contained a picture of Pope John XXIII and a small diary. The diary made it clear that 'Eugenio Cannata' was, in fact, a pseudonym. Its bearer was in reality a mafioso *– a Man of Honour, as he would have termed himself – who was on the run from the law on drug-trafficking charges. His taciturn friend was his bodyguard.*

It is highly unlikely that Graziella understood the lethal importance of what she saw. But 'Eugenio Cannata' probably found out that her brother was a Carabiniere, *and decided not to risk sparing her. He and his body- guard kidnapped her from the bus stop, took her into the mountains, interrogated her in the abandoned fort, and then murdered her.*

Graziella was blasted five times at close range with a sawn-off shotgun. The first shot hit her in the hand and arm. Presumably she had raised them instinctively when she realised what was about to happen. The next three shots hit her in the face, the belly and the shoulder. She was on the ground when the killer stood over her and fired for the final time – into her chest.

Graziella Campagna was a victim of Cosa Nostra, the mafia of Sicily.

Thirty thousand people. No library. No cinema. No park. Casal di Principe is a low-rise warren where buildings with planning permission are the exception rather than

the rule. Concrete and tarmac have long since won the fight for space with the peach and apricot orchards. The church of San Nicola di Bari is of a hard-faced piece with the town. Its featureless blocks and a square-columned portico are fit for a multistorey car park. The crucifix bolted to the roof bestows only an embattled air of determination.

But don Giuseppe Diana knew that it took something more than determination to bring hope to Casal di Principe. Don Peppino, as they called him, was a local man, a farmer's son. Priest. Literature teacher. Scout leader. Friend. He mustered the kids into games of five-a-side and ping-pong. He took them for trips into the countryside. He quietly galvanised them into working for their community – in a place where the word 'community' can scarcely gain any purchase on reality. Don Peppino's volunteers were even building a refuge for the most wretched of this wretched place, the illegal migrant labourers exploited by local gangmasters.

And then there was his articulate stand against organised crime. He and five other local priests put their name to a simple, typed document they called, 'For the love of my people, I will not keep silent.'

Don Peppino died, in the sacristy, early on the morning of Sunday 19 March 1994. He had just listened to his telephone messages in the tiny office space, and was minutes from beginning the Mass.

A few steps away, in the front pews, two Carmelite nuns were saying the rosary when they heard shots. They noticed a man, barely more than a shadow, slipping out of the main entrance. Once through the narrow corridor that led from the nave into the sacristy, they found don Peppino lying in a creeping slick of blood. He had been shot three times in the face at point-blank range.

Don Peppino Diana was a victim of the camorra, the mafia of Campania.

Giuseppe Grimaldi, age fifty-four, was a salumiere, *a butcher specialising in the Calabrian salami that bristle with chilli peppers like those of no other Italian region. One May afternoon in 1991, three men wearing ski masks and brandishing sawn-off shotguns burst into the food shop in Taurianova that Giuseppe ran with his brother. The three men ordered the Grimaldi brothers and their customers out into the street. As a judge would later rule, the Grimaldis 'had no criminal record and were entirely unconnected to any kind of crime'. So in those first moments, there was no reason to believe that the raid, terrifying as it was, was anything more than a robbery.*

It turned out to be a public execution, a 'transversal vendetta', as the newspapers in Italy call them – meaning the revenge killing of a mafioso's *innocent relatives. Once the Grimaldi brothers were in the tiny piazza in front of the shop, both were shot in the back several times from close range. Nor did the horror finish there . . .*

The following evening, the grief-stricken Grimaldi family were holding a vigil over Giuseppe's body when men claiming to be Carabinieri *called at the door. Mrs Grimaldi asked them to switch on their siren as proof of their identity. Their response was to fire wildly into the house. No one was killed, but the Grimaldis' twelve-year-old daughter was seriously wounded; she was still in intensive care when journalists from across the country descended on the home, its front door pock-marked with bullet holes.*

*Giuseppe's wife Luciana, head bowed, voice flattened
and quiet, responded simply to the journalists' probing.
Could she manage to forgive the men who did this?*

*'Sometimes I think I could manage it. Sometimes
not. But I think, in a case like this, God alone can
forgive.'*

*God alone knows where she got her composure. For
she must have had the appalling image of what had
been done to her husband tugging mutely at her
mind.*

*The shotgun blast that killed Giuseppe took away
most of his neck. The killers then fetched his butcher's
knife and hacked through the few remaining strands of
muscle and skin so that they could use his head for
target practice. Passers-by – and there were about
twenty of them in the centre of Taurianova – saw
Giuseppe's head repeatedly arc through the air, take
cruel deviations when the shotgun pellets hit it, and
tumble into the road.*

*Giuseppe Grimaldi was a victim of the 'ndrangheta,
the mafia of Calabria.*

Today's Italy came into being on 2 and 3 June 1946, when a
people battered by war voted in a referendum to abolish a
monarchy that had been profoundly discredited by its subservi-
ence to Fascist dictatorship. Here was a clean break with the
past: Italy would henceforth be a Republic. In the same poll,
Italians elected the members of a constituent assembly who would
draft a new constitution for the Republic based on democracy,
freedom and the rule of law.

The organisations that killed Graziella Campagna, don
Giuseppe Diana and Giuseppe Grimaldi are a monstrous insult

to the Italian Republic's founding values. The mafias' appalling cruelty is essential to what they are and what they do. There is no such thing as a mafia without violence. Yet violence is only the beginning. Through violence, and through the many tactics that it makes possible, the mafias corrupt the Republic's democratic institutions, drastically curtail the life-chances of its citizens, evade justice, and set up their own self-interested meddling as an alternative to the courts. In the areas of the country where mafia power is strongest, it constitutes nothing short of a criminal regime. In a secret dispatch from 2008 that found its way onto the Wikileaks site, the United States Consul General in Naples reported on Calabria, the region in the 'toe' of the Italian 'boot' which is home to the 'ndrangheta. One might quibble with one or two of his statistics, but the core of the diagnosis is as true as it is dispiriting:

> The 'ndrangheta organized crime syndicate controls vast portions of [Calabria's] territory and economy, and accounts for at least three percent of Italy's GDP (probably much more) through drug trafficking, extortion and usury . . . Much of the region's industry collapsed over a decade ago, leaving environmental and economic ruin. The region comes in last place in nearly every category of national economic assessments. Most of the politicians we met on a recent visit were fatalistic, of the opinion that there was little that could be done to stop the region's downward economic spiral or the stranglehold of the 'ndrangheta. A few others disingenuously suggested that organized crime is no longer a problem . . . No one believes the central government has much, if any, control of Calabria, and local politicians are uniformly seen as ineffective and/or corrupt. If Calabria were not part of Italy, it would be a failed state.

The 'ndrangheta's influence reaches far beyond the 'bleak and chaotic' cities of Calabria that were visited by the Consul General. Italy's poorest region has generated a criminal brotherhood that is more adept than any of the other mafias at establishing colonies in the wealthiest parts of the country. (Not to mention in a series of other rich countries, such as Germany, Canada and Australia.)

The mafias and the Republic have grown together. As the Republic's foundations were set in place, the mafias built themselves into the post-war settlement. As Italy recovered from the catastrophe of war, the mafias gained strength too. Soon, Italy would transform itself into one of the world's wealthiest capitalist economies. Italian goods were manufactured with an expertise, and designed with a style, that made them coveted the world over. The mafias too made themselves richer than they had ever been – albeit by trading in a more nefarious range of goods and services. In so doing, they made Italy's organised crime problem known the world over.

Since the 1960s, Italy has no longer been able to cite poverty as an excuse for harbouring the mafias. Indeed, it has no excuses at all. Post-war Italy has at times been a deeply troubled society. But it is not a banana republic in South America, or an impoverished warlord demesne in Asia, or some remnant of a shattered empire in Eastern Europe. Unless our maps are all calamitously wrong, the famous boot-shaped peninsula is not located in a region of the world where one might expect to find the state's authority undermined by a violent and rapacious alternative power. Italy is a full member of the family of Western European nations. Yet, alone among those nations, it hosts criminal organisations that have usurped the democratic state's authority over large tracts of its own territory.

Herein lie both the fascination and the urgency of mafia history. Mafia power is the antithesis of the *values* of freedom and democracy that underpin Europe's post-war prosperity. But in Italy, mafia power has been perfectly compatible with the day-to-day *reality* of freedom, democracy and prosperity.

In *Mafia Republic*, I tell the story of how Cosa Nostra, the camorra and the 'ndrangheta survived in the Republican era. Not only survived, but actually multiplied and spread, spawning new mafias and new infestations in parts of the national territory that had hitherto seemed immune. Not only multiplied and spread, indeed, but became stronger, more affluent and more violent than ever.

Mafia Republic is based on two simple principles:

On the one hand, there are a great many more differences between Italy's three major mafias than the casual observer might assume. Some of those differences are subtle, some are stark, but each is an adaptation designed to enable the particular criminal organisation in question to survive and prosper in its local environment. The result is that each mafia has followed a distinct path through history.

On the other hand, for all these intriguing differences between the criminal organisations, their histories make more sense when they are woven into one narrative. The mafias share very many things, most notably their perverse relationship with the Italian state, which they have by turns infiltrated, befriended and fought. Italy does not have solitary, static criminal organisms; it has a rich underworld ecosystem that continues to generate new life forms to this day.

'Mafia' is a Sicilian word, although it is frequently used as a general term for a criminal organisation, and therefore applied to the camorra and the 'ndrangheta as well as to the Sicilian mafia. I will follow the same convention here.

However, I don't want to begin this book with names and what they might mean, because names are not really very important to what the mafias do. Yet those names, and the confusion and reticence that has often surrounded them, *are* an integral part of the story to be told. The camorra has always been called the camorra but, until 1955, many people in Naples were reluctant to speak the word. The 'ndrangheta has only been known as the 'ndrangheta since the same year. It was not until a decade later that Cosa Nostra became popular among Sicilian *mafiosi* as a way of alluding to their group. Italian public opinion did not learn about the name 'Cosa Nostra' until twenty years after that. In the interests of clarity, in these pages I will sometimes use 'ndrangheta to refer to the Calabrian mafia, and Cosa Nostra to refer to the Sicilian mafia, at times when those names were not yet in wide circulation.

Whatever they have been called at different times, Cosa Nostra, the camorra and the 'ndrangheta all have a history that stretches back as much as a century before the foundation of the Republic in 1946. The mafias are more or less the same age as the Italian state, which officially came into being in 1861. I recounted the mafias' origins and early development in *Mafia Brotherhoods*, published in 2011. The scholar in me would love to use this preface to wag an admonishing finger at anyone who picks up a copy of this book without first having read its prequel, *Mafia Brotherhoods*. But, in truth, there is no justification whatsoever for such professorial crabbiness. *Mafia Republic* is a stand-alone book because, when mafia history began again after the Second World War, it did so with a blank page. Or perhaps it is more accurate to say that it began with a page on which the bloody traces of the past had been carefully erased. The Italian Republic completely forgot all of the lessons it should have learned from the previous century.

Mafia Republic opens with a tour of the different mafia strongholds in the 1940s – the years when Italy's institutions were being created, or revived after Fascism's fall. The following pages introduce each of the major mafias in turn. At the same time, they set out the ingenious ways in which a country reborn from the catastrophe of war proceeded to unlearn most of what it knew about the menace of organised crime. In the Italian Republic, mafia history began with an act of forgetting.

1

FUGGEDABOUTIT

Sicily: **Threats, terrorism, murder, arson, kidnapping and mayhem**

In the early hours of 10 July 1943, American and British landing craft crashed onto Sicilian beaches and disgorged their cargo of troops and tanks. Five and a half weeks later, on 17 August, the last ferries evacuating Axis soldiers and equipment across the straits to the Italian mainland chugged out of Messina's hooked harbour under heavy bombardment. Sicily had fallen to the Allies.

Newly liberated Sicily was already slipping towards chaos. The Allied Military Government of Occupied Territories (or AMGOT) found itself responsible for feeding the island's hungry population while struggling to douse an eruption of black-marketeering, banditry, prison-breaks, score-settling and extortion. As early as September 1943, the *New York Times* reported that the Sicilian mafia was profoundly enmeshed in the post-Liberation crime wave.

Back in the early 1930s, Fascism had loudly declared that its round-ups and mass trials had vanquished the mafia. Public opinion in much of the world agreed. In 1938 the Sicilian-American author of a travel guide explained that the mafia was 'officially extinct': 'the elimination of this canker is by far the greatest event in the recent history of the island'.

For their part, the British and American military authorities knew before they invaded Sicily that Fascist propaganda's boast about the mafia's demise was exaggerated. But it was hard for them to tell quite what state the mafia was really in – not least because Mussolini had made good his boasting in the only way he knew how: by banning organised crime stories from the Italian media. The truth behind the blackout, which has only emerged recently from the archives, was that the Sicilian mafia was as strong as ever in the 1930s. It was a secret, oath-bound brother-hood of criminals, modelled on Freemasonry, whose members referred to themselves as Men of Honour. It had branches, called 'Families', in most towns and villages across the west of the island. In the province of Palermo, where about half of the Sicilian mafia's strength was concentrated, its bosses, formally known as 'representatives', referred upwards to a governing 'Commission' presided over by a 'general president' or 'boss of all bosses'. Fascism had fought the Sicilian mafia, launching two major waves of repression against it. But in the end, the Duce's regime, like every previous Italian government, had learned to live alongside it.

In the chaos that followed Liberation, the fearsome silhouette of the Sicilian mafia once more became visible. AMGOT urgently needed to find out what it was dealing with. In October 1943, it commissioned a report on the mafia from military intelligence – a report of such secrecy that it was taken across the Mediterranean to Allied Forces Headquarters in Algiers by a personal messenger. Its author, Captain William Everett Scotten, was a thirty-nine-year-old career diplomat and lately US Army Military Intelligence officer from Pasadena, California. The report concluded that the mafia was a 'criminal system' that aimed 'to commit extortion and theft with impunity' using methods 'ranging from threats and terrorism to outright murder, arson, kidnapping, and mayhem'.

Scotten went on to explain how, in the weeks following the invasion of July 1943, the criminal system had given the Allies a lesson in how it could infiltrate the government machinery. When the Fascist state collapsed in Sicily, AMGOT needed locals they could trust to help maintain a semblance of order. Captain Scotten reported that many of the Sicilians – self-proclaimed victims of Fascism – who had been appointed mayors of towns under AMGOT were actually gangsters or their front men.

Sicilian *mafiosi* with experience in America had also volunteered to act as interpreters, and thereby wheedled themselves into positions of influence. Captain Scotten also knew of 'numerous cases' of Allied staff 'whose family connections or antecedents in the United States have led them directly into the sphere of Mafia'. What is more, even honest officials had been duped by Sicilian aristocrats with mafia links (the mafia's 'higher level', in Captain Scotten's words).

The mafia's economic power had grown too. Under AMGOT, grain was supposed to be requisitioned and held in warehouses for distribution through a rationing system. Captain Scotten learned that the mafia did not only run the vast black market in grain; in some places *mafiosi* had used their political contacts in Palermo to gain control over government grain banks too. *Both* the illegal *and* legal markets in agricultural produce were in criminal hands. In short, within weeks of the Allied occupation, the mafia had a grip on Sicily's throat. The detritus of the battlefield had equipped it with a formidable arsenal: 'machine guns, trench mortars, even light field pieces, land mines, field radios, and ample stores of munitions', according to Captain Scotten. Whatever business opportunities the war's aftermath might throw up, the Sicilian mafia was armed and ready to seize them.

Meanwhile, the Allied invasion of Sicily had started a chain reaction up in Rome. Duce Benito Mussolini fell from power and was arrested on the orders of the King. Then, on 8 September 1943, Italy capitulated to the Allies. The King, his ministers and some of his top generals fled. The state machinery dissolved, leaving disorientated soldiers and citizens to find their own way of surviving the rest of the war. In the early hours of the following morning, Allied forces landed on the southern Italian mainland, at Salerno, just below Naples. More German troops poured into the peninsula to resist: they were occupiers now, rather than Axis comrades. Italy was cut in two: the Allies in the South, the Germans in the North and centre. For the rest of the Second World War, the conflict would be slogged out on the soil of the

Italian mainland. Meanwhile, behind the lines in Nazi-occupied Italy, a civil war pitched the Resistance against die-hard Fascists.

Back in liberated Sicily, AMGOT came to an end in February 1944, and the island came under the authority of the coalition of anti-Fascist forces making up the new Italian civilian government, which was based in the portion of the mainland now held by the Allies.

Over the next couple of years, all of Italy made the transition from war to peace, and from Liberation to democracy, a transition marked by four key milestones:

April 1945: the war in Italy came to an end, only a few days before Hitler's suicide.

June 1946: the monarchy was abolished and the Republic was born.

March 1947: President Harry S. Truman announced that the United States would intervene to check Soviet expansion across the globe. In Italy, the Partito Comunista Italiano had won great prestige from its role in the Resistance, and was promising to create a Communist Party branch for every bell-tower. The peninsula found itself right on the front line of the newly declared Cold War.

April 1948: Italy's first democratic parliamentary election was decisively won by the American-backed Democrazia Cristiana (DC – the Christian Democrats) and decisively lost by the Communists.

Nowhere in Italy was the post-war transition more turbulent than in Sicily. Nowhere was organised crime more profoundly involved in the turbulence. Parts of the South had been strongholds of organised crime for generations by this time. In southern Calabria and Campania, as we will see, *'ndranghetisti* and *camorristi* carved out their own niche in the post-war settlement. But in Sicily, the mafia had grander designs. Many Sicilians are inclined to express doubts when the label 'organised crime' is applied to the mafia. *Mafiosi* are all criminals, and they always have been. But ordinary criminals, however organised they may be, do not have remotely the kind of political friendships that senior *mafiosi* have always enjoyed. It would be far, far beyond the mental horizon of any common-or-garden crook to try and shape the institutional destiny of his homeland in the way Sicilian *mafiosi* tried to do after 1943.

The most clamorous and bloody crime in which the mafia was involved was banditry. At the peak in 1945, hundreds of bandit bands roamed the Sicilian countryside, many of them well armed enough to best the police and *Carabinieri* in a firefight. Robbery, extortion, kidnapping and the black market gave these outlaws a rich income stream. As was traditional, rather than joining the bandits, *mafiosi* preferred, wherever they could, to 'farm' them through an exchange of favours. For example, the bandits might kick back a percentage of their earnings to the *mafiosi*, who in return offered tips on lucrative kidnapping or robbery targets, advance news on police round-ups, and mediators who could broker ransom payments with the necessary discretion.

Soon after the Allied invasion, *mafiosi* set about re-establishing their time-honoured stranglehold over the 'protection', rental and management of agricultural land in western Sicily. Many of Sicily's biggest landowners lived in decadent splendour in Palermo while leaving the running of their vast farms to brutal mafia middlemen. Hence, after the war, the landowners appointed men who would become some of the most notorious bosses of the 1950s and 1960s as leaseholder-managers of their land: like Giuseppe Genco Russo from Mussomeli, and the twenty-year-old killer Luciano Liggio from the agricultural town of Corleone, in the province of Palermo. (Liggio already had an arrest warrant out against his name when, after his predecessor's mysterious death, he became manager of the Strasatto estate in 1945.)

The business of land inexorably drew the mafia into politics. At every moment of political upheaval in recent Sicilian history, peasants had made loud claims to fairer contracts or even a share of the estates owned by the Sicilian aristocrats. In the end, mafia shotguns always voiced the definitive response to the peasants' demands.

The land issue was bound to resurface after the war and, when it did, the landowners and *mafiosi* turned terror into a political tool. With the pistol, the machine gun and the hand grenade, *mafiosi* went all out to eliminate peasant militants and intimidate their supporters into passivity. The appalling roll call of murdered trade unionists and left-wing activists began in the summer of 1944 and had not run its course a full decade later. For example, in the autumn of 1946, at Belmonte Mezzagno near Palermo, the peasants formed a cooperative to take over the management of land from a nearby estate. On 2 November, a death squad of thirteen men turned up in a field where many ordinary members of the cooperative were labouring. The brothers Giovanni, Vincenzo and Giuseppe Santangelo were led away to be executed one after another with a single shot to the back of the head.

Both the landowners and the mafia feared that a new, democratic Italian government would be forced to make concessions to the Communists, and therefore to the left-wing peasants in Sicily. Accordingly, from as early as 1943, the landowners and the mafia sponsored a movement to separate the island off from the rest of the peninsula. The road to Sicilian independence was plotted at a series of meetings held over the coming years. Scions of some of the oldest family lineages in Sicily welcomed the island's most senior mobsters to their luxurious country villas. At one of those meetings in September 1945, the bosses negotiated a deal to integrate some bandits into the Separatist movement's army. Salvatore Giuliano, the leader of the most notorious bandit gang of all, was offered a large sum of money, the rank of colonel, and the promise of an amnesty once the flag of a free Sicily was raised. There followed a series of assaults on *Carabinieri* barracks that were intended to prepare the ground for an insurrection.

In the end, there was no Separatist insurrection. The movement's ramshackle military wing was dispersed. More importantly, its political leadership was outmanoeuvred: in May 1946 Sicily was granted autonomy, and its own regional parliament, while remaining *within* Italy. *Mafiosi* who had supported Separatism began the search for new political partners.

If Separatism was in decline in 1946, Sicily's criminal emergency had become more serious than ever. Bandit gangs, often operating under the mafia's wing, were robbing and kidnapping at will. The police and *Carabinieri* in Sicily were sending information aplenty to Rome. The mafia was at the centre of the dark picture they painted. Like Captain Scotten before them, they were under no illusions about what the mafia was, as this report from October 1946 makes clear:

> The mafia is an occult organisation that traverses Sicily's provinces and has secret tentacles that reach into all social classes. Its exclusive objective is getting rich by unlawful means at the expense of honest and vulnerable people. It has now reconstituted its cells or 'Families', as they are referred to here in the jargon, especially in the provinces of Palermo, Trapani, Caltanissetta, Enna and Agrigento.

So these were the violent years that decided Sicily's future. Not coincidentally, these were also the years when Italy's rulers decided to forget everything they knew about Sicily's notorious 'occult organisation'. The most revealing illustration of that process of forgetting is not a mafia massacre or a secret report. To understand how the Sicilian mafia really worked in the late 1940s, to understand its unique ability to vanish into thin air, while at the same time seeping into the state apparatus, we need to watch Italy's first-ever mafia movie.

Sicily: *In the Name of the Law*

*It is September 1948, but the scorched expanses of the
Sicilian interior that stretch out before the camera seem
timeless. A young man in a double-breasted jacket, his
chiselled face shaded by a fedora, sits erect in the saddle.
Suddenly, he swivels to look out across a lunar landscape
of dust and rock. He sees eight figures on horseback
emerge over a hilltop to stand silhouetted against the sky.*

*'The mafia.' The young man speaks the dread word
aloud to himself, and his jaw sets with determination. His
name is Guido Schiavi, and he is a magistrate, a champion
of the law. This is the confrontation he has been expecting.*

The mafiosi, *riding beautifully curried thoroughbred
mares, come down the hill towards the magistrate at a
stately canter. The soundtrack provides an accompaniment
of stirring trumpets and driving strings to their cavalcade.
As they approach, Schiavi sees that each is dressed in
corduroy and fustian; each has a flat cap pulled down
over a craggily impassive face; and each has a shotgun
slung over his shoulder.*

The mafiosi *come to a halt on a low bridge. Their boss,
who goes by the name of Turi Passalacqua, is unmistake-
able on his statuesque white mount. He raises his cap
courteously to address the magistrate.*

Good day to you, voscenza. Welcome to our land. You
do us a great honour.

You are very young, sir. And my friends and I are
very happy about that. Because we know that the

*young are pure of heart. You are intelligent, and I'm
sure you have already understood the way of the world
here. Things have been like this for more than a
hundred years, and everyone is content.*

*The magistrate Schiavi is not impressed by this homily.
He objects that there are plenty of people who are far
from 'content' with this 'way of the world': the victims
of murder and blackmail and their families, for example;
or the brutalised farm labourers and sulphur miners. But
his words fail to provoke even a flicker of irritation on
the* mafioso's *serene countenance:*

*Every society has its defects. And besides, it's always
possible to reach an agreement between men of honour
. . . You need only express your desires.*

*Now it is the magistrate's turn to remain unmoved. In
tones of measured defiance he affirms that he has only
one desire, only one duty: to apply the law.*
*Clearly, there can be no compromise. Two opposing
value systems have deployed their forces in the field. A
great clash between the state and the mafia is inevitable.
All that remains is for the* capomafia *Turi Passalacqua to
restate his credo:*

*You are a brave man, but we make the law here,
according to our ancient traditions. This is an island.
The government is a long way away. And if we
weren't here, with our own kind of severity, then
criminals would end up spoiling everything, like rye-
grass spoils the wheat. Nobody would be safe in their
own home any more. We are not criminals. We are
honourable men: as free and independent as the birds
in the sky.*

> *And with that, the trumpets and strings swell once more. We watch as the posse of Men of Honour wheels round and gallops off into the distance.*

In 1940s Italy, the movies meant much more than just entertainment. The US studios had boycotted the Italian market in protest at Mussolini's attempts to control imports. During the last five years of Fascism, Italians were denied their weekly dose of Californian celluloid. When the theatres were reopened after the Liberation, and the supply from Hollywood resumed, Italians were soon going to the movies in greater numbers than ever – greater than in any other European country. The glamour of Rita Hayworth and Glenn Ford held out the promise of what freedom and democracy might bring to a country racked by war and demoralised by the debacle of Fascism.

Yet no country that had lived through such traumatic changes could ever be entirely satisfied with the products of the US studios. So, in the cinema, the years 1945–50 have come to be defined by the gritty homegrown poetry of Roberto Rossellini's *Rome, Open City* or Vittorio De Sica's *Bicycle Thieves*. Neorealism ('new realism') was the cultural buzz-word of the day. Neorealist directors took their cameras out into the bomb-shattered streets; they found moving dramas among the peasants toiling on the terraces or wading through rice paddies. Neorealist cinema seemed so true to life that it was as if the skin of history had peeled off as film (to quote what one critic evocatively wrote at the time). There has never been a moment when the movie screen was more important to how Italy imagined the light and the dark within itself.

Released in Italian cinemas in March 1949, *In nome della legge* (*In the Name of the Law*) was Italy's first mafia film. It is a strange muddle of a movie: it has many of the accoutrements of Neorealist cinema, notably in its use of the sun-blasted Sicilian landscape; but it also straddles the divide between Neorealism and Hollywood. The film's director, Pietro Germi, had never been to Sicily before his film went into production in 1948. Then again, his ignorance mattered little. Because when he got off the ferry and set foot on the island for the first time, he already knew exactly what he was going to find: Arizona. *In the Name of the Law* stages a shotgun marriage between Neorealism and the cowboy movie genre. Germi's Sicily is Tombstone with Mediterranean trimmings: a place of lone lawmen, long stares, and ambushes in gulches. Here trains pull into desert stations, gunshots echo across vast skies, and men stride into bars and drink glasses of Sicilian aniseed liqueur as if they were knocking back fingers of hooch whiskey.

Germi's reasoning was that the quasi-Wild West setting would dramatise the head-to-head between the lone lawman and his criminal foe. Muscular heart-throb Massimo Girotti, playing the young magistrate Guido Schiavi, was to be Italy's answer to John Wayne. But Germi's camera is even more obsessed with mafia boss Turi Passalacqua, played by French veteran Charles Vanel: he is always framed from below, cut out against a pale sky – as if he were part craggy rancher, and part Apache sage.

The cowboys-cum-*capos* formula clearly worked. 'Frenetic applause' was reported at the first public screenings. *In the Name of the Law* went on to become the third most popular movie of the 1948–9 season in Italy, taking a bumper 401 million lire (roughly €7 million in 2011 values) at the box office, and standing toe-to-commercial-toe with such Hollywood classics as *Fort Apache* and *The Treasure of the Sierra Madre*.

As mob movies go, *In the Name of the Law* may seem quaint at first glance – now that our tastes are attuned to *GoodFellas* and *Gomorrah*. Yet Germi's film is sinister too: it has a back-story full of dark surprises, and a context of unprecedented mafia violence and arrogance. More recent classics of the mafia movie genre, like *The Godfather*, are often criticised for glamourising organised crime. But in this respect Coppola's film has nothing on *In the Name of the Law*. The opening credits display a familiar disclaimer: 'Any reference to events, places and people who really exist is purely coincidental'. But that is some distance from the truth.

In the Name of the Law was based on a novel, and inspired by the example of the novel's author. Written in the early months of 1947, *Piccola Pretura* (*Local Magistrate's Office*) was the work of Giuseppe Guido Lo Schiavo, one of the country's foremost authorities on the Sicilian mafia. Born and brought up in Palermo, Lo Schiavo was a hero of the First World War who, when the war ended, went into the front line of the fight against organised crime on his island home.

Lo Schiavo's life was closely intertwined with the history of the Sicilian mafia under Fascism. In 1926 he was himself a young magistrate, like the hero of his novel. (The similarity between the names of author and protagonist – Giuseppe Guido Lo Schiavo/Guido Schiavi – is no accident.) In that year, Benito Mussolini's dictatorship launched a long overdue attack on the mafia. The 'cancer of delinquency' was to be cut out of Sicily by the Fascist 'scalpel', the Duce boasted. The police and *Carabinieri* led the assault, and prosecuting magistrates like Lo Schiavo had the job of preparing the evidence needed to convert thousands of arrests into convictions.

Lo Schiavo was among the most enthusiastic instruments of the Fascist repression. In 1930, one of the mobsters' defence lawyers, Giuseppe Mario Puglia, published an essay claiming that the mafia was *not* a secret criminal society. Indeed *mafiosi* were not even criminals. Rather the *mafioso* was an incorrigible individualist, 'a man who instinctively refuses to recognise anyone superior to his own ego'. What is more, the *mafioso* was a typical Sicilian, because this exaggerated pride and self-containment had seeped into the island's psyche as a form of resistance to centuries of foreign invasions. Therefore to repress the mafia was inevitably to repress the Sicilian people. Puglia's essay, in other words, reads like the words Lo Schiavo would later put into the mouth of mafia boss Turi Passalacqua in *In the Name of the Law*.

Lo Schiavo refused to let the defence lawyer's claims pass unchallenged, responding to them in a pamphlet that is a little masterpiece of controlled anger. The mafia, Lo Schiavo argued, was 'a criminal system'; it was not just illegal, it was an 'anti-legal organism whose only aim was getting rich by illicit means'.

Lo Schiavo went on to give the mafia lawyer a lesson in mafia history. The Sicilian mafia first emerged from the political violence of the *Risorgimento* – the nineteenth-century movement that turned Italy's disparate states into a unified nation. All revolutionaries need strong men to turn their ideals into reality, Lo Schiavo explained. The revolutionaries of pre-unification Sicily were no exception: they found the muscle they required among the fearsome wardens, overseers and bravoes who were already a law unto themselves in the Sicilian countryside. Thus a pact was formed between the island's toughest and most ambitious thugs on the one hand, and the patriots conspiring to make Italy into a nation on the other. The pact was not broken when Sicily became part of a unified Italian state in 1860, and the patriotic conspirators joined the national ruling class.

Many of the patriotic conspirators were members of the Freemasons or of Masonic-style sects, Lo Schiavo argued. The more unscrupulous among them taught their thuggish friends what huge advantages could accrue to a criminal network able to structure itself along the same lines as the Freemasons.

Lo Schiavo had also researched the economic history of the mafia. He learned that it had first grown rich by establishing protection rackets over the valuable lemon and orange groves surrounding Palermo. At the time, those lemon and orange groves constituted some of the most profitable agricultural land in Europe. *Mafiosi* would demand money to 'guard' the lemon trees on behalf of the landowner – just in case someone vandalised them. Someone like a *mafioso*, that is. These rackets would then give members of the mafia the power-base they needed to control the whole citrus fruit market.

Fear of the mafia pervaded society in western Sicily, reaching right up into parliament. Anything unfavourable said about the mafia would inevitably reach hostile ears. And that, argued Lo Schiavo, is why so many Sicilians could be found spouting the same drivel, along the lines that: 'the mafia does not exist; at worst, *mafiosi* are local problem solvers who embody the typically Sicilian pride and truculence towards authority'. Even the landowners who were, in theory, the mafia's most prominent victims, had bought into this fiction and espoused the belief that the mafia was somehow good for social peace, for law and order. On the contrary, Lo Schiavo asserted, the mafia was 'a programme to exploit and persecute honest members of society while hiding behind a reputation for courage and welfare that was only so much lying garbage'.

So, in the early 1930s, the man who would later inspire *In the Name of the Law* was an anti-mafia crusader with the bravery to engage in a public spat with the crime bosses' own defence lawyers. By 1948, Lo Schiavo had become one of the country's most senior magistrates, a prosecutor at the Supreme Court in Rome. In that year he published his novel, which was immediately adapted into a film.

Both novel and film tell a simple story about a young magistrate, Guido Schiavi, who is posted to a remote town deep in the arid badlands of the Sicilian interior. In this lawless place, the mafia rules unchecked, and runs a protection racket over the estate of the local landowner. When bandits kill one of the landowner's men, *capomafia* Turi Passalacqua hunts them down: the bandits are trussed up and tossed into a dried-up well, or simply shotgunned in the back in a mountain gully.

The young magistrate investigates this series of slayings, but he is frozen out by the terrified townspeople. When the courageous Schiavi confronts *capomafia* Turi Passalacqua on his white mare, he resists the boss's attempts to win him over to the mafia's way of thinking (the scene with which I began this chapter).

Eventually, Schiavi narrowly survives an assassination attempt. Resigned to defeat, he decides to abandon his post and return to the Sicilian capital, Palermo. But just as he is about to board the train to safety, he learns that his only friend in town, an honest seventeen-year-old boy called Paolino, has been murdered by a renegade *mafioso*. Indignant and distraught, Schiavi strides back into town. He rings the church bells to summon the whole population into the piazza for a do-or-die engagement. The state and the mafia are set to have their high noon – in what turns into perhaps the most bizarre climactic scene in the long history of gangster movies.

The church bell clangs out a continuous, urgent summons across the dust of the piazza, over the sun-weathered rooftops, and out into the surrounding fields. We are shown the unemployed sulphur miners, sitting and dozing in a line at the kerb, who raise their heads to listen. The camera then cuts to the women, young and old, who come out into the street wrapped in their black shawls; and then to the elegant club where the mayor and his cronies forget their game of baccarat and turn towards the source of the alarm.

Without discussion, everyone ups and walks towards the bells. The mule drivers scarcely pause to tether their beasts. Labourers drop their mattocks in the furrows. Soon streams of people are converging on the piazza. Led by Turi Passalacqua on his white mare, even the mafiosi – accompanied as always by the rhythmical trumpets of their signature theme – gallop into town to join the crowd gathering before the church steps.

There are loud murmurs of anxious curiosity as the young magistrate Guido Schiavi emerges from the church doors. Silence falls as he begins his address:

Now that you are all here, I declare that this is a trial. Half an hour ago we found Paolino's body, blasted by a double-barrelled shotgun. He was seventeen years old and he had never harmed anyone.

Schiavi scans the crowd as he speaks, seeking to look directly into the eyes of every person there. Then, staring with still greater intensity, the magistrate hails the group of stony-faced men on horseback.

> You there, men of the mafia. And you, Turi Passalacqua. Your bloody and ferocious brand of justice only punishes those who give you offence, and only protects the men who carry out your verdicts.

At these words, one of the mafiosi *levels his shotgun at the magistrate. But with a firm but gentle hand his boss pushes the barrels downwards again.*
Guido Schiavi does not hesitate for an instant:

> And you chose to put your brand of justice before the true law – the only law that allows us to live alongside our neighbours without tearing one another to pieces like wild beasts.
> Isn't that true, massaro Passalacqua?

Everyone in the piazza cranes to see how the capomafia *will react to this breathtaking challenge. A subtle change in his expression shows that he is troubled: his habitual composure is gone, replaced by solemnity. Silhouetted once more against the sky, Turi Passalacqua begins to make a speech of history-making gravity:*

> Those were tough words, magistrate. Until now, no one had ever spoken such tough words to us.
> But I say that your words were also just. My people and I did not come into town today to listen to your speech . . . But listening to you made me think of my son, and made me think that I would be proud to hear him talk in that way.

So I say to my friends that in this town the time has come to change course and go back within the law. Perhaps everyone here did kill Paolino. But only one person pulled the trigger. So I hereby hand him over to you so that he may be judged according to the state's law.

He turns and, with a mere flick of his head, gives the order to his crew. Amid clattering hooves, the Men of Honour corner the murderer before he can run away: it is the renegade mafioso, Francesco Messana.

The magistrate advances, flanked by two Carabinieri: 'Francesco Messana, you are under arrest, in the name of the law.'

The murderer is led away. The magistrate then turns, and with a look of glowing appreciation, gazes up towards the mafia boss to utter the film's final words:

In the name of the law!

And with that we cut to yet another shot of Turi Passalacqua silhouetted against the sky. His serenity has returned, and the suggestion of a smile plays on his lips. The mafia cavalcade music rises yet again. As the credits begin to roll, the boss turns his white mare to lead the mafiosi in their heroic gallop towards the sunset.

Mafiosi are not criminals, *In the Name of the Law* tells us. Turi Passalacqua is a man devoted to living by a code of honour that, in its own primitive way, is as admirable a law as the one magistrate Guido Schiavi is trying to uphold. If only *mafiosi* like him are addressed in the appropriately firm tone of voice, they will become bringers of peace and order. The mafia finds its true calling at the end of the film, the best way to live out its deeply held values: it becomes an auxiliary police force. If Sicily were

29

really Arizona, and *In the Name of the Law* were really a cowboy film, then we would not know which of the two men should wear the sheriff's badge.

In the Name of the Law is not *about* the mafia; rather it is mafia propaganda, a cunning and stylish variant of the kind of 'lying garbage' upon which Giuseppe Guido Lo Schiavo had poured vitriol in the 1930s. In the 1940s, each day of chaos in Sicily was adding to a mountain of proof that *mafiosi* were anything but friends to the rule of law. Yet this was precisely the time that Lo Schiavo's views on the mafia underwent an astonishing reversal. Lo Schiavo became a convert to the mafia's lies.

Now, anyone inclined to be generous to Giuseppe Guido Lo Schiavo might suppose that Pietro Germi's movie had twisted the meaning of the magistrate's novel by grafting a happy Hollywood ending onto a grimmer Sicilian tale. And it is certainly true that, in 1948, it would have been tough to create a genuinely realistic portrayal of the mafia. Rumours circulated during production that, when director Pietro Germi first arrived in Sicily, he was approached by several senior *mafiosi* who would not allow him to begin work until they had approved the screenplay. After the movie's release, during a press conference, a young Sicilian man in the audience argued with Germi about how true to life the Men of Honour in the film were: was the director not aware that the real mafia had killed dozens of people? Germi could only give a lame reply, 'So did you expect me to meet the same end?'

But the local difficulties that Germi faced in Sicily actually do nothing to excuse Giuseppe Guido Lo Schiavo. Indeed, his novel is *even more* pro-mafia than *In the Name of the Law*. In Lo Schiavo's tale, mafia boss Turi Passalacqua is 'the very personification of wisdom, prudence and calm . . . pot-bellied, shaven-headed and smiling like a benevolent Buddha'.

The conclusion is unavoidable: a magistrate who was a scourge of the mafia in the early 1930s was, by the mid-1940s, an enthusiastic mouthpiece for mystifications that could easily have been voiced by the mafia's slyest advocates. Once Giuseppe Guido Lo

Schiavo had been scornful about the way 'literature and drama glorified the figure of the *mafioso*'. Now he was himself writing fiction that did precisely that.

But why? What caused Lo Schiavo to upend his views so shamelessly?

Lo Schiavo was a conservative whose political sympathies had made him a supporter of Mussolini's regime in the 1920s and 1930s. After the Liberation, his conservatism turned him into a friend of the most murderous criminals on the island. The magistrate-novelist's bizarre rewriting of the mafia records in *Local Prosecutor's Office* testified to an unspoken and profoundly cynical belief: better the mafia than the Communists. This simple axiom was enough to drive Lo Schiavo to forget his own hard-won knowledge about Sicily's 'criminal system', and to relinquish the faith in the rule of law that was the grounding ethos of his calling as a magistrate.

Turi Passalacqua, the heroic bandit chieftain of *In the Name of the Law*, was laughably unrealistic. But, in a peculiarly Sicilian paradox, he was also horribly true to life. *In the Name of the Law* may have been a cinematic fantasy, but it nonetheless glorified a very real deal between the mafia and the state in the founding years of the Italian Republic.

Sicily is a land of strange alliances: between the landed aristocracy and gangland in the Separatist movement, for example. And once Separatism had gone into decline, the political and criminal pressures of 1946–8 created a still stranger convergence of interests: between conservatives, the mafia and the police. It is that alliance which is celebrated by *In the Name of the Law*, through the fictional figure of mafia boss Turi Passalacqua, sermonising from the saddle of his thoroughbred white mare.

In 1946, the police and *Carabinieri* were warning the government in Rome that they would need high-level support to defeat the mafia, because the mafia itself had so many friends among the Sicilian elite – friends it helped at election time by hustling votes. But these warnings were ignored. It may have been that conservative politicians in Rome were daunted by the prospect of taking on the ruling class of an island whose loyalty to Italy was questionable, but whose conservatism was beyond doubt. Or more cynically still, they may have reasoned that the mafia's ground-level terror campaign against the left-wing peasant movement was actually rather useful. So they told the police and *Carabinieri* in Sicily to forget the mafia (to forget the real cause of the crime emergency, in other words) and put the fight against banditry at the top of their agenda.

The police knew that to fight banditry they would need help – help from *mafiosi* prepared to supply inside information on the movement of the bands. For their part, *mafiosi* appreciated that farming bandits was not a long-term business. So when outlaws outlived their usefulness, *mafiosi* would betray them to the law in order to win friends in high places. Italian 'mafiologists' have a word for this traditional arrangement between the police and the mafia: they call it 'co-managing' crime.

Through numerous occult channels, the help from the mafia that the police needed was soon forthcoming. In the latter months of 1946, the bandits who had made Sicily so lawless since the Allied invasion in 1943 were rapidly eliminated. Until this point, police patrols had ranged across the wilds of western Sicily without ever catching a bandit gang. Now they mysteriously stumbled across their targets and killed or captured them. More frequently outlaw chiefs would be served up already dead. Just like the bandits of *In the Name of the Law*, they would be trussed up and tossed into a dried-up well, or simply shotgunned in the back in a mountain gully.

So at the dawning of Italy's democracy, the mafia was *exactly* what it had always been. It was *exactly* what the anti-mafia magistrate Giuseppe Guido Lo Schiavo, the US Army Intelligence officer Captain William Everett Scotten, and any number of police and *Carabinieri* had described it as: a secret society of murderous criminals bent on getting rich by illegal means, a force for murder, arson, kidnapping and mayhem.

Yet at the same time. give or take a little literary licence, the mafia was also *exactly* what the novelist Giuseppe Guido Lo Schiavo and the film director Pietro Germi portrayed it as: an auxiliary police force, and a preserver of the political status quo on a troubled island. Without ceasing to be the leaders of a 'criminal system', the smartest mafia bosses were dressing up in the costume that conservatives wanted them to wear. Hoisting themselves into the saddles of their imaginary white mares, *mafiosi* were slaughtering bandits who had become politically inconvenient, or cutting down peasant militants who refused to understand the way things worked on Sicily. And of course, most of the mafia's post-war political murders went unsolved – with the aid of the law.

The Cold War's first major electoral battle in Italy was the general election of 18 April 1948. One notorious election poster displayed the faces of Spencer Tracy, Rita Hayworth, Clark Gable, Gary Cooper and Tyrone Power, and proclaimed that 'Hollywood's stars are lining up against Communism'. But it was predominantly the Marshall Plan – America's huge programme of economic aid for Italy – that ensured that the Partito Comunista Italiano and its allies were defeated. The PCI remained in opposition in parliament; it would stay there for another half a century. The election's victors, the Christian Democrats (Democrazia Cristiana, DC), went into government – where they too would stay for the next half a century. Like trenches hacked into tundra, the battle-lines of Cold War Italian politics were now frozen in place.

A few weeks after that epoch-making general election, the most senior law enforcement officer in Sicily reported that, 'The mafia has never been as powerful and organised as it is today.' Nobody took any notice.

The Communist Party and their allies were the only ones not prepared to forget. In Rome, they did their best to denounce the

Christian Democrat tolerance for the mafia in Sicily. Left-wing MPs pointed out how DC politicians bestowed favours on mafia bosses, and used them as electoral agents. Such protests would continue for the next forty years. But the PCI never had the support to form a government; it was unelectable, and therefore impotent. In June 1949, just a few weeks after *In the Name of the Law* was released in Italian cinemas, Interior Minister Mario Scelba addressed the Senate. Scelba had access to all that the police knew about the mafia in Sicily. But he scoffed at Communist concerns about organised crime, and gave a homespun lecture about what mafia really meant to Sicilians like him:

> If a buxom girl walks past, a Sicilian will tell you that she is a *mafiosa* girl. If a boy is advanced for his age, a Sicilian will tell you that he is *mafioso*. People talk about the mafia flavoured with every possible sauce, and it seems to me that they are exaggerating.

What Scelba meant was that the mafia, or better the typically Sicilian quality known as 'mafiosity', was as much a part of the island's life as *cannoli* and *cassata* – and just as harmless. The world should just forget about this mafia thing, whatever it was, and busy itself with more serious problems.

For over forty years after the establishment of the Republic, Scelba's party, the DC, provided the mafias with their most reliable political friends. But the DC was by no means a mere mafia front. In fact it was a huge and hybrid political beast. Its supporters included northerners and southerners, cardinals and capitalists, civil servants and shopkeepers, bankers and peasant families whose entire wealth was a little plot of land. All that this heterogeneous electorate had in common was a fear of Communism.

In Sicily and the South, the DC encountered a class of political leader who had dominated politics since long before Fascism: the grandees. The typical southern grandee was a landowner or lawyer who was often personally wealthy, but invariably richer still in contacts with the Church and government. Patronage was the method: converting public resources (salaries, contracts, state credit, licences . . . or just help in cutting through the dense undergrowth of regulations) into private booty to be handed out to a train of family and followers. Through patronage, the grandees digested the anonymous structures of government and span them out into a web of favours. *Mafiosi* were the grandees' natural allies. The best that can be said of the DC's relationship with the mafias is that the party was too fragmented and faction-ridden to ever confront and isolate the grandees.

Under Fascism, as on many previous occasions, police and magistrates had painstakingly assembled a photofit of the mafia organisation, the 'criminal system'. Now, in the era of the Cold War and the Christian Democrats, that picture was broken up and reassembled to compose the Buddha-like features of Turi Passalacqua. Better the mafia than the Communists. Better the Hollywood cowboy fantasy land of *In the Name of the Law* than a serious attempt to understand and tackle the island's criminal system of which many of the governing party's key supporters were an integral part.

Thanks to the success of *In the Name of the Law*, and to his prestigious career as a magistrate, Giuseppe Guido Lo Schiavo went on to become Italy's leading mafia pundit in the 1950s. He never missed an opportunity to restate the same convenient falsehoods that he had first articulated in his novel. More worryingly still, he became a lecturer in law at the *Carabinieri* training school, the chairman of the national board of film censorship, and a Supreme Court judge.

In 1954 Lo Schiavo even wrote a glowing commemoration of the venerable *capomafia* don Calogero Vizzini, who had just passed away peacefully in his home town of Villalba. Vizzini had been a protagonist in every twist and turn of the mafia's history in the dramatic years following the Liberation. By 1943, when he was proclaimed mayor of Villalba under AMGOT, the then sixty-six-year-old boss had already had a long career as an extortionist, cattle-rustler, black-marketeer and sulphur entrepreneur. In September of the following year, Vizzini's men caused a national sensation by throwing hand grenades at a Communist leader who had come to Villalba to give a speech. Vizzini was a leader of the Separatist movement. But when Separatism's star waned, he joined the Christian Democrats. The old man's grand funeral, in July 1954, was attended by mafia bosses from across the island.

Giuseppe Guido Lo Schiavo took Calogero Vizzini's death as a chance to reiterate his customary flummery about the mafia. But intriguingly, he also revealed that, one Sunday in Rome in 1952, the fat old boss had paid a visit to his house. He vividly recalled opening the door to his guest and being struck by a pair of 'razor-sharp, magnetic' eyes. The magistrate issued a polite but nervy welcome: '*Commendatore* Vizzini, my name is—'

'For you, I am not *commendatore*,' came the reply, as Vizzini waddled into the book-lined study and lowered his meaty frame onto the sofa. 'Call me Uncle Calò.'

Uncle Calò's tone was firm, but his manner open-hearted. He praised Lo Schiavo as a man of the law who had played hard but fair. The two men shook hands as a sign of mutual respect. Lo Schiavo tells us that, as he gazed at Uncle Calò, he was reminded of a picture from the past, from his first years as an anti-mafia magistrate in Sicily, when he first met a corpulent old mafia boss who always rode a white mare. He concluded his memories of Uncle Calò with good wishes for his successor within the mafia: 'May his efforts be directed along the path of respect for the state's laws, and of social improvement for all.'

Lo Schiavo's account of the conversation between himself and don Calogero Vizzini is as heavily embroidered as any of his novels. But the meeting itself really happened. The reason for

Uncle Calò's visit was that he was caught up in a series of trials for the hand-grenade attack back in 1944. Only three days earlier, the Supreme Court had issued a guilty verdict against him. But the legal process was due to run on for a long time yet, and Uncle Calò knew that he would almost certainly die before he saw the inside of a jail. The real reason that he called in on Lo Schiavo may simply have been to say thank you. For the celebrated magistrate-novelist was involved in presenting the prosecution evidence at the Supreme Court. The suspicion lingers that, behind the scenes, he gave the mafia boss a helping hand with his case.

In today's Italy, if any magistrate received a social call from a crime boss he would immediately be placed under investigation. But in the conservative world of Christian Democrat Italy, affairs between the Sicilian mafia and magistrates were conducted in a more friendly way. The state and the mafia formed a partnership, in the name of the law.

Calabria: **The last romantic bandit**

The Calabrian mafia, like the Sicilian mafia, was a sworn secret society, modelled on the Freemasons. It shared some of the same criminal jargon as the Sicilian mafia – *omertà*, honour, and the like – and its affiliates engaged in the same day-to-day activities of extortion and smuggling. However, the two mafias were not directly related, and were far from identical: they had a different structure, different rituals and a different terminology. In Calabria, for example, bosses were known as *capibastone* – 'chief cudgels'. The Calabrian mafia was also born later than the Sicilian mafia, and came from humbler origins: it emerged from within the prison system in the 1880s to colonise the brothels and taverns. It surfaced first in Reggio Calabria, and in the agricultural towns of the region's thin coastal strip. Soon afterwards, it spread up into the mountains that occupy much of southern Calabria.

Quickly after it emerged, the Calabrian mafia set up cattle-rustling networks and protection rackets. Criminal fortunes began to accumulate. Political friends were won. And the police were persuaded to leave the bosses unmolested in return for information on petty delinquents. Successive governments in Rome did little to rectify the situation, because they relied on the support of Calabrian delegates when it came to building coalitions in parliament. The mafia became a facet of Calabria's ruling class.

Just as in Sicily, Fascism launched a campaign of repression against the mafia in Calabria. There were hundreds and hundreds of arrests. In one of many important trials, held in 1932, ninety defendants stood accused of membership of 'The Montalbano Honoured Family' – one of several titles, like the 'Honoured Society', or the 'Society of the Buckle', that the Calabrian mafia adopted at the time. (The name would change again: it was not until 1955 that the Calabrian mafia acquired the name 'ndrangheta that it bears today.)

Investigators in the 1932 case discovered that the organisation was divided into local cells or *'ndrine* (the word may well come from *malandrina*, the term for the section of a prison reserved for gangsters). Unlike the Families of the Sicilian mafia, the local Calabrian cells had a double structure: for greater secrecy, the senior members belonged to the so-called 'Major Society', while the 'Minor Society' comprised the less trustworthy recruits who were obliged to give 'absolute obedience to their ranking superiors'. Documentation from the trial paints an alarming picture of how the 'ndrangheta's internal discipline enabled it to infiltrate all corners of Calabrian life.

> That is how the mafia interfered in every imaginable issue – even, when one of the affiliates decided he had an interest, in the meanest squabbles within families that had nothing to do with the organisation. Government contracts, state construction projects, public bureaucracy: the organisation intruded into them all. Elections were a particular target. The most powerful campaigning weapon, and the surest path to victory at the polls, was this sect of bullying and rigorously disciplined felons.

Investigators in the 1932 case believed that the Calabrian mafia even had its own governing body, known as the *Criminale*, which intervened to settle disputes within the various *'ndrine* across the province of Reggio Calabria. On one occasion, during the First World War, the *Criminale* intervened in the affairs of the Santo Stefano *'ndrina* when two members of the sect were at loggerheads because both were engaged to marry the same woman. This was no criminal soap opera. There was nothing petty or comical in the dispute. By this time in its history, the Honoured Society of Calabria had learned just how politically important marriage was. By ceasing to make money from pimping, and settling down instead, *mafiosi* could found criminal dynasties and pass illegally acquired wealth down to their sons; they could make alliances within the organisation, or broker peace deals with bitter rivals. These were lessons that Sicilian mobsters had learned generations earlier. Now, in Calabria, mafia marriages were becoming as big a deal as they had long been in Sicily.

So the 'ndrangheta was no mere gang: like the Sicilian mafia, it was parallel government, a parasitical creeper that had wound itself so thoroughly around the branches of the state that it now formed a more solid structure than the tree off which it fed. Just as in Sicily, Fascism's enthusiasm for the task of taking on the mafia in Calabria could not be maintained. The party, like every other authority in the province of Reggio Calabria, was infiltrated and hollowed out. In the end, it proved much simpler to just pretend the problem had been dealt with, and to ban all mention of the mob in the press.

When the Second World War came, it largely bypassed Calabria. The Axis mounted only a token resistance, and the region was lightly garrisoned by the Allies after the Liberation. The local mafia was heavily involved in the black market. But few seemed to notice. Senior AMGOT officials were unaware that the Calabria mafia even existed.

When it came to organised crime, post-war Italy's amnesia was as deep and complex as the country's geology: its layers were the accumulated deposits of incompetence and negligence; the pressures of collusion and political cynicism sculpted its elaborate folds. By the time the Second World War ended, this geology of forgetfulness had created one of its most striking formations in Calabria.

In 1945, Italy's best-loved criminal lunatic returned to the land where he had made his name. Aged seventy, and now deemed harmless, Giuseppe Musolino was transferred from a penal asylum in the north to a civil psychiatric hospital way down south in Calabria.

Musolino's new home was an infernal place. Although it was a Fascist-era building, it was already crumbling by the time the Fascist dictator's battered corpse was swinging by its heels from the gantry of a Milanese petrol station. Bare, unsanitary and overcrowded, the psychiatric hospital's rooms and corridors echoed with the gibbering and shrieking of afflicted souls. But in the late 1940s and early 1950s, before today's encrustation of motorways and jerry-built apartments had sprouted around the Calabrian coast, the hospital did at least afford a lovely panorama: before it, the view down to the city of Reggio Calabria, across the Straits of Messina, and over towards Sicily; behind it, the wooded shoulders of Aspromonte – the 'harsh mountain' that had once been Musolino's realm.

The new arrival attracted a great deal more attention and sympathy than the other patients. He was, after all, one of the most famous Calabrians alive. 'Don Peppino', the doctors and nurses all called him, combining a respectful title and a fond nickname. Despite his mind's desolation, his frail body did its best to live up to this lingering aura. Musolino was thin, but unbowed by decades of incarceration. His scraggy beard stood out strikingly white against the olive darkness of his skin, making him look part Athenian philosopher and part faun, as one journalist noted. An actress drawn to visit the hospital was struck breathless by his resemblance to Luigi Pirandello, the great Sicilian dramatist, whose tales of masks and madness had earned him a Nobel Prize.

Musolino's own madness bore the blundering labels of mid-twentieth century psychiatry: 'progressive chronic interpretative delirium' and 'pompous paranoia'. He thought he was the Emperor of the Universe. He spent most of his day outside, smoking, reading, and contemplating the shadow of the cypress trees in the nearby cemetery. Yet when he found anyone with the patience to talk, he would grasp the chance to expound the hierarchy over which he presided: from the kings, queens and princes enthroned at his feet, to the cops and stoolies who grovelled far below.

Don Peppino had an obsessive loathing of cops and stoolies. And somehow, when he spoke to visitors, that very loathing often became a pathway to the corners of his mind that were still lucid. 'Bandits have to kill,' he would concede, 'but they must be honourable.' For Musolino, honour meant vendetta: all the crimes that had led to his imprisonment had been carried out to avenge the wrong he had endured at the hands of the police and their informers. Even in his insanity, he prized honesty above all: he would proudly point out that he had never denied any of his murders. After all, the victims were only cops and stoolies.

The newspapermen who made the long journey to the mental hospital in Reggio relished the chance to delve into the past and fill the gaps in don Peppino's fragmented memory for their readers. Born the son of a woodcutter in Santo Stefano d'Aspromonte in 1876, he was convicted at the age of twenty-two of attempting to murder his fellow villager Vincenzo Zoccali. From the dock, when he heard the judge issue a harsh twenty-one-year sentence, Musolino vowed to eat Zoccali's liver. In January of 1899, he hacked a hole in the wall of his jail, shinned down a rope of knotted bed sheets, and headed up into the Aspromonte massif. Musolino then spent two and a half years as a renegade. He killed seven people and tried to kill six more, all the while proclaiming that he had been framed in the Zoccali case. The longer he evaded capture, the more his reputation grew: he came to be seen as a brigand avenger, a wronged hero of the oppressed peasantry. Even those who found his ferocity distasteful, saw in him a symbol of desperate resistance to a heartless state. In the press, Musolino was crowned the 'King of Aspromonte'.

And this was the role that Musolino would continue to play when, after his capture in the autumn of 1901, the world's press gathered to watch him face justice. He confessed to the offences he committed in the mountains. His only care was to prove that he was innocent of the attempted murder of Vincenzo Zoccali for which he had originally been imprisoned. As a defence strategy, this was hopeless: no one was surprised when he received a life term. But Musolino's performance in court was guaranteed to add lustre to the King of Aspromonte legend.

At some point during the brutal years of solitary confinement that ensued, Musolino lost his mind. The state had inflicted yet more sorrow on the poor woodcutter's son, and his tragic stature was thrown into starker relief.

Then, in 1936, a Calabrian-born emigrant to the United States made a deathbed confession: it was he, and not Musolino, who had shot at Vincenzo Zoccali all those years ago. The King of Aspromonte had stuck heroically to the same story from the start of his murderous rampage, during his trial, and even through his descent into insanity. Now that story had been proved right.

Perhaps it is no wonder that the psychiatrist in Reggio Calabria was so angry on his behalf. 'Was Musolino antisocial?' he asked in one newspaper interview. 'Or was it society that forced him to become what he became?'

Don Peppino received many presents. The most generous – food, clothes and dollars – came from Calabrians who had emigrated to America and made it big. Occasionally, he was even allowed day release – when a sentimental Italian-American businessman in a fedora and pinstriped suit turned up to take the old bandit out on a motor tour of the mountain.

Looking back now, one has to suspect that the Americans who came to pay homage to Giuseppe Musolino knew the truth. He was no lone bandit hero: he was a member of the Calabrian mafia. The branch in Santo Stefano d'Aspromonte was founded by his father and uncle in the early 1890s. All the crimes Musolino committed were mafia business, in one way or another. Even the attempted execution of Vincenzo Zoccali, in which he was undoubtedly involved (though he probably did not pull the trigger), was a deed born of the Honoured Society's violent internal politics. Musolino was an 'ndrangheta killer.

When Musolino escaped from prison in 1899 and embarked on his murderous rampage, the King of Aspromonte fable grew up around him, relayed in song sheets and chap-books, perpetuated by folk poets and by children playing at bandits and *Carabinieri* in the street. By the time of his arrest in 1901, he was a national celebrity. His trial in 1902 represented an unmissable opportunity for the authorities to destroy the noble bandit myth, and for Italian public opinion to witness the growing power of Calabrian organised crime. But the opportunity was lost. The police tried to mount a prosecution against the 166 members of the mafia in Musolino's village, but could not prevent terrified witnesses from retracting their evidence. The King of Aspromonte was left free to act out his script at his trial, and thus keep the Calabrian mafia in the shadows.

Musolino's brother Antonio was an *'ndranghetista* too. Antonio was oathed in America soon after the King of Aspromonte's trial, and then returned to Calabria to rise through the ranks. After the First World War, Antonio was drawn into a feud with his boss that the Calabrian mafia's governing body, the *Criminale*, was unable to settle. There were two attempts on his life. At that point, he broke the code of *omertà* and turned to the authorities to get his revenge. He was the source of all the inside knowledge about the Calabrian mafia that led to the 1932 trial I outlined above.

Before Antonio Musolino, dozens of other Calabrian mobsters had given evidence to the authorities. (*Omertà* was not the iron law that the mob liked to pretend it was, either in Calabria or in Sicily.) Thousands of men were convicted of belonging to the Honoured Society over the years. But they were sent to serve short sentences back in the very same prisons where many of them had been recruited into the sect in the first place.

After 1945, with the war over, the transition to democracy under way, and the King of Aspromonte residing in Reggio

Calabria mental hospital, the 'ndrangheta operated in very much the same way that it had done when he was in his murderous prime. *Carabinieri* 'co-managed' petty crime with the underworld bosses. Grandees used the mafia to round up electors, and then returned the favour by testifying in court that there was no such organisation. For successive governments, it proved easy to just bank the votes of Calabria's mafia-backed members of parliament, and ignore the Honoured Society. Magistrates forgot all about the *Criminale*, the 'ndrangheta's coordinating body. Meanwhile, just as during Giuseppe Musolino's homicidal rampage, lazy journalists were content to churn out the King of Aspromonte fable, even now that their primary source was a crazy geriatric killer. Musolino, for his part, lived as the Emperor of the Universe, commanding interplanetary ships and deploying devices more destructive than the atomic bomb. In his psychologically damaged state, he became a metaphor for Italy's own cognitive failure. The reasons for that failure were ultimately very simple. In southern Calabria, the conflict between Left and Right had nowhere near the explosiveness that propelled Sicily up the political agenda and created such devilish intrigues between *mafiosi* and men of the law. Calabria remained Italy's poorest and most neglected region. The 'ndrangheta could be forgotten because the region it came from simply did not count.

Cinema proved unable to resist the story of the King of Aspromonte, however. In 1950, two of Italy's biggest stars, Amedeo Nazzari and Silvana Mangano, were cast in *Il brigante Musolino*. Filmed on location on Aspromonte, the movie told how Musolino was unjustly imprisoned for murder on the basis of false testimonies, and then escaped to become an outlaw hero. The film did well among the Italian community in the United States.

Giuseppe Musolino died in January 1956 aged seventy-nine. Up and down Italy, the newspapers told his story one more time, and called him 'the last romantic bandit'.

Naples: **Puppets and puppeteers**

In 1930, Italy's first great national encyclopedia, the *Enciclopedia Treccani*, included the following entry under *Camorra*:

> The camorra was an association of lower class men, who used extortion to force the vice-ridden and the cowardly to surrender tribute. Its branches spread through the old Kingdom of Naples; it had laws and customs, a rigidly organised hierarchy, specific obligations and duties, and a jargon and court system of its own . . . Moral education and environmental improvements succeeded, in the end, in destroying the camorra . . . Only the word remains today, to indicate abuses or acts of bullying.

The camorra was dead: for once, this proud claim had a strong basis in truth rather than in the propaganda needs of the Fascist regime. The Honoured Society of Naples, the old camorra's official name, was an oath-bound secret society of murderers, extortionists and smugglers like the Sicilian and Calabrian mafias. Like them, it was modelled on the Freemasons, spoke the language of honour and *omertà*, and was born amid political and economic turbulence in the middle of the nineteenth century. But the camorra was very much the poor relation. Whereas Sicilian *mafiosi* graduated from the wealthy lemon groves of the Palermo hinterland and quickly found friends among the aristocracy and magistracy, Neapolitan *camorristi* bullied their way out of the prisons, brothels and slums. Whereas Calabria's gangsters climbed the social ladder until they merged with the state, *camorristi* in Naples never quite left the alleys behind. Unable to call on the kind of political protection that the mafias of Sicily and Calabria could boast, the camorra was vulnerable. By the time the First World War broke out, the Honoured Society of Naples had collapsed.

In Naples in the late 1940s, one of the few places where the word 'camorra' was regularly used was in a tiny theatre, the San Carlino. Its entrance was hard to find: a doorway hidden among the bookstalls that crowded about the Porta San Gennaro. Inside, the auditorium could barely contain seven dilapidated benches. The stage was only just wider than the upright piano standing before it. This was the last poky outpost of a beleaguered art form for the illiterate: the only remaining puppet playhouse in the city.

Puppet theatre had been popular in Sicily and southern Italy for more than a century. Its stock stories told of chivalry and treachery among Charlemagne's knights as they battled against their Saracen foes. The marionettes, in tin armour and with bright red lips, would speechify endlessly about honour and betrayal, and then launch into a wobbly dance that signified mortal combat.

In Naples, the puppet theatres had another speciality too: tales of chivalry and treachery set in the world of the Honoured Society. Indeed, if the San Carlino was still holding out against the cinemas, it was largely because of the enduring appeal of camorra dramas. Outside, badly printed posters proclaimed the dramatic delights on offer:

TONIGHT
THE DEATH OF PEPPE AVERZANO THE WISE GUY.
WITH REAL BLOOD

Inside, the audience was integral to the spectacle. The loud cries of 'Traitor!' and 'Watch out!' from the stalls could as well have been written into the script. The punters knowledgeably applauded the knife-fighting skills of some *camorristi*, and angrily denounced the cowardly tricks of others: 'You should be ashamed of yourself! Ten against one!' The plots were repetitive: *camorristi* taking blood oaths, or fighting dagger duels, or saving marionette maidens from dishonour. The dramatic pay-off was always the same: good versus evil, the surge of righteous indignation versus the prurient thrill of violence. When the action was particularly moving, the San Carlino rocked and creaked like a railway carriage trundling over points.

Everyone knew the camorra heroes' names: the gentleman gang-ster, don Teofilo Sperino, and the mighty boss Ciccio Cappuccio ('Little Lord Frankie'); the devious Nicola Jossa, endlessly pitting his wits against the greatest *camorrista* of them all, Salvatore De Crescenzo. All of these puppet heroes and villains had once been real gangsters rather than gaudily painted puppets. Genuine episodes of nineteenth-century camorra history were reimagined on the stage of the San Carlino. The 'real blood' that spurted from the puppet's chest at the dramatic conclusion of the piece was in fact a bladder full of aniline dye. And whereas the good-guy *camorristi* would be given bright red gore, the bad guys bled a much darker shade, almost black.

Outside the San Carlino, in the bomb-ravaged streets of Naples, the real Honoured Society had not been seen for over thirty years. There were still a few old *camorristi* around. The most notorious of them was a familiar and pitiful sight, who recalled both the old camorra and the strange story of its demise.

Gennaro Abbatemaggio was a tubby little old man, almost bald. At first glance he seemed well turned out in a suit and open-necked shirt, or in a dark turtle-neck, sports jacket and sunglasses. But the threadbare tailoring fooled no one who saw him up close. For don Gennaro, as journalists called him with ironic reverence, was all but indigent. He lived hand-to-mouth, on petty theft and scams. No one would have cared about his fortunes – but for the fact that he was a living relic of a once fearsome criminal power.

In 1911, Gennaro Abbatemaggio was an initiated affiliate of the Stella chapter of the Honoured Society. But he betrayed his criminal comrades to become the star witness in the most sensational mob trial of the day. Newspapers and newsreels made his face known to millions across the world. During sixteen exhausting months of hearings, Abbatemaggio explained the camorra's rituals, ranks and methods, and furnished highly detailed evidence about the bloody crimes ordered by its leaders. His testimony led to dozens of convictions. Abbatemaggio struck a blow from which the Honoured Society never recovered. On the eve of the First World War, news filtered up from the underworld that the Neapolitan camorra had been formally disbanded.

In 1927, Abbatemaggio hit the headlines once more when he announced that he had made all of his evidence up on the orders of the *Carabinieri*. To this day, it is still uncertain just how much of his testimony was falsified. Nevertheless, as a result of this startling retraction, the *camorristi* convicted in the 1911 trial were released. But by this time, the Honoured Society of Naples was too far gone to be revived.

After the Second World War, Abbatemaggio did everything he could to keep himself in the limelight – at least he did when he was not in prison. In 1949 he staged a suicide attempt, and a conversion to religious faith; he later gave interviews on the steps of the Roman church where he was due to receive his First Holy Communion. When religion failed, he tried show business. But his repeated efforts to get his own story turned into celluloid came to nothing. In 1952 he had to be content with being snapped with the stars at the premiere of *The City Stands Trial*, a 1952 film retelling the story of the 1911 case that had destroyed the Honoured Society.

Shut out of the cinema, Abbatemaggio's last resort was to try and revive his moment of glory. He claimed to have sensational revelations about one of the biggest murder mysteries of 1953: the death of a Roman girl, Wilma Montesi. But it soon emerged that the old stool pigeon was at it again. He was arrested and tried for false testimony. Thereafter, he was seen begging. The press began to ignore him.

So if the word 'camorra' was used in post-war Naples, it was only to evoke its memory with the same mixture of amusement and pity that was conjured up by newspaper stories about the puppet theatre or Gennaro Abbatemaggio.

Today, more than half a century after Abbatemaggio's death, 'camorra' has changed its meaning. In the decades since the end of the Second World War, the camorra has re-emerged and adopted a new identity; it has become stronger and more insidious than ever. It is no longer an Honoured Society – a single sect of criminals with its initiation rituals, its formalised dagger duels, its ranks and rules. Today *camorrista* means an affiliate of one of many structured, but frequently unstable, gangster syndicates. The camorra is not just one secret society like the mafias of Sicily and Calabria, therefore. Rather it is a vast and constantly shifting map of gangs ruling different territories in Naples and the Campania region. Like the Honoured Society of old, these organisations run protection rackets and trafficking operations. But – at least when things are going well for them – they are far more successful than the old Honoured Society ever was at infiltrating the state institutions, politics and the economy.

To the audiences at the San Carlino in the late 1940s, such a future incarnation of the camorra would have seemed a highly unlikely prospect. Hoodlums were certainly active in Naples in the post-war years. But they were much less powerful than they are today – or indeed than they were in Sicily or Calabria at the time. Naples could not manage anything like the great Sicilian ruling-class conspiracy of silence about the mafia. There was no Neapolitan equivalent of a senior magistrate like Giuseppe Guido Lo Schiavo, who was prepared, in the teeth of everything he knew, to deny the mafia's very existence. And the great and troubled city of Naples was far from politically invisible in the way the towns and villages of Calabria were.

However, under closer examination, the hoodlums of post-war Naples do turn out to be the progenitors of today's Kalashnikov-wielding, cocaine-smuggling, suit-wearing *camorristi*. The seeds of the camorra's future revival had already been planted. Indeed, there was already something menacing there in the city's underworld – something that made it abundantly clear that the camorra was not as dead as all the encyclopedias claimed. A careful look at Neapolitan gangland in the 1940s and early 1950s also shows that Italy in general, and Naples in particular, had a guilty conscience when it came to organised crime. This was a city that refused to use the 'c' word (unless it was talking about the past, of course – about the San Carlino theatre or Gennaro Abbatemaggio). In short, Naples had *both* its own distinctive mobsters, *and* its own characteristic style of forgetting that they were there.

Stereotypes were the most powerful way to forget about the camorra. Naples is Italy's hardest city to decipher. Countless visitors have been lured into judging it by appearances, because those appearances are so obvious and so diverting. For hundreds of years, Europe has found the sunlit spectacle of Neapolitan street life irresistible. Here was a place where squalor seemed to come in colour, and sweet music to emerge miraculously from a constant din. The poor of the city had the reputation of using any shabby trick, putting on any demeaning act, in order to fill their bellies and live a life of *dolce far niente* ('sweet idleness'). The reason Gennaro Abbatemaggio appeared in the papers so often in the late 1940s was not just because he had destroyed the Honoured Society; it was also because, with his tragicomic ducking and diving, he seemed like a personification of everybody's archetypal Neapolitan. The San Carlino attracted attention because it too seemed peculiar and typical of the city. The Neapolitan poor were viewed as imps living in paradise: mischievous, sentimental, naïve, and endlessly inventive to the point of being unabashed about playing up to all the stereotypes about them. Before the war, Neapolitan urchins would charge a fee to foreigners who wanted to photograph them eating spaghetti with their hands, as a century and more of stereotypes dictated that they should.

The post-war generation also had its travellers keen to revive these commonplaces. The simple trick was to show a city encapsulated only in what first met the eye in the poor neighbourhoods like Forcella or Pignasecca. A city of beggars and pedlars, where from every windowsill or doorway, from orange boxes or trays, somebody would be trying to sell you something: chestnuts, or fragments of fried fish, or single cigarettes, or prickly pears, or *taralli* (pretzels). Poor Naples was an open-air bazaar where barbers and tailors plied their trade out in the street, and where passers-by could look in at the single-family sweatshops making shoes or gloves.

Foreigners were not the only ones responsible for rehashing the old clichés: there were always professional Neapolitans prepared to chip in too. One such was Giuseppe Marotta. He knew precisely how hard life in Naples could be: he and his two sisters had been brought up by a seamstress in one of the notorious *bassi* – the one-room apartments that opened directly onto the street. In 1926 he went north to become a writer in Italy's industrial and literary capital, Milan. By the late 1940s, after years of hack-work, he had made it: he was a regular newspaper columnist, and the man to whom editors turned when they wanted a colourful piece on some aspect of Neapolitan life.

In the stereotypical Naples that Marotta served up for his readers, lawlessness was not really crime, it was a part of the urban spectacle. Here pickpockets and endlessly inventive rip-off artists expressed a picturesque form of dishonesty – one that grew from hardship and not malice. There was something both creative and endearing about crime here. The poor of Naples could steal your heart as easily as lift your wallet.

In one article from 1953, Marotta marvelled at the agility of the *correntisti* – daring, agile young crooks who would swing themselves up onto the back of a passing lorry so as to offload the contents as it rumbled along. This type of crime was known in the alleys as *la corrente* ('the stream') because of the fluidity of the whole operation. A good *correntista*, Marotta remarked, needed a freakish range of skills:

The legs of a star centre forward, the eye of a sailor, the ear of a redskin, the velvet touch of a bishop, and the iron grip of a weightlifter – as well as hooked feet, rubber ribs, and the balance of a jockey. And to coordinate it all, the brain of the conductor Arturo Toscanini.

Marotta also smirked indulgently at the teetering pyramids of stolen tin cans that were the fruits of the *corrente*.

The truth that Marotta's stereotypes concealed was that criminal power was a threatening presence in Naples. The poor, the very inhabitants of those alleys who so charmed onlookers, were often its first victims, as one revealing episode from the everyday life of Naples allows us to see.

At around 6.30, one hot summer evening in 1952, Antonio Quindici, known as 'O Grifone (the Griffon), decided to buy some mussels. He presented himself at a stall in via Alessandro Poerio, not far from the station, but he found five workers from a nearby building site in front of him. He demanded to be served first, and the mussel-seller meekly obeyed. But the builders, who were from a different part of the city, obviously did not know who they were dealing with, because they objected loudly. 'O Grifone responded by grabbing the mussel-seller's knife and stabbing the most vocal builder twice in the heart. He then fled. He was chased by the victim's friends, but their pursuit was blocked by a coordinated group of accomplices. 'O Grifone vanished into the side streets. His victim bled to death where he lay, leaving a wife and a baby daughter.

The story of 'O Grifone is interesting for several reasons. First because the murderer was one of the *correntisti* that Giuseppe Marotta so admired. Men like 'O Grifone had learned their skills during the war, when Naples had been the major supply port for the Allied forces in Italy: around half of those supplies found their way off the backs of army lorries and onto the black market. The crowded area around via Forcella, where 'O Grifone came from, was where the wartime trade in stolen military supplies was concentrated: not for nothing did the Forcella area become known as the kasbah of Naples. Significantly, Forcella was once also a stronghold of the Honoured Society: it was home to all the earliest bosses. *Correntisti* like *'O Grifone* would become protagonists of the camorra's revival.

When the war ended, everyone confidently expected the *correntisti* to disappear. Yet they were still very much in business in 1952, when one newspaper commented:

> The *corrente* is fluid, as everyone knows, and omnipresent, especially in the streets where there is most traffic. Communications between the city and its outskirts are watched over by squads of criminals. Quick, well-equipped and scornful of danger, these men remove all kinds of goods from vehicles. It can be said that no road-train, lorry or car escapes the clutches of the *correntisti*.

Around each *correntista* there was a whole organisation that included teams of spies who tracked the path of valuable cargoes, porters who smuggled the goods away once they were dropped from the lorry, and fences who put the swag on the market. Long after the great days of military contraband came to an end, goods stolen by the *corrente* were still openly on sale in via Forcella.

The *correntisti* were not just agile, but also violent. They were often armed, for practical reasons: to protect themselves from gun-wielding truck drivers and rival gangs; and to discourage passers-by from trying to pick up anything they might have seen falling off the back of a lorry. But they were also armed because they had to impose themselves on the community around them, and establish a reputation for toughness. Back in the days of the Honoured Society, this reputation would have been referred to as 'honour'. It is one of the key ingredients of the mafias' power – of 'territorial control', as it is termed. *'O Grifone*'s row at the mussel stall displayed that 'honour' in an individualistic, undisciplined form.

After the stabbing, 'O Grifone spent several days on the run. Eventually he had a last breakfast in the bar next to the police station and gave himself up, having first concocted a story about how he had been grievously insulted and provoked by the man he knifed to death. Evidently his support network could not stand the strain of a high-profile police investigation and a public outcry. 'O Grifone and his friends still had limits to their territorial control.

Strikingly, the newspapers in Naples referred to 'O Grifone as a *camorrista*. Or at least they did so initially. This is one of the rare occasions when the word slipped into print in the late 1940s and early 1950s. Curiously, as the manhunt for 'O Grifone continued over the following days, the early references to the camorra disappeared. 'O Grifone started off as a *camorrista*, and then became a mere criminal.

There was a palpable unease about using the word 'camorra' in Naples in the years after the war, as there was about admitting just how serious the city's crime problem was. Naples was a key political battleground, where the soul of the Italian right was being fought over by opposing political machines. On the one hand, there was the creeping power of the Christian Democrats. On the other, there were the Monarchists, under the war profiteer, shipping magnate and football mogul Achille Lauro. (Naples, like many southern cities, had voted against the Republic in the referendum of 1946. Thereafter, the monarchy remained a powerful rallying cause for the city's right wing.)

The Naples these two political machines contested was scarred by chronic unemployment and homelessness, poor health and illiteracy. Neapolitan industry and infrastructure had not recovered from the devastations of the war, which were worse here than in any other Italian city. Yet politics found no answers because it was beset with instability and malpractice, mostly rotating around the lucrative construction industry. These were the years of '*maccheroni* politics'. At election time, political grandees would order their local agents to set up distribution centres in the kasbahs of the centre. Here, packets of pasta, or cuts of meat, or pieces of salt cod would be wrapped in the vague promise of a job or a pension and handed out in exchange for votes. Achille Lauro's election runners came up with the scheme of handing out pairs of shoes to their would-be supporters: the right shoe before the poll, and the left one afterwards, when the vote had been safely recorded.

The poor who sold their support so cheaply seemed almost as resistant to the benefits of education, social improvement and conventional party politics as they had been when Italy was unified in 1860. Their political loyalties were understandably fickle. One of the few ways of trying to win them over, other than *maccheroni* or shoes, was a tear-jerking local patriotism: the claim that the city's problems were all the fault of northern neglect. Achille Lauro, who also owned the second-biggest newspaper in Naples, *Roma*, was a master at playing up to the stereotype of Naples as a big-hearted city that history had treated harshly. Any talk of the camorra or organised crime was just old-fashioned northern snobbery.

There was another reason why Neapolitans insisted on confining the word camorra to the past: criminals were part of the ruling political machines. Even the old camorra stool pigeon Gennaro Abbatemaggio was an occasional electoral runner for Achille Lauro. But much more important than these grassroots agents were the so-called *guappi*. The only way to translate the term *guappo* is as 'wise guy' or 'hood'. But these American words don't really evoke the sort of authority that a *guappo* exercised over his corner of Naples. *Guappi* were fences and loan sharks, runners of illegal lotteries: they were the puppeteers of the city's lively criminal scene. But they were not *just* criminal figures: *guappi* also pulled political strings, fixing everyday problems by calling in favours from the politicians on whose behalf they raked in votes come election time.

The most famous *guappo* of them all was Giuseppe Navarra, known as the King of Poggioreale. He was a loyal electoral chief for the Monarchists and Achille Lauro, and collected honorific titles from his political protectors: *Commendatore*, and Knight of the Great Cross of the Constantinian Order. During the war, he had operated in the black market, making friends with the Allied authorities. He also made a great deal of money in iron and other scrap, which his people took (mostly illegally) from bombed-out buildings.

Navarra lived among the coffin-makers on the main thorough-fare of Poggioreale, the neighbourhood where the cemetery and the prison stand. He held court on wooden chairs on the pavement. It is said that on his saint's day, the tram would stop outside his house so that all the passengers could sample the sweets and liqueurs he offered. Navarra drove a gigantic Lancia Dilambda limousine with running boards down the side, a car of the kind we are used to seeing in American gangster movies of the inter-war years. Navarra bought it at an auction in Rome after the fall of Fascism; it used to belong to the Duce's oldest son, Vittorio Mussolini. In 1947, one northern newspaper gave a tongue-in-cheek portrait of this street-corner monarch:

> He is about fifty, dumpy, with a square face and thick salt-and-pepper hair. One of his eyes is lazy, and his nose starts off from a very wide base on his face, but comes to a rapid end in a sharp point – as if it started off wanting to be a huge Bourbon nose, and then repented along the way.

Navarra owed his fame, and quite a part of his popularity, to an extraordinary episode earlier in 1947, when he rescued the treasure of the city's patron saint, San Gennaro (Saint Januarius). San Gennaro is the martyr whose 'blood' is kept in a glass box in Naples cathedral so that it can miraculously liquefy a couple of times a year. Or not, if the citizens meet with the Almighty's displeasure for whatever reason. The saint's treasure is a collection of gifts from the faithful, which was taken to the Vatican for safe-keeping during the war. First-hand details of the King of Poggioreale's supposed act of heroism are sketchy because almost all newspapers, rather suspiciously, did not report it until later. But the story told is that, when the mayor asked the Chief of Police to help bring the treasure home, he was refused: the police could not spare the money or resources to send the armoured car, ten trucks and twenty-man armed escort that it would take to carry the treasure over the dangerous roads between the capital and Naples. At that point, the *guappo* Navarra volunteered his services, and did the job stealthily by car, with an aged Catholic aristocrat on the passenger seat next to him. He reportedly travelled in a FIAT 22, which was less conspicuous than his limo. But quite how he fitted all the treasure in its tiny boot is not entirely clear. Bizarrely, Ernest Borgnine later recreated the escapade when he played the title role in the 1961 movie, *The King of Poggioreale*.

Navarra was a figure enveloped in layers of legend and theatrical self-promotion – yet another picturesque landmark of the Neapolitan streets. Accordingly, the 'professional Neapolitan' journalist Giuseppe Marotta penned a typically indulgent portrait of him in 1947, saying that he was 'a man dedicated to charity work no less than he was to his wife and the Monarchist cause'. But Navarra had very real power, sustained by the threat of violence. Locals later remembered him strutting up and down the street in a fedora and waistcoat, brandishing a pistol.

So Navarra, like other *guappi* in the city, was a bridge between the streets, including the underworld, and the city's palaces of power. One of the things that sets Italy's mafias apart from ordinary criminal gangs is precisely this link with politics. Put the *correntisti* and the *guappi* together in a single system, and you would have every justification in using the 'c' word that the Neapolitan newspapers were determined not to use.

Gangsterismo

The mafia in the United States was founded by Sicilian emigrants in the late nineteenth century. In the big cities, crooks from Calabria and Naples were also recruited into what was soon an Italian-American mob. Ever since that time, Men of Honour have shuttled back and forth across the Atlantic, trafficking, investing and killing – and then running from the law or from their mafia enemies. The story of the mafia in the United States is not one I can hope to tell here. Nevertheless, some aspects of that story have a bearing on events in Italy.

America was a synonym for modernity in the backward Italy of the years that followed the Second World War. According to their political loyalties, Italians were either grudging or whole-hearted in their admiration for the United States' awesome warrior might, inconceivable wealth and unreachable movie stars. As one commentator wrote in 1958:

> People all over the world are looking to America, waiting expectantly for everything: for their daily bread or their tin of meat; for machines or raw materials; for military defence, for a cultural watchword, for the political and social system that can resolve the evils of the world. America provides the models for newspapers, scientific manuals, labour-saving devices, fashion, fiction, pop ditties, dance moves and dance tunes, and even poetry . . . Is there one single thing that we don't expect America to provide?

In fact there was one thing that Italy as yet refused to accept from across the Atlantic: a lesson in how to fight the mafia. In

1950, just when Italy had managed to forget about its organised crime problem, America started talking about the mafia again. For the first time in a very long time, Italian-American crime became news. But the perverse circumstances of the Cold War conspired to ensure that the noise surrounding the mafia in America only made the silence in Italy even more deafening.

On 6 April 1950, Kansas City gambling baron and local Democratic kingmaker Charles Binaggio, together with his enforcer Charles 'Mad Dog' Gargotta, were shot dead in a Democratic clubhouse. The press printed embarrassing photographs of Binaggio slumped at a desk under a large picture of President Harry S. Truman. On Capitol Hill, the Binaggio episode caused an outcry that removed the last opposition to Bible Belt Senator Estes Kefauver's efforts to set up a Senate Special Committee to Investigate Crime in Interstate Commerce, with the mafia as one of its main targets.

The Kefauver hearings, as they became known, were held in fourteen cities across the States over the following year. But it was the climactic nine days of testimonies in New York, in March 1951, that really propelled the mafia issue into the public domain. Underworld potentates such as Meyer Lansky and Frank Costello, plus a real live gangster's moll, and a host of other shady hangers-on, were hauled before the Senator and his sharp-tongued deputy Charles Tobey. At Kefauver's insistence, their testimonies were televised to a national audience that peaked at seventeen million. Housewives held afternoon 'Kefauver parties', their husbands left bars deserted to catch the evening résumé of the day's scandals, sales of home-popping popcorn more than doubled, and the Brooklyn Red Cross had to install a television set to prevent blood donations drying up.

The testimony of Frank Costello (born Francesco Castiglia in Calabria) made for a particularly captivating spectacle. While he refused to have his face on screen, the camera nonetheless showed lingering close-ups of his hands as they cruelly twisted pieces of paper or fiddled deviously with a pair of spectacles. This 'hand ballet', together with a voice 'like the death rattle of a seagull', made Costello loom far larger in the public imagination than if his rather nondescript features had been visible.

In Italy, the Communist press reported with undisguised glee on the evidence of political collusion with organised crime that was being uncovered by Kefauver. 'The "heroes" of American democracy on parade', ran one ironic headline.

> Everything is mixed up inextricably: political intrigues and police intrigues. The entire American system of government, both local and central, is prey to the gangs.

While the Cold War enemy was washing its dirty laundry in public, in Italy there had been no washing at all. The 1943–50 period had seen mafia violence and political collusion with organised crime on a scale greater even than the United States. Yet, in parliament as in the law courts, the Left had failed to take advantage from the mafia issue in their battle with the Christian Democrats. Kefauver, by contrast, exposed the long-standing mafia ties of William O'Dwyer, a former mayor of New York who was currently Ambassador to Mexico, and brought his political career to an end. Frank Costello, who at one time had been the 'respectable' face of the American mafia, its hinge with Democratic machine politics in New York, received a short stretch in prison for Contempt of Congress, and his tax affairs attracted the unwelcome attentions of the Internal Revenue Service. Costello's 'hand ballet' also gave him the kind of notoriety that Sicilian *mafiosi* had repeatedly managed to dodge. 'Kefauver is a master of publicity,' *L'Unità* commented. So while the PCI relished what the Kefauver hearings exposed, it also quietly envied their impact.

Many of the underworld figures interviewed by Estes Kefauver refused to incriminate themselves at the hearings – so many that the phrase 'take the Fifth Amendment' entered common parlance. To fill the huge gaps in these first-hand testimonies, the crusading Senator relied on several sources: information from the Federal

Bureau of Narcotics, whose ambitious head, Harry J. Anslinger, had been seeking to ramp up the mafia issue for years; the often muddled testimonies of a cluster of mafia informers; and a great deal of supposition. As a result, the profile of the mafia published in Kefauver's findings was alarming:

> Behind the local mobs which make up the national crime syndicate is a shadowy, international criminal organization known as the Mafia, so fantastic that most Americans find it hard to believe it really exists. The Mafia, which has its origins and its headquarters in Sicily, is dominant in numerous fields of illegal activity . . . and it enforces its code with death to those who resist or betray it . . . The Mafia is no fairy tale. It is ominously real, and it has scarred the face of America with almost every conceivable type of criminal violence, including murder, traffic in narcotics, smuggling, extortion, white slavery, kidnapping, and labor racketeering . . . The Mafia today actually is a secret international government-within-a-government. It has an international head in Italy – believed by United States authorities to be Charles (Lucky) Luciano . . . The Mafia also has its Grand Council and its national and district heads in the countries in which it operates, including the United States.

America was living through a period of Cold War paranoia at the time, and there is more than a hint of the Reds-under-the-bed world-view in what Kefauver wrote. The mafia: a sophisticated criminal conspiracy against America; a single, global organisation whose 'Kingpin' or 'Tsar of Vice' was Lucky Luciano.

Lucky Luciano's true story does not really fit Kefauver's image of him. In 1946, he had been released suspiciously early from a long sentence for pimping; he was expelled from the country and set up shop in Naples. There he did a bit of drug dealing with his Sicilian and Neapolitan friends, but he was certainly not the ruler of a criminal conspiracy, a super-boss whose every order was faithfully implemented in every corner of the world.

Many in the United States remained understandably unconvinced by Kefauver's sensationalist account, and some of them refused to believe that the mafia existed at all. Even the man charged with drafting the committee's recommendations called it a 'romantic myth'. The FBI would continue to remain sceptical about the existence of the mafia for several years yet. Kefauver had overplayed his hand.

Giuseppe Prezzolini, a professor at New York's Columbia University, was the Italian press's most prominent American correspondent. He was also much more representative than the Communists of the most widespread attitudes to organised crime in Italy. When he received calls from worried Americans wanting to know if the mafia really existed in Italy, he was moved to write a withering dismissal of Kefauver's 'grotesque legend'. The mafia in Sicily, Prezzolini explained, was not really a criminal organisation, but a product of centuries of bad government; it was 'a state of mind that expressed the resentment of a people that wanted to take justice into its own hands because it believed it had not received justice from its rulers'. Only in the dynamic capitalist environment of the United States could *mafiosi* be considered hoodlums:

> The modern felon in America, even if he bears an Italian name, is no longer an Italian felon. Rather he is a felon brought up in America and schooled in lawbreaking in America; he earned his degree at the American university of crime. America transformed his character.

The notorious Brooklyn waterfront gangster, Albert 'the Mad Hatter' Anastasia was a very good example. The fact that he was born Umberto Anastasio in Calabria in 1902 meant nothing because, 'I have never heard it said that a mafia has taken root in Calabria.'

Early in 1953, Kefauver's findings were translated into Italian as *Il gangsterismo in America*, the first book on the mafia to be published in Italy since the Second World War. Many commentators on all sides of the political spectrum passed over Kefauver's mafia-as-global-conspiracy in embarrassed silence, concentrating instead on what the Senator had to say about the United States. For most Italians, *gangsterismo*, as the ugly linguistic import implied, remained an exclusively American affair.

Something spectacularly newsworthy would be needed to succeed where the Kefauver hearings had failed, and break Italy's silence about the Sicilian mafia, the 'ndrangheta and the camorra. Something like a homicidal maniac. Or a gangland beauty queen. Or an alien invasion of Calabria. Suddenly, in 1955, all three of these things arrived, exposing at last just how deep-rooted the new Republic's mafia problem really was.

2

1955

The Monster of Presinaci

Late on the morning of 17 April 1955, a peasant called Serafino Castagna from the Calabrian village of Presinaci ate two fried eggs without even stopping to cut himself a slice of bread. He then kissed the crucifix on the wall before hugging his wife and nine-year-old son. 'The things of this world are no longer for me,' he told them. 'God has given them, and God takes them away.'

Moments later, armed with a Beretta pistol, a service rifle with bayonet fixed, and a haversack of ammunition, he loped out into the Sunday sunshine to find his first victim.

In a hovel just metres away lived Castagna's distant cousin Domenicantonio Castagna. When Serafino got there, he found only Domenicantonio's sixty-year-old mother, so he shot her six times.

He then caught sight of Francesca Badolato, who had once been his brother's fiancée. He fired and missed, and she managed to escape, scooping a baby into her arms as she ran. Castagna was not a quick mover because a congenital disability had made his right leg three centimetres shorter than the left. But he pursued Francesca all the same, and saw her take refuge in the house belonging to an aged barber. Castagna battered at the door and smashed a window while the barber and his wife pleaded with him to spare the girl. Finally, frustrated, he took a step back and shot the couple dead. Their names were Nicola Polito (71) and his wife Maria (60), and only two weeks earlier they had been reunited following Nicola's three-year stint in Argentina.

Castagna then followed the tinny murmur of a radio to the Communist Party centre. Peering in, he saw no one who had done him any harm and moved on. When he approached the Christian Democrat HQ nearby, they saw his pistol and begged for mercy. 'Don't be afraid,' he told them. 'I'm only looking for some friends of mine to say hello.'

Castagna now headed out of the village, making for the hay-barn where he had hidden more ammunition. When it dawned on him that his route ran past his father's plot, bitter childhood memories began to flash through his mind. His father had abandoned the family for other women, and wasted what little money the Castagnas had. Minutes later, Serafino was staring at his father and uttering a tearful sentence of death: 'Can you see what you've brought me to? You didn't give us a proper upbringing. Look at the abyss I'm in, at thirty-four years old . . . As a father, I adore you. But as a man, you must die.'

A single shot left the old man writhing on the ground. Serafino bayoneted him to end the agony, and then stooped to plant a farewell kiss on his father's hand.

On his way to the next target, he passed an old cowherd who enquired, 'What brings you by these parts, Serafino?' 'I'm hunting two-footed wolves,' came the reply. A short time later, Castagna found Pasquale Petrolo, who was sitting on the threshing floor in front of his farmhouse and chatting happily to his wife. Castagna shot him five times.

Then he went on the run.

Within hours, reporters across Italy were updating their readers on the manhunt. There were roadblocks at every crossroads. Patrols of *Carabinieri* scoured the slopes of Mount Poro, stopping to level burp guns at the goatherds, scrutinising each sun-weathered face to see if it matched the description: 'Medium height, robust physique, blond hair, blue eyes. Affected by heart disease and a duodenal ulcer.' The press called Castagna 'the Monster of Presinaci'.

Castagna's home village was a place of stunted peasants, black pigs and fat flies, a mountain hamlet of scarcely a hundred crude stone houses lost in a neglected corner of Italy's most neglected region. Inasmuch as most Italians knew anything about Calabria, they knew it as a region whose timeless poverty generated periodic explosions of savagery by brutalised peasants. Serafino Castagna's homicidal rampage bore all the signs of being just another Calabrian peasant tragedy. Indeed local legend even provided a script for the slaughter. 'Castagna has certainly read the story of the brigand Musolino, and would like to imitate his deeds', proclaimed the policeman in charge of the search. The 'Monster of Presinaci' became the 'Second Musolino', a candidate for the succession as King of Aspromonte. (At the time, the original King of Aspromonte was living out the last months of his life in the Reggio Calabria mental hospital.) Castagna even followed Musolino in issuing messages to the authorities. Before setting out on his rampage, he scribbled a list of twenty people he intended to murder, and left it behind for his wife to hand in to the police. He later wrote to the local sergeant of the *Carabinieri* to proclaim his plan of vengeance: 'I'll kill until my last cartridge.'

On the day Castagna's victims were buried, the only people in Presinaci who dared join the funeral procession were *Carabinieri* in their dark parade uniforms. A single child was spotted scuttling out from a doorway to throw a bunch of flowers onto the last coffin of the five. The sound of his mother's imploring wail followed him into the street, and he immediately hurried back indoors.

As the search for the Monster went on, the press began to ask questions. Something about the calm with which he had gone about the slaughter suggested that he was not entirely insane. But what logic could there possibly be to the murder of five seemingly innocent people, two of them women, and all of them old? Who were the 'friends' and 'two-footed wolves' that he said he was looking for? Initial speculation concentrated on Castagna's criminal record: he had served three years in prison for attempting to murder Domenicantonio Castagna, the distant cousin whose mother was the first to fall on that terrible Sunday. Some of the other victims seemed to have a connection with the same case. Was the Monster, like the King of Aspromonte all those years ago, taking vengeance on those who had testified against him? Another theory was that he was restoring his family's slighted honour by killing the woman who had spurned his brother.

The Communist press saw things differently, emphasising the social background to the tragedy. The correspondent for *L'Unità*, the Partito Comunista Italiano's daily, interviewed a comrade from the area who complained that bourgeois journalists from the north were having fun portraying Calabrians as a 'horde of ferocious people'. The real cause of Serafino Castagna's madness was poverty and exploitation. Why couldn't they make the effort to understand that?

Fragments of a more far-fetched explanation for Serafino Castagna's rage also surfaced from the well of village gossip. The first person to speak to journalists was, like Castagna, a farm labourer. Skulking by a wall, and refusing to give his name, he warily muttered something about a secret society in Presinaci. But the press remained sceptical:

> There have been rumours that Serafino Castagna is affiliated to the 'Honoured Society', a kind of Calabrian mafia. But the society's existence is very problematic. Supposedly this 'society' gave Castagna until 20 April to eliminate a man who had come into conflict with it. But it seems that these reports are baseless.

The Monster of Presinaci could not be a member of the Calabrian mafia for the simple reason that there was no such thing. On that count, the most authoritative voices were unanimous.

Then, some three weeks after going on the run, Castagna sent a forty-page memoir to the *Carabinieri* that explained that he was a sworn affiliate of what he called the 'Honoured Society of the Buckle'; he also referred to it as the 'mafia'.

Castagna was finally arrested after sixty days. Once in the

hands of the law, he told everything he knew about the Honoured Society, supplying the authorities with a great many names and evidence to incriminate them. Within forty-eight hours of Castagna's capture, fifty members of the criminal brotherhood were detained. More arrests followed. Apparently the existence of the Calabrian mafia was not quite so 'problematic' after all.

In jail, the Monster of Presinaci even went on to convert the memoir he had sent to the *Carabinieri* into an autobiography. Indeed, he was the first member of the Calabrian mafia ever to tell his own story. *You Must Kill*, as Castagna's autobiography is called, solved the mystery of why its author embarked on his desperate rampage. But it is also a very important historical document: it is post-war Italy's primer on the organisational culture of the criminal brotherhood that is now known as the 'ndrangheta.

Serafino Castagna wrote that he was born in 1921, and grew up in a downtrodden peasant family. He was taken out of school to herd goats, constantly taunted for his disability, and maltreated by his violent father. He first heard about the Honoured Society when he was fifteen. Already, at that age, he would spend long days hoeing the family's field. Working in the adjacent plot was Castagna's cousin, Latino Purita, who was ten years older, and who had just been released from a jail sentence for wounding. One day, when the time came for a rest, Latino started to talk to Castagna about 'the honesty that a man must always have', and said that 'to be honest, a man had to be part of the mafia'. Captivated by what his cousin had said, Castagna underwent a five-year apprenticeship, stealing chickens and burning haystacks on Latino's orders He asserted his manhood by stabbing another youth who had poked fun at his walk. Then, on Easter Monday 1941, he underwent the long oathing ritual that began as follows:

'Are you comfortable, my dear comrades?' the boss asked.

'Very comfortable,' came the reply from the chorus of *picciotti* and ranking *mafiosi* around him.

'Are you comfortable?'

'For what?'

'On the social rules.'

'Very comfortable.'

'In the name of the organised and faithful society, I baptise this place as our ancestors Osso, Mastrosso and Carcagnosso baptised it, who baptised it with iron and chains.'

Respecting the 'social rules' in Presinaci was a low-key business. There were meetings to attend, of course, and procedures to learn. But Presinaci *mafiosi* also spent a great deal of time hanging out in the tavern and spinning yarns. Castagna particularly loved to hear tales of Osso, Mastrosso and Carcagnosso. These three brothers, he was told, were medieval Spanish knights. They were gallant and invincible, but unjustly persecuted: because they avenged the rape of their sister, they were forced to flee Spain and seek refuge on the island of Favignana, just off the western tip of Sicily. There Osso, Mastrosso and Carcagnosso spent years drawing up the rules and rites of the Honoured Society before going their separate ways. Osso, whose name means 'Bone', crossed into Sicily, where he founded the mafia. Mastrosso ('Masterbone') voyaged as far as Naples, there to establish the camorra. And Carcagnosso ('Heelbone') came to Calabria, where the third branch of the Honoured Society was to find its home.

The Presinaci gang had a court, known as the 'Tribunal of Humility'. (The Italian word for humility, *umiltà*, is the origin of *omertà*.) Among the minor penalties that could be handed down by the tribunal were shallow stab wounds, or the degrading punishment known as *tartaro* – 'hell'. The leadership inflicted 'hell' on any affiliate who displayed cowardice, or arrogance towards his fellows. They summoned him to the centre of a circle of affiliates and told him to remove his jacket and shirt. A senior member then took a brush and daubed his head and torso with a paste made from excrement and urine.

Sex and marriage generated many of the tensions that the Tribunal of Humility tried to manage. One of Castagna's brothers was banned from the tavern for ten days and given a fine of one thousand lire. His offence was to have violated an agreement with another *mafioso* to take it in turns sleeping with a girl they both coveted.

In Presinaci, the Honoured Society always made its presence felt in public spaces, key moments of community life; it monopolised folk dancing, for example. Castagna recalled: 'During religious festivals we in the society always tried to take charge of the dancing, so as to keep the non-members away from the fun.' The *mastro di giornata* ('master of the day', the boss's spokesman) would call each of the gang's members to dance in order of rank. On one occasion that Serafino Castagna recalled, a non-member who tried too hard to join in was clubbed brutally to the ground.

In January 1942, the war brought an early interruption to Castagna's criminal career. Despite his health problems, which included recurrent malaria, he was conscripted into an artillery regiment. After the collapse of the Italian army in September 1943, he managed to escape through both German and Allied lines until, ragged and hungry, he reached home to resume his journey towards the bloodbath of 17 April 1955.

With the Second World War over, life in Presinaci returned to its grindingly poor normality. The Honoured Society began to intensify activities as its leaders came back from wherever they had been scattered by the conflict. The number of arson attacks and robberies increased. Contacts with branches in other places became more regular. The Tribunal of Humility held more frequent sessions. Crimes became more ambitious and violence more frequent: Castagna confronted and stabbed a man against whom he bore a petty grudge. A readiness to kill increasingly became an almost routine test that the gang's leaders set for the members. The climate grew more thuggish still when Latino Purita, Castagna's 'honest' cousin, became boss after his predecessor emigrated.

Castagna first got into serious trouble when he was ordered to exact a fine of one thousand lire from a new affiliate who had been gossiping about the society's affairs to a non-*mafioso*. Castagna's instructions were to execute the offender if the money was not forthcoming. The affiliate in question was Domenicantonio Castagna, the distant cousin whom Castagna tried to kill first of all on the day, five years later, that he committed his outrages. Castagna and Domenicantonio got into a scuffle over money, a municipal guard intervened, and Castagna ended up shooting Domenicantonio in the chest. As luck would have it, Domenicantonio survived. But Castagna was caught and imprisoned for wounding him.

Castagna tells us that the Society failed to help him in prison as he had been promised. Not only that, but when he was released in the final days of 1953, the Society immediately reprimanded him for failing to kill Domenicantonio. He was told that the only way to restore his reputation was by killing the municipal guard who had intervened in the scuffle. Castagna appealed against the decision, and obtained a little breathing space: the bosses decreed that he still had to kill the guard, but that he could wait until his period of police surveillance came to an end in the spring of 1955.

Castagna was trapped. If he committed the murder of a public official, he knew that he would probably spend the rest of his life in prison. But he could also envisage the catastrophic loss of face that would ensue if he betrayed his mafia identity and talked to the authorities: 'Nobody would give me any respect, not even people who did not belong to the Society.' As the deadline for vendetta grew near, he began to be tortured by nightmares about cemeteries, ghosts and wars. In the end, he made the irrevocable decision to refuse to obey, and to kill those who had ordered him to kill. He prepared himself for the coming battle by writing down everything he knew about the Honoured Society, and with it a list of the twenty members he wanted to murder. Then he prepared his last meal of fried eggs.

Castagna's plans misfired grotesquely. Only one of his victims, the last, was a member of the Honoured Society. The others were only obliquely connected to his real targets, if they had any connection at all. This was no grand gesture, but a venting of accumulated rage and desperation.

Much of the criminal subculture that the Monster of Presinaci described in his memoir is still in use in today's 'ndrangheta. The fable of Osso, Mastrosso and Carcagnosso, for example, is still the 'ndrangheta's founding myth. Rituals and fables help forge powerful fraternal bonds, moulding the identity of young criminals, giving them the sense of entitlement they need to dominate their communities. If Serafino Castagna's five murders teach us one thing, it is that the 'ndrangheta subculture can exert extreme psychological pressures.

But to the police and judiciary of the 1950s, much of Castagna's account seemed like so much mumbo jumbo. Indeed, this was a picture of the Calabrian mafia that flattered one of Italy's most enduring and misleading misconceptions. Even many of those who were prepared to admit that the mafia existed in places like Calabria and Sicily were convinced that it was a symptom of backwardness. At the time, it was not the problem of organised crime that dominated public discussion of southern Italy, but the issue of poverty. In the South average income stood at about half of levels in the North. In 1951, a government inquiry found that 869,000 Italian families had so little money that they *never* ate sugar or meat; 744,000 of those families lived in the South. If anyone thought about the mafias at all, they thought of them mostly as the result of poverty, and of a primitive peasant milieu characterised by superstition and isolated episodes of bestial violence. In the end, the story of the Monster of Presinaci raised few eyebrows.

The networks of patronage, including mafia patronage, that supported many politicians in southern Italy were an inherently unstable power-base. Inevitably, every so often, mafia activity would get out of hand, the violence would escalate, and loyal Christian Democrat supporters would begin to protest. At such times, even governments that were constitutionally averse to drawing attention to the mafia problem were forced to respond. It turned out that the Monster of Presinaci affair was by no means an isolated episode. The year 1955 was a very violent one in Calabria.

One or two journalists picked up signs that all was not well. A correspondent from the Naples newspaper *Il Mattino*, the most influential Christian Democrat daily in the South, visited Calabria a few weeks after Castagna was captured. He discovered that the province of Reggio Calabria was undergoing an alarming crime wave – or at least a crime wave that would have been alarming if it had being going on in any other Italian region. Buses and cars were being hijacked in the countryside, extortion payments demanded from farmers and factory owners, and witnesses were intimidated. Then there was the shocking case of Francesco Cricelli, a *mafioso* from San Calogero in the province of Catanzaro, who was beheaded for stealing a razor from his boss. *Il Mattino* demanded government action to reassert the authority of the law.

By the time these reports were published, somewhere within the courtyards, the loggias and the criss-crossing corridors of the Ministry of the Interior in Rome, the government machinery was already slowly turning its attention to the problem of law and order in the southernmost point of the Italian mainland.

Giuseppe Aloi was an entrepreneur from Reggio Calabria who employed some 150 people making bricks. The day before Serafino Castagna's rampage, Aloi wrote a letter to the Minister of the Interior. He was frightened and angry: his son had recently fought off a kidnapping attempt in the very centre of Reggio. Since then, the family had received threats and demands for money, and the police locally had not been able to identify the culprits. The situation was so bad that he was considering closing down his business. Aloi's letter also pointed out the rising crime in the area and said:

> It is a notorious fact that the underworld organisation has reappeared in almost every town in the province. There are numerous *mafiosi* who, despite not having any profession or trade that is useful to society, flaunt an easy and luxurious lifestyle based on suspect wealth; they offer their services to farmers or impose extraordinary tributes on them in return for assurances that property and belongings will be respected.

Two days after the brick-maker wrote his letter, plain-clothes police in two unmarked cars tried to trap the extortionists on a winding mountain road on the northern slopes of Aspromonte. One of the unmarked cars was targeted from the wooded slopes by bursts of machine-gun and hunting-rifle fire. Miraculously, four officers suffered only slight wounds. The Calabrian mafia was heavily armed and prepared to confront the forces of order directly.

Following a request for further information, the Prefect of Reggio Calabria (the Minister of the Interior's eyes and ears on the ground) responded with a report that confirmed Aloi's picture. Calabria had 'a vast network of underworld affiliates' that was able to assure its own immunity from the law through *omertà* and 'a well-ordered system of protection that even reached into politics'; 'often, at election time, these individuals [i.e. *mafiosi*] transform themselves into propagandists for one party or another, and try to influence the election results with the weight of their clienteles'. The Calabrian mafia was beginning to present a problem of public order that could not be dismissed as the work of a single, psychologically fragile peasant.

Soon after taking office in July, a new Christian Democrat

Minister of the Interior decided that urgent action was required. There would be an anti-mafia crackdown on a scale that Italy had not seen since the days of the Fascist repression of the late 1920s. A dynamic new Chief of Police, Carmelo Marzano, was lined up to lead what would become known as the Marzano Operation. Local wags, who could not resist a pun, joked that it was as if Martians (*Marziani*) had landed. Calabria was about to greet invaders from planet law and order.

Mars attacks!

The Minister who ordered the crackdown in Calabria was Fernando Tambroni, a Christian Democrat from the Marche region. A timid man in public, Tambroni attracted little press attention. His policy utterances were cagey and abstruse, even by Christian Democrat standards. The only obviously distinctive things about him were his alabaster good looks and his elegance. (He was a loyal customer of Del Rosso, the elite Roman tailor.) In private, Tambroni had a belief system with three pillars: the cult of San Gabriele dell'Addolorata, the influence of his personal astrologer, and a bent for compiling secret dossiers on his allies and enemies.

Despite these personal foibles, when Tambroni announced the beginning of the Marzano Operation it seemed like a good, old-fashioned, right-wing, law-and-order policy of a kind that could be witnessed in other Western European countries. The Marzano Operation was presented as a test run of Tambroni's law-and-order platform – a drive to reinforce the citizens' trust in the state (and thereby in the Christian Democrats). Early in the operation, Minister Tambroni gave a newspaper interview in which he denounced a 'government by organised crime' in Calabria, and promised that he would 'get to the bottom of things' and 'show no favours to anyone'.

Chief of Police Carmelo Marzano's early reports to Tambroni from Calabria were the manifesto of an ambitious man primed for vigorous action. It was no exaggeration, Marzano wrote, to say that the population was 'literally in the grip of terror'. The crime rate was alarmingly high. But many, many more offences went unreported because of public fear. Racketeering was systematic: forestry, taverns and restaurants, the state lottery, the bus service – nothing was allowed to work unless what Marzano called 'certain compromises' were reached. Hundreds of convicted criminals were at large in the province, including fifty-nine murderers; these fugitives paraded the state's failure to impose itself on the territory. One of them, the notorious Brooklyn-born Angelo Macrì, had walked up to a *Carabiniere* in the centre of Delianova and shot him in the head; his status within the Honoured Society had grown immeasurably as a result. Another convicted murderer on the run was the equally notorious boss of Bova, Vincenzo Romeo. Romeo lived openly in his territory, married in the presence of the bosses of the Honoured Society, fathered children, managed his business affairs and cared for his ten beloved dogs. On one occasion, when the *Carabinieri* came looking for him, the women of Bova simultaneously waved sheets from their windows to warn him of the danger.

The new Police Chief found the state of law enforcement even more shocking than the state of public order. He was horrified by his headquarters, the *Questura*: this poky, filthy building seemed half abandoned; it had no shutters on the windows to keep out the summer heat, and not even any railings on the balconies. Whereas a town of comparable size in the north or centre of Italy might have five or six local stations in addition to the *Questura*, in Reggio, a city that now had one of the highest crime rates in the country, there were no other police stations. So the *Questura* was permanently overrun by citizens from across the province clamouring to report a crime, or to apply for a licence or certificate. There were no cells, and no secluded space where a witness or informer could be interviewed. Visits from grandees making special pleas for arrested supporters were a regular occurrence. The *Questura* seemed less a command centre than a bazaar.

Many of the men now under Marzano's command had taken on the same dilapidated and immobile air as the furniture they sat on. They had close contacts in the community – friendships, family ties, business interests – and thus placed living a quiet life before applying themselves to their more abrasive duties. One officer suspected of conniving with criminals was still doing his job years after a transfer order had been issued. The Flying Squad – the plain-clothes unit whose responsibilities were supposed to include chasing after those fifty-nine convicted murderers – numbered only fourteen men, and less then half of them actually turned up to work with any regularity. Law enforcement in the province lacked even the most basic tools of modern policing: dogs, bicycles, or the radios that were essential if officers searching the wilds of Aspromonte were to coordinate their moves.

The Festival of the Madonna of the Mountain at Polsi was an obvious early opportunity for Police Chief Marzano to show that Minister Tambroni's alien invaders were no joke. The Sanctuary of the Madonna of the Mountain is one of the most atmospheric places in southern Italy. Lost high in the woods of Aspromonte, it was built on the spot where, in 1144, a shepherd had a miraculous vision of the Blessed Virgin. Every year in early September, pilgrims from across Southern Calabria would trek up here to show their devotion. The authorities were well aware that the festival was used by the Honoured Society to conceal an annual general meeting of some kind, although quite what happened at the meeting and why was not clear. In 1954, as so often in the past, the pilgrimage had seen a settling of mafia accounts: after the pilgrims had gone home, the corpses of two young men with multiple gunshot wounds were found near the sanctuary. This year, with Marzano in charge, there were roadblocks and patrols in the woods. Fourteen men were taken into custody on charges ranging from carrying weapons to attempted murder and kidnapping. Marzano's line manager, the Prefect of Reggio, telegraphed the Ministry to announce that the pilgrimage had passed off without incident.

Over the coming days and weeks, Minister Tambroni was scatter-gunned with telegrams announcing the recapture of one convicted Calabrian *mafioso* after another. Police arrested two of the men who had tried to blackmail Giuseppe Aloi, the brick manufacturer, and recovered numerous weapons in the same operation. They even managed to collar a town hall employee in Gioia Tauro who was stealing blank identity cards for gangsters who needed to become someone else. Vincenzo Romeo – the fugitive with ten dogs – was arrested, as (eventually) was Angelo Macrì, who had fled back to his native America. Marzano even went on a lone expedition up into Aspromonte, by car and on foot, and single-handedly brought back a renegade murderer from Bova.

Five weeks after arriving in Reggio, hyperactive Police Chief Marzano felt entitled to dictate a toadying despatch to Minister Tambroni:

> The face of the whole province has been transformed. The citizenry approve of the operation. There has been a tide of beneficial renewal, and trust in the state's authority has been reborn. The citizens know that they owe it all *exclusively* to Your Excellency's decisiveness and resolution. Without any trace of rhetorical exaggeration, I can guarantee that if Your Excellency came to visit Reggio, You would be literally carried shoulder-high.

The public seemed to like what was going on; the press certainly did. Correspondents arrived in Calabria in the kind of numbers previously only attracted by one of the region's frequent natural disasters. Remarkably, as a result of the Marzano Operation, Italy began its first-ever national debate about organised crime in Calabria. Naturally enough, journalists filed copy that contained lots of colourful material about the secret criminal sect that went by the name of 'mafia', or 'Honoured Society', or 'Fibbia' ('Buckle'). Indeed a new name emerged from interviews with local people: 'ndrangheta. Pronounced en-*drang*-get-ah, it means 'manliness' or 'courage' in the Greek-based dialect of the southern slopes of Aspromonte. The word has a long history, but there is no evidence that it was ever used about Calabria's Honoured Society before 1955. It is not entirely clear who applied the new name to the local mafia first: the *'ndranghetisti* themselves, or Calabrians who were not affiliated to the organisation, or even the visiting journalists. But whoever it was, 'ndrangheta was destined to win out as the brotherhood's official moniker, used by members and non-members alike. After some three-quarters of a century of growing in the shadows, Calabria's version of the mafia had at last attracted enough public attention to merit a name of its own.

The Marzano Operation also caused some Calabrians to recover their memories about the mafia. One notable example was Corrado Alvaro, the region's best-known writer. He was born in San Luca, the village on the slopes of Aspromonte whose criminals act as guardians of the Honoured Society's customs; San Luca is known as the Bethlehem of Calabrian organised crime. Alvaro was no 'ndrangheta sympathiser, but he learned all about its brutal reality as he grew up. After the Second World War, when he moved to Rome, he became an unofficial spokesman for the voiceless poor of his home region; he turned Aspromonte's downtrodden peasants into archetypes of human resilience. Perhaps through a misguided desire to protect Calabria from bad publicity, or perhaps for darker and more mysterious reasons, Alvaro kept a long silence about the region's criminal brotherhood. In 1949, denouncing the feudal squalor still endured by shepherds and peasants, he wrote that, 'There were attempts to set up criminal societies in imitation of the mafia, but they never took root. Still today, Calabria is one of the safest parts of the country, at any time, and in any isolated corner.'

In 1955, Alvaro changed his mind. He wrote about the 'ndrangheta in a column in the *Corriere della Sera*, and memories of the 'ndrangheta from his youth surfaced in his other writings. Indeed he probably did more than anyone to help the new name catch on.

In the end, restoring Corrado Alvaro's memory and naming

the 'ndrangheta turned out to be the Marzano Operation's only long-term achievements. And the key obstacle to achieving anything more lasting was Minister Tambroni's refusal to seriously tackle the 'ndrangheta's friends in politics.

The papers from Interior Ministry archives now allow us to peer behind the scenes of the Marzano Operation. Those documents show just how much information Tambroni's civil servants gathered about politicians who were hand in glove with gangsters in Calabria. The Martian invasion of 1955 revealed some darkly comic cameos of bad faith and connivance.

One case in point involved a typical southern grandee: Antonio Capua, an MP from the Liberal Party, one of the Christian Democrats' coalition partners. Indeed, what passed for the 'Liberal Party' in Calabria was actually Capua's personal clientele. Capua also sat across the Cabinet table from Fernando Tambroni, as Junior Minister for Agriculture and Forestry. Given that both agriculture and forestry played a big role in the local economy, Capua's job meant that he had a great many tax-funded favours to bestow on his friends. Tambroni discovered that Capua often pressed officials in private to grant driving and gun licences to known *'ndranghetisti*, and his local election agents mingled closely with thugs from the Honoured Society.

Capua was already in the headlines in Calabria before the Marzano Operation began. In a mysterious incident that reeked of the 'ndrangheta, a group of men fired shots at his wife's car as she was driving high on Aspromonte. Capua tried to cover the whole story up. When the press got hold of it, they published a garbled but even more worrying version, saying that Capua himself had been the target of a would-be assassination. An attempt on the life of a government minister was more than local news, and the national newspapers duly took an interest.

When Tambroni's Martians landed in the autumn, the new Chief of Police investigated both the shooting episode, and Capua's underworld friends. But worse was to follow for the Junior Minister: many people jumped to the conclusion that

Capua had called the Martians in as a result of the assassination attempt. The 'ndrangheta took the same view, and began to wonder why their favourite grandee had brought so much trouble down on their heads. The Junior Minister was in a desperate predicament; he looked like a crook to the police and a traitor to the 'ndrangheta.

On 14 September 1955, Junior Minister Capua made a desperate bid to save his credibility with *both* the 'ndrangheta and the police. He arranged to meet with Police Chief Marzano because he wanted to discuss the case of a suspect that Marzano was interrogating at the time. The suspect, an *'ndranghetista* called Pizzi who was also the mayor of Condofuri, was Capua's election agent for the whole Ionian coast of the province of Reggio Calabria. Capua presumably hoped that his prestige as a Junior Minister would intimidate the Chief of Police. That, after all, is just how countless *mafiosi* had been protected over the previous century. But the new Chief of Police was confident enough in his own political backing not to be intimidated. Instead, he calmly showed Capua the damning evidence he had already accumulated against Mayor Pizzi, who was sitting in the room with them. The Junior Minister responded with the kind of brass neck of which only a certain kind of Italian politician is capable. First, he feigned surprise and disappointment. Then he calmly told Marzano that his friend Mayor Pizzi was an honest man who had, despite good intentions, been corrupted by his environment. At that, he turned to Mayor Pizzi and gave him a finger-wagging in tones of plaintive sincerity, telling him to change his ways and collaborate with the police 'from now on'.

Alas, the records do not tell us Fernando Tambroni's reactions when he read this story about his Cabinet colleague. We do not know whether he was shocked, or whether he laughed fit to strain the seams on his Del Rosso suit. But we can make a guess at his thinking. Tambroni might have reasoned that exposing Capua would upset the delicate balance of the coalition government.

Or perhaps he simply followed one of the old, unwritten rules of Italian institutional life. Every governing faction, every party clique, had to get into bed at some point or another with politicians who were 'friends of the friends' in Sicily, Campania or Calabria. Start a serious investigation into one of them, and there was no telling where it would end. No matter that law enforcement on the ground in southern Italy said that the mafias could never be eradicated if their political protectors remained untouched. Better to let it all lie. The evidence against Junior Minister Capua was buried.

Capua also managed to smooth things over with his friends in the 'ndrangheta. Or so we must assume, for he was re-elected at the next poll.

Another politician whose nefarious dealings came to light during the Marzano Operation came from the Minister of the Interior's own party, the Christian Democrats. A top-secret report to Tambroni indicated that Domenico Catalano was part of a close-knit group of three DC chiefs who had managed to insert themselves into powerful positions in local quangos and Catholic organisations. There were strong suspicions that all three of these Christian Democrats had links to organised crime. Catalano even boasted publicly that he had arranged for a previous Chief of Police to be transferred away from Calabria when he became too enthusiastic in his pursuit of *'ndranghetisti*. Most worryingly of all, Catalano had a seat on the 'Provincial Commission for Police Measures'. The commission was a crucial body that ruled on cases in which the police asked for a dangerous suspect to be whisked off into internal exile on a penal colony without a proper trial. (Internal exile had been in use in Italy since the days when the *Carabinieri* were equipped with muskets and horses rather than machine guns and jeeps. It was not only highly dubious from a legal point of view, it was also totally counter-productive, since the penal colonies were notorious recruiting grounds for the mafias.)

During the Marzano Operation, the police filed requests for batches of 'ndrangheta suspects to be shipped to the remote penal colony of Ustica, off the northern coast of Sicily. But Minister Tambroni's man on the ground, the Prefect of Reggio Calabria, noticed that Domenico Catalano displayed what they called a 'certain indulgence' towards men with particularly blood-curdling criminal records. A number of parish priests also gave evidence before the Provincial Commission for Police Measures in the same strangely indulgent fashion. But rather than make trouble, the Prefect decided to act in a classic Christian Democrat fashion, and had a quiet word with the Archbishop.

Now the Archbishop of Reggio Calabria at the time was certainly no friend of the 'ndrangheta. He had only recently penned a pastoral letter denouncing 'shadowy secret societies that, under the pretext of honour and strength, teach and impose crime, vendetta and abuse of power'. We can only imagine how disturbed he would have been at the news that Domenico Catalano, a politician who was a senior member of local Church-backed organisations, was in league with organised crime. But rather than create a fuss, the Archbishop decided to act in classic Italian Church fashion, and have a quiet word with Catalano himself. The Archbishop gently persuaded Catalano to take his responsibilities on the Provincial Commission for Police Measures more seriously.

The little chain of quiet words seemed to work. For a while, Catalano voted the same way as everyone else on the commission, which began to send *'ndranghetisti* into internal exile.

But then the commission was asked to rule on the case of a notoriously powerful criminal called Antonio Macrì, known as don 'Ntoni. Not only was don 'Ntoni the 'chief cudgel' in the market town of Siderno, he was also one of the most powerful bosses in the whole of Calabria. In the autumn of 1953, don 'Ntoni was known to have presided over a plenary meeting of the 'ndrangheta during the Festival of the Madonna of Polsi. Sending a rank-and-file *'ndranghetista* to a penal colony was one thing; confining don 'Ntoni was quite another. On 3 September 1955, with the chief cudgel waiting in the corridor outside the room where the commission was sitting, Domenico Catalano got to his feet. He solemnly informed the commission's other members that he felt it was his duty to make a declaration that 'concerned the Vatican'. He then told a tale that left everyone else in the room open-mouthed.

Catalano's tale went something like this. Some years ago, the Bishop of Locri discovered that a number of priests had been stealing money from a Church charity. The Bishop forced the priests to give back the money, Catalano explained. At which the priests hired an assassin to do away with the Bishop. Luckily the Bishop heard tell of the plot to kill him, and wisely sought protection from the dominant *'ndranghetista* in the area, don 'Ntoni Macrì. Don 'Ntoni, Domenico Catalano revealed, had used his good offices to save the Bishop's life. Surely a man capable of such a noble gesture deserved merciful treatment from the Provincial Commission for Police Measures?

The other commissioners were not convinced. Don 'Ntoni Macrì was promptly dispatched to a penal colony, forcing a brief pause in his formidable criminal career. A full report was sent to Minister Tambroni in Rome.

Quite whether there really was any truth in Catalano's highly unlikely story about the plan to kill the Bishop of Locri we will never know, short of a documented declaration by the Papacy. But the whole affair is nonetheless exemplary. Italy's problem with organised crime was not just that mafia influence seeped into the state through private channels. It was also that prefects, politicians and archbishops preferred to use the very same private channels. Instead of respecting the law, they preferred to have a quiet word.

Once again, Minister of the Interior Tambroni read this report and did nothing. No matter that the case involved a clear instance of a politician trying to bend the law in an *'ndranghetista*'s favour. Domenico Catalano, the spinner of the strange tale of the bishop saved by the mafia boss, kept his seat on the Provincial Commission for Police Measures for years to come.

On 27 October 1955 – a mere fifty-four days after landing – Police Chief Marzano got back into his flying saucer and left Calabria for good. It was hopeless to imagine that less than two months of intensive police activity could make any long-term difference. All too soon, the *'ndranghetisti* would return from their penal colonies and everything would return to normal.

The Italian state could hardly have given a clearer demonstration of its desperately short attention span. Tambroni's policing apparatus did not even seem keen to really understand the 'ndrangheta as an organisation. The entire chain of command, right down from the Ministry of the Interior in Rome to the junior officers on the ground in Calabria, had at their disposal much of the information needed to build up a convincing picture of the Calabrian mafia. On 28 May 1955, only three months before the start of the Marzano Operation, police and *Carabinieri* had raided a house in Rosarno and found a notebook containing the 'ndrangheta's rules. Two and a half weeks later, the Monster of Presinaci was finally captured, and made clear his intention to tell the police everything. The authorities knew a great deal: the 'ndrangheta's cellular, territorially based structure; its extortion rackets and culture of vendetta; the way it set itself as an alternative to the law, and its ability to forge bonds with the feuding cliques and factions of Calabrian politics. Yet there is not a jot of evidence that Police Chief Marzano was even mildly interested in putting these precious new sources of intelligence to any practical use. Nor, in the small mountain of official correspondence generated by the Marzano Operation, is there any hint that the authorities had a historical memory of the Honoured

Society's development, or of the lessons to be learned from previous attempts to combat it. In short, no one associated with the 'Martian invasion' thought that to beat the 'ndrangheta, it might be a good idea to understand it from the inside.

In parliament in Rome, the Communists suspected that fighting the 'ndrangheta was never the Marzano Operation's real aim. They were convinced that Tambroni's promise to 'show no favours' was hollow and cynical from the outset. The most flagrant instances of organised criminal support for politicians involved Christian Democrats. One Socialist MP said in parliament that Vincenzo Romeo, the boss with ten dogs, had gone round with a machine gun shouting, 'Either you vote Christian Democrat, or I'll kill you.' Yet Marzano was being ideologically selective in the *mafiosi* he rounded up, the Communists protested. The DC mayor of the provincial capital Reggio Calabria had not been detained, despite serious evidence of links to organised crime. By contrast the Communist mayor of the mountain village of Canolo, Nicola D'Agostino, had been arrested and sent into internal exile.

There was definitely some substance in the Communist claims that Tambroni's Martian invasion had an ideological bias. However, the D'Agostino case was probably an unfortunate one for the Communists to cite, because it is clear that this particular mayor was a member of the PCI, while never ceasing to be an 'ndrangheta boss. The police claimed that he used the party to exert his personal power over the town. D'Agostino was not the only case of the kind: the Monster of Presinaci's last victim was a Communist *'ndranghetista*, for example. Communists in southern Calabria had fewer antibodies against mafia infiltration than did their comrades in western Sicily, who could count so many martyrs to the fight against organised crime. Here and there in Calabria, the 'ndrangheta had the power to hollow out even the ideology of its enemies.

That said, it seems that Tambroni had no particularly cunning political plan. He simply rushed into the Marzano Operation, and rushed out again when he realised just how profoundly rooted the 'ndrangheta was. Sensibly, Interior Minister Tambroni decided to take the plaudits for Marzano's easy early victories, dispatch a few gangsters to penal colonies for a couple of years, and then revert to managing Calabria in the normal way. Symptomatic of that return to normality was the final outcome of the Monster of Presinaci case. In September 1957, Serafino Castagna was sentenced to life imprisonment, as was inevitable. But of the sixty-five men implicated by his evidence, forty-six were acquitted and the other nineteen received suspended sentences of between two and three years.

The story of the Marzano Operation and the Monster of Presinaci is typical of the state's response when violence flared up from the underworld. Once the violence faded from the head-lines, the authorities resorted to their old habits of cohabiting with mafia power.

The President of Potato Prices (and his widow)

By the mid-1950s there were signs that the Italian economy had entered a period of sustained growth that would finally leave the hardships of wartime behind. In 1950, industrial production overtook pre-war levels. Inflation, which had reached 73.5 per cent per year in 1947, came down to single digits. Unemployment was dropping steadily too. The South still lagged well behind the North, but in the cities of all regions Italians were beginning to spend more. Better food was the first item on the national shopping list, notably the staples of what would later become known as the Mediterranean diet: pasta, and particularly fruit and vegetables.

One place that felt the effects of increased consumption was the wholesale fruit and vegetable market in the Vasto quarter of Naples: roughly 30 per cent of Italy's fruit and vegetable exports were funnelled through it. While other parts of Italy could manage a seasonal trade in one or two specialised crops, the hyper-fertile hinterland of Naples grew every conceivable food plant in year-round abundance. The fresh tomatoes, courgettes, potatoes, peaches and lemons emanating from the region every year were worth some 16 billion lire (roughly €225 million in today's values). A further 12 billion lire (€167 million) came from walnuts, hazelnuts, peanuts, raisins, figs and other dried foods.

Yet, for all its wealth, the wholesale market in Naples was a shambolic spectacle. Here was one of the city's economic nerve-centres, located at the railhead, within easy reach of the port.

Yet it was little more than a cluster of skeletal hangars, where rusting wire mesh and crumbling concrete still betrayed damage from the war. A variety of ramshackle vehicles skated through the permanent puddles in the hangars' shade: donkey wagons and lorries, barrows and tiny cars with comically outsized roof-racks – all of them loaded with teetering crate stacks of aubergines, lettuces, apricots and cherries. The market was serviced by a few cramped offices, a post office and a couple of bank branches in the surrounding streets. There were no teleprinters or rows of phones. Deals, however big, were done on the pavements of via Firenze and Corso Novara, face to face, in stagey exclamations of scorn and disbelief. Now and then, when a serious deal was in the offing or a major account had to be settled, a big-shot vegetable trader from a provincial market town would climb out of his sports car, smooth his hair and his suit, and receive the reverential greetings of agents and labour.

In 1955, one of the most famous murder cases of the era exposed just how powerful and dangerous a caste these fruit and vegetable dealers were. The trial of the 'new camorra', it was called. For, in 1955, Italy began hesitantly to use the 'c' word again. What the case demonstrated, to anyone who cared to look closely, was that the mafias were advancing in step with the growth of the Italian economy. Business was becoming one of the main drivers of mafia history.

Pasquale Simonetti was one of those fruit and vegetable dealers. Two metres tall and thirty-one years old, he had the bulk of a heavyweight and a physiognomy to match: his hard little eyes were pushed far apart by a thick nose (natural or broken, it was hard to tell); his square, burly head was mounted on a neck that defied his tailor's best efforts to restrain it in a shirt collar. He was known, unimaginatively, as Pascalone 'e Nola – 'Big Pasquale from Nola' (Nola being a market town not far from the city).

On the morning of 16 July 1955, Big Pasquale was shot twice as he peeled an orange he had just bought from a stall. The shooter, a young blond man in a slate-grey suit, fled unmolested. The victim, abandoned to haemorrhage into the gutter by his sidekicks, died in hospital near dawn the following day. Police moved his body straight to the morgue to avoid an unsightly pilgrimage of mourning by the criminal fraternity from the countryside.

As yet, nobody seemed to want to make the connection between Pasquale Simonetti's death and the huge fruit and vegetable economy. The traditional Neapolitan reticence about mob stories was still in force. The profiles of Big Pasquale that followed his murder did not make it beyond the crime pages of the local dailies. In addition to trading in the produce of Campanian farms, Big Pasquale was already familiar to the local press as a smuggler and enforcer. Some of his deeds had been as flagrantly public as his shooting. In 1951, near the main entrance to the railway station, he had bludgeoned a man with a wrench wrapped in a newspaper; the victim told the police he had not seen anything. Then there was the gun battle in the town centre of Giugliano that had earned him his time in Poggioreale prison, where he became the boss of his wing. In short, Big Pasquale seemed like just another thug from the province, and no one knew or cared much what went on out there. If he had been killed on his home turf rather than in the centre of the city, then the story would not have merited more than a few lines.

Nevertheless, Big Pasquale's death was just news enough for one or two journalists to want to bulk it out with human interest. There were rumours that he had gone straight before he died. The suggested explanation for this unlikely character transformation was his new wife: a broad-hipped, small-town beauty queen from Castellammare di Stabia. While Big Pasquale was in prison, she had written to him every day, vowing to keep him off the 'steep and painful path of sin', and gushing her teenage daydreams:

'I feel truly emotional, and even a little bit afraid, when I think my nice Tarzan will be able to carry me far, far away from this ugly place to go and live in an enchanted castle where fairies live.' Baptised Assunta Maresca, Big Pasquale's young widow was known by her family as Pupetta ('Little Doll'). She was expecting a baby when her husband died.

On 4 October 1955, two and a half months after her Tarzan's murder, a visibly pregnant Pupetta asked to be driven from Castellammare to the wholesale market in Naples; she stopped off on the way to put flowers on Big Pasquale's grave. In Corso Novara, only a few metres from the point where he had fallen, she encountered another prime exemplar of the fruit-and-vegetable-trader type: Antonio Esposito, aka 'Big Tony from Pomigliano'. An altercation ensued, it seems, during which Pupetta's driver ran away. Then the shooting started. Pupetta's FIAT 1100 was hit several times, including once through the seat that the driver had just vacated. Pupetta, who had been firing from the rear seat with a Beretta 7.65 that Big Pasquale had given her, was unharmed. She escaped on foot. However, her target, Big Tony from Pomigliano, caught five fatal bullets.

'Widowed, pregnant beauty queen in gangland gun battle': now here was a story to attract national attention to the strange world of Campanian wholesale greengrocery.

Pupetta toying with a string of pearls. Pupetta stroking her long dark hair. Pupetta leaning against a tree. Pupetta in a prison smock. Pupetta in happier days. Pupetta holding her prison-born baby. When both Corso Novara murders were brought to court in a unified trial, it was Pupetta's photo that newspaper readers were hungry to gaze at, and she obliged them by posing like a Hollywood starlet. But who was the cherubic girl in the pictures, and what had turned her into a murderer? Was she a gangland vamp, or just a widowed young mother, crazed by grief?

Pupetta Maresca gave her own response to these questions as soon as she took the witness stand: her opening gambit was 'I killed for love.' She admitted shooting Big Tony from Pomigliano, and maintained that he, along with another wholesale green-grocer called Antonio Tuccillo (known, prosaically, as *'o Bosso* – 'the Boss'), had ordered Big Pasquale dead. Big Pasquale had said as much to her on his deathbed, or so Pupetta claimed. Therefore this was a crime of passion, a widow's vengeance visited on her beloved husband's assassin. One correspondent, recalling Puccini's tragic opera about a woman driven to avenge her murdered lover, toyed with the idea that Pupetta was a rustic Tosca.

This was the Pupetta that the public wanted to see – or at least part of it did. It was blindingly obvious that there was a mob backdrop to the story. Newspapers in the north had started a full-scale debate about the 'new camorra'. But in Naples the idea that the camorra might not be dead after all still put people on edge. *Roma*, the newspaper that supported Mayor Achille Lauro, was as keen as ever to paint a sentimental gloss over organised crime. Lauro's Naples would never give in to any prejudiced northerner who tried to use these tragic murders as a pretext to bring up the camorra again. *Roma*, and with it part of Neapolitan public opinion, took Tosca-Pupetta to its heart and pleaded with the judges to send her home to her baby.

But this was not the real Pupetta. To many in court, it seemed that she was deliberately playing up to the Tosca comparison. She spoke not in her habitual dialect, but in a self-consciously correct Italian. As one correspondent noted, 'Pupetta is trying to talk with a plum in her mouth. She says, "It's manifest that" and "That's what fate decreed" – phrases that wouldn't be at all out of place coming from the mouth of a heroine in a pulp novel written to have an impact on tender hearts and ignorant minds.'

The cracks in both her courtroom persona and her line of defence quickly began to show. Her melodramatic posturing did not sit easily with her lawyer's best line of argument: that she had been threatened and attacked in Corso Novara by Big Tony from Pomigliano, and that she shot him in self-defence. Indeed Pupetta managed to put a hole in her own case with the first words she spoke to the court: 'I killed for love. And because they wanted to kill me. I'm sure that if my husband came back to life, and they killed him again, I would go back and do what I did once more.'

The prosecution did not need to point out that a homicide could be a crime of passion, or a desperate act of self-defence. But it could never be both.

Pupetta was asked whether her family had a nickname in Castellammare. She squirmed, and dodged the issue for a while. When she finally answered she could not help the look of pride that crossed her face: 'They call my family *'e lampetielli*,' she admitted – the 'Flashing Blades'. The Marescas were a notoriously violent lot, with criminal records to go with their nickname. Young she may have been, but Pupetta herself had already been accused of wounding. Her victim withdrew the charges, for reasons that are not hard to imagine.

One of Pupetta's main concerns during the trial was to absolve her sixteen-year-old brother Ciro of any involvement in the murder. Ciro, it was alleged, had been next to Pupetta in the back seat of the FIAT 1100, and had fired a pistol at Tony from Pomigliano. The boy's defence was not helped by the fact that he was still on the run from the law at the time of the trial.

But it may not just have been her brother that Pupetta was trying to shield. Ballistics experts never ascertained exactly how many shots were exchanged – twenty-five? forty? – because the holes spattered across the walls in Corso Novara could feasibly have been the result of previous fruit-related firefights. But it is quite possible that Pupetta and her brother Ciro were not the only people attacking Big Tony. If so, then 'Tosca' had actually been leading a full-scale firing party, and had embarked on a military operation rather than a solitary, impulsive act of vengeance.

Through the fissures in Pupetta's façade, post-war Italy was getting its first glimpses of a deeply rooted underworld system in the Neapolitan countryside, a system that no amount of stereotypes could conceal. Pupetta was a young woman profoundly enmeshed in the business of her clan. And that clan's business included her marriage: far from being a union of Tarzan and a fairy princess, this was a bond between a prestigious criminal bloodline like the 'Flashing Blades', and an up-and-coming young hoodlum like Big Pasquale. The world of the Campanian clans was one whose driving force was not the heat of family passions, but a coldly calculating mix of diplomacy and violence. Shortly before either of the fruit-market murders, a set-piece dinner for fifty guests was held. It seems that the dinner was a celebration of a peace deal of some kind between Big Pasquale and Big Tony from Pomigliano, the man Pupetta would eventually murder. No one could say with any certainty what had been said and agreed round the dinner table. What was obvious was that the peace deal quickly broke down. Yet even after Big Pasquale's death, the diplomatic efforts continued: there were frequent contacts between Big Tony from Pomigliano's people and Pupetta's family. Were they trying to buy peace with the young widow's clan? To stop the feud interfering with business?

These and a dozen other questions were destined to remain without a clear answer at the end of the hearings, largely because, once Pupetta had given evidence, the rest of the trial was a parade of liars. The refrain was relentless: 'I didn't see anything', 'I don't remember'. Only one man was actually arrested in court: he had flagrantly tried to sell his testimony to whichever lawyer was prepared to pay most. But many others deserved the same treatment. The presiding judge frequently lost his patience. 'You are all lying here. We'll write everything down, and then we'll send up a prayer to the Lord to find out which one is the real fibber.'

As the Neapolitan newspaper *Il Mattino* commented, whether they lied for the prosecution or lied for the defence, most of the witnesses were people 'from families where it is a rare accident for someone to die of natural causes'. The young blond man in the slate-grey suit who had gunned down Pupetta's husband was called Gaetano Orlando. His father, don Antonio, had been wounded in an assassination attempt six years earlier. In revenge, Gaetano ambushed the culprit, but only succeeded in shooting dead a little girl called Luisa Nughis; he served only three years of a risible six-year sentence. Big Tony from Pomigliano's family were even more fearsome: all three of the dead man's brothers worked in fruit and vegetable exports with him; all three had faced murder charges; and one of them, Francesco, gave evidence in dark glasses because he had been blinded in a shotgun attack in 1946.

Jailbirds and thugs they may have been, but these were people with drivers and domestic servants, accountants and bodyguards. They owned businesses, drove luxury cars and wore well-tailored suits. Big Pasquale's uncle, a man with an uncanny resemblance to Yul Brynner, now spent much of his time gambling in Saint Vincent and Monte Carlo – this despite having served twenty years for murder in the United States. The grey-suited Gaetano Orlando was the son of a former mayor of Marano, and the family firm had recently won a juicy contract to supply fruit and vegetables to a city hospital consortium. The young killer himself personally took charge of selling produce in Sicily, Rome, Milan and Brescia.

By this stage, the most astute observers of the case were less interested in the beguiling figure of Pupetta than in just how these violent men were making money from the vast agricultural production of the Campania region. Something Pupetta said early in proceedings opened a chink in the wall of *omertà*. She referred to Big Pasquale as the 'President of Potato Prices'. He was the man who determined the wholesale price of potatoes across the marketplace. The other man murdered in Corso Novara, Big Tony from Pomigliano, was also described as a President of Prices.

So what exactly did a President of Prices do? Pupetta put a

fairy-tale gloss on her husband's role. Her Tarzan fixed potato prices in the interests of the poor farmers, she said. He was an honest man, who was hated by other more exploitative business rivals. This account is no more credible than the rest of Pupetta's evidence. What seems likely is that a President's power, as is always the case with Italian mafia crime, was rooted in a given territory where he could build an organisation able to use violence without fear of punishment. His men would approach the small-holding farmers offering credit, seed, tools and whatever else was needed for the next growing season. The debt would be paid off by the crop, for which a low price was settled before it was even planted. Bosses like Big Pasquale or Big Tony were able to deploy vandalism and beatings systematically to quell any farmer who had enough cash or chutzpah to try and operate outside of the cartel. By controlling the supply of fruit and vegetables in this way, men who combined the roles of loan shark, extortionist and commercial middle-man could set the sums to be paid when the lorryfuls of produce were unloaded under the hangars in the Vasto quarter of Naples.

The many slippery testimonies at the Pupetta Maresca trial mean that we have to use educated guesswork to put more detail into the picture. It seems likely that the various Presidents from perhaps fifteen different towns in the Naples hinterland (Big Pasquale from Nola, Big Tony from Pomigliano, and so on) met regularly in Naples to hammer out prices between them. Because they all controlled the supply of a variety of different foodstuffs, they agreed to give the initiative in deciding the price of single fruits and vegetables to Presidents whose territory gave them a particular strength in that particular crop: hence Big Pasquale's potatoes.

While this might seem a corrupt and inefficient system, it had distinct advantages for any national or international company that came to source produce at the wholesale market in Naples. Firms such as the producers of the canned tomatoes used on pasta and pizza would look to the Presidents of Prices for guarantees: that supply would be maintained; that prices would be predictable; and that the deals done face to face on the pavements of Corso Novara would be honoured. In return for these services, the Presidents of Prices took a personal bribe. Big Pasquale is reputed to have taken a 100 lire kickback on every 100 kilos of potatoes unloaded at the market. According to one testimony, the President of Potato Prices could send as many as fifty lorry-loads of spuds a day to the market – equivalent to some 750,000 kilos. If these figures are right, Big Pasquale could earn as much as €10,000 (in 2012 values) on a good day. And this does not take into account the money he was bleeding from the poor farmers, and the profit he made on the fruit and vegetables he traded in.

Later investigations showed that livestock, seafood and dairy produce were as thoroughly controlled by the camorra as was the trade in fruit and vegetables. Indeed, Naples did not even have a wholesale livestock market – all the deals were done in the notorious country town of Nola from which Big Pasquale took his name. According to one expert observer, 'The underworld in the Nola area willed and imposed the moving of the cattle market from Naples to Nola.'

Among the questions that remained unanswered by the Pupetta affair was one concerning the links between the rural clans and politicians. It is highly likely that the mobsters of the country towns acted as vote-hustlers in the same way as the *guappi* of the city.

Then there was the question of the relationship between these country clans and the urban crime scene. The wholesale greengrocery gangsters certainly made the *correntisti* of the urban slums look like small-time operators by comparison. The past may provide a few clues as to the links between the two. Big Pasquale from Nola, Tony from Pomigliano and their ilk have a history that remains largely unwritten to this day. Nevertheless, in the days of the old Honoured Society of Naples, the strongest Neapolitan *camorristi* were always the ones who had business links to country towns like Nola. The real money was to be made not in shakedowns of shops and stalls in the city, but upstream, where the supplies of animals and foodstuffs originated. Outside Naples, major criminal organisations certainly survived the death of the Honoured Society, and may well have continued their power right through the Fascist era. So the 'new camorra' revealed by the Pupetta case was probably not new at all.

If there had been less muddle about the Sicilian mafia in the 1950s, then it might also have occurred to observers of the Pupetta Maresca trial that the camorra families of the Neapolitan hinterland bore a resemblance to the mafia cells of Sicily and Calabria. They all had power built on violence, wealth that straddled the legal and illegal economies, and an insatiable hunger for fruit and vegetables. In March 1955, just seven months before Pupetta shot her husband's killer, a *mafioso* called Gaetano Galatolo, known as Tano Alatu, was shot dead at the entrance to Palermo's new wholesale market in the Acquasanta quarter. A factional battle to control the market then ensued. Southern Calabria had no single wholesale market to compare with those in Naples and Palermo; nor was any blood shed in this period over lettuces and pears. But it is known that the local mob controlled the smaller local markets in Reggio Calabria, Palmi, Gioia Tauro, Rosarno, Siderno, Locri and Vibo Valentia. As Italy recovered from the hungry years of war and reconstruction, and made its first hesitant steps towards prosperity, the mafias established a stranglehold on the South's food supply.

After the events of 1955 in Naples, some of the best current affairs commentators who were not aligned with the PCI came close to these profoundly worrying conclusions. One example was the liberal intellectual and politician Francesco Compagna: his magazine *Nord e Sud* published a number of important analyses of organised crime in the following years. But at a time when the only women within the orbit of organised crime who made themselves visible were the black-clad mafia widows of Sicily and Calabria, even such serious observers struggled to see

Pupetta Maresca as anything more than an anomaly. The over-whelming view was that any women who might happen to asso-ciate with gangsters did so only because they were typical, family-bound southern females; that they played no active part in the mafia system.

Pupetta received an eighteen-year term for the premeditated murder of Big Tony from Pomigliano. And, despite her best efforts, her brother Ciro was eventually sentenced to twelve years. Many Italians remained hypnotised by the 'Tosca' version of her story. In the wake of the publicity surrounding the murder, the Italian film industry developed a minor obsession with her. The first film came out before the trial, in 1958. Two years after her release, in 1967, Pupetta herself starred in *Delitto a Posillipo* (*Murder in Posillipo*), based loosely on her life. In 1982, she was played in a TV movie by Alessandra Mussolini, the Duce's grand-daughter. Another TV dramatisation is due in 2012. Pupetta established a twin-track career that was destined to last for years: movie celebrity and mob queen.

3

THE MAFIAS' ECONOMIC MIRACLE

King Concrete

In the late 1950s and early 1960s, industry expanded faster in Italy than in any other western European nation. The European Common Market was a stimulus for exporters; cheap power, cheap labour and cheap capital created the right conditions for growth at home, and the north of Italy had traditions of entrepreneurship and craftsmanship to draw on. An agricultural country, much of which had still run on cartwheels in the 1940s, was now motoring into the age of mass production. Factories in the North began churning out scooters, cars and tyres in exponentially increasing numbers. This was Italy's 'economic miracle', the speediest and most profound social change in the peninsula's entire history.

Lifestyles were transformed. As tractors and fertiliser modernised agriculture, peasants abandoned the countryside in droves. Italy contracted the consumerist bug. Television began in 1954, and with it advertising for stock cubes, tinned meat, coffee pots, toothpaste . . . Italians learned to worry about armpit odour, lank hair and dandruff. Washing machines, fridges and food mixers promised an end to domestic drudgery for millions of women. Motorways were built for the legions of new car owners.

Italy even became fashionable. Brand names like Zanussi, Olivetti and Alfa Romeo conquered the continent. The Vespa and the FIAT 500 became icons. The world started to crave the peninsula's handbags and shoes. Soon Italy's much sniffed-at food would begin to win converts too.

During the economic miracle, Italy rapidly made itself into one of the world's leading capitalist economies. Here was a shining success story for the Europe that had risen from the rubble of the Second World War.

But the miracle also opened up roads to riches for the mafias. And the mafias' favourite industries knew few of the problems that would come to dog the lawful economy when the boom eventually subsided. No cycles of surge and recession. No bolshy unions. Little in the way of competition. Through the 1960s, 1970s and 1980s the history of the mafias traces an upward curve of relentlessly growing riches. The mafias' economic miracle would long outlast the first spurt of growth in lawful industry.

From the mid-1950s, Italy's three major criminal organisations followed one another into four new businesses – or at least newly lucrative businesses: construction, tobacco smuggling, kidnapping, and narcotics trafficking. The story of the mafias' economic miracle takes the form of an intricate fugue as, following a trend that was usually set in Sicily, each of the mafias moved in turn through the same cycles of greed, and each of these four businesses in turn increased mafia influence.

The two core skills the mafias deployed to exploit the construction industry, contraband tobacco, kidnapping and drugs were both highly traditional: intimidation and networking, which are what mafia crime has been all about since the outset. All the same, the new era of criminal business did not just make bosses more moneyed than they had ever been, it also profoundly altered the landscape of mafia power.

For one thing, wealth begat wealth. The profits from one illegal enterprise were ploughed into the others, and thereby multiplied. From construction, to smuggled cigarettes, to kidnapping, to narcotics: interlocking chain reactions were set in motion over the coming three decades. The mafias became what Italy's 'mafiologists' describe using an English phrase: 'holding companies'. In some senses that is what *mafiosi* ever were: 360-degree criminals who, in the nineteenth century, would take money from extortion and invest it in stolen cattle, for example. But from the late 1950s there was a quantum leap in the diversification and integration of mafia commerce.

Burgeoning criminal wealth wrought a whole series of other

changes. The liaison between organised crime and the Italian state grew both more intimate and more violent. The mafias themselves changed too. They experimented with new rules and new command structures. They grew to look more like one another. *Mafiosi* from different regions increasingly moved in the same circles, doing business together, learning lessons and, sometimes, fighting. *Mafiosi* began to operate more internationally. Entirely new mafias were spawned. In the end, these interlocking changes would plunge all of the mafias into violence of a scale and savagery that had never been seen before.

It all began with a commodity that is set hard at the very foundations of the mafias' territorial authority, and continues to this day to build many of their bridges into the lawful economy and the system of government: concrete.

Naples and Palermo have a great deal in common. Both were glorious capital cities in their time. Both are ports. And both are marked by a long-standing struggle to find an economic *raison d'être* in the era of industrial capitalism. In the early 1950s, Palermo and Naples had ancient enclaves of poverty at their heart: the alleys of the run-down quarters were bomb-damaged, crowded, filthy and poor. Typhoid and tuberculosis were regular visitors. Here the poky, precarious housing lacked proper kitchens and lavatories. In the alleys, barefoot children played amid open drains and rubbish. Many breadwinners, male and female, lived from hand to mouth as pickpockets, three-card tricksters, pedlars, prostitutes, chambermaids, laundresses and gatherers of firewood, rags or scrap. The bricklayers and plasterers who got occasional work, or the underemployed cobblers and tailors, were all too few. Child labour was one of the mainstays of the slum economy.

Change was urgently needed. To add to the pressure, Palermo was now Sicily's capital again, with the new regional parliament and its army of bureaucrats to accommodate. But instead of planned rehousing and strategic urban development, both cities were ransacked. Building speculation was rampant, and local government proved utterly incapable of imposing any order on the savage concrete bonanza. In the process, through the 1960s, the economic axes of both cities were shifted. Once their livelihoods had depended on land (for the wealthy) and improvisation (for the poor). Now they were rebuilt around state employment, meagre benefits, piecework, sweatshop labour, services – and, of course, construction. For the poor, the transformation meant years of waiting, protesting, and begging for a favour from a priest or politician, before finally moving from a city-centre slum to a bleak housing project a long walk from the nearest bus stop. For the middling sort, the reward was a rented apartment in one of many indistinguishably gaudy, jerry-built stacks on what had once been green space.

But when it comes to organised crime's part in the construction bonanza of the 1950s and 1960s, the contrasts between Naples and Palermo were more striking than the similarities.

In Naples, no one seized the mood of the building speculation boom better than film-maker Francesco Rosi, in his 1963 movie *Le mani sulla città. Hands Over the City* (as it was rather clumsily called in English) was both a prize-winning drama and a stirring denunciation of the political malpractice that fed off the construction industry in Naples. Rod Steiger snarls his way through the leading role as Edoardo Nottola, a rapacious councillor-cum-construction entrepreneur. The movie's opening scene shows Steiger barking out his plans as he gestures with both arms in the direction of a parade of brutalist tower blocks:

> That over there is gold today. And where else are you going to get it? Trade? Industry? The 'industrial future of the *Mezzogiorno*'? Do me a favour! Go ahead and invest your money in a factory if you like! Unions, pay claims, strikes, health insurance . . . That stuff'll give you a heart attack.

There could be no more vivid encapsulation of the cold-blooded credo of what Italians call an *affarista*: a profiteer, a wheeler-dealer, a cowboy businessman. *Affaristi* shirk the risks involved in real entrepreneurship, usually by working in the shadow of the political system where they can arrange little monopolies and sweetheart contracts.

Gangsters prefer to deal with *affaristi* rather than with real entrepreneurs. Yet, although *Hands Over the City* is a searing portrait of a Neapolitan *affarista*, it is telling that the word camorra is never used in Rosi's film; nor does anyone who could be considered a *camorrista* play a front-of-stage role in the story. For once, that absence is not the sign of a cover-up or of moral blindness: rather, it accurately reflects the facts on the ground. In Naples, *camorristi* simply lacked the clout to force their way into a major share in the building boom. At this stage in our story, there were no *camorristi* who doubled as construction *affaristi*.

In Palermo, the situation was strikingly different: here the councillors and construction entrepreneurs were invariably flanked by Men of Honour; *affaristi* and *mafiosi* were so close as to be all but indistinguishable.

In the late 1950s and 1960s, the mafia rebuilt Palermo in its own gruesome image in a frenzied wave of building speculation that became known as the 'sack of Palermo'. There were two particularly notorious mafia-backed politicians who were key agents of the sack. The first was Salvo Lima, a tight-lipped, soft-featured young man whose only affectation was to smoke through a miniature cigarette holder. He looked like the middle-class boy he was – the son of a municipal archivist. Except that his father was also a mafia killer in the 1930s. (That little detail of Lima's background had been buried, along with all the other important information from the Fascist campaigns against the mafia.) In 1956, Lima came from nowhere to win a seat on the city council, a post as director of the Office of Public Works, and the title of deputy mayor. Two years later, when Lima became mayor, he was succeeded at the strategic Office of Public Works by the second key *mafioso* politician, Vito Ciancimino. Ciancimino was brash, a barber's son from Corleone whose cigarette habit had given him a rasping voice to match his abrasive personality. In the course of their uneasy alliance, Lima and Ciancimino would wreak havoc in Palermo, and reap vast wealth and immense power in the process.

Men like Lima and Ciancimino were known as 'Young Turks' – representatives of a thrusting new breed of DC machine politician which, across Sicily and the South, was beginning to elbow the old grandees aside. In the 1950s, the range of jobs and favours that were available to patronage politicians began to increase dramatically. The state grew bigger. Government enlarged its already sizeable presence in banking and credit, for example. Meanwhile, local councils set up their own agencies to handle such services as rubbish disposal and public transport. Sicily's new regional government invented its own series of quangos. As the economy grew, and with it the ambitions for state economic intervention, more new bureaucracies were added. In 1950, faced with the scandal of southern Italy's poverty and backwardness, the DC government set up the 'Fund for the South' to sluice large sums into land reclamation, transport infrastructure and the like. Money from the Fund for the South helped win the DC many supporters, and put food on many southern tables. But its efforts to promote what it was hoped would be a dynamic new class of entrepreneurs and professionals were a dismal failure. As things turned out, the only really dynamic class in the South was the DC's own Young Turks. The Fund for the South would turn into a gigantic source of what one commentator called 'state parasitism and organised waste'. Government 'investment' in the South became, in reality, the centrepiece of a geared-up patronage system. Young Turks began to inveigle their way into new and old posts in local government and national ministries. Journalists of the day dubbed the Christian Democrat party 'the white whale' (i.e. Moby Dick) because it was white (i.e. Catholic), vast, slow, and consumed everything in its path.

In Palermo, for all these new sources of patronage, it was the simple business of controlling planning permission that gave Young Turks like Lima and Ciancimino and their mafia friends such a large stake in the building boom.

The sack of Palermo was at its most swift and brutal in the Piana dei Colli, a flat strip of land that extends northwards between the mountains from the edge of Palermo. It has always been a 'zone of high mafia density', in the jargon of Italian mafiologists. Indeed, it has as good a claim as anywhere to being the very cradle of the mafia: its beautiful lemon groves were where the earliest *mafiosi* developed their protection racket methods. A century on from those beginnings, the mafia smothered its birthplace in a concrete shroud. The scale of the ruin was immense. The gorgeous landscape of the Conca d'Oro, which for Goethe had offered 'an inexhaustible wealth of vistas', was transformed into an undifferentiated swathe of shoddily built apartment blocks without pavements or proper amenities.

In 1971, when the sack of Palermo was complete, a journalist climbed Monte Pellegrino, the vast rocky outcrop that surges between the Piana dei Colli and the sea. The view below him had once been stunning. Now it was shocking.

From up there you can cast your eyes across the whole city and the Conca d'Oro. Palermo seems much bigger than you would imagine: long rows of houses spreading out from the periphery towards the orange groves. Concrete has now devastated one of the most beautiful natural spectacles in the world. The huge blocks of flats, all alike, seem to have been made by the same hand. And that hand belongs to 'don' Ciccio Vassallo. More than a quarter of the new Palermo is his work.

Francesco Vassallo, known as 'don Ciccio' ('don Frankie'), or 'King Concrete', was by a distance the dominant figure in the Palermo construction industry in the 1960s. Between 1959 and 1963, under the Young Turks Salvo Lima and Vito Ciancimino, Palermo City Council granted 80 per cent of 4,205 building permits to just five men, all of whom turned out to be dummies. One of the five subsequently got a job as a janitor in the apartment block he had nominally been responsible for building. Behind those five names, more often than not, stood don Ciccio Vassallo.

King Concrete was a fat, bald, jowly man with a long nose, dark patches under his eyes, and a preference for tent-like suits and loud ties. He rose from very humble origins in Tommaso Natale, a *borgata* or satellite village that sits at the northern end of the Piàna dei Colli. Reputed to be only semi-literate, he was the fourth of ten children born to a cart driver. Police reports mention the young Vassallo as moving in mafia circles from a young age; his early criminal record included proceedings for theft, violence and fraud – most of them ended in a suspended sentence, amnesty or acquittal for lack of proof. His place in the local mafia's circle of influence was cemented in 1937 by marriage to the daughter of a landowner and *mafioso*, Giuseppe Messina. With the Messina family's muscle behind it, his firm established a monopoly over the distribution of meat and milk in the area around Tommaso Natale. Vassallo and the Messinas were also active in the black market during the war. When peace came, Vassallo started a horse-drawn transportation company to ferry building materials between local sites. His mafia kinfolk would be sleeping partners in this enterprise, as in the many lucrative real-estate ventures that would come later.

Suddenly, in 1952, Vassallo's business took off. From nowhere, he made a successful bid to build a drainage system in Tommaso Natale and neighbouring Sferracavallo. He had no record in construction; it was not even until two years later that he was admitted onto the city council's list of approved contractors. He was only allowed to submit a tender for the contract because of a reference letter from the managing director of the private company that ran Palermo's buses. The company director would later become Vassallo's partner in some lucrative real-estate ventures. At the same time, Vassallo received a generous credit line from the Bank of Sicily. Then his competitors withdrew from the tendering process for the drainage contract in mysterious circumstances. Vassallo was left to thrash out the terms of the deal in one-to-one negotiations with the mayor. Who would also later become his partner in some lucrative real-estate ventures.

In the mid-1950s, King Concrete started to work closely with the Young Turks. Construction was becoming more and more important to the economy of a city whose productive base, such as it was, could not compete with the burgeoning factories of the 'industrial triangle' (the northern cities of Milan, Turin and Genoa). By the 1960s, 33 per cent of Palermo workers were directly or indirectly employed in construction, compared to a mere 10 per cent in Milan, the nation's economic capital. However temporary the dangerous and badly paid work in Palermo's many building sites might be, there were few alternatives for ordinary working-class *palermitani*. Which made construction workers a formidable stock of votes that the Concrete King could use to attract political friends. Friends like Giovanni Gioia, the leader of Palermo's Young Turks, who would go on to benefit from a number of lucrative real-estate ventures piloted by Vassallo.

The notion of a 'conflict of interests' was all but meaningless in building-boom Palermo. The city municipality's director of works became King Concrete's chief project planner. From his political contacts, the rapidly rising Vassallo acquired the power to systematically ignore planning restrictions. Another Young Turk, Salvo Lima, was repeatedly (and unsuccessfully) indicted for breaking planning law on Vassallo's behalf. During the sack of Palermo, journalists speculated ironically about the existence of a company they called VA.LI.GIO (VAssallo – LIma – GIOia). They were successfully sued. Rather pedantically, the judges ruled that no such legally constituted company existed.

In the mid-1960s, the market for private apartments reached saturation point. By that stage King Concrete had built whole dense neighbourhoods of condominia that were without schools, community centres and parks. Ingeniously, he then turned to renting unsold apartments and other buildings for use as schools. In 1969 alone he received rent of nearly $700,000 from local authorities for six middle schools, two senior schools, six technical colleges and the school inspectorate. The DC press hailed him as a heroic benefactor. In the same year he was recorded as being the richest man in Palermo.

It pays to remember that don Ciccio Vassallo was an *affarista* rather than an entrepreneur. His competitive advantage lay not in shrewd planning and investment, but in corruption, in making useful friends, and of course in the unspoken menace that shadowed his every investment. Right on cue, unidentified 'vandals' would cut down all the trees on any stretch of land that had been zone-marked as a park. Any honest company that somehow managed to win a contract from under the mafia's nose would find its machinery in flames. Dynamite proved a handy way of accelerating demolition orders.

In 1957, just as the sack of Palermo was about to enter its most devastating phase, a mafia power-struggle began in King Concrete's home village of Tommaso Natale. His own family was soon drawn in. In July 1961 his brother-in-law, Salvatore Messina, was shot-gunned to death by an assassin who had sat in wait for him for hours in the branches of an olive tree. Another brother-in-law, Pietro, was shot dead a year later. A third brother-in-law, Nino, only saved himself from the same fate by hurling a milk churn at his attacker when he was ambushed; it is thought he then left Sicily. The fact that don Ciccio himself was not attacked (as far as we know) shows that his power now transcended any local base: he was a money-making machine for the entire political and mafia elite.

Mass migration was one of the most important characteristics of Italy's economic miracle. As the industrial cities of the North boomed, they sucked in migrants. About a million people moved from the South to other regions in just five years, between 1958 and 1963.

Mafiosi also became more mobile in the post-war decades: their trade took them to other regions of Italy. In some places, gangsters went on to found permanent colonies. Those bases in central and northern Italy, as well as in parts of the South not traditionally contaminated by criminal organisations, are one of the distinctive features of the recent era of mafia history. Nothing similar is recorded in previous decades.

Some of the American hoodlums who were expelled from the United States after the Second World War were the first to set up business outside the mafia heartlands of Sicily, Calabria and Campania. Frank 'Three Fingers' Coppola dealt in drugs from a base near Rome, for example.

The earliest signs of mafia colonisation from *within* Italy came in the great North–South migration during the economic miracle. In the mid-1950s, Giacomo Zagari founded one of the first cells of *'ndranghetisti* near Varese, close by Italy's border with Switzerland. The murder of a gangmaster in the early hours of New Year's Day in 1956 revealed the existence of mafia control among the Calabrian flower-pickers of the Ligurian coast near the French border.

Many northerners resented the hundreds of thousands of new arrivals from the South. Southerners, they said, had too many children and grew tomatoes in the bathtub. News of mafia-related crime, or indeed any crime as long as it was committed by an immigrant, merely served to confirm those anti-southern prejudices. Mafia appeared to be a kind of ethnic affliction that made everyone from 'down there' proud, vengeful, violent and dishonest.

The truth is that mass migration from the South was not to blame for the mafias' spread northwards. *Mafiosi* are a tiny minority of professional criminals; they are not typical southerners. There were plenty of places where immigrants arrived and the mafias did not follow. But migration did create many new opportunities for *mafiosi* – notably, as the flower-pickers of Liguria illustrate, in gangmastering, when immigrants were forced to work for low wages, untaxed, and without the protection of the law. As Italy grew during the economic miracle and afterwards, such criminal opportunities expanded and multiplied.

The criminal opportunities most conducive to long-term mafia colonisation of the North came from the construction industry. The most notorious case is the winter sports resort of Bardonecchia, in the northern region of Piedmont; it is situated in the Alps just a few kilometres from the French border. Bardonecchia is where the inhabitants of Turin, Italy's motor city and one of the capitals of the economic miracle, go to ski. Eventually, in 1995, Bardonecchia became the first town council in northern Italy to be dissolved by central government in Rome because of mafia infiltration. Strikingly, the mafia that had colonised Bardonecchia long before then was the 'ndrangheta. Italy's least-known mafia, the one most frequently associated with a disappearing world of peasant penury, was quick to spot the illegal profits to be made from construction, and put itself in the vanguard of the new era of expansion in the North.

The story of Bardonecchia is like a sequence of time-lapse photographs in a nature documentary. Narrowly focused, as if on the growth of a single poisonous weed, it nevertheless exposes the secret workings of a whole ecosystem. Played in rapid sequence, the images from Bardonecchia take us far ahead in our story. They illustrate how, from small beginnings, and in the right circumstances, the mafias can establish what they call 'territorial control' from virtually nothing.

The first hint of the 'ndrangheta's arrival in Bardonecchia came at past midnight, on 2 September 1963. A heavy rain was falling as Mario Corino, a young primary school teacher, turned into via Giolitti in the old part of town. He was approached by two men, both of them half hidden by umbrellas. The attack was swift – so swift that Corino did not see what type of blunt instrument flashed towards him. He instinctively parried the first blow with his umbrella and his forearm; the second grazed his head before smashing into his shoulder. His screams drove the attackers away. Evidently this was only meant to be a warning.

Initial speculation linked the attack with Corino's work as leader of the local branch of the Christian Democrat Party. More specifically, he had denounced what were politely called 'irregularities' in the local construction industry and the town plan. But within days the two men who attacked Corino had confessed, and the press was able to reassure itself that there was no political background to the assault. The culprits were both plasterers, paid by the square metre of wall they finished; they assaulted Corino because they objected to his attempts to enforce rules against piecework on building sites. Case closed. Or so it seemed.

As it turned out, the original suspicions were correct. Moreover, the assault on Mario Corino was only the first symptom of something much more menacing. The problems began, as Mario Corino had suspected, with a building boom in the early 1960s: tourists and second-homers needed places to stay if they were going to enjoy Bardonecchia's mountain air. Building firms needed cheap hands and a way round safety regulations and labour laws: they turned to 'ndrangheta gangmasters, who were more than happy to provide this service by recruiting from among the droves of Calabrian immigrants. The labourers in Bardonecchia, many of whom had criminal records and little chance of finding more regular employment, lived camped out in semi-squalor. By the early 1970s, an estimated 70–80 per cent of labour in the village was recruited through the mafia racket; many of those workers had to kick back part of their salary to the *capo*. Trades unions found it impossible to set up branches.

But long before then, the 'ndrangheta bosses had gone far beyond labour racketeering. First they set up their own companies to carry out subcontracting work: plastering and trucking were favourite niches. 'Ndrangheta-controlled construction firms were not far behind. Shadowy real-estate companies came and went from the record books. Then, at rival building sites, there were unexplained fires, machinery was vandalised and workers were threatened at gunpoint. Before long most of the honest building companies had been driven out of the market, or driven into the hands of the gangsters.

Meanwhile, the government had done its bit to fill the Calabrian mafia's coffers by building a new highway and a tunnel through the mountains. The 'ndrangheta recruited some local politicians and administrators to help them win contracts and get round regulations. Barely a stone was turned without the say-so of the local *capo*. One city council employee would simply hand out the boss's visiting card to anyone who applied for a licence to start up a new business – just to avoid any messy bureaucratic problems, he claimed. Mario Corino, the schoolteacher-cum-politician who had been attacked in 1963, led a heroic resistance to 'ndrangheta influence over local government when he became mayor in 1972. In 1975 the courts dismissed his alarm-calls as a politically motivated fiction: they said he was using the mafia as a pretext to throw mud at his rivals. Corino's opponents would feign disbelief and outrage when any journalist suggested that there might be a mafia problem in the town. Yet, at the same time, energetic policemen would be mysteriously transferred to other parts of the country. In a phone tap, the local boss was recorded as saying, 'We are the root of everything here, you understand me?'

It was remarkable that Bardonecchia had to wait until as late as 1969 for its first mafia murder. Forty-four deaths would follow between 1970 and 1983. On 23 June 1983, the 'ndrangheta proved how high, and how brutally, it was prepared to strike. Not long before midnight, Bruno Caccia was walking his dog when he was approached by two men in a car; they shot him fourteen times, and then got out to fire three *coups de grâce*. Caccia was an upstanding investigating magistrate who had refused any dialogue with what was now a thoroughgoing 'ndrangheta power system.

It is unlikely that there was a grand strategy behind the mafias' move north. Rocco Lo Presti, the *'ndranghetista* who led his organisation's rise to power in Bardonecchia during the building boom of the 1960s, had been there since the mid-1950s. It seems he came as a humble migrant, albeit one with some fearsome relatives. But he was less interested in getting a job than he was in handling counterfeit banknotes. Thereafter, *mafiosi* came north for many reasons: to hide from the police or their enemies; to set up temporary narcotics trading posts; to quietly launder and invest their ill-gotten gains, or to capitalise on criminal opportunities opened up by pioneers like Rocco Lo Presti. The full-scale colonisation of a town like Bardonecchia created a pattern to be followed elsewhere. In one bugged conversation, a friend of Rocco Lo Presti's was heard giving him a verbal pat on the back: 'Bardonecchia is Calabrian,' he said. The irony in this remark was that many of the entrepreneurs, administrators and politicians who had helped turn Bardonecchia Calabrian were as Piedmontese as Barolo wine and *agnolotti*.

In the political sphere, organised crime has always been a problem that affected the North and centre as well as the South. From soon after the birth of Italy as a unified state in 1861, coalition governments in Rome had to recruit clusters of supporters among southern MPs; and southern MPs – some of them, at least – used racketeers to hustle votes. Yet after the economic miracle, thanks primarily to infiltration of the construction industry, the mafias became a national problem in two dramatically new ways. On the one hand, as we have seen, the North became a theatre of operations for southern mobsters. On the other hand, the South became a theatre of cooperation between northern big industry and the mafias. For example, companies from the industrialised North were also dealing on friendly terms with the 'ndrangheta back in Calabria, where concrete proved even more lucrative than it was in Piedmont.

In the 1960s there began a major road-building programme. Its emblem was the so-called 'Motorway of the Sun' that ran down Italy from north to south. The last stretch of that motorway, covering the 443 kilometres from Salerno to Reggio Calabria, carried the burden of enormous hopes: a century on from Italian unification, the 'Salerno–Reggio Calabria' (as it is universally known) would finally end the deep South's isolation from the national transport network. Grand exploits of civil engineering were required to traverse the region's forbidding geology: no fewer than 55 tunnels and 144 viaducts, some of which soar over 200 metres above the forests at the valley floor.

Today the Salerno–Reggio Calabria is notorious – a prodigy of chaotic planning, pork-barrelling and broken political promises. It is still not finished nearly half a century after it was begun. Rather than taking the most logical and direct route along the coast, the Salerno–Reggio Calabria cuts tortuously inland to visit the electoral fiefdoms of long-forgotten ministers. At times the motorway's only purpose seems to be to join a chain of permanent construction sites. Long stretches are so narrow and winding that they have a 40-kilometre-per-hour speed limit. Jams are so frequent that the roadside is permanently lined with chemical toilets to allow desperate motorists to relieve themselves. During peak times, ambulances are parked ready to intervene. In 2002, magistrates in Catanzaro sequestered a whole section of recently modernised motorway because it was so shoddily built as to be acutely dangerous. The Bishop of Salerno recently called Europe's worst motorway a Via Crucis. The Salerno–Reggio Calabria shows the Italian state at its most incompetent.

Since the 1960s, the 'ndrangheta has profited handsomely from the mess. Yet very early on in the story of the Salerno–Reggio Calabria it became clear to law enforcement officers on the ground that the 'ndrangheta carried only part of the blame. One senior *Carabiniere* officer stationed in Reggio Calabria was interviewed by a national newspaper in 1970:

When northern entrepreneurs come down to Calabria to get their projects started, the first thing they do is to go to see the man they have been told is the mafia boss. They pay him a visit out of duty, as if they were calling on the Prefect. They solicit his protection, and pay for it by giving the *capomafia*'s friends the sub-contract for earth moving, and by taking on *mafiosi* as guards on their building sites.

Non-Calabrian construction entrepreneurs would offer other favours too: testimonies in favour of *mafiosi* in court; failing to report the many thefts of explosives from their building sites; offering guarantees to the bank when *'ndranghetisti* bought construction machinery on credit. The northern entrepreneurs would then fail to complete their work on time, and blame the local mafia for the delays. Those delays would then allow the entrepreneurs to charge the government more money, money of which the mafia would naturally receive its share. Along the Calabrian stretches of the Salerno–Reggio Calabria, the 'ndrangheta was educated into the ways of a particularly cynical brand of capitalism.

Construction is acutely vulnerable to the mafia's most rudimentary methods. Buildings and roads have to be built *somewhere*. And in any given somewhere, by merely smashing up plant or intimidating labour, *mafiosi* can force construction companies to sit down and negotiate. Nor, once those negotiations have borne fruit, does it require any great entrepreneurial nous for a boss to buy a few dumper trucks and set up an earth-moving company to take on some generously subcontracted business. More insidiously still, *mafiosi* do not find it hard to convince legal companies of the advantages that a friendship with organised crime can bring. An entrepreneur does not need to be exceptionally greedy or cynical to lapse into collusion with murderers. He just needs a preference for bending the rules, paying his workers in cash, and dodging red tape. And once he starts operating outside the law, who does he turn to when his machines are wrecked or his builders duffed up? His relief when he does a deal and the harassment stops merges easily with the satisfaction that comes when it is a competitor's turn to suffer. The truth is that there is often a *demand* for the mafias' services – a demand that the mafias themselves are past masters at cultivating.

So muscling in on the construction business is straightforward, up to a point. But success in construction can also be the measure of just how profoundly mafia influence has insinuated itself into the entrails of the state and the capitalist system. Getting zealous policemen moved, corrupting judges, adjusting town plans on demand, manipulating the awarding of government contracts, silencing journalists, winning powerful political friends: these are not activities for mere gorillas whose skills stop at pouring sugar into the fuel tank of a dumper truck. North or South, when a mafia masters these more refined arts, it can vastly increase its power to intimidate. Just as importantly, it can vastly increase the range of services it is able to offer to friendly firms: winning contracts at inflated prices, warding off inspections by the tax authorities, making new friends . . .

Gangsters and blondes

Italians got their first taste of imported American blend cigarettes like Camel, Lucky Strike and Chesterfield during the Fascist era. They named them 'blondes' because they contained a lighter-coloured tobacco than the dark, air-cured varieties that could be grown in Italy.

Blondes were immediately popular. The state had established a monopoly on the growing, importing, processing and sale of tobacco in 1862; and since that date the state had always struggled to keep pace with consumer demand and changing tastes. The arrival of blondes left the government further than ever from satisfying the public's craving. In fact, no sooner were these glamorous new gaspers introduced in the early 1930s than they disappeared from government tobacco outlets because of the sanctions imposed following Italy's invasion of Ethiopia in 1935. Rationing during the Second World War made smokers' lives even more difficult. And when the Allies invaded in 1943, and Fascism fell, Italy's own capacity to produce tobacco was devastated. Thus British and American troops arrived amidst a tobacco famine, and they arrived with cigarettes in their ration packs. Much of this tobacco was funnelled into the burgeoning black market. By the time rationing ended in the spring of 1948, and domestic production recovered, it was too late: Italy's rapidly growing number of smokers (14 million by 1957) were hooked on imported cigarettes. Perhaps just as damagingly, they were also hooked on the illegal supply channels that made those cigarettes available at tax-free prices. This vast criminal market has shaped the history of organised crime in Italy ever since. It has been compared to the Prohibition period in the United States

(1919–33), when the federal government banned alcoholic drinks, and in so doing created a bootleg bonanza. Naples, as the capital of the black market, is the place to watch the unfolding of the lucrative love affair between gangsters and blondes.

In 1963, cinema committed a captivating image of the Neapolitan contraband tobacco trade to popular memory in the first episode of Vittorio De Sica's three-part movie *Ieri, oggi, domani* (*Yesterday, Today and Tomorrow*), which won the Oscar for Best Foreign Film. Sophia Loren plays a girl who sells black-market cigarettes from an orange-box stall. For her, arrest is an occupational hazard. But she discovers that, by law, pregnant women cannot be held in prison, so she cajoles her husband into siring one baby after another, until their one-room apartment is bursting. Eventually, the poor man's reproductive apparatus gives out under the strain. (He is played, with typical harried charm, by Marcello Mastroianni.)

As a piece of cinema, the Loren episode of *Yesterday, Today and Tomorrow* is ultimately a sentimental cliché: yet another song to the gaudy anarchy of Neapolitan street life. Yet the story was rooted in truth all the same. The Loren character was based on Concetta Muccardo, who sold bootleg cigarettes in Forcella, the 'kasbah' quarter of Naples. Muccardo's reputed nineteen pregnancies (seven of them carried to term) kept her out of jail until 1957, when the police finally caught her without a baby on the way, or one in her arms. She was sent to prison for eight months and, harshly, a further two years were added to her sentence because she was unable to pay a fine. But Muccardo's notoriety quickly earned her freedom. The generous readers of two newspapers, one from Turin and one from Rome, paid off the money she owed. And in January 1958, following an appeal by Socialist and Communist women MPs, she was granted a pardon by the head of state, the President of the Republic. When

Concetta returned to her alley, vico Carbonari, pictures of President Giovanni Gronchi had been set up alongside the images of the Madonna in the local street tabernacles.

The experience of shooting *Yesterday, Today and Tomorrow* in the alleys of central Naples showed De Sica just how close the script came to reality. This was a city where the chronic failings of the economy had left many poor families reliant on contraband to put food on the table. De Sica gave a walk-on part to a well-known local woman with nine children: she boasted she had been in prison a record 113 times for contraband offences. In Forcella there were many other cigarette girls who entered local folklore. A certain 'Rosetta' was the most attractive of a number of women who charged extra for 'fun fags' – cigarettes that customers had to rummage for in her ample cleavage. (A Sophia Loren movie based on Rosetta's story would doubtless not have made it past the censors.)

While De Sica was staying in the Ambassador Hotel, Muccardo's husband introduced himself and demanded a percentage of the film's takings. Rather obliquely, De Sica replied by pointing to a magazine photo of Sophia Loren on set being fitted with a false baby belly. 'Don't you see how beautiful she is? As big as your wife was at that stage.' The husband refused to be wowed: 'Yes, Mr De Sica, but this is a belly full of millions: my wife's is full of air.' Writing to explain the episode to his family, De Sica could find nothing else to say than, 'They are poor people.'

Both De Sica's film, and his reaction to what he witnessed in Naples while shooting it, are a faithful reflection of the dilemma that the Italian authorities also found themselves in. The law against tobacco-trafficking was simply unenforceable at street level. A clampdown seemed to be impossible without hurting the people who were both its operatives and its first victims: the poorest inhabitants of the Neapolitan slums. Indeed this was a dilemma that the Italian state lacked the will to tackle in any other way than by sleep-walking into repression and then recoiling towards tolerance. There was an amnesty for illegal cigarette retailers in the year that *Yesterday, Today and Tomorrow* came out, and another one in 1966. Policies the world over that aim to prohibit or control substances like tobacco and alcohol are difficult to implement at the best of times. When those policies are widely disobeyed, they have a way of making the law seem draconian, unrealistic and inconsistent all at the same time. The precious principle that it is in everyone's interests for the state to create and enforce fair rules can only suffer, and the state itself falls into discredit. In Italy, where that principle has always struggled to hold its own, the damage to the state's credibility was very serious indeed. In Naples, contraband cigarettes were openly on sale in the corridors of government buildings.

Yesterday, Today and Tomorrow came out at a crucial historical moment for contraband tobacco, and thus for all of Italy's mafias. For this was the time when cigarette smuggling became an industry, and that industry became the primary occupation of organised crime.

The decisive event in the gearing up of Italy's bootleg tobacco trade happened in North Africa. In October 1959 Mohamed V, king of a newly independent Morocco, confirmed the fears of smugglers across the Mediterranean: he gave six months' notice that the port of Tangier was to lose its special privileges. Until that point Tangier, which is situated opposite Gibraltar at the mouth of the Mediterranean, had had a large 'International Zone' with few passport controls, very low taxes and no currency restrictions. Banks did not even have to present balance sheets. In short, Tangier was a smugglers' paradise, and the very hub of illegal commerce across the Mediterranean. As one resident, American novelist Paul Bowles, observed: 'I think all Europe's black-market profiteers are here . . . since the whole International Zone is one huge black market.' It was from the safe haven of Tangier that the 'mother ships' packed with contraband cigarettes could fan out along the southern European coastline. When they reached Naples, they would wait in international waters for tiny local craft to come and ferry the cargo to shore.

When King Mohamed announced the closure of the International Zone, the short-term result was that cigarette smuggling became more difficult. And when smuggling becomes more difficult, only the best-organised and best-resourced of smugglers can survive. The only wholesalers who could now prosper were those with international links to shipping companies, cigarette producers and officials in places like the Balkans. For different reasons, the local operators, who ferried the cases of cigarettes from ship to shore, also had to up their game: expensive speedboats were now needed to outrun the *Guardia di Finanza* (Tax Police). As competition in the tobacco business increased, so too did violence. Contraband was no longer a trade for amateurs.

Naples appealed to the new breed of professional trafficker of the 1960s for a number of reasons. One of the most important was the ready supply of cheap criminal labour in the alleys where Concetta Muccardo became a legend. Naples was also the gateway to an Italian market that was in the throes of its economic miracle, and consuming more and more cigarettes as a result. In the 1960s, Naples was also a free port, in the sense that the camorra in the city was still comparatively weak, and there was no dominant local criminal organisation able to throttle competition. So networks of big-time traffickers from Genoa, Corsica and Marseille were drawn to the city under the volcano to find outlets for their cigarettes. But the most important new arrivals after the closure of the International Zone of Tangier – men who would radically alter the course of criminal history in Italy – were from Sicily.

Cosa Nostra: **Untouchables no more**

In the late 1950s and early 1960s, Italy observed as the United States once more addressed its mafia problem. First, in November 1957, there was the spectacular episode at a large estate in Apalachin, upstate New York, when the state troopers stumbled upon a summit of some one hundred mafia bosses. One or two of them came from as far away as California, Cuba and Texas. Sixty men were taken into custody, and as a result the FBI finally admitted the mafia – or national crime syndicate, or whatever name might be applied to it – was something more than a romantic myth. As a result, in 1959, Vito Genovese, chief of the New York Family that bore his name, was sentenced to fifteen years for drug trafficking: the first major blow against a senior stateside boss in the decade and a half since the end of the Second World War.

Meanwhile Robert F. Kennedy, the energetic young chief counsel of a new Senate Labor Rackets Committee, was busy uncovering corruption in the Teamsters Union. Following the Apalachin summit, the committee again used television to good effect by interviewing several of the most prominent men who had been at Apalachin, such as Joe Profaci and Thomas Lucchese. Viewers also saw a federal agent explain the mafia's dynastic politics:

> The intermarriages are significant in that often times you wonder whether these people want to marry each other. Yet the marriages take place. Let's say two people of a prominent status within the Mafia if they have children, you will find that their sons and daughters get married. . . . a leader

within the organization would not have his child marry someone who is a nobody within the organization.

Bobby Kennedy's best-selling account of the investigation he led, *The Enemy Within* (1960), contained vivid cameo portraits of a series of Italian-American gangsters. One such was 'labor relations consultant' Carmine Lombardozzi, who had been ordered to wait in the garage during the Apalachin summit while the other *mafiosi* decided whether to kill him or merely fine him for covertly pocketing money from a juke-box racket. (They opted for the fine.)

In 1961, when his brother became President, Bobby Kennedy became Attorney General – in essence, the administration's top legal adviser and law-enforcement officer. The investigation and repression of organised crime was a key part of his programme. Where there had been nineteen organised crime indictments in 1960, the total rose to 687 in 1964.

Alongside these law enforcement and political developments, the mafia became a hot topic in American culture. In 1959, ABC began transmitting a drama series, based on Eliot Ness's *The Untouchables*, about Al Capone's Prohibition-era Chicago. The show became a hit, largely because it was studded with thinly disguised references to recent gangland news.

As always, there was a good deal of controversy and sensationalism in public discussion. The Order Sons of Italy in America, an ethnic lobby group that was desperate to play down the mafia issue, managed to get all Italian-American characters removed from *The Untouchables* in 1961. Deprived of this key element of authenticity, the show declined in popularity and was taken off air in 1963.

At the other extreme, some wrote about the mafia as if it were a centralised, bureaucratic, calculating monster – an IBM of crime. Ever since then, in both Italy and the States, it has made for good journalistic copy to see the mafia as a dark mirror of cutting-edge capitalism, and to see *mafiosi* as executives with guns. This is an oversimplification with undoubted imaginative power, to both the law-abiding and the outlaw. *The Godfather* – novel and movie – would later draw part of its insidious glamour from the same idea: 'Tell Mike it was only business.' Nothing could be better calculated to make middle-aged, middle-American middle-managers feel dangerous and clever than the suggestion that they and *mafiosi* are pretty much alike – give or take a few garrottings. Conversely, nothing could be better calculated to flatter a hoodlum's ego, and impress his young sidekicks, than the suggestion that he is the incarnation of some sleek, lawless ideal-type of the businessman. If *mafiosi* are entrepreneurs, then they are entrepreneurs who specialise not in competition, but in breaking and distorting the rules of the market.

The season of intense political and media interest in the mafia in the early 1960s also had a curious side effect: it changed the mafia's name. In 1962 Joe Valachi, a soldier in the Genovese Family, mistakenly suspecting that he was about to be killed on the orders of his boss, bludgeoned an innocent man to death in prison. He then began to talk to the FBI about the mafia, its initiation rituals and structure as he saw them from his lowly and relatively marginal position in the organisation. A non-Italian speaker, Valachi had heard other members of the brotherhood refer to *cosa nostra* – 'our thing'. Valachi took this vague description to be the mafia's official name: Cosa Nostra, or la Cosa Nostra. So too did the FBI. And then, once Valachi's testimony had been made public in 1963, so too did American *mafiosi* themselves. Only in 1984 would the world learn that this label had been adopted by the Sicilian mafia too.

The advent of the name Cosa Nostra is only the latest example of the way the mafias have learned their own language from the world outside. We have seen how the word 'ndrangheta only surfaced in the press during the 'Martian invasion' of Calabria in 1955. To the best of my knowledge, there is no insider testimony, trial document or newspaper article that refers to the Calabrian mafia by this name before that date.

Something similar happened a century earlier with the word 'mafia' itself. It only became the most commonly used of the many names for Sicily's elite criminal brotherhood as the result of being used in a successful play about prison gangsters in the 1860s.

Why are the mafias so bad at giving themselves a name? The main reason, as one defector from Cosa Nostra would later explain, is that secret criminal brotherhoods are the 'realm of incomplete speech'.

> Fragmenting information is one of the most important rules. Cosa Nostra is not just secretive towards the exterior, in the sense that it hides its existence and the identity of its members from outsiders. It is also secretive on the inside: it discourages anyone from knowing the full facts, and creates obstacles to the circulation of information.

Mafiosi habitually conduct their affairs in nods and silences, in language marked by an expertly crafted vagueness that can be understood only by those who are meant to understand. Communications within the mafia are like whispers in a labyrinth. So when the outside world says something about the mafia's affairs, it resounds through the labyrinth like a clarion call.

Despite the controversy, the oversimplifications and the perverse side effects, America's open discussion about the mafia in these years was a healthy sign. What it indicates is that the period of relative impunity and invisibility that Italian-American mobsters had long enjoyed was now over for good. The mafia in the United States was no longer untouchable. The question now was how long it would take for Italy to follow Uncle Sam's example.

Mafia diaspora

In October 1957, only weeks before the Apalachin summit in upstate New York, Men of Honour from the United States held several days of meetings with Sicilian bosses at the Grand Hotel et Des Palmes in the heart of Palermo. The head of the American deputation was Joe 'Bananas' Bonanno – *capo* of the New York Family that bore his name. Narcotics were almost certainly at the top of the agenda. Unlike what had happened at Apalachin, however, the heavy-lidded eyes of the Palermo police merely registered the meeting. Nothing was done about it.

Business was not the only thing discussed while Joe Bananas was in Palermo. According to the later confessions of a young drug trafficker called Tommaso Buscetta (a man destined to play an epoch-making role in Sicilian mafia history over a quarter of a century later), the 1957 Italo-American summit was the occasion for an important organisational innovation within the Sicilian mafia. It seems that, over dinner one evening, Joe Bananas suggested that Sicily should have a Mafia Commission – a kind of governing body – like the one that had overseen inter-Family relations in New York since Lucky Luciano brought it into being in 1931. The Commission has existed in Sicily, on and off, ever since. Not for the first time, Sicilian *mafiosi* had shown that they were better at learning lessons from America than were Italy's police or politicians.

However, the Commission, as Sicilian historians have now ascertained, was not the novelty that Tommaso Buscetta thought it was. Evidence that Cosa Nostra has had governing bodies of one kind or another is there in some of the earliest documentation we have about it. For example, there were forms of coordination between the different *cosche* of western Sicily – joint tribunals to settle disputes, summit meetings, marriage pacts and the like. In America, there seem to have been consultative meetings of senior East Coast Men of Honour before the First World War. Our best guess, using recent history as a guide to the mysterious moments in the past, is that the mafia has always had a lively constitutional life. Sicilian mafia bosses have constantly invented new rules and procedures to buttress their own authority and keep the peace with their neighbours. But equally, they have constantly broken their own rules and procedures, or found ways to use them as a political weapon against their enemies.

In the late 1950s, however, these nuances of mafia analysis had not even begun to dawn on Italy's rulers. The issue of Sicilian organised crime remained stuck in the political permafrost of the Cold War. Communist politicians took every opportunity they could to raise the mafia issue – and make it count against the DC. But without the power to govern, they remained isolated voices. One of the most astute and caustic of those voices belonged to Pio La Torre, the young leader of the PCI in Sicily:

The truth is that there is no sector of the economy in Palermo and in vast areas of Western Sicily that is not controlled by the mafia. This has happened in the course of a long process – the same process that has seen the DC regime prosper in Palermo and the rest of the island.

La Torre knew what he was talking about: he was born in Altarello di Baida, a village set amid the lemon groves surrounding Palermo – the mafia's nursery, in other words.

In response to charges like these, the DC all too often fell back on a contradictory rag-bag of myths: the mafia was dying out; it was merely a harmless Sicilian tradition; it was invented by the Left as a way of besmirching Sicily and the DC; it didn't exist; *mafiosi* only kill one another anyway; *gangsterismo* was an American problem.

The Left opposition had not forgotten the Kefauver hearings, and lobbied hard for something similar to happen in Italy: a parliamentary inquiry into the Sicilian mafia. The Christian Democrats were split into shifting and bitterly antagonistic factions. In the heat of the factional struggle, many DC chiefs were very reluctant to look too closely at the ethical standards of their Sicilian lieutenants. So the DC dragged its feet for years, and only gave ground when the Left's lobbying was given extra oomph by mafia dynamite.

Late in 1962, a conflict that later became known as the First Mafia War began in and around Palermo. The conflict's signature weapon was a tactical novelty for underworld wars in Italy: the car bomb. Invariably, it was an Alfa Romeo Giulietta that was stuffed with explosives. The Giulietta was one of the symbols of Italy's economic miracle. In 1962 it became a symbol of how the Sicilian mafia was keeping up with the pace of growth in the lawful economy.

Although a drug deal gone wrong is known to have been the trigger for the First Mafia War's outbreak, the underlying reasons for it baffled outside observers at the time, and are still uncertain today. Even many of the combatants did not know where the battle lines were drawn. In essence, it seems that the newly revived Commission had been unable to control conflicts over drugs, concrete and territory. Indeed some Palermo *mafiosi* regarded the Commission itself with justifiable suspicion: for them it was not an arbiter in disputes, but an instrument manipulated by some powerful bosses. The Sicilian mafia's constitutional wrangles had taken a bloody turn. Indeed, not for the last time, events in Palermo were pointing the way to the future for organised crime in Italy. Perhaps one hundred people were killed in the First Mafia War – more than in any other underworld conflict since the 1940s. Cosa Nostra had become more volatile in its internal politics, and more flagrant in its violence. Soon the other mafias would follow the same trend.

Against the background of the car bombings and other violence in Palermo, a parliamentary inquiry into the Sicilian mafia was grudgingly approved. Yet it still looked as if it would never get going. Then, on 30 June 1963, another Giulietta detonated in Ciaculli: it blew four *Carabinieri*, two military engineers and a policeman to pieces. The bomb's intended targets were probably the local mafia clan, the Grecos, one of Palermo's oldest and most powerful dynasties.

Remarkably, even on the day of the bomb, the DC remained very touchy about the word 'mafia'. The Christian Democrat notables who occupied the country's most senior institutional posts all issued messages of condolence to the victims' families, and of indignation to the general public. Not one of them mentioned the mafia.

Nevertheless, the public outrage that followed the Ciaculli massacre had rapid effects, both within Cosa Nostra and outside. The First Mafia War came to an immediate halt in the face of a massive police crackdown, with close to two thousand arrests. Cosa Nostra faced one of the worst crises in its history. As a *mafioso* who turned state's evidence later explained: 'After 1963 Cosa Nostra in the Palermo area didn't exist any more. It had been knocked out. The mafia was about to dissolve itself, and seemed to be in a shambles . . . The Families were all wrecked. There were hardly any murders any more. In Palermo, people did not even pay protection money.'

Mafiosi who were able to flee Palermo did so – men like the boss of the Commission, Totò Greco (known as 'Little Bird'), who emigrated to Venezuela. Others fled to Switzerland, the States, Canada . . . The mafia vanished from its birthplace, the province of Palermo.

The Ciaculli bomb also swept away the last resistance to the idea of a parliamentary inquiry into the mafia – an Italian Kefauver, at last. But anyone who expected the inquiry to achieve the kind of spectacular results seen on the other side of the Atlantic was in for both a very long wait and a dull disappointment. The political wrangling only seemed to intensify during the inquiry's hearings. Astonishingly, in 1966, Donato Pafundi, the Senator who chaired those hearings – a Christian Democrat by political affiliation and a magistrate by profession – denied the existence of the mafia as a criminal organisation, and even blamed Muslims for the problem:

> The mafia in Sicily is a mental state that pervades everything and everyone, at all levels of society. There are historical, geographical and social reasons behind this mentality. Above all there is a millennium of Muslim domination. It is hard to shake off the inheritance of centuries. The mafia has ended up in Sicilians' blood, in the most intimate folds of Sicilian society.

Considering views like this, it is hardly surprising that the parliamentary inquiry took no fewer than thirteen years to finish its work.

Nor did Italian politicians have any of the flair for the media that Estes Kefauver and Robert Kennedy had shown. The parliamentary inquiry's final report provided as good a definition of the problem as one could get without using insider sources. It certainly had none of the simplistic sensationalism of Kefauver's vision of a vast, centralised international conspiracy, or of Donato Pafundi's ignorance. But its abstruse wording was indicative of the problems the inquiry had had in bringing public opinion along with it:

> The mafia has continually reproposed itself as the exercise of autonomous extra-legal power and the search for a close link with all forms of power and in particular state power, so as to collaborate with it, make use of it for its own ends, or infiltrate its structure.

Anyone who was still awake after trying to read a couple of paragraphs of prose like this deserved a medal for endurance.

Predictably, the parliamentary Left also disagreed with the report and issued its own version, placing much more emphasis on the mafia's ties to the highest spheres of Sicilian society: 'The mafia is a ruling class phenomenon.' This, in its own way, was also an oversimplification. The point about the Sicilian mafia, like the nineteenth-century Freemasonry on which it was based, is that it includes members of all classes: both cut-throats and counts can become Men of Honour.

Perhaps the most damning criticism to be made of the 1960s parliamentary inquiry into the Sicilian mafia is that its terms of reference did not include the camorra and the 'ndrangheta. Underestimating the organised crime issue outside Sicily would have dire consequences. And those dire consequences were set in motion scarcely two years after the parliamentary inquiry started work, when the first piece of legislation to issue from the post-Ciaculli climate was passed. Law 575 of 1965 was a parcel of anti-mafia measures that included the policy of 'forced resettlement': suspected *mafiosi* could be compelled to leave their homes and take up residence somewhere else in Italy. Forced resettlement was based on the highly questionable theory that the fundamental cause of the mafia was the backward social environment of western Sicily. If *mafiosi* could be transplanted from that environment into healthier surroundings, so the theory went, then their criminal inclinations would shrivel.

Rather than shrivelling, the mafia spread. As one Man of Honour would later explain: 'Forced resettlement was a good thing for us, because it gave us a way to contact other people, to get to know different places, other cities, zones that weren't already contaminated by organised crime.'

It was not just 'uncontaminated' zones of Italy that hosted resettled *mafiosi*. Incredibly, some of them were even sent to the hinterland of Naples. Despite the fearsome traditions of criminal enterprise that had become visible during the Pupetta Maresca affair, Campania was now deemed socially healthy enough to reform the Sicilian gangster elite. In the late 1960s and early

1970s, some of Sicily's most powerful criminals were forcibly resettled around Naples: *mafiosi* of the calibre of Francesco Paolo Bontate, the boss of Santa Maria di Gesù, and later his son Stefano, a future keystone of Cosa Nostra's Palermo Commission. They were joined there by other *mafiosi* who were on the run from the law. One of these was Gerlando Alberti, who later became famous for a *bon mot*: asked about the mafia by a journalist, he replied, 'What's that? A brand of cheese?'

Through the repression following the Ciaculli bomb, and then by the policy of enforced resettlement, Italy had involuntarily created a new diaspora of criminal talent. Naples during the contraband tobacco boom would be one of that diaspora's favourite ports. The stage was set for a crucial new convergence of interests between Sicilian and Campanian organised crime.

The mafia-isation of the camorra

Michele Zaza, known as 'o Pazzo ('Mad Mike'), was the son of a fisherman from Portici who became the dominant Neapolitan cigarette smuggler of the 1970s. He had a vast villa in Posillipo, with one of the most splendid views over the bay of Naples – *La Glorietta*, he called it. Interviewed there by a local TV station, he once famously quipped that tobacco smuggling was 'the FIAT of southern Italy'. What he meant was that it created as many jobs as did the Turin-based car giant. Naples could no more survive without smuggling than Turin could without the automotive industry. This was a wisecrack pitched at a ready audience, both in the alleys of central Naples, and in the communities far beyond Naples that had once enjoyed Sophia Loren's sassy performance in *Yesterday, Today and Tomorrow*. As had been the case during Prohibition in the United States, gangsters who operated in a clandestine market, trading a commodity that had a great many non-criminal customers, could easily pose as the good guys.

Mad Mike was no Robin Hood, however. On 5 April 1973, he was part of an assassination squad that tried to kill Chief of Police Angelo Mangano, a Sicilian lawman who had distinguished himself in the fight against the mafia in Corleone. (Mangano survived, despite being shot four times, including in the head.) Why would a Neapolitan *camorrista* try to kill an enemy of the Sicilian mafia? Because that *camorrista* had recently become an initiated affiliate of Cosa Nostra.

By the early 1970s, the Sicilian *mafiosi* who had ended up in Campania had become intimate friends with a number of *camorristi*. The police and *Carabinieri* reported a regular series of meetings between Neapolitan and Sicilian hoods in Naples. The

Sicilians even acquired a taste for the sentimental pop melodies that their Neapolitan hosts adored.

The links between the mafia and the camorra were soon formalised. In the Sicilian mafia's traditional fashion, *mafiosi* established kinship alliances with the *camorristi*, based on marriage and *comparatico* ('co-parenthood' – i.e. becoming godfather to one another's children). Big Neapolitan smugglers were also formally initiated into Cosa Nostra. At least two Cosa Nostra Families in Campania were created and authorised by Palermo. One had its seat in the city itself, and was grouped around an extended family, the Zaza-Mazzarellas, including 'Mad Mike' Zaza. The other was based in Marano, a small town on the northern outreaches of Naples. Marano was home to the man who had shot dead the 'President of Potato Prices' in 1955. The murderer's relatives, the Nuvoletta brothers, were now in charge in the town, and were duly initiated into Cosa Nostra.

Thus Cosa Nostra's new Campanian Families inherited the two main criminal traditions in the region. 'Mad Mike' Zaza represented the urban camorra revived by the black market during the Second World War. The Nuvoletta brothers were just the type of *camorristi* who had long been involved in controlling supply routes from the countryside to the city markets. So in one sense, the novelty of Cosa Nostra's branches in Campania was also a highly significant return to the past. For the first time since the days of the old Honoured Society of Naples, a single organisational framework embraced both the urban and rural camorras.

The scaling-up of the trade in bootleg cigarettes, and the close links between the Sicilian and Neapolitan underworlds, was 'mafia-ising' the camorra. Indeed, not for the first time in history, the very meaning of the word 'camorra' was undergoing a transformation. Once, if it was used at all, it referred to small local gangs, or networks of smugglers, or even to isolated *guappi*. Now *camorristi* were increasingly functionaries of much bigger groups, with a bigger range of criminal activities and greater financial sophistication.

To the Neapolitans, the incoming *mafiosi* brought many things, such as organisational skills, and particularly prestige. For who has not heard of the Sicilian mafia? And who, among criminals, is not afraid of it?

To the Sicilians, Neapolitans like 'Mad Mike' offered excellent smuggling contacts and a vast distribution network. Bringing them inside Cosa Nostra was a way of keeping a close eye on them. Indeed, they also did the same thing, and for the same reason, to a major Palermitan cigarette smuggler, Tommaso Spadaro.

The Sicilian mafia's decision to absorb some *camorristi* also had strategic military motives. The dominant players in Neapolitan contraband during the late 1960s were multinational traffickers known collectively as the Marseillais – because one of their previous bases had been in the French port of Marseille. Between 1971 and 1973, Cosa Nostra's men in Campania deployed their firepower to cut out the competition. A handful of Neapolitan cigarette smugglers were executed, and at least six Marseillais. By mafia standards, this was a very small investment in violence that would reap very big returns. Soon Cosa Nostra and its Campanian friends had the contraband tobacco market to themselves.

Business ballooned. One estimate suggests that, in the late 1970s, the annual turnover of the illegal cigarette business in Campania was some 48.6 billion lire (very roughly €175 million in 2012 values), and net profit stood at somewhere between 20 and 24 billion (€72–€86 million). In 1977, the *Carabinieri* found 'Mad Mike' Zaza with an account book, according to which mafia-camorra tobacco smuggling turned over an astonishing 150 billion lire a year (over €500 million). Between 40,000 and 60,000 people in the Campania region are thought to have found employment in the smuggling economy. The FIAT of southern Italy indeed.

Cosa Nostra got more than its share of the bonanza. Naples, according to a *mafioso* heavily involved in contraband, became the

'El Dorado' of Sicilian organised crime. As Tommaso Buscetta, a veteran cigarette smuggler, recalled:

> The volume of business in the illegal cigarette trade became enormous. In the 1950s, 500 cases were considered a big consignment. Now we'd reached as many as 35–40,000 cases unloaded every time a contraband ship travelled between Naples and Palermo.

Managing the flow of wealth that came to Sicily from across the Tyrrhenian Sea also had profound effects on the Sicilian mafia. For by 1969, most of the Men of Honour charged as a result of the First Mafia War had been acquitted, and they were free to pick up where they had left off at the time of the Ciaculli bomb. They wasted little time letting everyone in Palermo know they were back. At a quarter to seven on the evening of 10 December 1969, five men in stolen police uniforms machine-gunned the occupants of a construction company office in viale Lazio. Five were killed, including one of the attackers and their intended target: the mafia boss Michele Cavataio, who many within Cosa Nostra thought was the mastermind behind the car-bombing campaign of the early 1960s. We now know that the men who carried out the viale Lazio massacre were delegates from different mafia Families – as if to demonstrate that Cavataio's execution had been decreed by Cosa Nostra as a whole.

Thus, after a six-year hiatus following the Ciaculli bomb, the Sicilian mafia resumed its constitutional life. The first formal shape that Cosa Nostra's politics took was a triumvirate of senior bosses who were entrusted with reawakening the organisation's dormant structures in the province of Palermo. The first triumvir, and probably the most prestigious, was Stefano Bontate, known as the 'Prince of Villagrazia', *capo* of the largest Family in

Palermo, a job he had inherited from his father. Bontate was mafia aristocracy. The second triumvir was Gaetano 'Tano' Badalamenti, the boss of Cinisi, where Palermo's new airport provided a huge source of revenue; Badalamenti had long-standing links with Cosa Nostra in Detroit. The third was Luciano Liggio from Corleone.

The triumvirate gave way to the full Commission in 1974, with Cinisi mobster Tano Badalamenti sitting at the head of the table. It was now a subtly different kind of body. When the Commission was set up in the late 1950s, there was a rule that no Family *capo* could have a seat. The ostensible objective was to hear complaints from individual Men of Honour about their bosses, and to protect them from unwarranted bullying. The Commission activated in 1974, by contrast, was composed of the most important bosses in the province of Palermo. It is no coincidence that this new shape emerged at the time that smuggling cigarettes through Naples was one of the mafia's major sources of income. For as well as being a body devoted to managing relations between the Families, the Commission became a tobacco-smuggling joint-stock company.

Mafia sources have given us a remarkable insight into the tense politics of contraband tobacco within Cosa Nostra in the 1970s. Each of the interested parties would take it in turns to take possession of a shipload coming into Campania: one for the Neapolitans, one for each of the groups of *mafiosi* operating in Naples, and then one as a tribute to the Commission. Thus every two months or so, the ship carrying the cigarettes for Palermo would make its way towards Sicily. Tano Badalamenti, in his role as head of the Commission or 'provincial representative', would take responsibility for divvying up the cargo: 1,000 cases for Michele 'the Pope' Greco from Ciaculli; 1,000 for the Corleone Family; 2,000 for the Bontate group, and so on. In other words, each boss who was prestigious enough to be included on the Commission, and rich enough to have the capital to buy cigarettes upfront, became a stakeholder in the portion of the cigarette market that the Commission claimed as its right.

In addition to the Commission's 'joint-stock company', many *mafiosi* ran contraband cigarettes independently, as traffickers in their own right. Rings of smugglers were formed by Men of Honour from different Families, as and when business opportunities presented themselves. The picture was further complicated by the need to work closely with non-*mafiosi* who were not as dependable, and not subject to the mafia's rules. Initiating men like 'Mad Mike' Zaza did not entirely solve the problem.

Mad Mike had manifestly not undergone the same rigorous selection process as the Palermo criminal elite, and he occasionally needed reminding of the self-discipline he was expected to show now that he was a Man of Honour. On one occasion, he was spotted playing cards for large sums in the casino of a luxury hotel on the island of Ischia. The Catania boss Pippo Calderone, one of his partners in the cigarette business, angrily reminded him that ostentatious gambling on that scale was not permitted behaviour for a member of Cosa Nostra.

Mad Mike and other smugglers never lost their reputation for slipperiness within Cosa Nostra. According to Tommaso Buscetta, they had a 'fraudster mentality', and tended 'to play it sly'. Of course, sly behaviour was not an exclusively Neapolitan trait. It is likely that Mad Mike's semi-detached status vis-à-vis Cosa Nostra also made him the perfect accomplice and scapegoat for Men of Honour who were just as sly as him, and who wanted to get more than their allotted share of any given cargo.

Thus the mafia-camorra cigarette oligopoly was born already fissured by mutual suspicion. Some years later, it would become clear that the tensions in the contraband tobacco business had also exposed fault lines *within* Cosa Nostra that would open up into the bloodiest conflict in mafia history.

But in 1978 the tobacco-smuggling boom slowed because an international accord now allowed the authorities to pursue smugglers into international waters. Seizures of cigarettes hit a peak in that year. More significantly, by that time, heroin was opening up a new, more profitable, and much more divisive chapter in Italy's underworld history.

There is a postscript to the story of Concetta Muccardo, the Forcella cigarette-seller played by Sophia Loren in *Yesterday, Today and Tomorrow*. On 27 June 1992, aged sixty-seven, she was arrested for retailing heroin from a doorway in the Sanità neighbourhood; behind the door the police found another fifty wraps of heroin and 350,000 lire (€280 in 2011 values). Long before that date, narcotics were being funnelled through the same channels once used to bring contraband cigarettes into Italy.

The mushroom-pickers of Montalto

Meanwhile, in Calabria . . .

The 'ndrangheta, as we have seen, had begun to make inroads into the construction industry in the 1960s. Southern Calabria's long coastline also afforded plenty of sheltered places where cases of contraband cigarettes could be off-loaded. Just as was happening in Sicily and Campania, the money flowing in from concrete and tobacco created a new political climate in Calabrian organised crime.

In 1969, the judicial authorities were given a rare glimpse of the Calabrian mafia's internal politics when, for the first time in history, the police mounted a full-scale raid on the 'ndrangheta's annual general meeting on Aspromonte. The episode briefly propelled Italy's least visible mafia into the headlines for the first time since the 'Martian invasion' of 1955. The story of that 1969 raid, and the trial that resulted from it, allows us to catch up on a crucial process of political change under way within the Calabrian underworld. Just as importantly, it illustrates how the Italian law viewed the sworn criminal sects of both Calabria and Sicily at a time when they were becoming both richer and more dangerous.

At nearly 2,000 metres, Montalto is the highest point on Aspromonte. From here, a statue of the redeeming Christ – were he able to revolve on his axis to follow the line of the horizon – would enjoy one of the most beautiful 360-degree panoramas on the planet: the Aeolian Islands off the northern coast of Sicily, the wooded slopes of Calabria's Serre mountains to the north-east, and the quietly smoking peak of Mount Etna across the Straits. Somewhere in the woods below lies the Sanctuary of the Madonna of the Mountain at Polsi, where the 'ndrangheta has always held an annual reunion early in September. In 1969, the increased attentions of the police had forced a change of date and venue. This year, the chief cudgels of the Calabrian underworld convened in a woodland clearing just below Montalto, on a damp Sunday morning, 26 October. But their counter-measures turned out to be in vain.

A team of twenty-four police and *Carabinieri*, acting on clues derived from weeks of surveillance, came across thirty-five cars parked higgledy-piggledy on the edge of the road near Montalto. Moving swiftly and silently, the police overpowered and gagged the five lookouts. Advancing further into the forest, they heard shouting and applause: the underworld conference was still in session.

The team split into two groups to try and encircle the broad clearing where they could glimpse more than a hundred men, sitting in a circle in animated discussion. But someone gave the alarm. Six officers advanced into the clearing shouting 'Nobody move! Police!' The gangsters ran off in every direction, firing wildly with pistols, shotguns, automatic rifles and machine guns. No one was hit and, amid chaotic scenes, the police managed to arrest twenty-one of the men at the summit. They also had the cars abandoned by the fleeing *'ndranghetisti* to work with. Eventually seventy-two of the estimated 130 men in attendance would face trial. Most of them claimed they had been out picking mushrooms. Some of the younger affiliates cracked under interrogation. One of them, a builder from Bagnara, told police of his initiation ceremony He and a few others also revealed the gist of what had been discussed at Montalto.

The first striking thing about the debate is how *procedural* some of it was. Before the summit got under way, as tradition dictated, each man present had to stand up and formally greet the others in the name of the clan he represented. An important item on the agenda was the annual meeting itself. Should the Honoured Society continue to gather at the Sanctuary of the Madonna of Polsi every year, now that the police were clearly taking a close interest? Someone proposed a change of location. And surely, with a change of location should come a change of name: it should now be termed the 'Aspromonte meeting' and no longer the 'Polsi meeting'. After much discussion, the conservatives won out: Polsi would remain the venue of choice, although the date could be switched to throw the authorities off. Perhaps understandably, when the men arrested at Montalto came to court, the judge described this discussion as 'formalistic' and 'pedantic'.

Yet there were more substantive issues discussed at the summit, like how to respond to the threat posed by the forces of law and order. The circle of bosses complained loudly about the activism recently shown by the Chief of Police of Reggio Calabria. This called for a united response, for a show of force. A variety of tactical options were tabled, such as blowing up police vehicles with dynamite, or ambushing the Chief of Police's car.

Planning dynamite outrages against the common enemy may well have lightened the mood among the 'mushroom-pickers' of Montalto. But the main issue at the summit was potentially much more explosive: addressing the potential for disunity within the 'ndrangheta's ranks. Investigators learned that one of the older bosses from Taurianova in the plain of Gioia Tauro, a veteran felon called Giuseppe Zappia who had been entrusted with the task of chairing the meeting, made a passionate appeal for unity: 'There's no Mico Tripodo's 'ndrangheta here! There's no 'Ntoni Macrì's 'ndrangheta here! There's no Peppe Nirta's 'ndrangheta here! We should all be united. Anyone who wants to stay, stays. Anyone who doesn't want to stay, goes.'

Apart from what is probably a veiled threat in the last line (one wonders what the price of leaving the meeting would have been), this plea sounds very bland: the gangland equivalent of motherhood and apple pie. The police and magistrates looking into the Montalto summit sensed that the appeal was in reality highly significant. But before they could find out much more, the few men arrested at Montalto who had confessed retracted their statements: they had been bullied by the police, they said. As had almost always been the case in the first century of organised crime history in Italy, such vital witnesses were not properly cultivated and protected by the magistrates handling the case; no one will ever know how much more they could have told us about the 'ndrangheta. Instead they joined the chorus of gangsters who claimed to have been picking mushrooms.

To his great credit, the judge in the case, one Guido Marino, would have none of these feeble alibis. Nor did he take very seriously the defence's claims that the 'ndrangheta was like the Rotary Club or the Lions. Judge Marino meant business. He made some devastating criticisms of the way the fight against the 'ndrangheta was being conducted. Investigations were 'superficial' and 'desultory', meaning that the mafia remained 'elusive' in court. Rather than 'solid and patient' investigation, the police all too often fell back on police cautions and internal exile. These preventive measures were entirely counterproductive, he said. 'They have acted like a restorative vaccine in the bodies of these criminal societies, which today are more vigorous and efficient than ever.'

It was the same scandalous story that had been carrying on since Italy had become one country in the nineteenth century. In Calabria, as elsewhere in southern Italy, mafia organisations were thriving on the half-cocked tactics designed to contain them.

Astutely, Judge Marino latched on to what might seem the least sinister aspect of the Montalto summit: the 'formalistic' and 'pedantic' procedural discussion. In his view, this betrayed the fact that the 'ndrangheta was an 'institutionalised' association. Moreover, Judge Marino went on to argue, the gangsters' debate about shared traditions showed that the world of Calabrian organised crime was much more than a scattering of isolated gangs. There was only one 'ndrangheta, and it was a criminal organisation with a long history behind it. (At this point, no one knew how long that history was.)

There is a striking contrast here with the 'Martian invasion' of Calabria in 1955, when the authorities seemed to have only a passing interest in the 'ndrangheta's history and structure. Judge Marino's ruling is the first small sign of what the Italian judicial system could learn by treating the mafias of Calabria and Sicily as what they were: criminal sects that had been embedded in society for decades.

Judge Marino was so keen to delve into the 'ndrangheta's secrets that he compiled biographies of the two most powerful bosses named in the plea for unity at Montalto. Those biographies – the first ever detailed portaits of 'ndrangheta chief cudgels – are worth looking at closely.

We have already met one of the bosses: don 'Ntoni Macrì, the Siderno boss who reputedly saved the Bishop of Locri from being murdered by a gang of vengeful priests before the Marzano Operation in 1955. Don 'Ntoni was born in Siderno in 1904. By the time he reached his forties, he was in his pomp. He induced the local landowners to use his own henchmen as guards on their olive groves. He forcibly regulated lemon prices to suit his own needs as a trader in agricultural commodities. He also had interests in agricultural machinery and construction. In short, don 'Ntoni was rich.

In the autumn of 1953, anonymous reports said that don 'Ntoni had presided over the Honoured Society's plenary meeting on Aspromonte. In 1957 his political protection came into operation to rescue him from the internal exile he had been sentenced to during the Marzano Operation. A year later he was on the run, charged with murder. In 1961 he was found not guilty, and also acquitted of the supplementary charge of being a member of a criminal association. An arrest for attempted murder came in 1965. Then, in 1967, three of his rivals were shot dead and another two wounded in what became known as the 'massacre of piazza

Mercato' in Locri: two men armed with a shotgun and a machine gun opened fire on a group of people who were striking a deal in the wholesale fruit and vegetable market. As always, Macrì was found not guilty on the grounds of insufficient evidence.

But don 'Ntoni's most jaw-dropping coup was yet to come. In 1967, he defrauded the Bank of Naples with the help of the Siderno branch manager. Although the manager was sacked as a result, the Bank of Naples refused to help the police with their investigations. Reviewing the evidence in that case, Judge Marino could only conclude that there was a mafia in the Bank of Naples alongside the mafia run by don 'Ntoni Macrì. The judge was shocked by the number of times, through the 900 pages of don 'Ntoni's criminal record, that he had been shown leniency after important people had defined him as a reformed character. By the time of the summit at Montalto in 1969, the Siderno boss had become what Judge Marino called a 'living symbol of organised crime's omnipotence and invincibility'.

Don Domenico 'Mico' Tripodo was the second boss invoked at the Montalto summit whose biography was assembled by Judge Marino. In the judge's words, Mico Tripodo was a 'proud and indomitable villain, entirely devoted to the mafia cause'. He derived his income from extortion, fruit-market racketeering, armed robbery, counterfeit money and cheques, and, of course, construction and tobacco smuggling. One of the more remarkable features of Tripodo's career is that he escaped confinement three times by the same trick of feigning illness and getting himself transferred to clinics, which were less well guarded and much easier to slip away from. Much of the rest of his time was spent in hiding: he changed his name several times, and even contracted a bigamous marriage in Umbria before finally being recaptured in Perugia. The fact that he was behind bars at the time of the Montalto summit did not stop him running his empire and ordering murders on his turf.

Poring over these biographies understandably left Judge Marino angry and disbelieving. The authorities knew an awful lot about the 'ndrangheta: the summit at Polsi had been an open secret for a while, for example. Yet, as Judge Marino observed, they seemed incapable of making any progress towards hampering its operations and resisting the rise of don 'Ntoni, Mico Tripodo and their ilk.

Judge Marino's diligent and penetrating ruling on the mushroom-pickers of Montalto contrasts strikingly with the trials against Cosa Nostra that took place around the same time. A notable example is the 1968 trial that was intended to bring to justice the participants in the First Mafia War, when Palermo's delinquent elite had blown one another up with booby-trapped Alfa Romeo Giuliettas. The prosecutor who prepared the case against the participants in the mafia war, Cesare Terranova, was certain that the mafia had a centralised coordinating council of some kind. According to a report prepared by the *Carabinieri* in 1963, fifteen senior *mafiosi*, of whom six came from the city of Palermo and nine from the towns and villages of the province, had seats around the table. This council, of course, was what we now know is called the Commission. Yet, as so often in mafia history, this picture of the mafia's inner workings was based on confidential information leaked from within the mafia rather than on formal testimony given in open court. For that reason, it was all but useless as prosecution evidence.

Accordingly, the judge in this case remained agnostic on the question of whether the Sicilian mafia existed or not. He discounted the far-fetched theory that the mafia had 'norms' and 'criteria' common to all its members. He also made concessions to the defence's argument that the mafia was 'a psychological attitude or the typical expression of an exaggerated individualism'. But he also thought it was something more, something illegal but hard to define with any clarity. So he concluded, fuzzily, that it was a 'phenomenon of collective criminality'. All but ten of the 114 defendants were acquitted for lack of evidence.

Law enforcement took its cue from this verdict. In 1974, the very year when, as we now know, the Palermo Commission of

Cosa Nostra was reconstituted, the Chief of Police of Palermo argued that the mafia was only a loose set of unstructured local gangs that coalesced for specific criminal enterprises and then quickly dissolved. It was hopeless to try and fight the mafia *as such*, because it was just a part of Sicilian culture. 'It is impossible to repress the general phenomenon of the mafia! Repress what? An idea? A mentality?' Cosa Nostra, as so often in its history, was proving very, very adept at concealing its real nature.

So Judge Marino's account of the Montalto summit case gave the Italian authorities a picture of a highly structured and ritualised 'ndrangheta. Moreover, the criminal records of don 'Ntoni Macrì and Mico Tripodo bore a striking resemblance to those of many Sicilian mafia bosses of their generation and earlier: the same violence, the same powerful friends, the same curious train of acquittals for lack of evidence, the same ability to insinuate themselves into the richest sectors of the lawful economy. Yet no one seems to have wondered whether a similar picture of a structured and ritualised criminal brotherhood might fit the evidence in Sicily. The raw truth was that nothing that happened in far-off Calabria was ever likely to wake Italy up to the gravity of its organised crime problem.

Alas, when it came down to it, the revelations that followed the Montalto case did not change anything in Calabria either. Even Judge Marino, who had proved so painstaking in his research and so withering in his condemnation of the state's failings, handed out risible sentences to the 'ndrangheta's leaders. Italy's laws against mafia organisations were feeble. Although a crime of 'mafia association' existed, and made membership of a mafia group illegal, it carried very light penalties. Most of the 'mushroom-pickers' were given two and a half years, and most had two of those two and a half years remitted. The bosses invoked in the chair's appeal for unity, including don 'Ntoni Macrì, were all acquitted of belonging to a criminal association: lack of evidence, yet again. Don 'Ntoni and the others had been *mentioned* at the summit, but they were not arrested at the scene, and there was no proof that they had actually been there. Mico Tripodo was acquitted because he was in prison at the time of the meeting. The judge seemed to be speaking to his own conscience when he tried to explain his reasoning:

> This is an argument that might seem like a travesty if one takes into account the reality that is felt and seen by everyone in this part of the world. But that reality has not been recognised by the criminal justice system in the few extremely serious cases that it has dealt with.

The judge, in other words, was a prisoner of history. The authorities' repeated failure to create a legal precedent by describing the 'ndrangheta accurately, and to convict men like don 'Ntoni, meant that they could not be convicted now.

As well as feeble legislation, Italian law enforcement would continue to betray the same weaknesses that Judge Marino had so acutely identified in his account of the 'ndrangheta's Montalto summit. The mafias would continue to be policed in the haphazard and discontinuous way that had allowed the 'ndrangheta to grow so strong. Much blood would have to be shed before Italy was ready, finally, to create investigating methods and laws that were adequate to the threat it faced.

Years after the summit at Montalto was raided, the memories of a small group of *'ndranghetisti* who turned state's evidence helped magistrates understand just how quickly the threat of organised crime was growing in the late 1960s.

For example, the criminal profiles of don 'Ntoni and Mico Tripodo were even more alarming than Judge Marino could know. For, as well as being chief cudgels of the 'ndrangheta, both were also fully initiated members of Cosa Nostra. Here is how one 'ndrangheta defector later recalled don 'Ntoni:

This man was the overall boss. He embodied what people thought was the Honoured Society – and he wasn't unworthy of embodying it, in my view. We could say that he was the boss of all bosses, and I'm not the only one who has magnified his qualities . . . He was the one and only representative, a fully qualified member of Cosa Nostra . . . He was a personal friend of Sicilian mafia bosses like Angelo and Salvatore La Barbera, Pietro Torretta, Luciano Liggio, and the Grecos from Ciaculli.

Don 'Ntoni's relationship with the Sicilian hoodlum elite was close. He smuggled cigarettes with them. He also borrowed killers from them: it is thought that the shooters in the massacre of piazza Mercato were Sicilians.

Mico Tripodo was a member of Cosa Nostra too. But the Sicilians were not his only friends. Later in his career, Mico Tripodo would spend periods of 'forced resettlement' in various regions. He was arrested for the last time in 1975 in Mondragone, on the northern coast of Campania – a town that had been one of the region's most notorious camorra strongholds for a century. When he was caught, Tripodo was in hiding with two leading *camorristi*. This was just one indicator of the way in which cigarette smuggling and other businesses were weaving high-level ties between the camorra and the 'ndrangheta that were almost as densely meshed as those between Cosa Nostra and the other two organisations.

Gradually, southern Italy was developing a criminal system that was much more unified than it had ever been in the past. Members of Italy's three historic mafias have always had contacts with one another, chiefly through the prison system. But from the 1960s, the cases of 'double affiliation' and even 'triple affiliation' would become more and more common. What was happening was *not* the development of a single master mafia, an umbrella organisation of the underworld. Rather it was something much more subtle and efficient: the pooling of contacts, resources and expertise. Because of cigarette smuggling, *mafiosi*, *camorristi* and *'ndranghetisti* were rapidly learning how to work together. The new economic frontiers of mafia power could be exploited more thoroughly when Men of Honour from different criminal organisations worked together.

The evidence of later 'ndrangheta defectors also revealed more about the crucial political changes going on in the Calabrian mob. For about a decade before Montalto, the 'ndrangheta in the province of Reggio Calabria was divided into three territories. Those territories corresponded to the three coastal areas at the bony toe of the Italian boot, and thus to what is almost the natural geographical layout of 'ndrangheta power. In Sicily, about half of Cosa Nostra's total numerical strength is concentrated around the island's capital, Palermo. In southern Calabria, power was and is shared roughly equally between the strip of land facing Sicily that includes the provincial capital of Reggio Calabria; the Ionian coast, looking out into the Mediterranean; and the Tyrrhenian coast, or the top of the boot's toe, which included the plain of Gioia Tauro – the largest and most fertile lowland in the region.

In the 1960s a triumvirate of three bosses, one from each of these three territories, had a great influence over 'ndrangheta affairs. We have already encountered two of the three triumvirs in Judge Marino's conclusions about the Montalto summit. The first was the venerable don 'Ntoni Macrì, from Siderno, the 'living symbol of organised crime's omnipotence and invincibility', the underworld patriarch whose authority extended along the Ionian coast. The second member of the 'ndrangheta triumvirate was Mico Tripodo, the bigamist whose power centred on the city of Reggio Calabria and its environs.

The third member of the triumvirate was neither present nor mentioned at the Montalto summit (a fact which itself betrayed tensions within the organisation). His name was don Girolamo 'Mommo' Piromalli. Piromalli was the dominant boss in the plain of Gioia Tauro, where the work for the Salerno-Reggio Calabria stretch of the 'Motorway of the Sun' was concentrated. Roughly the same age as Mico Tripodo, he too was a major smuggler of tobacco who had been initiated into Cosa Nostra.

Mommo was the oldest of seven siblings, five of them male. His father Gioacchino, who died in 1956, sat at the root of a vast and spreading genealogy. By the 1960s the Piromallis were busily consolidating their dominant role in the plain of Gioia Tauro by marrying themselves into its major 'ndrangheta blood-lines. Across the province of Reggio Calabria, the spider's web of kinship bonds grew both wider and thicker as the 'ndrangheta immersed itself deeper into the new economic reality.

Together, the three bosses of the triumvirate guaranteed what one *'ndranghetista* called a 'certain equilibrium' in the Calabrian underworld – an equilibrium that was becoming increasingly deli-cate as the Honoured Society grew richer on concrete and tobacco.

Coordination between the different territorially based cells of Italian criminal organisations is not new. Indeed it has been integral to the mafia landscape since the beginning. Even the most traditional of criminal affairs tend to go better when *mafiosi* from different territories cooperate: rustling cattle, hiding fugi-tives, borrowing killers from one another, and so on. Nevertheless, the new businesses of the mafias' economic miracle made the rewards of coordination even greater. The Calabrian stretch of the Motorway of the Sun is an obvious example, cutting as it did through numerous 'ndrangheta fiefs along the Tyrrhenian coast. As one senior *Carabiniere* observed in 1970: 'There is always someone who rebels against the monopoly held by some *cosche*, and who then goes and puts dynamite in a cement mixer, under a digger, or in a truck.'

Conflict like this is costly for everyone concerned. So greater cooperation between the rival criminal clans can bring big rewards. The cry for unity that went up at Montalto was one symptom of that new need. And unity, whatever form it actually took, also required more concentrated forms of power. The authority wielded by the triumvirs was a symptom of a drive for greater centralisation. Mommo Piromalli is a good example. In the 1970s, his mighty clan took 55 per cent of the earth-moving and transport subcontracts spun off from a new wave of construction on the plain of Gioia Tauro; the rest went to keep less powerful groups on adjacent territories fed.

Cosa Nostra was undergoing similar changes, a similar distillation of power. As we have already seen, in 1969 the Sicilian mafia created a triumvirate of its own to rebuild the organisation following the dramas of the 1960s. In 1974, the triumvirate was superseded by a full Commission, which was a much more powerful body than the one dissolved in 1963. It was now a direct manifestation of the power of the sixteen or so mightiest bosses in the province of Palermo. Hence the Sicilian Honoured Society underwent a top-down restructuring. Entire Families that had proved troublesome during the early 1960s were disbanded, and their cadres absorbed into neighbouring *cosche*. When a representative was arrested or killed, the Commission reserved the right to impose a temporary replacement, a 'regent', as he was termed.

Yet there is a lethal paradox at the heart of the drive for greater criminal unity in the 1960s and 1970s. For when power became concentrated in fewer hands, then it also brought the risk of greater violence when unity broke down. Mafia history was now caught in a terrible double bind. Criminal organisations had more reasons to negotiate and pool their resources. But greater unity meant that when mafia in-fighting did explode – as it inevitably would – then the blood-letting would be on a much bigger scale. Where once there had been local squabbles, now there would be all-out conflict. The Italian underworld's intensified peacemaking activity – its appeals for unity, its summits, its rules, its governing bodies, its Machiavellian politics of the marital bed – was all a way of inventing war. And war became all the more likely because Italy itself was descending into the worst civil strife it had seen since the fall of Fascism. As the 1960s gave way to the 1970s, growing political violence in Italian society helped accelerate the approach of a mafia hecatomb.

Mafiosi on the barricades

In the late 1960s, Italy entered an age of political turbulence. It all began in the autumn of 1967 with the birth of an anti-authoritarian, counter-cultural student movement; a series of occupations of university buildings followed. The protests gained pace in 1968 with a wave of working-class action that culminated in the so-called 'hot autumn' of 1969. There were wildcat strikes, mass meetings, pickets and street demonstrations. New groups of Marxist revolutionaries sprang up to guide the struggle, convinced that – from Vietnam, to South America, to Europe – the Revolution was just around the corner. Agitation on all fronts continued into the early 1970s.

The most sinister response to the new climate of militancy came on the afternoon of 12 December 1969: a terrorist bomb placed in a bank in piazza Fontana, a stone's throw from Milan Cathedral, killed sixteen people and wounded eighty-eight more. Crude police attempts to blame anarchists for the massacre unravelled, but not before one anarchist suspect, Giuseppe Pinelli, had inexplicably fallen to his death from a fourth-floor window in police headquarters. (This was the 'accidental death of an anarchist' on which Dario Fo's famous play is based.) Italy's establishment showed a marked reluctance to dig for the truth about who planted the bomb in piazza Fontana. What remained was the widespread and almost certainly justified suspicion that neo-Fascists linked to the secret services were responsible. This was the 'strategy of tension': an attempt to create a climate of fear that would draw Italian society away from democracy and back towards authoritarianism.

A year later, Junio Valerio Borghese, a recalcitrant Fascist with friends in the military and secret services, mounted an attempted *coup d'état* in Rome. The putsch was a flop in the end, but Italians did not even get to hear about it for months: there were suspicions of a secret-service cover-up.

The strategy of tension produced further outrages later in the decade. In May 1974, in Brescia's piazza della Loggia, a bomb was detonated during a demonstration against right-wing terrorism: eight people were killed. Eighty-five people were murdered by a massive bomb placed in the second-class waiting room of Bologna station in August 1980. A familiar sequence of smokescreens and artfully laid false trails ensued. Many in Italy were convinced that these were state massacres, and the credibility of Italy's institutions suffered enduring damage as a result.

In the South, the most shocking result of this dangerous destabilisation of Italian society came in July 1970 when the city of Reggio Calabria rose in revolt. Demonstrations led to police charges, which brought barricades and Molotov cocktails, which in turn provoked gunfire. A few days after the revolt broke out, a train derailed just outside Gioia Tauro station, killing six passengers. There were strong suspicions that a bomb had caused the accident, and troops were sent to guard Calabrian railways. Back in Reggio, there were dynamite attacks on the transport infrastructure and occupations of public buildings. No less than eight months of street fighting were only brought to an end when tanks rumbled along the sea front.

The cause of all the violence was the decision that Reggio would *not* be the administrative headquarters of the new regional government of Calabria. People in Reggio were convinced that politicians from the other two major Calabrian cities, Catanzaro and Cosenza, had formed a devious pact to divide out the prizes of regional government between themselves. At a superficial level, what this meant was that the inhabitants of three of Italy's poorest cities were tussling for the thousands of public-sector jobs that would come with the status of Calabrian capital. But the causes of the Reggio revolt went much deeper than that. Beset by chronic

unemployment and a housing crisis that had lasted for generations, Reggio's population had staged a mass rejection of their
political representatives. National party leaders were dismayed
and baffled by the uprising, which undoubtedly enjoyed widespread local support. It was led first by local dissidents within
the Christian Democrat party, and then by a Committee of Action
under a rabble-rouser from the Movimento Sociale Italiano, the
neo-Fascist party.

Recent testimonies from Calabrian *mafiosi* who have turned
state's evidence strongly suggest that there was a criminal subplot
to the story of the 1970 Reggio revolt. In the summer and autumn
of the year before, Junio Valerio Borghese paid a series of provoc-
ative visits to Reggio in the run-up to the coup that he would
mount in Rome in 1970. On 27 October 1969, he organised a
rally that ended in a riot after a small bomb destroyed a Fascist
eagle that dated back to Mussolini's first visit to the city. It later
emerged that neo-Fascists themselves had planted the charge as
a pretext for the disturbances. It seems that Borghese established
contacts with 'ndrangheta leaders at around this time. Some sort
of deal between the 'ndrangheta and Junio Valerio Borghese's
movement may have been discussed at the 'mushroom-picking'
summit at Montalto, which happened the day before the October
rally. Sicilian *mafiosi* have also reported discussions with Borghese
in the lead-up to his failed putsch.

We do not know whether there was an understanding between
Borghese and the Calabrian mafia. What we do know for certain
is that 'ndranghetisti helped man the barricades in Reggio; that
'ndranghetisti supplied guns and dynamite to the revolt's
Committee of Action; and that it was 'ndranghetisti who provided
the explosives used by Fascist terrorists to derail the train near
Gioia Tauro. The 'ndrangheta, therefore, had added its weight
to the strategy of tension.

But what on earth did 'ndranghetisti have to gain by allying
themselves with Fascists, or indeed with the Reggio revolt? The
first thing is that they too had reason to protest about the fact

that the privilege of being regional capital was awarded to another, less mafia-infested, city. Several other aspects of this profoundly murky affair seem certain. In the first place, the revolt gave the 'ndrangheta a chance to discredit the police, which had recently stepped up its activity against organised crime. That said, support for the revolt involved only one segment of the 'ndrangheta in Reggio Calabria, whereas outside the city bosses like the old criminal patriarch don 'Ntoni Macrì wanted nothing to do with Borghese. Quite sensibly, rather than the highly risky and uncertain project of plotting an insurgency to bring author-itarian politicians to power, most *'ndranghetisti* preferred the humdrum and much more lucrative business of doing deals with corrupt politicians who already *had* power. What is more, where there *were* contacts between gangsters and right-wing insurrec-tionaries, they tended to be about one of the few things the two parties genuinely had in common: weaponry. Quite how far beyond this basic convergence of interests the contacts went is unclear. There is much else to this story that is still cloaked in mystery. In subsequent years, some *'ndranghetisti* undoubtedly moved in the same circles as Fascist subversives and their friends in the secret services. However, the main lines of 'ndrangheta history moved along a rather more familiar pathway following the events in Reggio in 1970.

The Reggio revolt is a lesson in how unstable a political system based on patronage, faction politics and mafia influence can be. Eruptions of popular anger are always a possibility, because there are never enough favours to go round.

The national government's response to the Reggio revolt was to increase the supply of favours through a massive programme of investment: the 'Colombo package', named after the Prime Minister of the day. The centrepiece of the Colombo package was a gargantuan new steelworks to be situated on the Tyrrhenian coast at Gioia Tauro.

In the end, as the economic crisis of the 1970s unfolded, the Colombo package would be cut down in size. The steel plant would never actually be completed – a crash in steel prices saw to that. Subsequent plans for a coal-fired power station also failed to materialise. Eventually, the site was transformed into a vast container port – the biggest in the Mediterranean – which opened in 1994. The Piromalli family estate sits on a ridge overlooking both the container port and the cemetery situated next to it: the symbolism is lost on no one.

'Ndranghetisti like the Piromallis could not have dreamed of a better outcome to the crisis of 1970: a seemingly permanent building site, right in the middle of one of the most mafia-dominated areas in the whole of Calabria. When the Colombo package was announced, the chief cudgels of the plain of Gioia Tauro scrambled to gather up diggers, cement mixers and dumper trucks faster than toddlers let loose in a toyshop. The frenzied grab at the contracts and subcontracts generated by the Colombo package would be one of the major causes of what has become known as Calabria's First 'Ndrangheta War.

The First 'Ndrangheta War had other causes too. One of them was the growth of the third big sector of the mafias' economic miracle: after construction and cigarette trafficking came kidnapping.

The kidnapping industry

Up and down Italy, around 650 citizens were kidnapped by criminals in the 1970s and 1980s. Some of the most famous names in the country became victims, like the singer-songwriter Fabrizio De André, and no less than three members of the Bulgari jewellery dynasty. Of the untold billions of lire paid in ransoms, only the tiny proportion of eight billion (very roughly €28 million in 2011 values) were ever recovered, despite precautions like marking or microfilming banknotes. No wonder that the phrase 'the kidnapping industry' became a journalistic cliché.

From the early 1970s, the kidnapping industry brought organised crime even more riches. Yet it also made the tensions in the whole Italian underworld much more volatile. The lines of cause and effect between the newly profitable business of kidnapping and the risks of mob warfare were not the same in Calabria and Sicily. The 'ndrangheta and Cosa Nostra had very different attitudes to the art of taking hostages. As Antonino Calderone, a Sicilian *mafioso*, explained in 1992:

> The [Sicilian] mafia doesn't run prostitution, because it's a dirty business. Can you imagine a Man of Honour living as a pimp, an exploiter of women? Maybe in America *mafiosi* have got involved in this business . . . But in Sicily the mafia just does not do it, full stop.
>
> Now kidnapping is another matter. Cosa Nostra has no internal rule against abductions. Deep down inside, a Man of Honour accepts kidnapping. He does not view it as something dirty like prostitution.

Sicilian *mafiosi* have a century and a half of collective kidnapping experience; they have snatched away men, women and children since their Honoured Society began. So they know that taking hostages can have many meanings and many motives. A big ransom is always appreciated, but sometimes it is only part of the story. A more important consideration may be the desire to make friends.

To make friends through kidnapping means deploying a role-playing game. The first role is the bad guy: the screaming blackmailer who peremptorily threatens to make your children disappear unless you hand over a fortune. The second role is the mediator who promises to reason with the kidnappers, the quietly spoken friend who can negotiate a reduction in the ransom, get your loved ones home safe and, of course, make sure you are protected from any future dangers.

Both of these roles are played by *mafiosi*. Whether through kidnapping or through extortion (which often works by the same role-playing rules), the mafia has a genius for making itself into *both* your greatest dread *and* the best friend you could hope for in the circumstances. As Machiavelli wrote, 'Men who are well treated by one whom they expected to treat them ill, feel the more beholden to their benefactor.' By simple means like these, the Honoured Society of Sicily has infiltrated the island's ruling class since the mid-nineteenth century. The term 'Stockholm syndrome' – used to describe cases in which kidnap victims form a strong bond with their kidnappers – was only invented in 1973. But for more than a century before that date it could quite easily have applied to large sections of the Sicilian elite.

However, kidnapping tends to be a messy crime. A large team of accomplices is often needed. Hostages have to be restrained, hidden and fed, perhaps for long stretches of time. Those victims are by definition wealthy and, like as not, powerful too – the sort of people whose disappearance embarrasses politicians, leading to loud anti-crime rhetoric and the deployment of large numbers of police. Any mafia boss who pulls off a big kidnapping and does not compensate other bosses for the inconvenience is likely to make himself very unpopular. Any ordinary criminal with an atom of sense knows that carrying out an abduction without the mafia's permission is suicide. In the 1970s, a *mafioso* in prison heard tell that another inmate without mafia connections was thinking about kidnapping someone; his response was simply to mutter *chistu 'avi a moriri*: 'this bloke must die'. The would-be kidnapper was shot dead a week after he was released.

For all these reasons, kidnapping has had its seasons in Sicily: short phases when it has been frequent, and longer periods when it has been rare. For example, *mafiosi* – or bandits who were working for them willy-nilly – took many Sicilian dignitaries hostage in the decade and a half following Italian unification in 1860. In 1876, the kidnapping of an English sulphur merchant helped trigger a major crackdown on organised crime on the island. Many bandits were betrayed by their mafia protectors and shot down. Kidnapping largely fell out of favour thereafter: a sure indicator that the mafia had reached an accommodation with its friends in the island's ruling class.

So kidnappings, whether they are on the increase or in decline, may also tell us that historically significant change is under way in the Sicilian underworld. That is particularly true of the early 1970s. Most of the bosses released from prison following the trials of the late 1960s – the trials relating to the events of the First Mafia War – were very hard up. As Antonino Calderone, a Man of Honour who knew them all, later recalled:

Mark my words. When I say that there was no money around at that time, that the mafia didn't have any money, I'm not just saying it by way of exaggeration. After the arrests of 1962–63, after all the men who'd been sent into forced resettlement or who'd spent time in prison, and after the Catanzaro trial in 1968, the money was gone. It had all been spent on lawyers, prison and stuff like that . . . So when they started being released, around 1968, Cosa Nostra's bosses were all skint. Maybe Luciano Liggio had the odd house or property, but he wasn't going to sell. I can tell you that 'Shorty' Riina cried when he told me that his mother couldn't come and see him in prison, in 1966 or 1967, because she couldn't afford the train ticket. So in 1971 or thereabouts a series of kidnappings was organised.

The authors of the new wave of kidnappings were from Corleone, a town in the hinterland some fifty-five kilometres by road from Palermo. We have already had intermittent glimpses of the Corleone Family in mafia history. Kidnapping would turn them into its protagonists. Luciano Liggio began as a petty criminal whose skill with a gun endeared him to the town's boss, Dr Michele Navarra. In 1958 Liggio machine-gunned Navarra to death, triggering a violent fissure in the Family that would make Corleone notorious: 'Tombstone', the press dubbed it. Eventually Liggio emerged triumphant, thanks in good measure to his fierce young lieutenants, Totò 'Shorty' Riina and Bernardo 'the Tractor' Provenzano. The *corleonesi* had a close working relationship with Vito Ciancimino, the Christian Democrat Young Turk who was instrumental in the sack of Palermo in the early 1960s. Liggio's power-base was such that, when Cosa Nostra was reconstituted in 1969, he was one of the triumvirs entrusted with rebuilding the organisation's structure. Since Liggio was often away from Sicily, his place at the triumvirate's meetings, and later on the Commission, was often taken by 'Shorty' Riina, a man who would develop into the most powerful and violent Sicilian mafia boss of all time.

The *corleonesi* first attempted to remedy their shortage of cash on 8 June 1971, when a twenty-eight-year-old man, who had just pulled up outside his home after buying a chilled cake, was grabbed by five assailants and bundled into a car; passers-by were threatened with pistols. Suddenly, bourgeois Palermitans began going out less and wondering who would be taken next. The reason for their fears was that the victim was Pino Vassallo, the son of the notorious 'Concrete King' don Ciccio Vassallo – the very man who had built many of the apartment blocks where much of the Palermitan bourgeoisie now lived. Vassallo had strolled unscathed through all the battles of the 1960s. Now, it seemed, his protection had failed him.

A mafia-backed businessman like the 'Concrete King' (or his son, for that matter) was the perfect hostage. Yet at the same time, abducting him was also a potentially catastrophic move. On the one hand, the crimes that lay behind the Vassallo fortune guaranteed that the whole affair would be handled with discretion. Don Ciccio was never likely to try and involve the police. A ransom estimated at between 150 million and 400 million lire (€1.2 million–€3.2 million in 2011 values) was duly paid, and Pino Vassallo was released. But on the other hand, kidnapping someone protected by another boss was flagrantly offensive. To snatch away someone else's meal ticket was tantamount to a declaration of war. If fighting did not break out after the Vassallo abduction, it might have been because his protection was in abeyance – in that the *mafiosi* closest to him had been the La Barbera brothers, who were the losers in the First Mafia War.

When they received the ransom from the Vassallo kidnapping, Liggio and his boys demonstrated impeccable mafia manners in the way they distributed it equally between the neediest Families in the province of Palermo. So the Vassallo operation served two peaceful purposes: it redistributed wealth, and it cemented the new balance of power that had emerged after the turmoil of the 1960s. But soon the issue of kidnapping would become much more divisive.

After organising the Vassallo kidnapping, the *corleonesi* went on to mount unauthorised operations – such as the August 1972 abduction of Luciano Cassina, the son of the entrepreneur whose contracts to maintain the city's drains and roads made him Palermo's biggest taxpayer. Curiously, the man who posed as a 'friend' to help the Cassina family negotiate with the kidnappers was a priest, Agostino Coppola, who was a nephew of Frank 'Three Fingers' Coppola and close to Luciano Liggio's allies in the Partinico Family of Cosa Nostra. This time, the *corleonesi* kept the profits from these escapades for themselves.

In mafia terms, there could be little justification for how the *corleonesi* were behaving. Although they were deceitful and evasive when talking to other *mafiosi* about what was going on, it was nonetheless clear that they were mounting a challenge to their rivals' authority that was both calculated and flagrant. In 1972 the other two members of the triumvirate, Tano Badalamenti and Stefano Bontate, were both temporarily behind bars, and therefore less able to react to the provocation. Just as importantly, even if they had wanted to take measures against the *corleonesi*, they would have had trouble finding them. Luciano Liggio had gone on the run again in the summer of 1969. His two lieutenants, Totò 'Shorty' Riina and Bernardo 'the Tractor' Provenzano, had been in hiding since 1969 and 1963 respectively.

The years 1974–5 were politically important for Cosa Nostra. In 1974, after Stefano Bontate's release from prison, the triumvirate that had presided over the organisation in the province of Palermo since 1969 was superseded by a full Commission, largely comprising Bontate allies; Tano Badalamenti sat at the head of the table as provincial representative. Then, in February 1975, a villa set in the central Sicilian countryside near the lofty city of Enna hosted the first meeting of an entirely new body, the Regional Commission, or Region. The Region comprised six bosses representing the six most mafia-infested provinces of Sicily: Palermo, Trapani, Agrigento, Caltanissetta, Enna and Catania. In effect, the mafia Commissions in these six provinces were each sending a delegate to sit on an island-wide coordinating committee for mafia crime. The Region's authority over island-wide mafia affairs was relatively limited, as was symbolised by the fact that the boss chosen to preside over its meetings took the title of 'secretary' rather than *capo*.

The strategic brains behind the Region belonged to Pippo Calderone, whose younger brother Antonino would later turn state's evidence, giving us a priceless insight into this remarkable phase of mafia history. Pippo Calderone, a businessman and Man of Honour from the eastern Sicilian city of Catania, even went to the trouble of drafting a constitution for the new body. The most important article in that constitution, and the first item on the agenda at the Region's first meeting, was an island-wide kidnapping ban – on pain of death. The reasons for the ban seemed wise. Kidnappings might be lucrative in the short term, but made the mafia unpopular with civilians. More importantly, they drew down more police pressure – roadblocks and the like – that made life particularly difficult for *mafiosi* who were in hiding from the law. So it was hard for any of the bosses at the Region's first meeting to disagree with such a statesmanlike measure, and six hands were duly raised to approve it. However, as always in mafia affairs, the kidnapping embargo was a tactical move as well as a practical one: it was aimed at the *corleonesi*, and intended to isolate them within Cosa Nostra. Liggio, Riina and Provenzano took note.

On 17 July 1975, only a few months after that first meeting of the Region, a little old man was driving an Alfa Romeo 2000 through the crackling heat of a Sicilian summer afternoon. His destination was Salemi, a town clustered round a Norman fortress on a hill in the province of Trapani. But he never reached it: by a petrol pump just outside town, he found the road in front of him blocked by ten men armed with machine guns. As he was being forced out and bundled into another car, the bus from Trapani arrived. Two of the snatch team flagged down the terrified driver and climbed aboard the bus. Silently they then showed their weapons to the passengers. Words were superfluous: nothing had happened, and nobody had seen it happen.

The *corleonesi* had struck again, showing their contempt for the manoeuvres against them in the Region. Moreover, they had struck at a more illustrious victim than ever before. The old man in the Alfa Romeo was Luigi Corleo, a tax farmer. In Sicily, tax collection was privatised and contracted out. Since the 1950s, Corleo's son-in-law, Nino Salvo, had turned the family tax-collecting business into a vast machine for ripping off Sicilian taxpayers. Together with his cousin, Ignazio, Nino Salvo ran a company that now had a near monopoly on revenue gathering, and took a scandalous 10 per cent commission. In effect, one lire in every ten that Sicilians paid in tax went straight into the pockets of the Salvo cousins. Not only that, but the Salvos managed to engineer a two- or three-month time-lag between harvesting the taxes and handing them over to the state – two or three months in which these huge sums attracted very favourable interest. The pharaonic profits of the Salvos' legalised swindle were invested in art (Van Gogh and Matisse, apparently), hotels, land, and in the political support network needed to ensure that the Sicilian Regional Assembly continued to rubber-stamp the tax-collecting franchise. Both Salvo cousins were also Men of Honour, and both were very close to two members of the triumvirate: Tano Badalamenti and Stefano Bontate, the 'Prince of Villagrazia'. In other words, by kidnapping Luigi Corleo, the *corleonesi* had taken aim at the very heart of economic, political and criminal power in Sicily. Antonino Calderone would later explain that the Corleo kidnapping was 'an extremely serious matter that created a huge shock in Cosa Nostra'. The ransom demand was shocking too: 20 billion lire (not far off €100 million in 2011 values).

The Corleo kidnapping was initially a grave embarrassment for Badalamenti and Bontate, and quickly become an utter humiliation. Despite sowing the countryside around Salemi with corpses, Badalamenti and Bontate failed to either free the hostage, or find any evidence in support of their suspicion that the *corleonesi* were responsible. To cap it all, old man Corleo died while he was still in captivity, probably from a heart attack. Yet Badalamenti and Bontate proved unable even to recover the body.

The *corleonesi* may not have bagged the ransom they had hoped for, but they did gain something that in the long term would prove far more valuable: a high-profile demonstration that Badalamenti and Bontate had not mastered the basics of territorial control. Plainly, the *corleonesi* could ignore Cosa Nostra's lawmakers with impunity. Across Sicily, other mafia bosses heard the rumours and started to draw conclusions.

The brief sequence of high-profile kidnappings in Sicily coincided with one more important development: a new generation of leader took control in Corleone. Luciano Liggio was gradually sidelined by his deputy, Totò 'Shorty' Riina, who was ably assisted by Bernardo 'the Tractor' Provenzano. Riina it was who directed operations for the Cassina and Corleo kidnappings.

Meanwhile Liggio was still very busy, but in places where Cosa Nostra's rules against kidnapping did not apply. In July 1971 he moved to Milan, where he could orchestrate the hijacking of as many hostages as he liked. Furthermore, in Milan, there were many more rich people available to abduct. Kidnapping in Sicily was more politically significant than it was lucrative or frequent. Between 1960 and 1978, there were only nineteen abductions in Sicily, a very small proportion of the terrifying 329 in Italy as a whole. The word inside Cosa Nostra was that Liggio grew fantastically rich on the off-island trade in captives, and that he was working with the organisation that was rapidly becoming the Italian underworld's kidnapping specialist: the 'ndrangheta.

Cosa Nostra and the camorra were involved in kidnapping to a comparatively limited extent. Cosa Nostra, as we have seen, had severe constitutional reservations about harbouring captives on its own manor. *Camorristi* in the early 1970s performed a number of abductions, but kidnapping did not become a typical camorra crime, probably because they did not have the colonies in the North that would enable them to create a national network for hostage-taking.

To anyone who bothered to read the crime pages of the Calabrian dailies, a pattern of kidnappings had already established itself in the region in the late 1960s. But the victims were all local figures, the ransom demands relatively small, and the periods of captivity short. Things began to change in December 1972 with the abduction of Pietro Torielli, the son of a banker from Vigevano in the northern region of Lombardy. Luciano Liggio and the 'ndrangheta are thought to have been involved. From now on, kidnapping would be a nationwide business for Calabrian organised crime.

There were several reasons why kidnapping became a favourite business for the 'ndrangheta. It had the great advantage of being cheap to organise, for one thing. The ransoms it rendered often served as seed capital for more investment-intensive initiatives, like construction or wholesale narcotics dealing. No mafia had a network of colonies in the North to match the 'ndrangheta's. Nor did any other mafia have Aspromonte. The mountain massif at the very tip of the Italian peninsula had long been a reliable refuge for fugitives. Its crags, its grottoes and its wooded gorges became internationally notorious as hiding places for kidnap victims. Captives would report hearing the same distant church bells from their prisons. A bronze statue of Christ on the cross, situated among the beeches and firs of the Zervò plain above Platì, became a kind of postbox where ransoms would often be deposited. For years the statue had a single large bullet hole in its chest. On Aspromonte the 'ndrangheta's reign of fear and complicity was so complete that the organisation could be confident of keeping hostages almost indefinitely. More than one escaped victim turned to the first passer-by they encountered for help, only to be led back to his kidnappers. The poor 'ndrangheta-controlled mountain villages began to live off the trickle-down profits of kidnapping. Down on the Ionian coast, Bovalino had an entire new quarter known locally as 'Paul Getty' – after the famous hostage whose abduction first propelled the 'ndrangheta to the forefront of the kidnapping industry.

In central Rome, in the early hours of 10 July 1973, John Paul Getty III – the sixteen-year-old, ginger-haired, hippy grandson of American oil billionaire Jean Paul Getty – was bundled into a car, chloroformed and driven away. After an agonising wait, the kidnappers finally communicated their demands in a collage of letters cut out from magazines: ten billion lire, or around $17 million at the time. The eighty-one-year-old Jean Paul Getty, a notoriously reclusive and avaricious man, refused to negotiate: 'I have fourteen grandchildren, and if I pay a penny of ransom, I'll have fourteen kidnapped grandchildren.'

The stalemate dragged on until 20 October when the boy's captors sliced off his right ear, dropped it in a Band Aid packet full of embalming fluid, and mailed it to the offices of the Roman daily newspaper, *Il Messaggero*. The gruesome package included a note promising that the rest of him would 'arrive in tiny pieces' if the ransom were not paid. To increase the Getty family's agony further, the ear was held up by a postal strike and did not arrive for nearly three weeks. The savage mutilation had the desired effect: a month later a ransom amounting to two billion lire ($3,200,000) – a fifth of the sum originally demanded – was deposited with a man wearing a balaclava helmet standing in a lay-by.

John Paul Getty was released. But the psychological impact of his ordeal was profound. He was fragile and very young: he had spent his seventeenth birthday in captivity. The trauma seems to have tipped him into drug and alcohol addiction. In 1983 his liver failed, precipitating a stroke that caused blindness and near total paralysis.

It was never proved beyond all doubt that Luciano Liggio masterminded the Getty kidnapping. Nor, for that matter, was anybody ever convicted apart from a handful of small-time crooks – the hired hands rather than the orchestrators. But one thing is certain nonetheless: Getty was held in the mountains of Calabria, and his captors were Luciano Liggio's friends in the 'ndrangheta. And once Luciano Liggio was removed from the scene (he was

A noble and tragic desperado: Giuseppe Musolino was known as the 'King of Aspromonte'. His famous story was acted out by major Italian star Amedeo Nazzari in the 1950 crime drama, *The Brigand Musolino*.

Meanwhile, the real Musolino lived out his last years in a Reggio Calabria mental hospital.

The wealthy Italian-American visitors who came to pay him homage may just have known the truth behind the myth: he was an 'ndrangheta killer.

Mafia media frenzy. Calabrian-born mobster Frank Costello testifies before the Kefauver Hearings, New York, 1951.

Friends in politics. *Mafioso* Giuseppe Genco Russo stands as a Christian Democrat (DC) candidate (late 1950s). The close ties between the DC and the Sicilian mafia prevented an Italian version of the Kefauver hearings.

Fruit and vegetable racket. The wholesale market in Naples was a major source of income for the camorra in the 1950s.

The Monster of Presinaci. Following his murderous rampage in 1955, Serafino Castagna told the authorities about the Honoured Society of Calabria.

Camorra bride. Pupetta Maresca marries her 'President of Potato Prices', Big Pasquale from Nola (1954). She would soon be a widow, and a killer.

Sophia Loren, in the role of a Neapolitan cigarette-seller. Tobacco smuggling, a crucial business for organised crime, is portrayed sympathetically in the 1963 movie *Yesterday, Today and Tomorrow*.

Silent grief. Palermo turns out en masse in 1963 for the funeral of four *Carabinieri*, two military engineers and a policeman murdered by a Sicilian mafia bomb.

The sack of Palermo. From the late 1950s, the construction industry propelled organise crime in Sicily and Calabria to new levels of wealth and power.

Giuseppe Zappia, pictured after his arrest at the 1969 Calabrian underworld summit, where he made this famous plea for unity: 'There's no Mico Tripodo's 'ndrangheta here! There's no 'Ntoni Macrì's 'ndrangheta here! There's no Peppe Nirta's 'ndrangheta here! We should all be united.'

Reggio Calabria erupts. In 1970, an urban uprising marked a turning-point in 'ndrangheta history. The revolt was eventually quelled by tanks.

Corleonese kidnap king. Sicilian mafia boss Luciano Liggio ran kidnapping operations in northern Italy with his friends in the 'ndrangheta.

Kidnap victim. John Paul Getty III was taken in July 1973. His 'ndrangheta captors cut off his ear before releasing him.

In the 1970s, many wealthy people armed themselves as a defence against mafia kidnappers. Here a young Berlusconi is pictured with a gun on his desk (circled).

Head of a crime dynasty. Girolamo 'Mommo' Piromalli pictured in 1974, the year the First 'Ndrangheta War broke out. Don Mommo would emerge victorious.

The face of the new 'ndrangheta? Paolo De Stefano in 1982.

r Champagne. Gaspare Mutolo became one of Cosa Nostra's ding heroin brokers in the 1980s. With him (left, with striped tie) Boris Giuliano, a brilliant policeman murdered later in 1979.

'Ice Eyes', early 1980s. Luigi Giuliano led his crime family from their base in the Forcella quarter of Naples – the historical home of the camorra in the city.

The greatest footballer of the age, Diego Armando Maradona, poses with members of the Giuliano camorra clan, who were keen to show off their taste in bathroom fittings (mid-1980s).

recaptured in 1974 and never freed again), the 'ndrangheta showed that it was more than capable of running highly lucrative kidnapping schemes on its own.

Kidnapping proved less divisive in the 'ndrangheta than it did in Cosa Nostra. But the new criminal industry did attract media and police attention to Calabria, and therefore controversy within the local underworld. It seems that the Siderno boss and triumvirate member, don 'Ntoni Macrì, made his misgivings about having hostages on his territory known to the other bosses not long after the Getty kidnapping. These misgivings further increased the rivalries between the 'ndrangheta factions that were trying to get their hands on the Colombo package.

Gangsters from the South and Sicily were by no means the only people to profit from the wave of abductions across the country in the 1970s and 1980s. For example, bandits from the island of Sardinia, some of the most active of them operating off-base in Tuscany, had their own tradition of hostage-taking and were particularly active in the 1970s. Many ordinary delinquents latched on to the idea that taking a hostage or two was a short cut to riches. Kidnapping became a criminal craze that was profoundly damaging to Italy's weakened social fabric.

Luigi Ballinari, a drunken, small-time cigarette smuggler of Swiss nationality, recalled the buzz in prison in 1974: 'Our conversations always came back to the crime of the moment, which was now a fashion in Italy: extorting money by kidnapping. It was everyone's dream! We fantasised, we organised, we analysed the mistakes that other kidnappers had made.'

Soon after being released, Ballinari became involved in one of the most atrocious kidnappings of the era. Cristina Mazzotti, nineteen-year-old daughter of an entrepreneur from near Como, on the Swiss border, was taken on 26 June 1975. Her captors stripped, blindfolded and manacled her, blocked her ears, and lowered her into a tiny space below a garage floor. There she was made to consume sleeping pills dissolved in fruit juice for more than two weeks during negotiations with her parents. The plan – one common to many improvised kidnapping groups in the North and centre of Italy – was to sell the hostage on to the real experts: the 'ndrangheta. But in this case, before Cristina could be bartered and sent to a new prison on Aspromonte, her body slowly shut down under the cumulative effect of the drugs; she was loaded into a car boot and buried in a rubbish dump. Her parents, unaware that she was already dead, paid a ransom of 1.05 billion lire (€5.2 million in 2011 values).

Ballinari was later caught trying to launder some of the profits from Cristina's abduction. By the time he buckled under interrogation, and told the whole story, Cristina's body was so decomposed that it proved hard to tell whether she had actually been dead when she was interred.

The horrors of the kidnapping industry were legion. The captives on Aspromonte were particularly badly treated. Shackled and fed on scraps, they were not allowed to wash and their clothes were never changed. In intercepted phone conversations, their 'ndrangheta captors were heard referring in code to the prisoners as 'pigs'. The longest kidnapping was that of teenage student Carlo Celadon from near Vicenza, who was snatched in his own home in 1988. Carlo was kept for a mind-boggling 828 days in a rat-infested grotto scattered with his own excrement. With three chains round his neck, he was subject to constant threats – and to beatings if he dared cry or pray. When he was released, his father commented that he looked like the inmate of a Nazi concentration camp. Carlo's comment on his ordeal was harrowing: 'I asked, I begged my jailers to cut my ear off. I was totally destroyed, I had lost all hope.'

In Italy as a whole, between 1969 and 1988, seventy-one people vanished and were never seen alive again; it is thought that in roughly half those cases, a ransom was paid. In 1981 Giovanni Palombini, an eighty-year-old coffee entrepreneur, was kidnapped by a Roman gang who probably intended to pass him on to the 'ndrangheta. He managed to escape, but was so disorientated that when he knocked on the door of a villa to ask for help, it turned out to be his kidnappers' hideout. He was given a glass of champagne, and then executed. His body was thrown in a freezer so that it could be pulled out for the photographs his family wanted to see to be certain that he was still alive.

Children were not spared: there were twenty-two abductions of children, some no more than babes in arms. Marco Fiora was only seven years old when 'ndranghetisti grabbed him in Turin in March 1987. His ordeal lasted a year and a half, during which time he was kept chained up like a dog in an Aspromonte hideaway. His captors did their best to brainwash him, telling him that his parents did not want to pay the ransom because they did not love him. It seems that the long delay was due to the fact that the 'ndrangheta's spies had greatly overestimated how rich Marco's father was, and refused to believe his claims that he could not afford the ransom. Marco was skeletal when he was released near Ciminà, and his legs were so atrophied that he could barely walk. He knocked on a few doors, but the inhabitants refused to open. So he just sat down by the roadside until a patrol of *Carabinieri* happened upon him. His first words to his mother were, 'You aren't my mummy. Go away. I don't want to see you.'

Some children fared even worse. A little girl of eleven from the shores of Lake Garda, Marzia Savio, was taken in January 1982. Her captor turned out not to be a gangster, but just the local sausage butcher who thought he had found a neat way to make some quick money. He strangled Marzia, probably while he was trying to restrain her, and then cut her into pieces that he scattered from a flyover.

Kidnapping became so common that it acquired its own rituals in the news bulletins and crime pages. The victims' families giving anguished press conferences. Or, conversely, desperately attempting to shun the limelight and avoid provoking whoever was holding their father, their son, their daughter. There was the long, anguished wait for the kidnappers to make known the ransom demands. There were hoax calls from ghoulish pranksters.

Kidnapping is a crime that creates and spreads mistrust. Many families rightly suspected that friends and employees had leaked information to the criminals. Finding reliable lines of communication and intermediaries was often agonising. The family of Carlo Celadon, the young man who was held for a record 828 days, alleged that the lawyer they delegated to transport the ransom had pocketed a proportion of it. (He was convicted of the crime but later benefited from an amnesty before his appeal.) The 'ndrangheta sometimes seemed to know more about how much their hostages earned than did the tax man. For that reason, the media tended to cast suspicion over the finances of even the most honest victims. Hostages' families were often warned against going to the police. And the police were often frustrated by families' silence: some had the indignity of being arrested for withholding information after seeing their loved ones freed.

The poison of mistrust leaked into the public domain. Each high-profile abduction triggered a vitriolic and, for a long time, entirely inconclusive debate between journalists, politicians and law-enforcement officials. There were those who favoured the hard line on kidnapping: refusing to pay ransoms, freezing victims' assets, and the like. Ranged against them were those who thought the 'soft line' (i.e. negotiation) was the only humane and practical option. Some of the more bullish entrepreneurs of the North underwent weapons training. The situation became so bad that, in 1978, one magistrate discovered that some wealthy families were taking out special insurance policies so that they would have enough money for a ransom when the masked bandits paid their seemingly inevitable visit. Wealthy citizens – the class of person who, in other Western democracies, would almost automatically be loyal to the powers that be – were angry, alienated and afraid.

There is a photo that makes for an intriguing memento of

that terrible era of fear and mistrust. It shows a self-confident young Milanese construction entrepreneur leaning back in a chair. His serious expression shows no hint of the permanent matinée idol smile that would later become his worldwide trademark. He has just removed a pair of aviator sunglasses, and the flared trousers of his suit reveal the trendy ankle boots on his feet. But it is not his dress and accessories that really make the photo symptomatic of the 1970s. Rather it is the holstered pistol that sits on his desk. The entrepreneur's name is Silvio Berlusconi, and around the time the photo was taken, he had the well-grounded dread of kidnapping that was common to many wealthy Italians. However Berlusconi's business factotum, a Sicilian banker called Marcello Dell'Utri, found a more effective way to calm these fears than a pistol in a desk drawer. From 1974 to 1976 Vittorio Mangano, a *mafioso* from Palermo, took a not terribly clearly defined job (groom? major domo? factor?) at Berlusconi's newly acquired villa at Arcore. The Italian courts have recently ascertained that, in reality, Mangano was a guarantee of Cosa Nostra's protection against kidnapping. Moreover, he was also there with the intention of making friends. Or, in the language of a judge's ruling, Mangano was part of a 'complex strategy destined to make an approach to the entrepreneur Berlusconi and link him more closely to the criminal organisation'.

Marcello Dell'Utri has been convicted of a long-standing collaboration with Cosa Nostra that included recommending Vittorio Mangano's services to Berlusconi. He still denies the charges, which he says are the result of a judicial plot against him. The case will almost certainly go to the Supreme Court.

Vittorio Mangano was later sentenced to life for two murders, and died of cancer in 2000. He died like a good *mafioso* should, without shedding any light on the case.

Silvio Berlusconi's own public utterances on the affair have been disturbing, to say the least. For example, he gave his view of the *mafioso* in a radio interview in 2008:

[Mangano] was a person who behaved extremely well with us. Later he had some misadventures in his life that placed him in the hands of a criminal organisation. But heroically . . . despite being so ill, he never invented any lies against me. They let him go home the day before he died. He was dying in prison. So Dell'Utri was right to say that Mangano's behaviour was heroic.

Quite whether the kidnapping season was the beginning of a direct long-term relationship between Berlusconi and the Sicilian mafia is not clear. It should be stressed that Berlusconi has never been charged with anything in relation to the Mangano affair.

Every kidnapping was a clamorous demonstration of the governing institutions' inability to protect life and property. Italy was getting visibly weaker at the very same time that the mafias were getting stronger, richer, more interlinked, and closer to descending into war. The state seemed to have lost its claim to a 'monopoly of legitimate violence', as the jargon of sociology would have it. In the 1970s, while the wave of kidnappings spiralled out of control, a new wave of economic and political troubles brought further discredit on the state.

Italy, like the rest of the developed world, had to face a grave economic crisis following a dramatic hike in crude oil prices in 1973. There ensued a decade of stuttering growth, high unemployment, raging inflation, steepling interest rates and massive public debt. Violent social conflict was on the rise. The trades unions that had been so pugnacious since the 'hot autumn' of 1969 now went on the defensive. As a result, some members of Italy's revolutionary groups lost patience with peaceful forms of militancy; they opted instead to form clandestine armed cells. These terrorists, as ruthless as they were deluded, thought of themselves as a revolutionary vanguard who could hasten the advent of a Communist society by maiming or assassinating strategically chosen targets. Italy had entered its so-called 'Years of Lead' (i.e. years of bullets).

The Red Brigades (or BR) would turn out to be the most dangerous of these groups, and many of their earliest actions were kidnappings. The victims – usually factory managers – would typically be subjected to a 'proletarian trial', and then chained to the factory gates with a placard daubed with a revolutionary slogan round their necks. In the spring of 1974, under the new slogan of 'an attack on the heart of the state', the BR hit the headlines by kidnapping a judge from Genoa. The BR's demands were not met, but the judge was released unharmed.

After a wave of arrests brought a lull in their activities in the middle of the decade, the Red Brigades returned with more terroristic resolve than ever. On 16 March 1978, they brought the country to a standstill by kidnapping the former Prime Minister and leader of the Christian Democrat Party, Aldo Moro. Moro's driver and his entire police escort were murdered in the assault. On 9 May Moro was himself shot dead, and his body was abandoned in a car in the centre of Rome. The BR and other groups continued their murder campaign into the following decade. Many young people, in particular, could not find it within themselves to identify with the authorities in their fight against terrorism: 'Neither with the state, nor with the Red Brigades' was one political slogan of the day. This was the state that would soon have to face up to unprecedented mafia violence. Calabria was to be the first place where war broke out.

The Most Holy Mother and the First 'Ndrangheta War

When evidence of organised crime's vast new wealth emerged in the 1960s and 1970s, many observers claimed that, in both Sicily and Calabria, the traditional mafia was being replaced by a new breed. The mafia was now no longer rural, but urban; it was a 'motorway mafia', rather than a donkey-track mafia; these were gangsters in 'shiny shoes' rather than the muddy-booted peasants of yesteryear. The new model *mafioso*, it was claimed, was a young, aggressive businessman. In particular, he had no time for the quaint, formalistic concerns of the Honoured Societies, or for the antediluvian cult of honour. Backward Calabria was where the transformation appeared to be most marked. Here, even many who took the mafia threat seriously thought that initiation rituals, Osso, Mastrosso, Carcagnosso, and the meeting at the Sanctuary of the Madonna of Polsi were bound to be consigned to the folklore museum − if they hadn't been already.

The De Stefano brothers, Giorgio, Paolo and Giovanni, fitted most people's idea of the emergent gangster-manager. The brothers came from Reggio Calabria, the town that was bigamist don Mico Tripodo's realm. As we have already seen, Tripodo spent much of his time away in Campania, cementing close friendships with the *camorristi* of the Neapolitan hinterland. But a boss can only remain away from his territory for so long before the ground shifts behind him. In don Mico's absence the De Stefanos emerged as a power in their own right.

Giorgio, the oldest of the brothers and the most cunning, was referred to by one 'ndrangheta defector as 'the Comet' − the rising star of Calabrian organised crime. The De Stefanos were the most enthusiastic participants in the Reggio revolt, and the keenest to make friends with Fascist subversives. And they were certainly young: none of them was out of his twenties at the time of the Montalto summit. The triumvirs whose authority the De Stefanos would come to challenge were from an older generation: don 'Ntoni Macrì could just about have been their grandfather.

One *'ndranghetista* also remembered the De Stefanos as being educated, at least by the standards of the Calabrian underworld, recalling that: 'Paolo and Giorgio De Stefano attended university for a few years. Giorgio was signed up to do medicine, and I think Paolo studied law.' That education was visible. Pictures of Giorgio ('the Comet') and Paolo, the two oldest and most powerful De Stefano brothers, show men with large, sensitive faces and black hair parted neatly at the side. Their up-to-date, clean-cut image could hardly be more starkly different from the grim physiognomies of the triumvirs: Mico Tripodo and the others all had mean little eyes, cropped hair and sagging, expressionless faces; each seemed to have been assembled from the same old kit of atavistic hoodlum features.

As it turned out, these contrasting faces, and the switch from tradition to modernity that they seemed to make visible, proved to be no guide to the winners and losers who would emerge from the unprecedented criminal wealth and violence of the 1970s. The simplistic 'modernity versus tradition' template that was used to make sense of the events of the 1970s was just a bad fit with reality. For one thing, the rise of ambitious young thugs like the De Stefanos from within the ranks of the organisation is not a novelty. For another, even in Calabria, there is nothing new about *mafiosi* with middle-class credentials. Nor are the mafias traditional in the sense of being very old. On the contrary, they are as modern as the Italian state.

It is much nearer the mark to say that the 'ndrangheta, like Cosa Nostra, is *traditionalist*, in the sense that it has manufactured its own internal traditions that are functional to the demands of extortion and trafficking. When the 'ndrangheta grew richer, through the construction industry, tobacco smuggling and kidnapping, it did not simply abandon its traditions and embrace modernity. From their origins, Italy's mafias have always *mixed* tradition and modernity. Their response to the new era was to *adapt* the mixture. Or indeed, in the case of the 'ndrangheta, to invent brand-new traditions like the one that is the subject of this chapter: the Most Holy Mother. That newly minted tradition is significant for two reasons. First, it provides evidence of just how many friends the mafias, with their new wealth, were making among the Italian elite. Second, the Most Holy Mother became the trigger of the First 'Ndrangheta War. And to understand it, we need to grasp some subtle but important differences between the 'ndrangheta and Cosa Nostra.

The 'ndrangheta and Cosa Nostra are very similar in that they are both Honoured Societies – Freemasonries of crime. Both organisations are careful about choosing whom they admit to the club. No one with family in the police or magistracy is allowed in. No pimps. No women.

Yet there are also some differences in the way the two select their cadres. *'Ndranghetisti* tend to come from the same blood families. Cosa Nostra, by contrast, has rules to *prevent* too many brothers being recruited into a single Family, in case they distort the balance of power within it. In some cases, two brothers may even enter *different* Families.

Cosa Nostra tends to monitor aspiring gangsters carefully before they cross the threshold of the organisation, often making a criminal wait until his thirties so that he can prove over the years that he is made of the right stuff. The Calabrian mafia admits many more people. A police report from 1997 estimated that in Sicily there were 5,500 *mafiosi*, or one for every 903 inhabitants.

By comparison, there were 6,000 *'ndranghetisti* in Calabria, or one for every 345 citizens. In the most 'ndrangheta-infested province, Reggio Calabria, there was one affiliate for every 160 inhabitants. In other words, proportionally speaking, the 'ndrangheta admits two and a half times as many members. The male children of a boss are initiated willy-nilly. Some even go through a ritual at birth. But that does not mean that the Calabrian mafia has watered-down membership criteria. Rather it suggests that it does much of the business of monitoring and selecting members *once they are inside*. A winnowing process continues through each *'ndranghetista*'s entire career. Only the most criminally able of them will rise through the ranks. Young hoods may learn to specialise either in business or in violence.

As they acquire more prestige, they progress through a hierarchy of status levels. An *'ndranghetista* starts off as a *giovane d'onore* ('honoured youth' – someone marked out for admission into the organisation, but who is not yet a member). Through day-by-day service to his superiors – issuing threats and vandalising property as part of extortion demands, collecting protection payments, hiding weapons and stolen goods, ferrying food up to the mountain prisons where hostages are kept – he rises to become a *picciotto* ('lad'), and then on up the ladder through a long list of other ranks.

These ranks are called *doti* ('gifts'). Being promoted to a higher gift is referred to as receiving a *fiore* (a 'flower'). The giving of each flower is marked by a ritual. But secrets, rather than gifts, are the true measure of status in the 'ndrangheta. Since it began in the nineteenth century, each 'ndrangheta cell has had a double structure made of sealed compartments: the Minor Society and the Major Society. Younger, less experienced and less trustworthy recruits belong to the Minor Society. Minor Society members are insulated from understanding what goes on in the Major Society to which the more experienced crooks belong. Promotion through the ranks, and from the Minor Society to the Major Society, implies access to more secrets.

As profits rose within the 'ndrangheta in the early 1970s, and tensions increased, so too did the tinkering with these peculiarly complicated protocols. Until the early 1970s, the highest gift that any affiliate of the 'ndrangheta could attain was that of *sgarrista*. Literally, *sgarrista* means something like 'a man who gives offence, or who breaks the rules'. (The terminology, like so much else about the 'ndrangheta, dates back to the nineteenth-century prison system.)

Around 1972–3, some chief cudgels began to create a new, higher gift for themselves: *santista* ('saintist' or 'holy-ist'). With the new status came membership of a secret elite known as the Mamma Santissima ('Most Holy Mother') or Santa for short. In theory, the Mamma Santissima had a very exclusive membership: no more than twenty-four chief cudgels were to be admitted. Becoming a *santista* involved a new ritual, an upmarket variant of the 'ndrangheta's existing initiation rites. It also entitled the bearer of this new flower to certain privileges, the most important being the right to join the secret and deviant Masonic brotherhoods that were springing up in 1970s Italy.

The most notorious of the new Masonic groups was Propaganda 2 or P2, a conspiracy of corruption and right-wing subversion that reached right to the heart of the Italian establishment. When, in March 1981, a (probably incomplete) P2 membership list of 962 people was found, it included:

> all the heads of the secret services, 195 officers of the various armed corps of the Republic, among whom were twelve generals of the *Carabinieri*, five of the Tax Police, twenty-two of the army, four of the air force and eight admirals. There were leading magistrates, a few prefects and Police Chiefs, bankers and businessmen, civil servants, journalists and broadcasters.

There were also forty-four members of parliament, including three government ministers. Among the businessmen on the list was an entrepreneur who could not yet be called a member of the establishment: Silvio Berlusconi. It is often not clear what individual members of P2 like Berlusconi thought its aims really were. But the power of the lodge is not in question: in 1977 it took control of Italy's most influential newspaper, *Corriere della Sera*. The very least that can be said about P2 is that it showed how, in the face of the growing influence of the Communist Party (which reached its highest ever percentage of the popular vote in the general election of 1976), key members of the elites of both power and money were closing ranks and establishing covert channels of influence.

P2 was far from the only aberrant Masonic society to emerge at this time. *Mafiosi* wanted in on the act. Cosa Nostra was making similar moves to the 'ndrangheta. According to several defectors from the ranks of the Sicilian mafia, between 1977 and 1979 a number of its most senior men joined Masonic organisations too. The issue of Masonic affiliation was discussed at Cosa Nostra's Regional Commission in 1977.

The mafias' alliance with Freemasonry in the 1970s showed underworld history coming full-circle. For the very origins of Italy's secret criminal brotherhoods lay in contacts between Masonic conspirators who successfully plotted to unite Italy in the first half of the nineteenth century, and the hoodlums those patriotic conspirators recruited as revolutionary muscle. Then, as now, the thing Italy's hoodlums prized most about Freemasonry was contacts. As Leonardo Messina, a Sicilian *mafioso* who defected from Cosa Nostra in 1992, explained:

Many men in Cosa Nostra – the ones who managed to become bosses, that is – belonged to the Freemasonry. In the Masons you can have contacts with entrepreneurs, the institutions, the men who manage power. The Masonry is a meeting place for everyone.

So for the 'ndrangheta, the Mamma Santissima was a new

constitutional device for regulating the Calabrian underworld's connections with the upper world of politics, business and policing.

When it was first introduced, the Mamma Santissima was highly controversial: many considered it a 'bastardisation' of the Honoured Society's rules. Indeed the innovation drove a wedge between the members of the triumvirate. Mommo Piromalli supported it, whereas Mico Tripodo was against it. It is said that don 'Ntoni Macrì, the 'ndrangheta's patriarch, the 'living symbol of organised crime's omnipotence and invincibility', was viscerally opposed.

Why the resistance? Some say that the grounds for don 'Ntoni's opposition to the Mamma Santissima were simply that he was traditional, a man loyal to the old rules. This explanation seems implausible to me, dripping in nostalgia for some good old mafia that has actually never existed. If don 'Ntoni was like every other *mafioso* there has ever been, then he obeyed the traditional rules only for as long as it suited his interests.

No, the real reason why don 'Ntoni Macrì was opposed to the Mamma Santissima was simply that he was excluded from it. In fact, I suspect that the new gift was invented with the precise aim of cutting him out, of isolating him from important secrets. And behind that manoeuvre lay a plan to stop don 'Ntoni meddling in other people's kidnappings, and – even more importantly – to keep his grasping hands away from the Colombo package (the publicly funded construction bonanza that came following the Reggio revolt of 1970). It was through contacts with the local ruling class, and in particular with Masonic brotherhoods, that the bonanza was to be distributed. It is no coincidence that among the main proponents of the Mamma Santissima was don Mommo Piromalli, the triumvir who hailed from Gioia Tauro where the new steelworks was going to be built. In the world of the mafias (and not just the mafias), constitutional innovation is often just a mask for skulduggery.

Between them, the De Stefano brothers' ambitions in Reggio

Calabria and the tensions between the triumvirs over the Mamma Santissima and the Colombo package would push the 'ndrangheta into war.

In September 1974, Mommo Piromalli hosted a meeting of the 'ndrangheta's chiefs in Gioia Tauro. Among those in attendance were not just the other triumvirate members – don 'Ntoni Macrì from the Ionian coast and the bigamist Mico Tripodo from Reggio – but also don Mico's pushy underlings, the De Stefano brothers. Unanimously, the bosses rejected an offer from major construction companies: a 3 per cent cut of profits from construction of the Gioia Tauro steelworks. The 'ndrangheta would not be happy unless its share was fattened out by contracts and subcontracts. Nonetheless tensions within the brotherhood in Reggio spilled over: Mico Tripodo and Giorgio De Stefano exchanged acid words, and only the intervention of don 'Ntoni Macrì – posing, as ever, as the peacemaker – prevented a violent confrontation.

Another attempt to preserve the peace in Reggio Calabria soon followed. This time the occasion was not a business meeting but a wedding reception in the Jolly Hotel in Gioia Tauro. The father of the bride was one of the Mazzaferro clan, close allies of Mommo Piromalli, and the celebrations were attended by chief cudgels from across Calabria. Fearing an ambush, Mico Tripodo did not attend, and paid for his absence by being insulted by the Comet's younger brother Paolo. Again don 'Ntoni tried to calm the waters, and plans were laid for a third meeting on neutral territory – Naples.

But by this time it had become clear to all involved that any outbreak of fighting between the De Stefanos and don Mico Tripodo in Reggio Calabria would draw other *ndrine* in. Behind don Mico stood 'Ntoni Macrì. And behind the De Stefanos stood Mommo Piromalli in Gioia Tauro. So what had initially seemed like a local matter, a familiar confrontation between an older boss and younger men trying to oust him, had grown into a fracture dividing the whole 'ndrangheta into two alliances, both of them prepared for war. The equilibrium that the triumvirate had guaranteed for a decade and a half had been fatally destabilised.

On 24 November 1974, at around eight o'clock in the evening, two killers entered the fashionable Roof Garden bar, a notorious 'ndrangheta hang-out in Reggio Calabria's piazza Indipendenza. Scanning the room, the two quickly identified the table where their targets were sitting. The first assassin pulled out a long-barrelled P38 and shot Giovanni De Stefano in the head from about a metre away. When the gun jammed, his accomplice raised another weapon and blasted two more bullets into Giovanni De Stefano's prostrate form before firing at Giovanni's brother Giorgio, 'the Comet'. Although the Comet was badly wounded, he survived the Roof Garden assault; Giovanni died at the scene. Retaliation could not wait long. The conflict was now unstoppable.

Don 'Ntoni Macrì had the habit of playing bowls with his driver every day on the edge of town before heading back home to hold court. On 20 January 1975 he had just finished his game and climbed back into the car when an Alfa Romeo 1750 screeched to a halt in front of him. Four men got out and let rip with pistol and machine-gun fire. Siderno shut down for the old chief cudgel's funeral, and some 5,000 people paid their respects.

The First 'Ndrangheta War, as it is now known, caused more fatalities than Sicily's First Mafia War of the early 1960s. There were 233 murders in three years. Local feuds in Ciminà, Cittanova, Seminara and Taurianova added to the body count. There was savagery on all sides. In one phone tap, Mommo Piromalli was heard telling his wife how he fed one of his victims to the pigs: *'L'anchi sulu restaru'* ('Only his thigh bones were left over'), he explained. 'Oh yes!' she replied.

A score of the old bosses fell. The last (and the most important after 'Ntoni Macrì) was the bigamist and triumvir don Mico Tripodo. In the spring of 1976, he was arrested with his camorra friends in Mondragone and sent to Poggioreale prison in Naples. Five months later, on 26 August, two Neapolitan petty crooks cornered him in his cell and stabbed him twenty times on the orders of a camorra *capo*. The De Stefanos had shown that they too had friends in the Neapolitan underworld, and by using them to eliminate their boss and enemy Mico Tripodo, they brought the war to a close.

Or not quite to a close. On 7 November 1977, Giorgio 'the Comet' De Stefano took the risk of leaving his patch in Reggio Calabria to attend an important meeting of the 'ndrangheta's upper echelons up on Aspromonte. Before proceedings got under way, he sat down on a rock to light a cigar. Suddenly, there came a shout: *'Curnutu, tu sparasti a me frati'* ('You cuckold, you shot my brother'); it was followed immediately by gunshots. The Comet, the apparent victor of the First 'Ndrangheta War, and the supposed epitome of the modern *mafioso*, had only been allowed a year to enjoy the fruits of his military success.

For a moment, it looked as if the Comet's surviving brother Paolo De Stefano would push the 'ndrangheta into another war. But internal investigations soon discovered that the hit-man was a low-ranking affiliate called Giuseppe Suraci. Paolo De Stefano was told that Suraci just had a personal beef. The other bosses who had seen the Comet die placated Paolo De Stefano's vengeful wrath by presenting him with Giuseppe Suraci's severed head. This grisly gesture re-established the peace that had taken shape after the war of 1974–6.

We now know, however, that the version of the Comet's murder told to Paolo De Stefano by the other 'ndrangheta bosses was an ingeniously crafted lie. The killer Giuseppe Suraci had not acted out of personal vendetta, but because he was ordered to by the De Stefanos' allies in the First 'Ndrangheta War, the Piromallis. He was then beheaded to prevent him from being interrogated by Paolo De Stefano about why he had *really* killed his brother.

By the time of the Comet's death, Mommo Piromalli was semi-retired, leaving the clan's day-to-day business to his younger brother Giuseppe. And Giuseppe had taken objection to the way Giorgio 'the Comet' De Stefano had extorted a bribe from a building contractor who was already under Piromalli protection. Thus the Comet had committed a *sgarro*: an insult to a mobster's authority and honour. That *sgarro* was enough to draw a death sentence down on its perpetrator. The Piromallis had, deviously and ruthlessly, cut their upstart former allies down to size.

So it was Mommo Piromalli's clan who were the real winners of the First 'Ndrangheta War. The core reason for the Piromallis' success was their political shrewdness. Mommo Piromalli joined the triumvirate in keeping the equilibrium for as long as it suited him. He then proposed the Mamma Santissima when the time came to isolate his enemies. He used the Comet against his enemies too; and then used a trick to dispose of him.

Mommo Piromalli was the only member of the triumvirate that ruled the 'ndrangheta since the 1960s who died of natural causes. Cirrhosis of the liver carried him away in a prison hospital in 1979. He left behind him a clan more powerful than any in Calabria. Still to this day, the Piromallis are a major force. As, for that matter, are their allies in the First 'Ndrangheta War, the De Stefano family.

By the late 1970s, however, the Mamma Santissima had already been overtaken. As one 'ndrangheta defector has explained, the number of *santisti* rapidly increased, making it necessary to introduce new, higher gifts above:

A few years after the Santa was recognised, there was a certain inflation in bestowing the rank of *santista*. Indeed there were no longer just the thirty-three *santisti* envisaged by the rules: more *santisti* were created to keep everyone who aspired to hold that rank happy. So in 1978–80 I heard that a new body was created, called the Vangelo (Gospel). I was awarded the rank of *vangelista* ('gospel-ist') between 1978 and 1980 in Fossombrone prison.

In practical terms the Vangelo was restricted to a smaller number of people than the Santa, which had gone from thirty-three people to a much higher number. But then the same thing happened with the creation of the Trequartista ('Three-quarterist') and Quintino ('Fifther').

And so it went on: the business of tweaking and bending the 'ndrangheta's traditional rules so as to suit the needs of the moment. In the mafia world, there is nothing more traditional than that. Tradition helps bind the mafias together. But it can also be used to prepare for civil war. The First 'Ndrangheta War was only a rehearsal for what was to come when narcotics propelled the Italian mafias to the greatest riches they had ever known.

A brief history of junk

Then Zeus' daughter Helen . . . drugged the wine with the herb nêpenthes, which banishes all care, sorrow, and anger. Whoever drinks wine thus drugged cannot shed a single tear all the rest of the day, not even though his father and mother both of them drop down dead, or he sees a brother or a son hewn in pieces before his very eyes.

Homer, *Odyssey* IV, 220–21

Opium is a very ancient oriental drug that has appalled and enthralled occidental civilisation since the ancient Greeks. The drug nêpenthes, which Helen administers in Homer's *Odyssey*, is probably opium.

Heroin, by contrast, is a child of modern, global capitalism; it is a brand name that was first coined by the German pharmaceutical company Bayer at the end of the nineteenth century. What Bayer *thought* they were putting on the market was a new, safe version of the opium derivative morphine – one that did not carry the same risks of dependency. What they were *actually* selling was even more addictive than morphine. But it was so reassuringly packaged and so roundly endorsed by medical opinion that, for the next decade and more, even many children's cough syrups contained it. No wonder that the United States could count over 200,000 heroin addicts by the time the First World War came to an end.

In China, the problem of opiate addiction was at least a century older. By the time heroin was invented, those Chinese hooked on smoking opium numbered in the millions. Throughout the nineteenth century, British merchants had ferried opium from India to the Celestial Kingdom. At the behest of those merchants, the British government fought two wars to force China to accept the free trade in a drug that was tearing holes in its social fabric. The *Cambridge History of China* calls the British opium trafficking business 'the most long-continued and systematic international crime of modern times'.

In 1912, the United States, China and Britain all signed the first international treaty aimed at controlling narcotics production and distribution; in 1919 its provisions were included in the Treaty of Versailles that sealed the peace at the end of the First World War. A new era of drug control had dawned across the world. From now on, the main suppliers and distributors of heroin and other narcotics would not be pharmaceutical companies, merchants and governments (not openly, at least), but instead criminal syndicates.

The Sicilian mafia was among the earliest players in the world's biggest consumer market for illegal heroin, the United States. With their bases in western Sicily and New York, their transatlantic commercial ties and their wide network of contacts in the United States, *mafiosi* were ideally placed to smuggle. Between the wars, morphine was hidden in hollowed-out oranges, or in crates of other Sicilian exports like anchovies, olive oil and cheese.

But the mafia's heroin business remained artisanal. What is more, the market shrank. By 1924 the number of addicts to all narcotics in the United States was probably no greater than 110,000. The Second World War so badly disrupted supplies of opiates that, at its end, the number of addicts had plummeted to an estimated 20,000.

Trade resumed after the Second World War, as did the mafia's involvement in it. Italy did not have much of a domestic consumer market for drugs at the time. Moreover, until 1951, pharmaceutical companies in the peninsula were able to produce heroin legally for medicinal purposes. Some of that legal heroin found its way to the United States for sale on the black market. Lucky Luciano, like several other *mafiosi* sent back to Italy after the war, was a heroin exporter. Nevertheless, heroin use remained restricted largely to America's black and Puerto Rican ghettoes, and as a result the drug was just one business interest among many for *mafiosi*.

Heroin started to play a more prominent role in Sicilian criminal enterprise after 1956, when the Narcotics Control Act was introduced in the United States. Because the Act established severe new penalties for drug trafficking, the heroin traders of the New York mafia were keen to outsource as much work – and risk – as possible to their Old World cousins. As we have seen, a delegation from New York's Bonanno family came to Palermo in 1957 for a high-level sit-down at the Hotel delle Palme. As a US Attorney would later remark, everyone at the hotel was a 'narcotics track star'. There were other clear signs that Sicily had become a major heroin entrepôt. In 1961, the *Guardia di Finanza* (Tax Police) dismantled an international dope-smuggling ring that was based in Salemi, in the province of Trapani, but included Canadian and American Men of Honour. In February 1962, the First Mafia War was triggered when a mafia drug-dealing consortium comprising bosses from different Palermo Families fell out over a package of heroin destined for the United States. When Cosa Nostra in Palermo disbanded itself following the Ciaculli bomb in 1963, many of the most senior Men of Honour fled to the Americas to immerse themselves full time in trafficking for the United States market. Thus in the drugs business, as in tobacco smuggling, the Sicilian mafia diaspora of the 1960s dramatically increased the geographical range and profitability of mafia enterprise.

Underlying the Sicilian mafia's increasing commercial activism there also lay a new epidemic of heroin use in America. That epidemic gathered pace from the mid-1960s, as the drug-friendly counter-culture grew, and as American ground forces were deployed in Vietnam. During the war, Laos-based refiners linked to corrupt officers of the South Vietnamese Air Force controlled a fat heroin pipeline to Saigon. In 1971, US Army medical staff calculated that 10–15 per cent of all US troops were using heroin. By the same time, addicts back home in the American market had climbed to half a million – two and a half times the number recorded when heroin was a legal ingredient in many patent medicines. Dope was not a cottage industry any more.

The world's opium poppy fields are to be found almost exclusively in the highlands that snake across the southern edge of Asia: from the Anatolian Plateau of Turkey in the west, through Iran, Pakistan, Afghanistan and India, to end in the highly productive region known as the 'Golden Triangle', where Burma, Laos and Thailand meet. In the 1960s, most of America's heroin came from Turkey, where the opium poppy could be cultivated legally, but where a large slice of production found its way onto the illegal market. Between Turkish farmers and American junkies there was a long, long chain of middlemen, smugglers and profiteers. Like the police and border guards paid to look the other way. And the camel drivers who fed plastic bags of opium paste to their animals in order to smuggle it over the Turkish border. Or the first-stage refiners, who boiled the raw opium paste with quicklime to precipitate out the morphine. Or the truck drivers who created secret compartments in loads of fruit and vegetables bound for Turkish markets in Germany. Or the technicians who refined the morphine into heroin – a delicate operation that involves heating it with acetic acid to a precise temperature for a precise time. At each of these stages, the price – and the profit margin – rose in geometric progression. Depending on where you were in the chain and, just as importantly, how *many* links of that chain you controlled, heroin could generate shepherd money or oil-magnate money.

At this stage of heroin's history, Sicilian *mafiosi* were not the dominant suppliers to the United States. In the 1960s, the bulk of the heroin consumed in North America came through Corsican hands. The Corsicans were enterprising, with a worldwide network of contacts and a secure base for their refineries in Marseille. Here the Corsican clans won a political shield for their operations by hiring themselves out as strike-breakers and anti-communist thugs, turning the French port city into one of Europe's great criminal capitals. By 1970, Marseille heroin had become famous among American addicts. *Mafiosi* provided access to a distribution network in the United States. Thus the Sicilians were an important but essentially subordinate part of a Corsican business.

The Corsican system was thrown into chaos in the early 1970s. With American public opinion alarmed by the rise in heroin addiction, particularly among combat troops, President Richard Nixon declared a 'war on drugs'. The Turkey–Marseille–New York channel, known as the French Connection, was picked out as the war's strategic objective. The US first offered the Turkish government generous financial persuasion to stop legal opium cultivation, which ceased after the harvest of 1972. Meanwhile, in France, the Corsicans were losing their friends in high places. In November 1971, a French secret-service agent who had been running heroin from Marseille with the Corsicans was indicted in the United States, creating a huge political scandal in France. Moreover, the growing heroin problem in French cities increased the pressure on government to order a clampdown. One by one, the Marseille refineries were shut down and the chemists were arrested.

The Sicilians, who occupied a less strategic segment of America's heroin supply lines than did the Corsicans, looked to have been marginalised by the destruction of the French Connection. American junkies suffered a heroin drought, and the Sicilians occupied a smaller segment of that reduced market. In 1976, the long-awaited final report of Italy's parliamentary inquiry into the mafia used evidence from drug seizures in the States in the early 1970s to argue that 'much of the heroin destined for the United States market is no longer forwarded through Italy as it once was'. The war on drugs, it seemed, was being won.

In reality, all that had happened was that the law of supply and demand was taking its time to work through the global narcotics system. The scarcity of heroin on the American market pushed up the price, which made the risks of setting up new pipelines more worthwhile. Turkish production soon revived after the initial assault. Worse still, as American troops were withdrawn from Vietnam, suppliers of morphine and heroin from the Golden Triangle were avidly seeking new outlets. Between the Asian suppliers and the desperate American addicts there were tempting new opportunities for brokers and refiners. Which is where the Sicilian mafia came in. After the French Connection came the Pizza Connection. Cosa Nostra was about to become addicted.

Mr Champagne: **Heroin broker**

Gaspare Mutolo, son of a ticket collector on the Palermo tram system, was eased gently into the psychological rigours of life as a professional assassin. Not long after being initiated into Cosa Nostra, he was shown what went on inside a mafia torture chamber. Then he took a hands-on lesson in garrotting technique. He retched as blood started to come out of the victim's nose and ears just before death. Mutolo was then taught how to truss up a body so it could be transported in the boot of a car, and how to bury it with quicklime (so that it would rapidly decompose beyond the reach of forensic science) and fertiliser (so that the site of the burial would be covered in vegetation). He was even shown what a body looks like when it has spent two or three months in one of these specially prepared pits.

The toughening-up process paid dividends when Mutolo carried out the first of many solo murders with calm efficiency, cutting the throat of a dissident Man of Honour during a carefully faked robbery. Giving death soon became routine, as it had done for so many *mafiosi* of previous generations.

> I've never felt fear the evening before a murder. You just have to be convinced about what you are going to do. Sometimes, I've been more thoughtful the night before, and have reflected on how easy it is to kill and be killed . . . On occasions, I've experienced a strange sense of pity, especially when I've had to kill youngsters whose family I maybe knew.

Mutolo was then given a fast-track apprenticeship in all of the major criminal businesses that had been transforming Italy's mafias since the 1950s: making them richer, broadening their geographical horizons, bringing them into relationships with one another, thickening their ties with politicians. Sent to Naples, he quickly became involved in cigarette smuggling with *camorristi*. Then he was sent into the wealthy northern region of Lombardy to gather information on possible kidnapping targets. Back in Palermo, Mutolo also learned how to make money from public construction projects.

> All you have to do is set up good relationships with a few local administrators. When the Sicilian regional government puts a contract out to tender, there are men linked to Cosa Nostra who manage the negotiations. That way ghost companies win the contracts and pass them on to the mafia group hiding behind them. To give you an idea of the profits: if a contract is worth a billion lire [€1.65 million in 2011], 10 per cent goes to the politician who obstructs the competition and makes sure the contract goes to the right people, and the rest goes to a *mafioso* who will double his money in a year.

Mutolo proved an obedient underling to his boss, Saro Riccobono of the Partanna-Mondello Family. All was progressing well with a good, but unexceptional, mafia career.

Suddenly, in 1975, a new business exploded, a business that would earn the mafia more than tobacco smuggling, kidnapping and construction put together. Mutolo remembers being in a meeting, chatting with other Men of Honour about routine extortion rackets, when Tano Badalamenti burst in. 'Gentlemen, we have the chance to earn ten times as much with drugs.' Badalamenti, head of the Palermo Commission, well connected in the United States, had spotted the gap in the market created by President Nixon's war on drugs, and he was perfectly placed to exploit it.

Initially, Cosa Nostra stepped up its involvement in heroin

through the same channels it used to smuggle cigarettes. The merchandise travelled in the same containers as the 'blondes'. Palermo Families pooled their investments in joint-stock ventures in just the same way as they had done for major cigarette cargoes. Payments were made through the same Swiss banks that were used to pass money to some of the major tobacco multinationals. As Mutolo quipped, 'If there are any rascals in the story, it's the Swiss.' Tano Badalamenti himself took charge of the first expedition to meet suppliers in Turkey. The scheme was a roaring success. Within forty days, all of the investors had tripled their money. Cosa Nostra's heroin rush had begun.

Mafiosi plunged headlong into the tide of white powder, adapting their old techniques of networking and corruption, and rapidly acquiring lucrative new skills. Nunzio La Mattina, a Man of Honour from the Porta Nuova Family, underwent retraining of a historically resonant sort. Where he had once used his knowledge of chemistry to test the exact composition of Sicily's lemon juice, now he became a large-scale heroin refiner. Other *mafiosi* learned the same trade by taking lessons from Corsicans who were brought over from Marseille. Among them was Francesco Marino Mannoia, from the Santa Maria di Gesù Family. Each time a bulk delivery of morphine base arrived, Marino Mannoia would spend a week at a time amid the vinegary fumes of one of many laboratories that had sprung up across the island. When he emerged, his skin would be scaly and his lungs scoured. He was known as 'Mozzarella' because he was simple and unflashy, and in restaurants always ordered mozzarella and tomato salad, the simplest and safest item on the menu. His personal habits did not change even when, as Cosa Nostra's most important chemist, he became fabulously rich.

Gaspare Mutolo chose another specialism: he became a broker, contacting the wholesale suppliers in the Near and Far East, bringing batches to Sicily and selling them on to traffickers within Cosa Nostra who had access to America. As a leading heroin broker, Mutolo had a reliable map of the politics and economics of the mafia's trafficking. What that map shows is that Cosa Nostra did not enter the heroin business *en bloc*. Nor was it transformed into a top-down multinational dope corporation by the late 1970s heroin boom. Rather it acted like what it is, and what it has always been: a Freemasonry of criminals. Each individual member of the club, each little network of friends within it, each of its Families, and each of the high-level coordinating structures like the Palermo Commission, had the capacity to carve out a role. As Mutolo would later explain:

> When it comes to drug trafficking, if deals are small then they can be managed by a Family. Everyone is independent and does what they want. But sometimes someone gets involved in a big consignment that could interfere with other *mafiosi* and their work, with what a whole organisation is doing. Some big deals can take over a whole market. In such cases the Commission may intervene. Members of the Commission can step in to impose organisation on the deal. So the Commission intervenes in all the most important sectors.

A kind of internal market among Men of Honour developed. Some wholesalers would sell consignments of morphine base to refiners they knew in the brotherhood. When it had been transformed into heroin, they would then buy it all back from them. Often the Family bosses did not deal directly in heroin at all, but were content to sit back and 'tax' the dealers they knew: a much less risky way to make money.

In 1976, just as his heroin ventures were really taking off, Mutolo was arrested; incarceration brought a quantum leap in his criminal standing. 'God bless these prisons!', he later proclaimed. Mutolo's cell mate in Sulmona in central Italy was a long-haired Singapore Chinese heroin importer called Ko Bak Kin. Though neither spoke the other's language, Mutolo took a liking to Kin. Over shared meals and through little gestures of generosity, they began to develop the most precious thing in the treacherous world of international narcotics dealing: trust. When Kin had learned enough Italian to talk business, he said to Mutolo: 'Gaspare, promise me: as soon as you get out, call me. I'll let you have all the drugs you need.' In 1979, just before Kin's sentence ended, Mutolo gave him his gold watch and jewellery to pay for somewhere to stay in Rome, and for a plane ticket to contact his suppliers in Thailand. Kin reciprocated by leaving Mutolo a postbox address in Bangkok.

Soon afterwards, in 1981, Mutolo himself was allowed out on day release. To reintegrate him with the world of honest work, he was allotted a job in a furniture factory in Teramo, in central Italy. But the position of assistant bookkeeper was not best suited to Mutolo's abilities, so he persuaded the owner to make him the factory's Palermo agent. He was also granted periods of leave in Sicily for 'family' reasons. Mutolo had his Ferrari Dino and his Alfa Romeo GTV 2000 brought up to Teramo, so he would roar down to Sicily for his business meetings. He also rented a huge villa by the sea near Teramo, and used a suite in the five-star Michelangelo Hotel as his office. From there he would make calls to Australia, Brazil, Venezuela and Canada.

Mutolo's drug business rocketed. He quickly put together an organisation of common criminals, friends and relatives to handle the hundreds of kilos of heroin imported from Thailand by Ko Bah Kin. When the authorities began to discover some of the Sicilian laboratories, Mutolo and Kin latched on to a scheme that would make refining much safer, and put even more links in the supply chain into their hands. Kin sourced the morphine base in Thailand. A mafia partner of Mutolo's arranged for it to be transported to Europe by ship. On board, there would be a Man of Honour from Mutolo's Family of Cosa Nostra to act as guard. Just as importantly, there would also be a chemist, so that the heroin – as much as 400 kilograms in one go – was ready to put on the market as soon as it arrived.

'1981: my magic moment, the best year of my life,' Mutolo remembered. Armani suits, silk scarves, designer shoes, Cartier watches for his friends . . . Among the lawyers, doctors and professors of Teramo whose company he kept, Mutolo became known as 'Mr Champagne'. Today, having turned state's evidence, he lives a humble life under an assumed identity, and rides a scooter rather than driving a Ferrari. So perhaps it is understandable that he is nostalgic for the luxuries of his past. But he knows deep down that these were fripperies. The phone taps and other evidence that would eventually convict him of heroin trafficking show him carefully using his wealth to dispense favours and make friends. To avoid political tensions within Cosa Nostra, Mutolo made sure that the Palermo Families always got the chance to invest in a new cargo, and that the heroin reaching Sicily was distributed fairly. Mutolo kept his boss sweet. He rose in Saro Riccobono's estimation, becoming one of the leading members of the Partanna-Mondello Family. In the end, in Cosa Nostra, money means nothing unless it is converted back into power.

The huge amounts of cheap heroin being channelled through Italy in the 1970s caused an explosion of drug use in the peninsula. In 1970, the presence of a heroin problem had barely registered. By 1980, Italy had more heroin addicts per head of population than did the United States. Anyone who visited a major Italian city in the 1980s can remember the sight of plastic syringes littering the gutters in quiet streets.

Despite the growth in Italian domestic consumption (and therefore in overdose fatalities), the United States market remained the biggest consumer market in absolute terms. Gaspare Mutolo was a big player in the complex pass-the-parcel game of trafficking heroin from the East, through Sicily, and into the United States. But he was a long way from being the biggest. In fact,

Mutolo learned very quickly that the *mafiosi* who occupied the most strategic place in the supply chain to America were the ones who straddled the Atlantic.

The Transatlantic Syndicate

On 22 April 1974, a small group of *mafiosi* sat down to chat in an ice-cream bar in Saint-Léonard, Montreal's Little Italy. Two of them led the discussion. One was the bar's owner, Paolo Violi, underboss of Cosa Nostra in Quebec. Violi's guest had come directly from Sicily: he was Giuseppe 'Pino' Cuffaro, a Man of Honour who also hailed from the province of Agrigento. The two spoke a common jargon of mafia power politics. A jargon which – through a hubbub of background conversation, a clatter of crockery and the hiss and crackle of a secret microphone – Canadian police were able to record.

Violi began the pleasantries: 'So the journey went well then? Let's kiss one another.'

In reply, Pino Cuffaro could hardly wait to unload his news from Sicily. 'Well, Paolo, before you drink this cappuccino, I've got to announce a nice surprise, an affectionate surprise that is naturally close to our hearts . . . Carmelo has been made representative in our village.'

Then, between sips of coffee, there followed a long bulletin on the latest Cosa Nostra appointments in the far-off province of Agrigento. Who was provincial boss, who were the *capimandamento* (precinct bosses), who were the *consiglieri*, and who had been initiated. They discussed the state of Cosa Nostra across Sicily, remarking on how the Palermo Commission was still suspended. And they dropped the names of mutual friends, like don 'Ntoni Macrì – the 'ndrangheta boss from Siderno who was also a member of Cosa Nostra (and who, unbeknownst to all, would enjoy his last game of bowls just a few months later).

But Pino Cuffaro had not come all the way to Quebec just to

bring his Canadian friends up to speed with the ins and outs of
the old country. He had come to resolve a delicate issue of diplomatic protocol. Could a Man of Honour from Sicily arrive in
America and assume full citizenship of the Cosa Nostra community there? Underlying this question was the fundamental issue
of whether Cosa Nostra was a single transatlantic brotherhood,
or whether the American and Sicilian branches were separate
entities. The positions were so entrenched, and the argument so
strained, that the men had to meet twice.

Paolo Violi, the Canadian gangster, argued for a five-year rule:
any Sicilian who arrived in Canada would have to spend five
years being monitored before he was granted full status. The
Sicilian visitor wanted no barriers to be put up between Sicily
and the New World.

Who was right? The short answer is that it does not really
matter. In the mafia world, rules are very important, but they
are also pliable: *mafiosi*, like the rest of us, tend to interpret rules
in ways that suit their own interests. Even a rule as basic as the
relationship between the American and Sicilian arms of Cosa
Nostra was not permanently fixed.

It is significant that Paolo Violi, the ice-cream-bar owner who
was such a stickler for the five-year rule about admission to the
American Cosa Nostra, was actually a living example of the
rule's flexibility. For he was Calabrian. His bar was called Reggio
– after the city in southern Calabria, birthplace of the 'ndrangheta. Like many young Calabrian hoods who emigrated to major
centres of organised crime in the Americas, Violi made his career
not in the 'ndrangheta, but in the American Cosa Nostra. America
was where closer ties between the Calabrian and Sicilian mafias
were pioneered, and where those ties persisted. But despite the
American mafia's long history of openness to newcomers, even
Calabrian newcomers, in the spring of 1974 the Calabrian immigrant Paolo was adamant that Sicilian *mafiosi* would have to
spend five years under observation before they were entitled to
full membership of Cosa Nostra in the United States.

So the constitutional rights and wrongs of Violi's position are much less important than the question of why he was arguing in that way – of what naked self-interest he was trying to drape in constitutional clothes.

By the time of the ice-cream-bar meeting, the collapse of the French Connection was already beginning to intensify mafia involvement in importing heroin to the United States. Violi was a territorially based boss, not a narcotics trafficker. As such, he felt threatened by this massively lucrative cross-territorial business that he could not entirely control. In the specific case of Quebec, the people who worried Violi were the Cuntreras and Caruanas: two Sicilian mafia bloodlines intertwined over several generations into a single clan-cum-business network. Two members of that clan, Pasquale and Liborio Cuntrera, had moved to Canada in 1951 – more or less when Paolo Violi arrived. Subsequently, many more members of the Cuntrera-Caruana clan joined the Sicilian mafia diaspora that followed the Ciaculli bomb in 1963. Yet rather than settling permanently in one place, the new exiles converted themselves into roving heroin smugglers, a shifting international network that financed, sourced and shipped heroin in bulk, and then laundered and invested the profits. Over the coming years, their traces would be found in Canada, the USA, Mexico, Brazil, Honduras, the Bahamas, Antigua, the Caribbean tax haven of Aruba, India, Germany, Switzerland – and Woking in Surrey. Venezuela was the clan's long-term base, an offshore heroin trading post for the US market. Here the Cuntrera-Caruanas owned a vast, fortified cattle ranch near the Colombian border that had its own airport. When Pasquale Cuntrera's son got married, the event was covered on television and the Venezuelan President was a witness.

Giuseppe Cuffaro, the *mafioso* who argued with Paolo Violi at the ice-cream-bar meeting, was a travelling salesman for the Cuntrera-Caruana group. That is why he wanted free entry to the Canadian market for mafia emissaries.

The Cuntrera-Caruana network centred on a set of smart,

well-connected and mobile *mafiosi* whose spectacular wealth allowed them to win friends anywhere in the world. The Cuntrera-Caruanas and the other roving heroin traders have been referred to as a mafia in their own right. They formed what we could call a Transatlantic Syndicate whose power floated dangerously free of the territories controlled by the Sicilian and American branches of Cosa Nostra. Such men could dictate terms to local bosses like Violi in whichever territory they found market or investment opportunities. The loyalty of soldiers to their captain or boss could easily be bought. Thus it was that, on 22 January 1978, Paolo Violi paid the ultimate price for his finicky, protectionist interpretation of the mafia's rules when he was shot dead as he played cards in his ice-cream bar.

Canada was not the only place where wire-taps registered the way in which the Transatlantic Syndicate was upsetting the mafia balance of power in the late 1970s. In a justly famous undercover sting, FBI Special Agent Joseph D. Pistone infiltrated New York's Bonanno Family by posing as 'Donnie Brasco'. The memorable 1997 movie of Pistone's story, starring Johnny Depp and Al Pacino, fails to capture the operation's crucial historical context. Pistone/Brasco was a first-hand witness to the rise of the 'zips' or 'greasers'. These were derogatory terms that local *mafiosi* used to refer to Sicilian Men of Honour who had recently set up shop in America. There were two reasons why New York *mafiosi* were anxious about the new arrivals. First, because the zips had been granted the exclusive right to supply wholesale heroin for New York's Bonanno and Gambino Families. Second, because they formed an autonomous faction whose power within American Cosa Nostra was on the rise. What soldiers in the Bonanno Family called 'zips' were actually members of the Transatlantic Syndicate.

Pistone's body mike recorded two New York wise guys as they

reacted to the news that some of the Sicilians were going to be awarded ranks within the American organisation:

> Those guys [the zips] are looking to take over everything. There's no way we can make them captains. We'd lose all our strength.

> Them fucking zips ain't going to back up to nobody. You give them the fucking power, if you don't get hurt now, you get hurt three years from now. They'll bury you. You cannot give them the power. They don't give a fuck. They don't care who's boss. They got no respect.

The zips had names and faces. John Gambino was one: he had moved from Palermo to Cherry Hills, New Jersey, in 1964. Salvatore Inzerillo was another: he was the nephew of a Palermo boss. Like the Cuntrera-Caruana clan, these were mobsters with a great many exotic stamps in their passports, and a vast international skein of relatives by blood and marriage to support them. Members of the Transatlantic Syndicate like these were responsible for what became known as the Pizza Connection, a tag coined during the huge US police investigation that eventually cut out a small part of the Transatlantic Syndicate in the mid-1980s.

The members of the Transatlantic Syndicate were frighteningly powerful, and they also worked together. As early as 1971, the Venezuelan secret services looked into the Cuntrera-Caruana cattle ranch, and found that its shareholders included the following: Nick Rizzuto, the Cuntrera-Caruanas' man in Montreal (he would eventually take the reins in Quebec after the murder of Paolo Violi); John Gambino from Cherry Hills; and Salvatore 'Little Bird' Greco, the head of the Palermo Commission at the time of the Ciaculli bomb, who had abandoned Sicily to become a South America-based narcotics importer.

The Transatlantic Syndicate had the keys to the United States heroin market: anyone who wanted to supply bulk dope to the East Coast had little choice but to go through them. Our Sicilian broker, Gaspare 'Mr Champagne' Mutolo, knew that from experience. In 1981, the first of his ships delivered 400 kilograms of ready-refined heroin from Thailand: half of it went to the Cuntrera-Caruanas, and half to John Gambino in Cherry Hills.

Back in Sicily, the Transatlantic Syndicate carried even more clout than it did in Canada or the United States. One member, Salvatore Inzerillo, returned to Palermo in 1973, and his uncle immediately ceded to him his job as representative of the Passo di Rigano Family and then his seat on the Commission. Other bosses who were part of the Transatlantic Syndicate included triumvirate members Tano Badalamenti and Stefano Bontate.

The Transatlantic Syndicate enjoyed the cream of Cosa Nostra's contacts in the world of banking. Some of their narcotics profits were laundered and invested by the notorious fly-by-night financiers and P2 Masonic Lodge members, Michele Sindona and Roberto Calvi. Both Sindona and Calvi would end up dying in circumstances that remain mysterious to this day: Calvi was found hanging under Blackfriars Bridge in London in 1982; Sindona drank a coffee laced with cynanide in prison in 1986.

The Transatlantic Syndicate enjoyed enormous traction in business and politics too. They were close to the Salvo cousins, fabulously wealthy barons of Sicily's privatised tax-collection system. They were also close to Salvo Lima, the Young Turk. Through Lima and the Salvos, but also directly, they had the ear of the most powerful politician in Italy: Giulio Andreotti, seven times Prime Minister by the end of his parliamentary career, and the man whose faction in the Christian Democrat Party included Lima and his Sicilian followers. According to the Italian Supreme Court, in a verdict from 2004, Andreotti displayed 'an authentic stable and friendly availability' towards Stefano Bontate et al until 1980, when Cosa Nostra's increasing violence alienated him.

Never in the long history of the Sicilian mafia has there been a concentration of might and opulence to compete with the Transatlantic Syndicate. That is why, in 1981, the Transatlantic Syndicate became the target of a war of extermination.

But before war broke out once more in Sicily, the camorra in Campania was revolutionised by the most influential boss of the twentieth century.

The Professor

Raffaele Cutolo was the creator of possibly the largest criminal organisation in Italian history, the Nuova Camorra Organizzata ('New Organised Camorra'). At its peak in 1980, according to a police estimate, the Nuova Camorra Organizzata (or NCO) counted 7,000 members. Its leader evaded the full force of the law with a regularity that was shocking even by Italian standards. His speciality was obtaining psychiatric reports that absolved him of full responsibility for his deeds. 'While committing criminal acts', one diagnosis declared, 'Cutolo falls under the influence of a typical impulsive-aggressive crisis that completely overcomes and nullifies his will power.' Or, in lay terms: he often gets angry and has people killed – but it isn't his fault. The NCO boss compared himself to Christ and said he could read minds. It is unclear whether he believed this or was merely acting out the psychiatric script.

Whatever Cutolo's precise mental equilibrium was, in 1980 he decided to flaunt his authority architecturally. Overlooking Ottaviano, the town on the north-eastern slopes of Mount Vesuvius where the NCO boss had grown up, was the dilapidated Medici Castle; it had a room for every day of the year. Cutolo bought it through a front company and turned it into both his organisation's HQ and the grandiose symbol of a rise to criminal power as fast and brutally successful as any in the annals of Italian organised crime. And the astonishing thing is that Raffaele Cutolo did it almost entirely from prison.

In 1963, at the age of twenty-one, Cutolo had earned himself a twenty-four-year prison sentence for shooting a man dead in a road-rage incident of illustrative viciousness. Newspaper reports tell us that in Ottaviano's main thoroughfare, Cutolo deliberately drove his car at four young women, braking only at the last minute. When one of the women remonstrated with Cutolo about the stupid stunt, he set about her with his fists. A passing firefighter intervened to save the woman, and Cutolo responded by pulling a Beretta 7.65 pistol from his pocket and firing twice. But what really earned Cutolo the judge's indignation was the way in which he followed the wounded fireman as he staggered into a doorway to take refuge. There, Cutolo emptied the rest of the clip into the luckless man, who died in hospital leaving a widow and three children.

In 1970 Cutolo was freed, pending a ruling on his case by the Supreme Court, and went on the run. He became a junior camorra boss, dealing in extortion and cocaine. Upon his recapture, after a firefight with the *Carabinieri* in March of the following year, he was sent to the infamous penitentiary at Poggioreale. There he would begin to build what became known as the NCO. By 1974 he had already earned the nickname 'the King of Poggioreale' and was involved in a major drug-trafficking ring with senior *mafiosi* from both Sicily and Calabria. By 1977 he had enough power to have himself transferred to the cosier surroundings of the state mental institution in Aversa near Naples. In February 1978 his men blew a wall down with TNT and he scrambled over the rubble to freedom. One plausible theory is that the breakout was staged to avoid the embarrassment that would have been caused had Cutolo merely strolled out of the main gate – as he probably could have done. Be that as it may, the fugitive was not recaptured for fifteen months. In 1981 an appeal verdict said he could not be punished for the escape because of his mental infirmity. As Cutolo himself put it, 'I did not "escape". I wandered away. A little noisily.'

After his recapture, Cutolo never tasted freedom again. Thus, apart from two brief periods on the run, his entire adult life was spent in captivity. But he understood that prison was the perfect base for a criminal empire. Dominate the prison system, and you dominate the underworld. Confinement is an occupational hazard for criminals. And if they cannot go to jail without the fear of being raped in the showers or stabbed in the yard, they become acutely exposed.

In a sense, Cutolo perfected the methods used by prison camorras since the early nineteenth century. At the simplest level, the NCO offered safety in numbers to terrified youths doing their first stretch in an adult jail. Indeed Cutolo specialised in cultivating isolated youngsters who were not affiliated to other gangs. One of his fellow prisoners in Poggioreale described him as a 'talent scout'. Once outside, those young men would kick back part of their earnings to Cutolo so he could support others by sending cash and food to relatives, by corrupting guards and administrators, and by arranging transfers, lawyers and medical visits. So began the circulation of tributes and favours that bound the NCO together. Cutolo's organisation extended its reach from Poggioreale to many other prisons across Italy, and gained the manpower and discipline in the outside world to manage crime on an industrial scale.

The NCO engaged in all kinds of business, ranging from drug dealing and truck theft to defrauding the European Economic Community of agricultural subsidies and infiltrating government building projects. But for the NCO – as for the Sicilian mafia and for the Neapolitan Honoured Society of yesteryear – extortion was the key tool of authority. Cutolo's rackets were run by trusted lieutenants, including his big sister Rosetta. She looked for all the world like the frumpy embroiderer her brother claimed she was. But this was a façade created in part because there were those within the NCO hierarchy who were reluctant to take orders from a woman. Many observers believe that Rosetta was one of the camorra's most powerful female bosses. The money she sent to her brother allowed him to live out his confinement in luxury: in the course of just over a year in 1981–2, he received nearly 56 million lire (equivalent to €100,000 in 2011 values) to take care of his daily expenses; he reputedly spent over half of it on food and clothes.

Cutolo's conspicuous consumption was intended to publicise his power, as was the transparent irony he deployed in interview. During the trial for his escape from Aversa asylum, Cutolo gave an impromptu press conference. Surviving news footage shows him to be well groomed, with a face both weaselly and self-satisfied. He shifts his weight repeatedly from one foot to the other behind the bars of the defendants' cage, and casts rapid, smirking glances to either side – as if he were a back-row schoolboy seeking complicity from his classmates during a scolding.

'I'm someone who fights injustice. Me, and all my friends.'
'A Robin Hood, so to speak?'
'So to speak.'
'What about the Nuova Camorra Organizzata, the NCO?'
'I dunno. Maybe NCO means *"Non Conosco Nessuno"* – "I don't know anyone".'
'Are you in charge in the prison system?'
Cutolo feigns disbelief with an unpersuasive snigger. 'I'm not in charge, the prison governor is.' [. . .]
'What about the murder of the deputy prison governor? You had previously slapped him and threatened to kill him.'
'Yes I did. Because he was doing some really . . . ' There follows an oily mellowing in Cutolo's tone. 'But he's dead now. It's unkind to talk ill of the dead . . . Anyway, I may be insane, but I'm not stupid-insane. I'm intelligent-insane. So I'm hardly going to slap someone, threaten to kill him, and then go ahead and murder him. I don't fancy collecting life sentences like that.'

Even among professional criminals, there are very few with a public persona as odious as Raffaele Cutolo. Yet his distinctive trait as a boss was the adoration he inspired. The Nuova Camorra Organizzata was founded on a cult of personality and an ideological fervour that no other mafia in Italy has ever matched. At the height of Cutolo's power, a legion of *camorristi* would gladly have died for him. What was the secret of his charisma? For one thing, he had a keen organisational intelligence and used it to construct an elaborate internal culture for the NCO. Its recruits felt they belonged, that they had a shared cause. And for the purpose of building this esprit de corps, Cutolo borrowed rituals and terminology from the Calabrian mafia. Indeed he was almost certainly affiliated into the 'ndrangheta while in prison: two *'ndranghetisti* have spoken to the authorities about how Cutolo was given his 'second baptism' in 1974. Later, Cutolo would put the NCO's new recruits through a very similar ceremony. From the 'ndrangheta, Cutolo also borrowed the terminology that defined ranks within the organisation: *giovane d'onore*, *picciotto*, *cuntajuolo*, *contabile*, *santista*, etc. Cutolo it was who, on behalf of his Calabrian friends, arranged to have the triumvir Mico Tripodo stabbed to death in Naples prison in 1976 during the First 'Ndrangheta War.

Camorra history came full circle with Raffaele Cutolo. From Calabrian gangsters, he learned rituals and terminology that the 'ndrangheta had itself inherited from the prison camorra of the early nineteenth century. He then reimported them into the Neapolitan prison system whence they had first come, and where they had died out before the First World War.

Indeed, for a crime boss, Cutolo had a quite extraordinary sense of history. He was dubbed 'the Professor' by his men, partly because he sought out books on camorra history in the prison library, and partly because he wrote verse and short meditations on life, love and *omertà* for his admirers. In 1980 he had his jottings published as *Poems and Thoughts*. The book was seized by the police and possessing it was treated as incriminating. It is not difficult to work out why: Cutolo does little to conceal the terror he wielded. Less obviously, the book also shows the

Professor putting his time in the prison library to good use. By way of example, it is worth citing the verses written in praise of the NCO's principal enforcer within the prison system, Pasquale Barra, known as *'o Sturente* ('the Student') or, more appropriately, as *'o 'Nimale* ('the Animal'). Barra was a gaunt, darkly bearded man with a very prominent nose and eyes like a mole's. He had been Cutolo's devoted friend since their teenage years in Ottaviano, and was the first recruit to the NCO. His primary role was stabbing people to death on his old friend's orders. The poem dedicated to him is called simply, 'A Man of the Camorra':

Pasquale Barra: in our town
He was called 'the Student'
When it comes to a *zumpata*, no one is better
He can even face down an army
He always pulls off the same move
His knife-thrusts are totally lethal
Up under your lungs, so you start to cough
He makes you spit out a bit of red froth
He sees you fall to the ground, then leaves you . . .

In his own devious way, Cutolo was here using verse to bestow a certain literary and historical grandeur on his vicious henchman. For 'A Man of the Camorra' is actually cobbled together from lines stolen from a much older poem about the long dead *camorrista* Gennarino Sbisà. The original author, journalist Ferdinando Russo (1866–1927), often celebrated individual *camorristi*, mixing just enough realistic grit into the verse to make his portraits of noble hoodlums feel authentic and dangerous.

In Russo's day, the camorra – with its hierarchical management structure and its ceremonial *zumpate*, or knife duels – was very unlike the loose gangs and street-corner bosses that had dominated Neapolitan criminality for most of the twentieth century. Before it was destroyed by a famous trial in 1911–12, the camorra was an Honoured Society. And through his poems, Ferdinando

Russo became the man most responsible for creating a popular cult around it.

The echoes of that popular cult still resounded in the 1970s. Cutolo devoured the dewy-eyed fables about the old-time bosses such as Salvatore De Crescenzo and Ciccio Cappuccio ('Little Lord Frankie') – the same *camorristi* once celebrated in the puppet theatres of Naples. As both plagiarising poet and gangster, the Professor was bent on bringing the camorra's historical memory back to life. He explicitly sold the NCO to recruits as a revival of a proud gangster tradition. To be a *cutoliano* was to have roots in the past.

On one intriguing occasion, Cutolo even stage-managed a violent close encounter with camorra history – as personified by Antonio Spavone. Born in 1926 into a family of fishermen in the Mergellina quarter, Spavone and his older brother led a band of black marketeers during the chaos of Allied Military Government in 1943–5 that had launched so many criminal careers. When Spavone's brother was killed during a feud with a rival outfit, Antonio took vengeance in spectacular fashion, by raiding a family celebration in a restaurant and stabbing the opposing gang leader to death in front of a crowd. His gesture earned him both a long prison sentence and the right to inherit his brother's simple but effective nickname: *'o Malommo* – 'the Bad Man'.

At some point in 1975, when both *'o Malommo* and Cutolo were in Poggioreale prison, the younger man chose to issue a challenge to a *zumpata*, a knife duel – just like the *camorristi* of the old days. This may well have been a deliberately archaic gesture: the equivalent of slapping *'o Malommo* in the face with a glove. Cutolo's challenge was refused, either because *'o Malommo* was about to be released, or because he did not want to dignify the uppity young hoodlum's impudence with a response. Recalling the episode much later, a prisoner who was in Poggioreale at the time gave a shrewd analysis of how Cutolo managed the prison rumour-machine:

Nobody witnessed the episode. It was a completely 'virtual' event. Somebody, maybe Cutolo himself, put the rumour into circulation that the duel had not happened because of *'o Malommo*'s cowardice. In cases like this, different versions do the rounds – versions that always suit one side or the other. Cutolo went a long way thanks to a fame that was often built on made-up events. He was skilful at making exploits that never existed seem credible and legendary. He had an extraordinary talent for promoting his own image.

Even within the straitened confines of a prison, organised crime – however organised it may be – is a domain where information circulates in a confused and fragmentary form. The Professor was a master at making the gaps in any story work for him, in writing his own history.

Cutolo's *Poems and Thoughts* are repulsive, and often trite and clumsy. But they would be much less dangerous if all they did was prompt fake duels in prison corridors or trumpet a killer's feats of savage dexterity. Cutolo's writings did much more. Copies circulated among his acolytes like the scriptures of a new messiah, and provided a seductive emotional script for the Nuova Camorra Organizzata. Analysing that script brings us to the heart of the Professor's charismatic appeal.

Nihilism is the base note of the Cutolo philosophy. We are all beasts, ready to tear one another apart for filthy money. Man is the most treacherous and cruel of all the animals; he ought not to exist. But the psychological trick that the Professor pulls off in *Poems and Thoughts* is to create a criminal value-system that seems redemptive when set against this background of fear and despair.

A good portion of Cutolo's verse voices a prisoner's yearning for his freedom, his mum, and the sights, sounds and smells of home. All of which may seem self-pitying. But it shows that Cutolo was a smart enough leader to identify with the underlying mental vulnerability of his fellow cons. His mawkishness was the first means to a very unsentimental end: moulding a disciplined criminal army.

The sentence: life imprisonment
As a youth
You entered
The tomb-like cell
The silent cell
The suffering cell
You felt alone, and lost

Cutolo blames social inequality and especially the prison system for the fact that he, like so many others, has turned to crime. But this persecution has had an ennobling effect. As in the following Cutolian maxim: 'Take note: the best men end up as outlaws, fugitives or prisoners. While the people who have done this to them are the hypocrite defenders of the law.'

Cutolo presents the NCO as a fellowship of the downtrodden, bound together against the onslaughts of a hostile world; it is a group of Friends. For Friendship is the supreme good in the Professor's charismatic world. 'Friendship is sacred, because it is beautiful to share your own moments of bitterness, joy, pain and triumph with a friendly heart.'

And if Friendship came under threat, then death must become the best Friend of all: 'When a battle begins, a boss's first thought must be to make "Death" a Friend . . . Death, my Friend, help me to plant seed in your land.'

On April Fool's Day 1982, the *Carabinieri* in Ottaviano discovered that Friend Death had planted a seed a few hundred metres away from the Cutolo castle. The body was in the boot of a stolen car. The head, wrapped in cellophane and covered with a towel, was in a plastic basin placed on the front seat. Even in the violence-weary Italy of the early 1980s, a camorra decapitation was guaranteed to attract a deal of media attention. But in this case the victim's name turned the event into front-page news.

Professor Aldo Semerari was the criminal psychiatrist responsible for some of the most clamorous expert opinions on Raffaele Cutolo's mental health. He was also a prime example of the kind of figure who, in the 1970s and 1980s, seemed to be spawned from the murk where organised crime and subversive politics overlapped. An extreme right-wing agitator with links to Italian military intelligence, Semerari had tried to enlist a number of criminal organisations to his Fascist cause. But in the end he only managed to arrange a simple swap: the gangsters received the benefit of his psychiatric expertise and, in return, Semerari's friends were given weapons. But the psychiatrist had been rash enough to try and make the same deal with both Raffaele Cutolo and his camorra enemies. When his headless corpse was found in Ottaviano, it was not clear who had punished him for playing off both sides.

The Semerari case gave Ottaviano a reputation as the town 'where heads fly'. Ten men were murdered there in the first five months of 1982. Journalists flocked to try and diagnose the malaise. But only one of them – a young Milanese writer called Luca Rossi – was patient enough to trace just how deeply the ideas expounded in *Poems and Thoughts* had been imbibed by many of the locals. For the rootless youth that grew up in the 'South Bronxes' of the Neapolitan periphery, Cutolo's poisonous credo was strong magic. The economic downturn of the mid-1970s put thousands of young men onto the market for criminal labour. During Cutolo's reign, Campania was the region with the highest number of juvenile inmates in the country. These *camorristi*-in-the-making were poor, from dysfunctional families, and educated early to the value of violence. By the time these kids were officially recruited, and had the NCO's five-dot insignia tattooed at the base of their right thumb, they professed an indifference to Friend Death that was as pitiful as it was terrifying:

> What I've already seen in my twenty-three years is enough for me. I'm already dead. Now I'm just living an extra bit, a bit of life that's been gifted to me. They can kill me if they want.

> We're already living corpses. Someone's already got half a foot on my head. And if you put the other half of your foot on my head, then I'll kill you.

> You ask me why I behave like this, and why I do certain 'jobs' that even other *camorristi* won't do. The reason is very simple. It doesn't matter to me if I live or die. In fact, in some ways, I'm actually trying to get killed.

An anonymous twenty-year-old girl from Ottaviano interviewed by Luca Rossi set out the most perceptive and chilling dissection of the NCO mentality. This was the voice of a young woman both immersed in camorra culture, and yet able to distance herself from it, as if it were all just a nightmare:

> The camorra has some really beautiful things about it. It's an instinctive, animal response. We take what they don't give us, and we take it with force. There are extraordinary, powerful feelings in the camorra. I've seen incredible acts of love and solidarity. They believe in what they are doing like no one believes in political ideologies . . . The strongest among them are the ones who are afraid. You see these kids with a pistol in their hand, and you realise they're fucked. Of all the *camorristi* I know, the most sensitive ones are the most violent. I mean really violent: machine-gun violent, massacre violent.

Raffaele Cutolo gave sensitive, wasted youths an elemental narrative – a reason to die where there seemed no reason to live. His *Poems and Thoughts* was a collective manifesto for living fast and going out in an expensive shirt and a hail of gunfire. The NCO came as close as any mafia has ever done to being a death cult.

And in 1978, Cutolo sent the NCO into a battle that turned into the bloodiest underworld war in Neapolitan history – a war against the Sicilian mafia.

4

THE SLAUGHTER

Blood orgy

First tobacco. Then construction. Then kidnapping. And finally heroin. The new sources of criminal wealth that developed between the late 1950s and the late 1970s offered huge rewards to *mafiosi*, *camorristi* and *'ndranghetisti* who could think big and collaborate to achieve their aims. New business networks were assembled: like the joint-stock ventures that pooled investments first in tobacco and then heroin; or the kidnapping gangs that took victims in the north before smuggling them into captivity on Aspromonte; or the heroin-trafficking rings that traversed the globe, linking the Golden Triangle to the United States via Sicily. New economic partnerships were forged, including partnerships that crossed the lines between Cosa Nostra, the camorra and the 'ndrangheta.

Alongside these cycles of commercial inventiveness, there came cycles of political inventiveness too. In Italy, no gangster would last long if he lapsed into believing that he was exclusively a criminal entrepreneur, and forgot that he has no choice but to take part in the permanent scheming and jockeying for position among his criminal peers. Thus, as the mafias grew richer, new arrangements of power were shaped: like the triumvirates in Calabria and Sicily, or Cosa Nostra's Regional Commission, or the Sicilian mafia Families that were set up in Campania. Underworld rules and traditions were overhauled or even invented, such as the ban on kidnapping in Cosa Nostra, or Raffaele Cutolo's revival of the nineteenth-century Honoured Society of Naples, or the 'ndrangheta's Mamma Santissima.

The faster the wheels of the criminal economy turned, and the more frenetic the politicking became, the more the pressures in Italy's underworld increased. The stakes and the risks grew greater and greater until, in the 1980s, there came an explosion of violence without precedent in the annals of mafia history.

How many died? Precision is impossible. Given the number of disappearances, and of mob assassinations that were artfully disguised as crimes of passion or robberies that got out of hand, we will never have an accurate sum. Not unless all the unmarked graves and skeletons in the deep can be located, and some sorcery invented to make the acid baths tell their story. Estimates for the number of fatalities during just the first two years of Sicily's Second Mafia War range between 500 and 1,000 people. More than 900 died in the camorra wars of 1979–83. One journalist has reckoned the total number killed by organised crime across the whole of southern Italy in the 1980s at 10,000. A guess, certainly. But by no means a wild one. More conservatively, the parliamentary inquiry estimated that, between 1981 and 1990, 2,905 murders were committed in Sicily, 2,621 in Campania, 1,807 in Calabria and 757 in Puglia. The vast majority of these were committed by organised crime. If that number is near the truth, it tells us that there were about twice as many victims of organised crime in southern Italy in the 1980s as there were victims of three decades of religious and political strife in Northern Ireland.

Any chronicle of that decade of slaughter must begin in Palermo, where Corleone's Totò 'Shorty' Riina was continuing his ascent. As we have seen, already in the 1970s the kidnappings perpetrated by Riina or his boss Luciano Liggio had begun to split Cosa Nostra into two factions. The make-up of the triumvirate demonstrated the balance of power clearly enough: on the one hand, Riina; and ranged against him Stefano Bontate, the Prince of Villagrazia, and Tano Badalamenti, the first head of the Palermo Commission after it was reconstituted in 1974. On the face of it, the two factions were unfairly matched. Although they were not close allies, Bontate and Badalamenti were nonetheless both part of the greatest concentration of wealth and connections that the Sicilian mafia had ever known. They had the politicians, both local and national. They had the ties with the shadowy world of Freemasonry. They had Palermo's oldest citadels of mafia power in their hands, and – at least in Bontate's case – the prestige that comes with a venerable mafia lineage. Crucially, they were also connected to the Transatlantic Syndicate with its near monopoly on access to the United States heroin market. Riina hailed from Corleone, which historically had been on the edges of the map of mafia power in the province of Palermo. Of the eleven men who had seats on the Commission in 1975, only three, including Riina himself, could be considered opponents of the Bontate and Badalamenti power system.

But Riina had luck and, above all, cunning on his side. Luck, because both Bontate and Badalamenti were arrested in the early 1970s, giving him the time and space to make his initial kidnapping moves. And cunning, because when the narcodollars really began to flood into Sicily, Riina was quick to divine the submerged currents of envy they set in motion.

Everyone in Cosa Nostra was involved in heroin, or at least wanted to be involved in heroin. But not everyone had access to the American market. The Transatlantic Syndicate had created a bottleneck, and was profiting handsomely from it. Many *mafiosi* became rich in the late 1970s drug boom, but only a few became opulent: those like Badalamenti, Bontate and Inzerillo, who were part of the transatlantic heroin elite.

Shorty planned to turn his economic weakness into political strength. He aimed to capitalise on the envy and frustration inspired by the Transatlantic Syndicate so as to win friends and territory in Sicily, and so take control of the Commission. By steadily recruiting the marginal players in the heroin industry, Riina was to transform the *corleonesi* from being just a Family, into being a great alliance of Men of Honour recruited from all the Families.

There was nothing startlingly new about this strategy. In New York, during the Castellammarese War of 1929–31 (the war that ended with Lucky Luciano installing himself at the apex of the New York underworld), Salvatore Maranzano's *castellammaresi* were just such a cross-Family alliance. In the battle for supremacy in Palermo that happened at more or less the same time as the Castellammarese War, Ernesto 'the *generalissimo*' Marasà infiltrated the Families of the province of Palermo in his campaign to become boss of all bosses.

Like his strategy, Riina's tactics were traditional too. The Sicilian mafia is a territorial organisation, and the cult of territory is as old as the mafia itself. As one nineteenth-century policeman put it: 'One of the mafia's canons is respect for another man's territorial jurisdiction. Flouting that jurisdiction constitutes a personal insult.' The point here is that it is not just the mafia's *rules* that are traditional, but also the reasons why those rules are regularly broken – the signals that *mafiosi* send when they break them. Riina showed himself to be a master of maintaining his own territorial authority while sending out signals that undermined other people's. One of those signals was murder.

In January 1974, a retired policeman called Angelo Sorino was shot dead in San Lorenzo, in the Piana dei Colli. (His devotion to the cause was such that he had been helping his former colleagues with their investigations into Riina's allies.) Whoever was responsible for Sorino's death had not informed Cosa Nostra's Commission beforehand, as was supposed to happen with significant hits like this. It was obvious to the police who the culprit was, because of the principle of territorial jurisdiction: Filippo Giacalone, boss of the Family whose realm included the murder scene. Giacalone, a friend of Stefano Bontate's, was duly arrested. Needless to say, Giacalone's involvement was even more obvious to his peers in Cosa Nostra. While he was in prison, Bontate demanded an explanation on behalf of the Commission.

As it turned out, Giacalone had not ordered Sorino's death; in fact he was only a patsy in a much bigger plot. Once he was freed, and had time to investigate, he told Bontate that a top *corleonese* killer called Leoluca Bagarella had carried out the murder. But before Bontate could refer these findings back to the Commission, Giacalone vanished. His place on the Commission was taken by the boss of neighbouring Resuttana, a friend of the *corleonesi*.

The Sorino murder was a dual-purpose homicide. It eliminated a threat to one of Riina's friends. More importantly, it loudly proclaimed Bontate and Badalamenti's political weakness.

In 1977, the *corleonesi* carried out another dual-purpose homicide. They killed a zealous colonel of the *Carabinieri* on their own territory, thus eliminating a threat to their own interests. But they also failed to ask permission from the Commission before acting: another political snub to their enemies.

Having used kidnappings and murders to discredit the Bontate-Badalamenti-controlled Commission, the *corleonesi* looked to take it over themselves. By now they already had a prestigious ally: the boss of Ciaculli, Michele 'the Pope' Greco, who proved adept at befogging Bontate with seemingly reasonable explanations for what the *corleonesi* were doing. Behind the smokescreen created by Michele Greco, more and more bosses were coming over to Riina's side.

In 1978 the extent of *corleonese* influence within the Commission became obvious to all when – sensationally – Tano Badalamenti, the boss of all bosses, was expelled from Cosa Nostra. Badalamenti was almost certainly punished because he had failed to give everyone a share of the heroin bonanza. Being expelled – the word *mafiosi* use is *posato* or 'laid down' – is a relatively rare sanction, and often a temporary one. Among men for whom one murder more or less is no cause for handwringing, this was a demonstratively mild penalty. Riina was making a show of playing by Cosa Nostra's traditional rules; he was showing just how *reasonable* he was. Accordingly it was a man of reason, Michele 'the Pope' Greco, who took Badalamenti's place as provincial representative. Greco was little more than a front for *corleonese* power.

Later the same year, the *corleonesi* once more played tricks with the rules of territorial sovereignty. A team of *corleonese* hit men shot dead Giuseppe Di Cristina, a boss who was particularly close to Stefano Bontate. Crucially, the murder took place on territory belonging to another Bontate ally, the zip Salvatore Inzerillo. The killers even abandoned the car used in the assassination in Inzerillo's domain. The message in the murder humiliated a key Bontate ally, and a central figure in the Transatlantic Syndicate. Di Cristina's death also showed that the *corleonesi*'s ambitions were not restricted to the province of Palermo. The son and grandson of mafia bosses, Di Cristina was from the inland town of Riesi in the province of Caltanissetta.

After central Sicily came the turn of the eastern city of Catania. In September 1978, Pippo Calderone – the local boss of Cosa Nostra and the man who had instigated the kidnapping ban at the Regional Commission in 1975 – was shot dead by his deputy, another covert member of the growing *corleonese* alliance. At the banquet held by Calderone's men to mark their boss's passing, Shorty Riina had the front to give a speech. He eulogised the dead *capo* as a peacemaker in the best mafia traditions. Many of the gangsters present were moved to tears.

By 1979 the *corleonesi* had won a clear majority on the Palermo Commission. Just as significantly, they had begun to make inroads into their enemies' own closest circles. One Man of Honour from Stefano Bontate's own Santa Maria di Gesù Family serves as a measure of just how far the *corleonesi* now reached. He was a lawyer, and a major drug trafficker, who resented his boss's overweening manner, and found a sympathetic ear for his complaints among Totò Riina's friends. His name was Giovanni Bontate, and he was the younger brother of the boss.

Cunning exploitation of the mafia's rules and conventions, calculated insults, alliance-building and betrayal: all of the ingredients in the measured *corleonese* advance upon the centres of underworld power in Sicily can be found in the archives of mafia history going back to the nineteenth century. In that sense, the events of the late 1970s and early 1980s were nothing new. All the same, there were at least two novelties. The first was the value of the prize that would accrue to the victors. For once Sicily was won, the Americans would have no alternative but to talk business with Salvatore 'Shorty' Riina. The heroin pipeline would flow through Corleone. The other novelty in Riina's rise to the top was the relentless ferocity with which he executed his plans, the unrelenting brutality of Sicily's Second Mafia War.

On the evening of 23 April 1981, Stefano Bontate, well dressed as ever, drove his brand-new limited edition Alfa Romeo Giulietta Super through the rain and the habitually frenetic traffic on the Palermo ring road. He had spent the evening quaffing champagne at his own forty-second birthday party, and was now on the way home. When he turned off into a side road, he was stopped dead by blasts from a sawn-off shotgun and a Kalashnikov.

Two and a half weeks later, another Kalashnikov victim was found lying by the gate of a large housing block in via Brunelleschi. The head was so badly pulped by bullets that it took the police five hours to make an identification on the basis of fingerprints and a blood-caked medallion with initials engraved on it: it belonged to Salvatore Inzerillo, boss of Passo di Rigano, whose name had just begun to appear in the papers in association with a major investigation into heroin smuggling.

National public opinion took a while to wake up to the fact that this was something more than another seasonal bout of gangster-on-gangster violence. In newspapers in the north, Salvatore Inzerillo's death attracted coverage comparable to a moderately serious motor accident in Milan or Turin. But as the killings continued in Palermo, people sought explanations for what was happening. Heroin obviously had something to do with it. Not much else made sense.

One by one, all the old journalistic templates for mafia violence were applied, and discarded. Was this a tit-for-tat: perhaps the Bontate and Inzerillo clans were at war with one another? But then it was discovered that the same Kalashnikov was used to kill both bosses.

Another theory – a very old one – was that this was an inter-generational conflict, and that a young mafia of 'forty-some-things' was making an attack on the power of the 'old' mafia. The fact that Bontate was forty-two when he died, and Salvatore Inzerillo thirty-seven, did not square easily with this interpreta-tion.

Some explanations were so wildly off target as to be comical, or exasperating, depending on your point of view. Interviewed by the *New York Times*, the novelist Alberto Moravia argued that 'The Sicilian as such – including the honest Sicilian – is by inclination a Mafioso, in the sense that he shares with the mafia man the yearning for, and obsession with, the "prestige of power".' Nowadays it seems mystifying that anyone should consider a Roman novelist to be an authority worth consulting on the complexities of the mafia. But Moravia's ignorance should serve as a reminder of the appalling state of public knowledge in this key phase of the organisation's century-old history.

The police themselves were more astute than Moravia, but hardly revealing. The chief of the Flying Squad said only that, 'What we have here is a blood orgy: when the war ends, we will manage to understand the new balance of power.' This was the police's traditional approach to the cyclical blood-letting among Palermo's criminal elite: wait for the shooting to stop, and then count the bodies and hope for a tip-off.

The shooting did not stop. The newspapers became a daily catalogue of horrors. Bodies abandoned in slicks of blood in the street, or found crumpled behind shop counters, or left amid burning rubbish on waste ground. Antonino Ciaramitaro was discovered in the boot of a car in two plastic bags – one for his trunk and one for his head. Giovanni Prestigiacomo was shotgunned to death as he parked his FIAT 1100. His wife heard the detonations and ran outside; she would continue to hold him, screaming 'Don't die. Don't die', long after the life had ebbed from his riddled cadaver.

Desperate for certainties, the newspapers tried to keep a tally. Seventy bodies in the six months between April and October 1981; 148 by the end of the year. But the 'white shotguns' (meaning cases in which a victim simply vanishes and their body is never found) made the counting difficult. Perhaps 112 disappearances in the first nine months of 1982, plus 108 murders. But the numbers were only a veil for confusion.

We now know that what was really going on was not actually a mafia war at all: it was a programme of annihilation. Riina was systematically eliminating his enemies and anyone close to them. The day after Inzerillo's murder, the boss who had stepped into Stefano Bontate's shoes in Santa Maria di Gesù called the dead *capo*'s six most loyal soldiers into a meeting to discuss what was happening. Four of them obeyed and were never seen again: the new boss was Riina's appointment.

The drug broker Gaspare 'Mr Champagne' Mutolo was a witness to what happened next. Emanuele D'Agostino, one of the two men who had wisely decided not to answer the call to visit the new boss of Santa Maria di Gesù, went into hiding. He sought refuge with Rosario Riccobono, Mutolo's *capo*. Riccobono had always tried to maintain a neutral position in the mafia power struggle of the late 1970s. But the initial success of the *corleonese* assault persuaded him it was time to come off the fence: he killed D'Agostino as a token of his new-found loyalty to Shorty Riina. Just in case Riina needed more convincing, Riccobono then set a trap for D'Agostino's son by telling him to bring some clean clothes to his father's hideout. The son followed the father into a shallow grave.

A couple of weeks later, the only survivor from among the six

Bontate soldiers, a *mafioso* by the name of Totuccio Contorno, was driving through Brancaccio with a little friend of his eleven-year-old son in the passenger seat. Suddenly, a powerful motorbike pulled out from a side street, and the pillion passenger raked the car with a Kalashnikov as it sped past. Contorno pushed the boy out of the car (miraculously, he had not been hit) and returned fire with a pistol before escaping. Totuccio Contorno would, in time, become one of the most important witnesses who enabled investigators to reconstruct the dynamics of the slaughter.

Hardly had the *corleonesi* finished with the active members of the opposing faction than they moved on to their relatives. Santo Inzerillo, brother of murdered zip Salvatore, was strangled when he tried to make a peace offering to Riina. Another brother, who was only sixteen, had his arm cut off before he was put out of his agony.

News of the blood-letting in Sicily caused consternation in New York. John Gambino, the Transatlantic Syndicate boss from Cherry Hills, bravely came back to Palermo to express the American Cosa Nostra's concerns. Shorty Riina's response was an order: the Americans must kill anyone from the Bontate or Inzerillo clans who had managed to escape across the Atlantic. Thus it was that Salvatore Inzerillo's uncle and cousin disappeared; then Pietro Inzerillo, a brother, was taken from a restaurant in Trenton New Jersey, beheaded by gunfire, and his body dumped in the boot of a Cadillac. One particular detail of Pietro Inzerillo's grisly end caught the public's imagination: dollars were placed in his mouth and on his genitals to show that he had been too greedy. The message here was that his American killers (among whom numbered yet another Inzerillo cousin) were dutifully parroting the *corleonese* justification for the war: the greed of the *mafiosi* who controlled access to the American heroin market.

Having turned the Inzerillo clan against itself, Shorty Riina next purged anyone whose loyalty to him was even remotely in doubt. Just before Christmas in 1982, Saro Riccobono, the

Partanna-Mondello representative who had been so keen to cosy up to Riina by betraying and killing Emanuele D'Agostino and his son, was invited to a great barbecue amid the mandarin orange trees of Michele Greco's Ciaculli estate. After a hearty meal and a nap, he was woken by men placing a rope around his neck: 'Saru, your story ends here', they told him. At the same moment, Riccobono's soldiers were being strangled one by one by the other guests at the barbecue. When the stragglers had been hunted down, only three members of Mr Champagne's entire Family remained alive.

The cull extended to other provinces of Sicily. In September 1981, the international heroin traffickers of the Cuntrera-Caruana clan suffered their first victim when Leonardo Caruana was murdered. The *corleonesi* also sponsored particularly vicious fighting in the province of Trapani, where they slowly encircled and conquered the town of Alcamo – the capital of the Bontate-Badalamenti-Inzerillo faction in that province.

Although the Sicilian blood-letting peaked in the years 1981–3, it did not abate entirely, but transformed itself into an endless state of terror. As Riina's power grew, so did his fear. He began to see the young killers who had taken a leading role in the first waves of killings as a potential threat. The prime case in point was Pino Greco, known as 'Little Shoe'. Little Shoe was the man whose Kalashnikov had put paid to both Stefano Bontate and Salvatore Inzerillo. He was also the Kalashnikov-wielding pillion passenger who led the attempt to eliminate Totuccio Contorno. Little Shoe it was who cut off the sixteen-year-old Inzerillo brother's arm. He is thought to have killed some eighty people. But he was more than just a sadistic butcher. He was also a power in his own right. While he was formally the under-boss of Michele 'the Pope' Greco's Ciaculli Family, Pino Greco was in reality the power behind the Pope's throne, making sure that Corleone's will was done. At some point, late in 1985, Little Shoe's own men decided to eliminate him before his ambitions put them in the way of Shorty Riina's wrath.

Such was the dread inspired by the Corleone boss. Shorty had established a kind of military dictatorship. Cosa Nostra would never be the same again. By the time of Little Shoe's death, the new tide of underworld war in Italy had long since engulfed Campania too, and the Sicilian mafia had been drawn into a proxy war against the Professor and his Nuova Camorra Organizzata.

The New Family: **A group portrait**

When Raffaele Cutolo 'noisily wandered away' from the mental hospital in Aversa in February 1978, the growth of his Nuova Camorra Organizzata (NCO) accelerated. The Professor recruited hundreds more young followers, reorganised his command structure, vastly increased the pressure of his extortion rackets, and even made a trip to the United States to seek closer business ties with his contacts in the American Cosa Nostra. All of these initiatives prepared the ground for the audacious demand he then issued to every other camorra organisation: he wanted tribute, in the form of 20,000 lire (equal to some €65 in 2011) for every case of contraband cigarettes that was unloaded in the region. There was no mistaking the scale of the ambition implicit in Cutolo's ultimatum: he was making a bid to become the absolute ruler of the whole Campanian underworld.

Cosa Nostra was the biggest force standing in Cutolo's way. In the early 1970s, the clans affiliated to the Sicilian mafia held the criminal balance of power in Campania, a region traversed by many different gang territories. Canny propagandist that he was, the Professor sold his campaign to his followers as underworld patriotism: the Nuova Camorra Organizzata, heir to the traditions of the Neapolitan Honoured Society of old, was to lead a crusade to free the region of Sicilian influence: 'One day the people of Campania will understand that a crust of bread eaten in freedom is worth more than a steak eaten as a slave. And that day Campania will truly have victory.' Cutolo branded *camorristi* who were loyal to any outside criminal force as traitors: 'In my eyes they were "half *mafiosi*", because they took orders from Sicilian bosses and in that way sold out their own land.' The

Professor's rhetoric was backed by the firepower of his legions of young gunmen. Fighting began to break out across Campania.

The first clans to bond together to resist Cutolo were those from central Naples. The anti-Cutolo front then grew to embrace Cosa Nostra's Campanian Families and other clans in the Neapolitan hinterland too. As it did so, it adopted the name Nuova Famiglia – the New Family – or NF. By early in 1980, the whole of the region was divided between two armed camps, the NF and the NCO. The scale of the armies was absolutely unprecedented in the whole long history of Campanian organised crime. So too was the scale of the bloodshed: an estimated 1,000 dead in the course of five years.

The battle in Campania in the early 1980s was a much messier affair than Shorty Riina's *coup d'état* in Sicily. Most of the confusion derived from the fact that Nuova Famiglia was a loose alliance rather than a single underworld organisation. It did use improvised initiation rituals. But that fact tells that its leaders were desperate to use any means they could to manufacture loyalty among the recruits they needed to stand up to the greatly superior numbers of the Nuova Camorra Organizzata. The Nuova Famiglia was held together (when it did hold together) only by its opposition to the Professor. Some of the underworld barons within it soft-pedalled on the war-making when it suited their own selfish purposes. Some switched sides halfway through. Cosa Nostra tried to manage the conflict from the outside, while going through a savage conflict of its own back in Palermo.

In 1980, Cosa Nostra first tried to drum up the kind of united resistance to Cutolo's ambitions that would have brought a quick end to the struggle. But the Commission found that even some of the Sicilian mafia's own affiliates in Campania were loath to throw men and money into a war. The leading tobacco smuggler Michele 'Mad Mike' Zaza had been one of the founding members of the anti-Cutolo alliance. But by now he preferred to strike a deal with the Professor based on dividing out territory: the Nuova Camorra Organizzata could have the province to itself, as long as it left the city alone. Lorenzo Nuvoletta, leader of the other Campanian Family of Cosa Nostra, probably had different motives. For narcotics were more important to him than the declining revenue from tobacco smuggling that the Professor wanted to tax.

Frustrated by this lack of warrior zeal, the Palermo Commission sent a killer to dispatch the Professor. But someone must have leaked news of the assassin's arrival, because the assassin himself was shot dead by two men on a motorbike not long after arriving in Naples.

In the summer of 1980 Cosa Nostra tried a different approach. Having failed to nudge Zaza and Nuvoletta into the attack, it urged them to broker an accommodation. But the resultant peace-making seems to have been almost as half-hearted as the war-making, for the cycle of punitive expeditions was not interrupted for long. In the end, Cosa Nostra would sponsor at least three peace conferences attended by large numbers of representatives from both the NCO and NF. Two of those conferences were attended personally by Shorty Riina and his lieutenants, despite the massacre that they were orchestrating in Sicily. But it was all in vain. Once started, the fighting in Campania proved too bitter to stop.

The camorra would go on to murder 364 people in 1982 – very nearly one a day. And lest the many innocent victims get lost in the tales of gangland retribution, it is worth citing the case of someone else who died in January 1982: Annamaria Esposito, aged thirty-three, a mother of two who was executed for the sole reason that she witnessed a *camorrista* being murdered in her bar.

A group portrait of the Nuova Famiglia bosses who were fighting against the Nuova Camorra Organizzata for control of this terri-tory tells us a great deal about the past, the present and the future of Campanian organised crime. The story of the camorra stretching forwards into the twenty-first century has its roots in the NF.

The camorra war of the early 1980s brought Pupetta Maresca back to the national headlines again. In 1955, she had first made herself notorious by killing the man who killed her husband, the President of Potato Prices. Pupetta's fame carried weight in the Campanian underworld. In 1970, she started a long-term relationship with a major narcotics trafficker, Umberto Ammaturo. With her new beau, Pupetta was able to turn her fame into a luxurious prominence as a *femmena 'e conseguenza* (a woman with stature), a First Lady of the underworld. The police believed that 'many of the crimes carried out by Umberto Ammaturo were, in reality, dreamed up in her head'.

Pupetta's consort, Umberto Ammaturo, was one of the most aggressive members of the NF. Near Christmas in 1981, he planted a bomb outside Cutolo's Ottaviano palace as a provocation. He would later confess to being the man behind the murder of criminal psychiatrist Aldo Semerari, whose beheaded corpse was also found near Cutolo's palace on April Fool's Day 1982. Raffaele 'the Professor' Cutolo demanded Ammaturo's own head as the price for any peace deal with the NF.

In February 1982, in the middle of this confrontation between Ammaturo and Cutolo, Pupetta Maresca's brother Ciro was arrested and sent to the very maw of the NCO monster: Poggioreale prison. Although he was kept in isolation, his life was in obvious and immediate danger. Pupetta's response showed that she had lost none of her gift for publicity. On 13 February 1982 she called a media conference, no less, in the Naples press association headquarters. Arriving alone, she made a statement entrance: nearly an hour late, her jewels sparkling as the camera flashbulbs ignited, she was dressed in a black leather skirt and black fur coat, with a leopard-skin choker at her throat and a white blouse that exposed her cleavage. No sooner had she come into the room than she started picking fights with the journalists, responding angrily to queries about her jewellery ('I'd like to see anyone with the courage to mug me') and then demanding order: 'Gentlemen, a bit of silence please! If Cutolo was here instead of me, you wouldn't be making such a racket. Of course, it's because you're afraid. He has shut your mouths with lead.'

The Professor was the target of her unrestrained rage: 'bastard', 'madman', 'he wants to become the emperor of the city'. When journalists asked Pupetta if she was speaking on behalf of the Nuova Famiglia, she replied: 'I'm not part of any group. But if some people think like I do – and you tell me that means the Nuova Famiglia – then they are my partners.'

Fighting back tears, she returned to the main purpose of the press conference: to issue an ultimatum to Cutolo. 'I want to let that gentleman know that, if he dares touch anyone close to me, I will destroy him and his family down to the seventh generation, women and children included.'

We can only wonder about the emotions that helped drive this extraordinary performance. Rage or sorrow? Defiance or fear? Nor do we have an idea whether these emotions were real or staged. Yet it seems certain that they were at least partially the symptom of the psychological strains of a lifetime spent as a camorra queen. Maresca enjoyed status and very probably real power. She also paid a heavy price. She had two children by Ammaturo, twins. She also lost a child: her first son Pasqualino (the baby she had been carrying during the notorious events of 1955) vanished in 1974 during the tobacco-smuggling war between Cosa Nostra and the Marseillais. Pupetta herself strongly suspected that Ammaturo had killed him. Yet she stayed with her man, either because he beat her (above the hairline, so the damage would not show) or because she was too attached to her furs and jewels.

The Professor was even less shy of publicity than Pupetta, and much better than her at getting under his enemies' skin. Dressed in a grey double-breasted suit, he issued his response to her challenge from a Naples courtroom: 'Maybe Pupetta said those things to attract attention. Maybe she wants to make another film. You have to say that she's chosen the right moment: Carnival kicks off in a few days' time.'

As the spat between Pupetta Maresca and the Professor demonstrated, the war in Naples was an extraordinarily *public* affair. In Sicily, where Shorty Riina's death squads emerged from nowhere to exterminate his enemies, the citizenry and even the police struggled to make out who was fighting whom. In Campania, by contrast, there were open challenges and proclamations, and nobody was in any doubt where the battle lines were drawn. These contrasting styles of warfare corresponded to a long-standing difference between the public images of the two crime fraternities. The soberly dressed Sicilian *mafioso* has traditionally had a much lower public profile than the *camorrista*. *Mafiosi* are so used to infiltrating the state and the ruling elite that they prefer to blend into the background rather than strike poses of defiance against the authorities. The authorities, after all, were often on their side. *Camorristi*, by contrast, often played to an audience.

There is no clearer illustration of this point than the Giulianos, a clan centred on Pio Vittorio Giuliano and a number of his eleven children, plus some of their male cousins. With its criminal roots in the smuggling boom that took place during the Allied military occupation, the family hailed from Naples's notorious 'kasbah', Forcella.

The Giulianos' reign would persist into the 1980s and 1990s, when the clan eventually began to fall apart amid arrests, deaths and defections to the state. The brashness of their power – the family occupied an apartment block that loomed like the prow of a huge ship at a fork in the road at the very centre of Forcella – would not have been unfamiliar to nineteenth-century *camorristi* with their gold rings, braided waistcoats and flared trousers.

The second Giuliano boy. Luigi (born in 1949), took charge of the family business in his twenties. He was a wannabe actor and poet, a medallion man whose success with the ladies earned him the nickname 'Lovigino' – an untranslatable coupling of the English word 'Love' and the affectionate form of Luigi. Lovigino's menacing good looks and his startlingly blue irises explain his other moniker: 'Ice Eyes'.

It is no coincidence that the Giulianos have left many eloquent photographs of their pomp. By far the most famous image from the Giuliano family album was confiscated during a police raid in February 1986. It shows two of the curly-haired Giuliano boys, Carmine 'the Lion' in a bright red V-neck, and Guglielmo 'the Crooked One' in white jeans. Both are beaming with delight as they recline in the most flamboyant bathtub in the history of plumbing: it takes the form of a giant conch-shell, its top half lifted back to reveal a gold-leaf interior, its surround in black stone, its base in pink marble with a pattern like stone-washed jeans. But the most remarkable thing about the photo is not the questionable taste of the Giulianos' bathroom fixtures and fittings. Lounging between the brothers is a muscular little man wearing a grey and red tracksuit and an even bigger grin than them: Diego Armando Maradona, the greatest talent ever to lace up a pair of football boots.

Argentinian superstar Maradona played for Napoli at his peak, between 1984 and 1992, and won the Serie A national championship twice. He became a demigod in the city, worshipped as no other sportsman anywhere has ever been: still now, his picture adorns half the bars in Naples. The notorious bathtub photo was not the only occasion during his time in the sky-blue shirt of Napoli when his name was associated with organised crime. In March 1989, he put in an appearance at the swish restaurant where Lovigino's cousin was getting married: 'Maradona at the boss's wedding' ran one headline. Four months later, he claimed that the camorra was threatening him and his family, and that he was too afraid to return to Naples for the start of the new season. There were unsubstantiated rumours of match-fixing. This was the summer when the conch-shell bathtub photo was made public. (Mysteriously, it was kept in a drawer in police headquarters for over three years.) It is also worth recalling that it was in Naples that Maradona's well-documented problems with cocaine took a grip.

At the time, 'the Hand of God' denied knowing that the Giulianos were gangsters. His autobiography, published in 2000, is more forthcoming:

> I admit it was a seductive world. It was something new for us Argentinians: the Mafia. It was fascinating to watch . . . They offered me visits to fan clubs, gave me watches, that was the link we had. But if I saw it wasn't all above board I didn't accept. Even so it was an incredible time: whenever I went to one of those clubs they gave me gold Rolexes, cars . . . I asked them: 'But what do I have to do?' They said: *Nothing, just have your picture taken*. 'Thank you,' I would say.

The point here is not whether Maradona's links to organised crime were more substantial than he claims. His very visible friendship with the Giulianos was more than enough for their purposes. Many *camorristi*, particularly urban *camorristi*, have always sought good publicity; they have always sought to win the admiration of the section of the Neapolitan population that identifies with well-meaning miscreants. Whether by loud, expensive clothes and flagrant generosity, by shows of piety, by grand public funerals and weddings, or by rubbing shoulders with singers and sportsmen, generations of *camorristi* have won legitimacy in the eyes of the very people they exploit. Maradona's own story, as the pocket genius risen from a shanty suburb of Buenos Aires, was a perfect fit with the camorra's traditional claim that it was rooted in, and justified by, poverty. If the camorra from the slums of Naples had an official ideology, it would be the kind of cod sociology that Lovigino 'Ice Eyes' Giuliano himself articulated:

> In Forcella it isn't possible to live without breaking the state's laws. But we Forcella folk aren't to blame. The blame goes to the people who prevent us doing a normal job. Because no one from a normal company is prepared to take on someone from Forcella, we are forced to find a way to get by.

Needless to say, 'getting by' involved extorting money from every money-making activity in Forcella; it involved illegal lotteries and ticket touting for Napoli games; it involved mass-producing fake branded clothes; it involved theft and drug dealing on a huge scale; and it involved appalling acts of violence. When Lovigino 'Ice Eyes' eventually turned state's evidence in 2002, he confessed to the murder of an NCO killer called Giacomo Frattini. Frattini's fresh-faced looks earned him the nickname of *Bambulella* – Doll Face – despite a body covered in jailhouse tattoos. The NF spent a long time planning what they would do to him. One idea was to crucify him in front of the Professor's palace on the slopes of Mount Vesuvius. In the end, in January 1982, an execution party lured him into a trap, tortured him, and then summoned a friendly butcher to lop off his head and hands and cut out his heart. They left the pieces in separate plastic bags in a FIAT 500 Belvedere just off piazza Carlo III. A note from an imaginary left-wing terrorist group was left in a telephone box nearby: it called him the 'prison executioner', the slave of a 'demented, diabetic fanatic' – meaning Raffaele 'the Professor' Cutolo.

Being flash like the Giulianos has never been the only style of criminal authority in Naples. Historically, the area to the city's north is home to a quieter brand of *camorrista* who would also become part of the Nuova Famiglia.

Marano is a small agricultural centre that has long been notorious for camorra influence. In 1955, the son of the town's former mayor, Gaetano Orlando, shot dead Big Pasquale, the 'President of Potato Prices'. During the 1970s and 1980s, Gaetano Orlando's nephews, Lorenzo, Gaetano, Angelo and Ciro Nuvoletta, became the most powerful criminals in Campania. They were initiated into Cosa Nostra during the tobacco-smuggling boom. Their farmhouse, which stood shrouded by trees on a hill just outside town, was the theatre of all the most important meetings during the war between the NCO and the NF.

The Nuvolettas preferred the subdued public image of their brethren in Cosa Nostra. Their wealth was vast, and as was the case with the many criminal fortunes built in the same part of Campania over the previous century, it straddled the divide between lawful business and crime. The clan earned from construction as well as smuggling, property as well as extortion, farming as well as fraud. Sicilian heroin broker Gaspare 'Mr Champagne' Mutolo was initiated into Cosa Nostra on the Nuvolettas' farm. He saw their riches at first hand: they had vast hangars of battery hens because they had a contract to feed all the military barracks in Naples. Thus, even during the new wealth of the 1970s, *camorristi* from the hinterland had not relinquished their traditional grip on the city's food supplies.

This combination of lawful and illegal income explains the Nuvolettas' preference for passing unobserved. For all their riches, their profile was so low that when, in December 1979, the *Carabinieri* captured Corleone *mafioso* Leoluca Bagarella in possession of a photograph of a businessman with salt-and-pepper hair, it took them months to put Lorenzo Nuvoletta's name to the face. No wonder, then, that Lorenzo Nuvoletta was entrusted with being the *capomandamento* ('precinct boss') of the three Campanian Families of Cosa Nostra, the man whose job was to represent Neapolitan interests to the Palermo

Commission, through his prime contact, Michele 'the Pope' Greco.

So the Nuova Famiglia reflected all the traditional diversity of organised crime in Naples and Campania. And that diversity also explains why it seemed that the atrocities might carry on without anyone ever achieving a military victory.

Catastrophe economy

Giuseppe Tornatore's 1986 film *Il camorrista* is a rambling, rise-and-fall gangster melodrama based on the career of Raffaele 'the Professor' Cutolo. It plays back the embellished highlights of the Nuova Camorra Organizzata story to a soundtrack of plaintive trumpet and clarinet melodies that owe more than a little to *The Godfather*'s genre-defining score. Since *Il camorrista* first came out in 1986, endless reshowings through local TV, bootleg videos, and now YouTube, have irretrievably confused reality and myth in the popular memory of the Professor's reign. The movie's most resonant lines ('Tell the Professor I did not betray him' and 'Malacarne is a cardboard *guappo*') have become slogans – the Neapolitan equivalent of 'I'll make him an offer he can't refuse' and 'Leave the gun, take the *cannoli*.'

Perhaps *Il camorrista*'s most visually arresting scene takes place in prison. The Professor is shown reading a history book in bed, in an immaculately pressed pair of sky-blue pyjamas. A low rumble in the background causes him to look up. The rumble becomes a shaking: first the ornaments on his bedside chest vibrate, then his metal bed frame starts clanking repeatedly against the wall, and his cell window shatters. Wails of panic rise in the background: 'Earthquake!' Staggering to his feet, Cutolo opens his cell door to watch Poggioreale prison plunge into anarchy. Clouds of dust rise from the floor of his wing, and chunks of plaster drop from the ceiling. The guards run hither and thither releasing screaming inmates from the cells. Within seconds, Cutolo has his arms around his two chief enforcers: 'This is a chance sent to us by the Lord above! It's gotta be the apocalypse for the old camorra!'

There then follows a ghastly chiaroscuro carnival of stabbings, clubbings, lynchings and garrottings, as Cutolo's men take advantage of the chaos to dispatch their enemies. From the din and mass panic inside the prison, we then cut to the morning after, to watch a dozen or so pine coffins being loaded into vans in the prison yard.

The earthquake of 23 November 1980 was no cinematic fantasy. With its epicentre in the mountains east of Naples, it killed 2,914 people across Campania. But the film director's job is what it is: Tornatore used a deal of artistic licence when he edited the disaster into his mob movie. The historian's job being what it is, I must indicate a couple of the points at which art and fact diverge. The numbers murdered for example: there were 'only' three fatalities in Poggioreale; plus another three on 14 February 1981 when Cutolo's men went hunting again following a major aftershock. Tornatore makes room for all the extra deaths by stretching the ninety seconds that the real quake lasted into nearly three minutes; he also adds in a few implausible thunderclaps and lightning flashes for effect. In reality, the reign of terror in Poggioreale was more prolonged. NCO killers did not pursue their victims while the quake itself was happening, but rather during the night that followed, after the guards abandoned many wings, leaving the rival criminal factions to battle it out.

Il camorrista embroiders the truth in more insidious ways than these. For example, it turns the squalid road-rage murder that earned Cutolo his first life sentence into an episode where he kills a man for groping his sister. Since the very origins of Italy's mafias, underworld prestige has constantly been confused in the public mind with the defence of women's sexual honour.

Yet even the most nit-picking historian would have to admit that Tornatore's artistic licence was justified in some cases. He was absolutely right to make the earthquake one of the movie's major set pieces, for example. The twenty-third of November 1980, when Cutolo, dressed in his silk dressing gown, directed his teams of killers to eliminate his enemies, was indeed an important date in the Nuova Camorra Organizzata's battle with its enemies. The reason the NF hated Giacomo 'Doll Face' Frattini so much that they beheaded him was because he was one of the Professor's prison killers in November 1980.

The earthquake also marked a seismic shift in the nature of camorra power in Naples. After the earthquake, because of the earthquake, the camorra at last joined the mafia and the 'ndrangheta in plundering the construction business and thereby merging with the political class. One of the many remarkable things about the Professor is that his organisation made that leap into construction while his war against the NF was still going on.

Back in the 1950s, Italy had great hopes that state investment could help the backward South industrialise. By the mid-1970s, the international economic crisis and a long history of politicking, corruption and incompetence in the allocation of the cash had brought these hopes to an end. Italian governments abandoned the long-term ideal of economic development and instead embraced the short-term aims of propping up consumer spending, while giving politicians enough money to keep their clienteles happy. From now on, the stream of taxpayer's money that went towards the South would no longer be directed in targeted squirts at training and infrastructure. Instead, it would descend as a fine drizzle of benefits and pensions. The same system would prevail even when the Italian economy recovered in the 1980s.

The earthquake of 23 November 1980 cruelly exposed Campania's ills. Prestigious buildings put up with central government money turned out to have been too shoddily built to resist the tremors. An entire wing of one public hospital in the village of Sant'Angelo dei Lombardi flopped to the ground, killing dozens. Clearly, in this, as in many other cases, distributing contracts and jobs had been a higher priority than actually providing an edifice worthy of the name.

The state's response to the challenges of post-earthquake reconstruction was a lesson in bad planning. The professed aim was not just to rebuild, but also to create new economic opportunities for the stricken area. But a proliferation of confused emergency laws created a messy ensemble of spending programmes. Powers and responsibilities were scattered among different special commissars, ministries, regions, provinces and town councils, so that it became impossible to monitor the reconstruction programme properly. Avid politicians rushed to cash in. Two months after the earthquake, in February 1981, 316 town councils were deemed eligible for reconstruction funds; nine months later, the total had risen to 686. The number of damaged buildings reported increased from 70,000 to more than 350,000 over roughly the same period. Either the earthquake had had some very peculiar delayed effects, or a lot of people were telling fibs about the extent of the destruction.

Actually spending the reconstruction money involved a multiplicity of official roles. Technicians to estimate the work required. Commissioners to evaluate those estimates on behalf of the town councils. Planners. Administrators who had to approve the planners' plans. Lawyers to draw up contracts. Construction entrepreneurs. Works supervisors and inspectors. And so on. But because the agencies given money to spend were largely unaccountable, many of these separate roles turned out to have been performed by the same people wearing different hats. Or by groups of friends. Or by narrow party cliques. The regime of emergency measures that had opened the door to these vultures turned into a permanent state of affairs.

The results of the shambles were grim. At the end of 1990, ten years after the quake struck, 28,572 people were still living in emergency caravans. Few of the thousands of jobs that were promised had materialised. Costs had skyrocketed. Parasites had made fortunes. And vast new political clienteles had been created. The earthquake gave birth to the worst financial scandal in 1980s Europe. But that scandal was only in its infancy when the most violent elements in Campania decided that they too could profit from the disaster.

The episode that exposed the camorra's links to the catastrophe economy was a terrorist kidnapping.

Ciro Cirillo stood at the very centre of the Christian Democrats' patronage system in Campania. After the 1980 earthquake, he was given responsibility for handling the massive funds channelled through the Campanian regional government for reconstruction. Soon afterwards, on the evening of 27 April 1981, he was abducted by the Naples column of the Red Brigades. Five *brigatisti* were waiting for him as he arrived in the underground garage of his house in Torre del Greco, a town lying on the strip of land between Mount Vesuvius and the sea. When Cirillo's bodyguard, as usual, stepped back outside to check that all was well, he was shot dead. Before the driver could react, he was also killed, and his secretary shot several times in the legs. Cirillo was pulled from the back seat, pistol-whipped, and led away.

Italy was by then grimly familiar with the routine of terrorist kidnappings. First the call to a newspaper to claim responsibility. Then a short interlude of worry and speculation: was the claim genuine? Then the proof. The afternoon after Cirillo was kidnapped, another call was made, this time to the editorial offices of *Il Mattino*, the biggest circulation daily in Naples. The instructions were terse: 'At number 275, Riviera di Chiaia, under a rubbish bin, you will find communiqué number one.' When it was retrieved, communiqué number one contained a Polaroid photo of the captive sitting in front of the crude, five-pointed star of the Red Brigades, and a slogan, 'The executioner will undergo a trial'. In nearly 150 typed pages of rambling pseudo-Marxist economico-political analysis of the state of Naples, Cirillo was described as 'the point man for imperialist reconstruction in the Naples metropolitan pole'.

The frightened face staring out from the Polaroid did not betray the power the BR attributed to him: a bald dome of a head, a toothbrush moustache and features too small for his face. Yet the *brigatisti* had chosen their target well, and despite their delusional ideology, there was a strategic intelligence to their 'Cirillo campaign' (as they termed it). The earthquake had left 50,000 homeless in Naples alone: the terrorists hoped to appeal to this pool of vulnerable and angry people. The BR's regular communiqués denounced the earthquake profiteers and railed against what it called 'deportation of proletarians' from the overcrowded and quake-damaged housing of the city centre. There were other acts of propaganda too: BR posters went up in areas where the caravans of the homeless were concentrated, and two more functionaries involved in the reconstruction were kneecapped. The BR subjected Cirillo to a 'people's trial', tapes of which were released to the media; it showcased DC greed and maladministration. The Christian Democrats in Campania had very good reason to worry. The kidnap victim was a man with many secrets: there was no telling what he might be terrified into saying while in the BR's hands.

On the face of it, Cirillo's chances of surviving his ordeal were not at all good. The DC was officially wedded to a policy of not negotiating with political kidnappers – the same policy that it had adopted when the Party Secretary Aldo Moro had been kidnapped in 1978. Moro ended up dead, as did many other victims. On 9 July 1981 yet another BR communiqué trumpeted that the people's trial had reached 'the only just verdict possible' and that Cirillo's death sentence was 'the most elevated humanitarian act in the circumstances'. He was doomed.

Then, at dawn on 24 July 1981, Cirillo was released, and the BR announced that they had received a ransom of 1 billion 450 thousand lire (€1.9 million in 2011).

The Interior Minister indignantly rejected the notion that Cirillo had been traded for money, saying that he had been freed 'without any negotiation and without any concession on the part of organs of the state faced with blackmail from an armed band'. It would take another twelve years for Italy to learn just how unfounded those denials were. The truth would only emerge after a succession of further denials, of unreliable testimonies, of murdered witnesses and destroyed evidence. During Cirillo's captivity, 'organs of the state' had not just negotiated with the Red Brigades. They had also negotiated with Raffaele 'the Professor' Cutolo's Nuova Camorra Organizzata.

The story goes something like this. A mere sixteen hours after Cirillo's disappearance, a secret agent from Italy's internal intelligence and security agency, SISDE, visited Raffaele Cutolo in prison in Ascoli Piceno. There were further meetings with Cutolo, when the agent was accompanied by two people. The first was a local mayor from Cirillo's faction of the DC who was close to the NCO. The second was the deputy leader of the NCO, Enzo Casillo. Known as *'o Nirone* ('Blacky') because of his dark hair, Casillo was the son of a trouser-factory owner; despite these comfortable origins, he had become the NCO's military chief during the war with the Nuova Famiglia.

After these initial meetings, Blacky Casillo and another senior officer in the Nuova Camorra Organizzata roamed the country over the coming weeks under the protective wing of the secret services so that they could take part in negotiation between the state, the BR and the NCO – as well as carrying on their duties in the camorra war.

Yet despite the best efforts of the secret agents of SISDE, the Professor remained standoffish. So a second phase in the negotiations opened on 9 May, when the military intelligence service, SISMI, took over. SISMI had no jurisdiction over domestic security issues, and thus no right to intervene in the Cirillo kidnapping. Nonetheless, things suddenly started to move. Imprisoned BR sympathisers were transferred to Ascoli Piceno to talk to the Professor, and then moved again to jails where BR leaders were being held. Blacky Casillo carried on his work as a roving mediator. Eventually, the ransom was paid and Cirillo was released.

The Cirillo affair illustrated the depths to which the Italian state sank in the course of the 1980s. 'Organs of the state' negotiated with left-wing terrorists through the good offices of the biggest criminal organisation in the country. A dastardly list of characters took part in the talks. The final phase of the negotiations was conducted by a wheeler-dealer called Francesco Pazienza, who had somehow become a consultant for SISMI. (Among other things, he would later be convicted for misleading investigations into the 1980 right-wing terror outrage at Bologna station in which eighty-five people were killed.) Through channels like these, money changed hands – money that the BR then used to pursue its campaign of murder and kidnapping. The DC's reconstruction money magus was saved. But shamefully and tragically, other victims paid the ultimate price instead of him.

Although a parliamentary inquiry could find no direct evidence of a *quid pro quo* between the secret services and the NCO, very big questions remain unanswered. The Cirillo story is made of many profoundly worrying suspicions and relatively few certainties. A great deal of murk remains. Here are two of the reasons why.

At the time of the Cirillo kidnapping, many senior officers in both SISDE and SISMI were members of the P2 Masonic lodge, which makes their motives very difficult to read. No combination of blackmail, right-wing subversion and corruption can be ruled out.

When Cirillo was released, in a semi-derelict building in the Poggioreale quarter of Naples, he flagged down a passing traffic police patrol. The orders were to take Cirillo straight to police headquarters where he could be cared for and interviewed by the magistrates investigating the kidnapping. But the journey had barely begun when the car was blocked off and surrounded by four more police cars. Citing orders from on high, the officer in charge of the four cars took Cirillo home instead. Once home, Cirillo was examined by a doctor who declared that he was in a state of shock and could not be interviewed by investigating magistrates. These health problems did not, however, prevent senior figures in the DC, including Flaminio Piccoli, the party's national leader, from going to see Cirillo forty-eight hours before the magistrates were eventually allowed access. The timing may have given Cirillo and his DC friends an opportunity to get their story straight about the whole negotiation saga.

What did the Professor have to gain from getting himself involved in the deal to free Cirillo? One thing he definitely pocketed was the chance to boast to the criminal world that he had the ear of the authorities. Irrespective of the real nature of any bargain behind Cirillo's release, the Professor could now present himself as a man with a seat at the top table. But did he receive anything else? And did he give the BR more than money? Several witnesses, including *brigatisti* and *camorristi* turned state's evidence, have cited a whole list of bargaining counters. Such people may of course have been lying. But there is nonetheless evidence to back up what they said.

Some *brigatisti* claimed that Cutolo passed them useful information on potential targets. There are facts that seem to support this allegation. On 15 July 1982, the BR machine-gunned police commander Antonio Ammaturo along with his driver Pasquale Paola. Ammaturo was a common enemy for both the BR and the NCO. He had investigated left-wing terrorism. Moreover, soon after being appointed to the Naples job, he had even had the impudence to raid the Professor's castle in Ottaviano – the first policeman to do so. Ammaturo was also probing into the Cirillo affair at the time of his death. When asked about the murder in court, the Professor was his usual, slippery self:

> I did not give the BR Ammaturo's name so that he could be killed. I'm not ruling out the fact that bumping him off would have been a pleasure for me. But I would have done it myself, directly, because it was a personal vendetta.

The likely scenario – one that illustrates the twisted logic in force in the shadows where violent subversion and violent crime overlapped – is that a left-wing terrorist group killed two good policemen on behalf of the NCO.

According to one *camorrista*, the Professor also converted his intervention as a mediator in the Cirillo affair into a series of favours that further extended his influence within the prison system. Hence, perhaps, the fact that on 27 October 1981, the Appeal Court in Naples ruled that Cutolo was 'semi-insane', and thus deserving of more lenient treatment.

But the biggest item on the Professor's shopping list was a slice of the earthquake reconstruction bonanza. It must be stressed that investigations did not reveal smoking-gun proof of such an exchange. Nevertheless, the courts ruled that entrepreneurs close to the NCO, including the Professor's own son Roberto, *were* awarded contracts worth sixty-seven billion lire (€129 million in 2011 values) to put up prefabricated housing in the Avellino area.

The question of reconstruction contracts leads us into the last, and most controversial, of the mysteries surrounding the Cirillo kidnapping: the question of who authorised the negotiations. Which politicians were involved, and how deeply?

A parliamentary inquiry would conclude that, while there had definitely been negotiations with the BR through Cirillo, there was no absolute proof that favours were exchanged as part of a deal. A number of senior Christian Democrats emerged with their reputations badly damaged by the verdict. For example Flaminio Piccoli, the party's national leader, *must* have known about the negotiations. Francesco Pazienza, the wheeler-dealer linked to right-wing terrorism who conducted the last phase of the bargaining, was a regular visitor to the DC leader's house. But the figure at the epicentre of the controversy, and one of the most powerful politicians in Campania, was Antonio Gava. Gava had just won his first national Cabinet post when Cirillo was kidnapped, and he went on to hold a series of senior Cabinet positions, including Interior Minister and Finance Minister, in the 1980s.

Gava was chief of the local DC faction whose main man on the ground was none other than Ciro Cirillo. Gava went on trial for having links with the camorra in 1993. No less than thirteen years passed before he was finally acquitted in 2006. Gava was suing for damages when he died in 2008. One cannot help but sympathise with the plight of a man on the receiving end of such an appallingly protracted judicial ordeal. Alas, such judicial sagas are all too common in Italy, particularly when it comes to the delicate business of ascertaining the relationship between organised crime and politics. However the final ruling that marked Gava's acquittal, for all its opaque legal phrasing, showed him in a very poor light indeed.

> The court maintains that it has proved with certainty that Gava was aware of the arrangement of functional reciprocity between local politicians in his faction of the DC and the camorra organisation . . . There is also proof that [Gava] did nothing incisive and concrete to fight or limit that situation, and that instead he ended up enjoying the electoral benefits it brought his political faction.

Gava's behaviour, the judges concluded, was morally and politically reprehensible, but he had done nothing to deserve a criminal conviction.

Camorristi had their hands on the post-earthquake reconstruction before the BR's 'Cirillo campaign' began. On 11 December 1980, a mere two and a half weeks after the quake, the mayor of one damaged town was shot dead because he tried to block companies linked to organised crime from winning rubble-clearing contracts. So the Cirillo kidnapping was ultimately only one symptom of the way the camorra seized hold of the opportunities that came with the disaster of 23 November 1980. In Sicily, the mafia war of the early 1980s was fought for control of the heroin pipeline to the United States. In Campania, the Nuova Camorra Organizzata and the Nuova Famiglia battled for control of the reconstruction riches.

Yet the Cirillo affair would prove to be decisive in another respect: it would bring about the final defeat of Raffaele 'the Professor' Cutolo.

On 18 March 1982 – eleven months after the Cirillo kidnapping, and with the mysteries surrounding it still unsolved – the Italian Communist Party daily *L'Unità* published what purported to be an Interior Ministry document that gave full details of the negotiations leading up to Cirillo's release. The letter turned out to be a fake – fake enough to cost the newspaper's editor his job. But many of the details it contained were true – true enough for a formal investigation into the negotiations leading to Cirillo's release to be launched. We now know that the Professor was the likely author of the fake. He created it because he did not feel that he had received his just reward for helping out in the Cirillo kidnapping affair. Leaking the letter to the opposition press was a sly way of sending a warning: if the Professor did not get what he wanted, new revelations, documented revelations, would follow.

The letter backfired horribly. The President of the Republic, outraged by the stories of Cutolo's cushy life behind bars that were then beginning to emerge, arranged for him to be sent to the forbidding prison island of Asinara. From now on, communicating with the rest of the NCO would be impossible. The Nuova Famiglia moved in for the kill. Within days of Cutolo's being transferred to Asinara, Alfonso Rosanova, the construction entrepreneur who managed the business arm of the NCO, was shot dead in the Salerno hospital where he was recovering from a previous attempt on his life; six or seven killers entered the building, disarmed the policemen on duty at his bedside, and shot him many times where he lay. In January 1983 came the mortal blow, when Enzo 'Blacky' Casillo – the Professor's top military commander and the roving negotiator of the Cirillo affair – was blown to pieces by a car bomb in Rome. The Nuova

Famiglia officer who rigged the booby trap would later turn state's evidence and explain to a parliamentary inquiry why Casillo was dispatched in such a spectacular fashion. The message in the murder, he explained, was 'to demonstrate to Cutolo that he was finished, and that he had to stop once and for all with blackmailing the politicians or the people in the state institutions that he had dealt with during the Cirillo kidnapping business'. The same *camorrista* also suspected that the secret services had been the source of the information that allowed him to identify where Blacky Casillo lived.

The Professor had overplayed the hand he had been dealt in the Cirillo affair. The Nuova Famiglia were now determined to punish him, and thereby win over his political friends. The Nuova Camorra Organizzata began to fall apart. Leaderless, Cutolo's zealous young followers were slaughtered by the Nuova Famiglia's well-organised hit squads.

The Professor's legacy was nonetheless enormous. His reign saw the camorra reach a level of wealth and influence that bore comparison with the mafias of Calabria and Sicily. He also had lasting effects outside his own region of Campania. Indeed, the Professor was one of the main reasons why Italy witnessed the birth of two entirely new mafias.

The Magliana Band and the Sacred United Crown

The late 1970s and 1980s were not just a period of record violence within Italy's historic mafias. They were also a time when, for the first time in a century, entirely new criminal organisations were created in regions outside the home turf of the Sicilian mafia, the Neapolitan camorra and the Calabrian 'ndrangheta.

Rome was a special case when it came to the spread of mafia power. All three major mafias were present there, kidnapping, dealing in drugs, laundering money, and the rest. Yet none of the three tried to oust the others. Contrary to what one might expect of such ferocious clans, there was no direct military confrontation between *camorristi*, *mafiosi* and *'ndranghetisti* on Roman soil. In Rome, as elsewhere, the three major mafias preferred to profit from peaceful cohabitation rather than endure the costs and dangers of a 'foreign' war. The capital became a kind of free port of criminal influence, its riches open to all for exploitation. In those peculiar circumstances, Rome generated a criminal fraternity of its own in the late 1970s – one entirely independent from the mafia, the camorra and the 'ndrangheta, although deeply indebted to them when it came to methods and contacts.

On 7 November 1977 Duke Massimiliano Grazioli Lante della Rovere, the former owner of Rome's major newspaper, *Il Messaggero*, was kidnapped just outside the city. One night the following March, after months of negotiations, his son heaved a bag containing two billion lire (more than €7 million in 2011 values) over the parapet of a road bridge. From below came a voice: 'Go home and wait. Your father will be freed in a few hours.'

The Duke was never freed. In fact, when the ransom was handed over he was already dead, killed by his kidnappers because he had seen one of them without a mask. His body was propped in a chair, his eyes forced open, and a recent newspaper lodged in his hands so that a photograph proving that he was alive could be sent to his relatives.

The macabre abduction of Duke Grazioli was the first major action carried out by a group named the Banda della Magliana (the Magliana Band), after the newly built suburban neighbourhood of Rome whence some of its members came. The Banda della Magliana's chiefs – variously loan sharks, drug dealers, fences and particularly armed robbers – explicitly set themselves the goal of dominating the capital's underworld. Before long, they achieved their aim.

The Banda della Magliana bore many similarities to the mafias of Sicily and Calabria. Its leaders divided out the capital into districts for the purposes of drug distribution, and eliminated any dealers who refused to come under their control. They had a common fund, and used it to support imprisoned members and their families, to corrupt policemen and *Carabinieri*, and to make important friends. Like the traditional mafias, the Banda della Magliana decided its murders centrally, keeping in mind the organisation's strategic aims. They were also a 'holding company' that exploited opportunities for money-making wherever they came, reinvested their profits in new criminal ventures, and laundered cash through formally lawful ventures, notably property.

From its origins, the Banda della Magliana had an intense pattern of relationships with the traditional mafias. It sourced wholesale heroin from Cosa Nostra – both from the group close to Stefano Bontate and, once Bontate and his friends were exterminated, from Shorty Riina's *corleonesi*. As early as 1975, the police spotted one of the band's future leaders chatting in a Roman restaurant called Il Fungo with *'ndranghetisti* of the highest level, including Giuseppe Piromalli from Gioia Tauro and Paolo De Stefano from Reggio.

The Banda della Magliana also drew inspiration from the Nuova Camorra Organizzata. One of its founders had known the Professor in prison and was a great admirer. Some of the others shared his vision: as one would later confess, 'We decided to try and carry out the same operation in Rome that Raffaele Cutolo was carrying out in Naples.' In 1979, when the Professor was on the run after 'noisily wandering away' from Aversa asylum, he hired a whole floor of a hotel in Fiuggi, a spa town south of Rome, and there held discussions with the Banda della Magliana. The aim of the meeting was to 'find a strategy that was compatible with both groups' aims'. Shortly after the meeting, the Banda della Magliana deferentially did the Neapolitans a favour by disposing of a metallic green BMW 733 whose interior was covered in bloodstains – the blood in question had belonged to a construction entrepreneur that Cutolo himself had shot. The NCO and the Banda della Magliana shared a useful friendship with Aldo Semerari, the fascist subversive, ally of the secret services, and professor of forensic psychology who would end up being decapitated near Cutolo's Ottaviano villa. As with the NCO, the Banda della Magliana was offered the chance to take an active part in violent right-wing politics by Semerari; the Romans declined the offer but exchanged weapons for favours instead – just as the NCO had done.

Unlike the NCO or the traditional mafias of Sicily and Calabria, the Banda della Magliana did not use initiation rituals or arcane mythology. Perhaps partly for this reason, despite its wealth and its violence, it failed to set down roots for the long term: in that narrow sense, the Banda della Magliana did not constitute a mafia. By the mid-1980s, it had begun to fall apart, amid the kind of internecine bloodletting and rattings to the state that the traditional mafias have always shown a remarkable ability to survive.

The Sacra Corona Unita ('Sacred United Crown') or SCU is the mafia of Puglia, the region that forms the stacked 'heel' of the Italian boot. Its story begins in 1978 when the conflict between the Nuova Camorra Organizzata and the Nuova Famiglia got under way in neighbouring Campania. The prison authorities tried to defuse the tensions in prisons by moving camorra-affiliated inmates to facilities in other regions, including Puglia. Once installed in Puglian jails in numbers, the Professor's pupils quickly put themselves at the top of the jailbird pecking order, and then began to initiate local crooks into the NCO. In January 1979, Cutolo himself visited Puglia, and held a meeting in a hotel in Lucera at which he 'legalised' more than forty local criminals – meaning he put them through the Nuova Camorra Organizzata initiation ritual. At a second meeting, this time near Lecce, another ninety Puglian criminals were initiated.

In 1981 the Professor, by now back in prison, formally instituted a Puglian branch of the NCO, the Nuova Camorra Pugliese, whose leaders were obliged to kick back 40–50 per cent of their profits to Cutolo. Not content with trying to establish his hegemony over Campania, in other words, the Professor was trying to dominate the entire Puglian underworld too. But in Puglia, as in Campania, the Professor's megalomania was eventually thwarted. As the NCO began its slide to defeat in the wake of the Cirillo kidnapping, some Puglian *camorristi* increasingly hankered after greater autonomy.

The authorities found the first signs that something strange was happening in the Puglian criminal fraternity early in 1984 when a handwritten document was found in a prison cell. Entitled 'The S Code', it listed the articles of faith of a new brotherhood of crime called the Famiglia Salentina Libera (Free Family of Salento – Salento being the furthest part of the 'heel' of Italy). Article 7 of the S Code stipulated that the organisation's aim was 'never to allow any family from other regions to lord it over our territory'. The resistance to the Professor was beginning to take organisational form.

Just a few weeks later, in a prison in Bari, Puglia's biggest city, another statute of another new mafia was found: the Sacra Corona Unita. The statute's author, and SCU's founder and supreme leader, was a murderer called Giuseppe Rogoli. Rogoli was partly driven to found the SCU in 198 by a desire to resist the Nuova Camorra Organizzata's power in prison. As he would later remark:

> At the time, Cutolo's men felt like they were Lord God Almighty, and wherever they entered the prisons they wanted to commit abuses – things that didn't go down well with us. So a group of us, not just me, decided to constitute this Sacra Corona Unita in opposition to the NCO's excessive power in the prisons.

Looking for a counterweight to the Professor's influence in his region, Rogoli sought backing for his new fraternity from the 'ndrangheta. Rosarno 'ndrangheta boss Umberto Bellocco initiated Rogoli into the Calabrian mafia, and then dictated the rules of the Sacra Corona Unita to him. The Calabrians reserved the right to preside over the rituals that marked the promotion of SCU members to the highest ranks within the Puglian organisation, and also demanded the SCU's collaboration in a series of kidnappings. The SCU, in other words, was a semi-autonomous Puglian branch of the 'ndrangheta.

Rogoli's men embraced the SCU's borrowed mystical rituals with the zeal of converts. One of the new mafia's early leaders, Romano Oronzo, commissioned a painting crammed with the new mafia's symbols. The artist who took the commission would later describe it to a court:

> He wanted me to draw a triangle, the sign of the Holy Trinity, with Jesus's face and a dove, plus the world, and his own eyes, and a hand stopping a bolt of lightning. Before painting it, I asked him to explain why he wanted those themes, and he told me he felt that he had been sent by God to help the world.

Like the Professor whose power over Puglian territory he sought to resist, Rogoli built his organisation behind bars in the first instance, and then moved on to seek territorial dominance in the outside world. The SCU soon grew to absorb the Famiglia Salentina Libera, and unite criminals from all the provinces of Puglia.

The Sacra Corona Unita did not have a tranquil life, all the same. Members from different parts of Puglia were often reluctant to submit to Rogoli's authority. Rivalries over the growing income from narcotics were also a cause of friction. New mini-mafias were set up in Puglia in opposition to the SCU. In 1986, the internal wrangling had become so bad that Rogoli felt obliged to refound the SCU, renaming his new brainchild, imaginatively, the *Nuova* Sacra Corona Unita. The SCU was given a command body, the Società Riservatissima (or 'Very Confidential Society') which comprised eight senior bosses – 'eight unknown, invisible and well-armed men', in Rogoli's words. They were well armed because they could call on a dedicated death squad, paid for out of the organisation's central fund, to enforce discipline. But even these drastic measures did not stop the internecine conflict and fragmentation.

Thus the Sacra Corona Unita repeated the same basic developments that other mafias had been going through since the 1950s: more profits, greater centralisation and more bloody divisions. Between 1984 and 1992, the number of mafia-related homicides in Puglia tripled, from 45 to 135 per year.

The SCU is still an underworld force today, albeit one that has suffered some heavy blows in recent years. It is too early to tell whether the Sacra Corona Unita will pass the ultimate test of mafia longevity and allow some of its leaders to hand their authority down through the generations.

Puglia, like Rome, was a territory where all three major mafias had a presence. The region's Adriatic coast was a vital point of entry for bootleg cigarettes, as well as other illegal goods. Geographically speaking, it was in the back yard of the 'ndrangheta and the camorra. One of the striking things about the story of the Sacra Corona Unita is that, as in Rome, *camorristi*, *mafiosi* and *'ndranghetisti* did not come to blows on Puglian soil. There was even diplomatic cooperation between them. It seems that emissaries from the 'ndrangheta and Cosa Nostra were present as observers when the Professor ceremonially initiated ninety Puglian criminals in Lecce.

Nonetheless, Cosa Nostra, camorra and 'ndrangheta took different approaches to the business of operating on new terrain. As the number and power of mafia outposts in other regions grew during the 1960s and 1970s, through businesses like kidnapping and narcotics, one of the three showed itself to be markedly more successful than the other two at occupying new ground.

Perhaps surprisingly, given that it was the richest and most powerful of the mafias, Cosa Nostra showed only an intermittent interest in formally establishing branches in other regions. In various parts of Italy there were authorised *decine* (ten-man platoons) of Cosa Nostra which were mostly run and staffed by Sicilians. But when they left Sicily for whatever reason, Men of Honour tended *not* to set up their own formalised embassies. Instead, they got along very well by relying on their personal criminal prestige to bind collaborators in the local underworld to them on an ad hoc basis. That is just what Corleone *capo* Luciano Liggio did in the kidnapping phase of his career. Gaspare 'Mr Champagne' Mutolo operated in a similar way when he ran his heroin trafficking from a base near his prison in the Marche region.

Only in Naples were Families of Cosa Nostra established, and non-Sicilians like the Nuvolettas and Zazas put in charge. That unusual move was due to the importance of Naples as the 'El Dorado' of contraband cigarettes. And, as we have seen, Cosa Nostra's influence generated violent resistance from the Professor's NCO. It also spread resentment even among the Sicilian mafia's

Neapolitan allies. 'The Sicilians looked down their noses at us,' one camorra boss recalled. 'But what a race there was to suck up to Cosa Nostra. And you call these people *camorristi*! They were ready to offer their arses to the Sicilians just so they could feel a little bit stronger.'

Despite his opposition to the Sicilian influence in his homeland, Raffaele Cutolo adopted a centralised and rather dictatorial strategy when it came to operating outside Campania. Hence the Puglian branch of the Nuova Camorra Organizzata had to pay a heavy tribute to the Professor. His high-handedness backfired when the Sacra Corona Unita was formed to resist him.

The 'ndrangheta took a more subtle and yet also more thorough approach to the problem of expanding outside its home territory. It had powerful emissaries in Campania and Puglia. Yet none of the local criminal groups revolted against the Calabrian presence. Indeed, like the SCU's founder Giuseppe Rogoli, they actively sought it out. A minor mafia, the Rosa dei Venti ('Wind Rose') was set up in Lecce prison in 1990 and also asked for the 'ndrangheta's blessing. Clearly, recognition from Calabria was a great prize for newly formed gangs.

The 'ndrangheta is the mafia that has the richest and most complex repertoire of symbols, traditions, ranks and rituals: it has been collecting them since the nineteenth century. The 'ndrangheta is the last survivor of a broad kin group of Honoured Societies from the Italian mainland that included the original Honoured Society of Naples, and even an organisation called the Mala Vita (literally 'Bad Life', but more accurately, 'the Criminal Underworld'), which was a short-lived nineteenth-century forerunner of the Puglian mafia, the Sacra Corona Unita. Some of the most important new mafias of the 1970s and 1980s, including the NCO and the SCU, drew on the 'ndrangheta's great library of gangland style and structure.

Together with a great many business opportunities in drugs, kidnapping and the like, these cultural offerings were enough to satisfy both the Puglians of the SCU and the *'ndranghetisti* they adopted as sponsors. The 'ndrangheta, in short, preferred a hands-off approach. It did not want an empire, just a select band of reliable business partners. Perhaps 'franchising' is the best way to describe the Calabrian approach to the Puglian crime scene.

In the wealthy regions of the North, the 'ndrangheta had long been setting down roots through its involvement in construction and kidnapping. Here the 'ndrangheta spread directly and not by recognising local gangs like the SCU. By the 1980s, *'ndranghetisti* had established branches called Locals in many towns and cities across Lombardy and Piedmont. These northern colonies were closely linked to individual Locals back in Calabria by blood ties, organisation and business: through such channels a regular to-and-fro of drugs, money, assassins, fugitives and kidnap victims was established. Young men born into 'ndrangheta families in the North would come back home to be initiated into the brotherhood. The northern *'ndranghetisti* also met among themselves to settle disputes and make sure that Calabrian rules were applied. As one 'ndrangheta defector from the North testified:

> In 1982 I took part in a meeting of all the Locals in Piedmont. About 700 people were there . . . The reason for the meeting was because in Turin at that time many Calabrians who were affiliated to the 'ndrangheta were pimping – an activity that the 'ndrangheta considers dishonourable . . . It was decided to order the affiliates to stop pimping. And if they did not obey the order, they would either be expelled from the 'ndrangheta or physically eliminated.

The 'ndrangheta's strategy made it by far the most successful of the three major mafias in other regions. According to one Sicilian *mafioso* who did business in the North: 'In Piedmont, the Calabrians have taken over the region. The little groups of Sicilians don't give any trouble to their organisation.' The Calabrians were so confident in their power in the North that they accommodated groups of Sicilian *mafiosi* within their structure. The 'ndrangheta, once the poor relation of the mighty Sicilian mafia, had come a long, long way.

While all this was actually going on, the Italian authorities had very little idea of just how far the 'ndrangheta had spread. The Calabrian mafia's softly-softly brand of colonisation proved to be the right formula for expansion into the regions at the heart of the national economy.

However colonisation was not the only measure of mafia reach. The 'ndrangheta may have planted its piratical flag in towns and cities across the North, but Cosa Nostra's narco-dollars had earned it a place at the highest tables of Italian finance. Aldo Ravelli was a famously ruthless stockbroker who ran into trouble with the law on several occasions in the course of a career on the Milan Bourse that traversed the decades. In an interview he ordered to be published only after his death, he gave an insider's take on Italy's financial bourgeoisie, dividing it into three camps. The first was 'semi-clean'. The second was 'unscrupulous'. The third was the Sicilian mafia.

5

MARTYRS AND PENITENTS

Mafia terror

In the 1980s, the mafias achieved greater wealth, more awesome military power, a wider geographical range, and more profound penetration of the state apparatus than at any other moment in their long existence. The story of the people who stood against them at that time is the most tragic and most stirring page in the history of the Italian Republic. Its key dramas took place in the home of what was still the most dangerous of the mafias, Cosa Nostra. The years between 1979 and 1992 were Sicily's longest decade. The island had set the pace of organised crime history since long before the Second World War. Now it was to set the pace of the struggle against the mafias.

The tale told in the following pages was first reconstructed by investigators – the very people who were at the centre of the unfolding events. By journalists too: for many of them, the task of trying to make sense of what was happening around them with such fearful speed in the 1980s became a sacred cause more than a job. Since those terrible days, the story has been told and retold. It is there in the monuments to the fallen, in street names and plaques, and in the ceremonies that mark each passing anniversary of a mafia outrage. It is there in the famous video clips and photographs that have become icons of collective memory. Its grip on the public imagination is no mystery: this, after all, is a narrative that pits good against evil. Nor should we be surprised if, like all great stories, this one is sometimes emptied of its real meaning, hollowed into mere ritual by indifference, turned bland by the cynical lip-service of politicians, or by the cheesy conventions of television dramatisation. All the same, the truths of this story are far too important to be uncontroversial even today; its lingering mysteries still make headline news.

The people who died fighting Cosa Nostra during Sicily's longest decade were martyrs. The word may sound overblown. In those Western countries lucky enough to be able to treat the mafia as if it were little more than a movie genre, such vocabulary now belongs only to the mind-set of religious fanatics. But in the Italian context, it is the only word one can use. The martyrs of the struggle against mafia power died for a cause – one that in luckier European countries might seem banal: the rule of law. They also changed lives by setting an example for others to follow. Inspired by them, many young people found a calling in the police or magistracy – or simply by refusing to rub along with the mafia system that confronted them in their day-to-day lives.

The sacrifices made in the anti-mafia battle changed history too. For what happened in Sicily broke patterns that had remained obstinately in place since Italy first became one country in 1861. The most significant progress was in understanding the mafia. The struggle against Cosa Nostra was also a struggle to find out what it really was. In the 1970s, because more than a century of evidence had been covered up, neglected or forgotten, nobody really knew. Italy did not even know that the Sicilian mafia was called Cosa Nostra by its members. The most widely read academic study of the mafia at the time was written by a German sociologist and translated into Italian in 1973. Filled with penetrating insights into Sicily's social structure, the book was nonetheless dismissive of the suggestion that the mafia might be a secret society: only 'sensation-hungry journalists, confused northern Italian jurists, and foreign authors' made that mistake. There were *mafiosi* in Sicily, of course – mediators, protectors and thugs. But they were part of the island's culture. There was no single organisation that could be labelled 'the mafia'. The results of the most recent trials in the late 1960s seemed to back that view up. By 1992, however, such falsehoods had been decisively overturned: enough proof had been assembled to convince even Italy's Supreme Court to confirm that the Sicilian mafia was indeed a criminal organisation, a secret society. By the end of the longest decade, the Sicilian mafia's most astonishing crime – the claim that it did not even exist – had been exposed at long last.

The years of bloodshed and polemic in Palermo that led to that crucial Supreme Court verdict would have profound repercussions for the camorra and 'ndrangheta, and for Italy's entire criminal power system. In its wake, Italy established institutions whose very founding principle was the need to view the Italian underworld, with its connections to the 'upper world' of politics, the institutions and business, *as a whole*. Finally, after well over a century, the mafias would be viewed as aspects of the same underlying problems.

Such changes are unquestionably profound – profound enough to mark the long 1980s as the bloody passage between two entirely different eras in mafia history. Yet more time must pass before we can tell whether the progress made at such appalling cost is irreversible. That is why the titanic struggle between the mafia and the anti-mafia in those years is a story that must continue to be told. For it will retain its relevance, its urgency, until the day when Italy can say that the mafias have been vanquished for good.

Sicily's longest decade began with five high-profile murders in the space of nine months: 'eminent corpses', as they were called.

In Palermo, on 26 January 1979, Mario Francese was shot in the head outside his house. Francese was the crime correspondent of Sicily's main daily, the *Giornale di Sicilia*. With him when he died was his twenty-year-old son Giulio, who was just a few weeks into his own career as a journalist.

Six weeks later, on 9 March, Michele Reina, the leader of the Christian Democrat Party in the province of Palermo, died in a hail of dum-dum bullets at the wheel of his car. His wife, who was beside him, saw the killer grinning as he fired. Reina was the first post-war politician to be murdered by the Sicilian mafia; he left three young children.

The third assassination took place at the other end of the country, in the banking centre of Milan, on 11 July. Giorgio Ambrosoli, a lawyer, had been appointed by a court to dig into the affairs of disgraced Sicilian banker, Michele Sindona. A team of three killers was waiting for Ambrosoli when he got home late in the evening; he too left a wife and three small children.

Ten days later, back in Palermo, Boris Giuliano, the commander of the Flying Squad (a plainclothes investigative unit) was shot seven times at the counter of his local bar.

Cesare Terranova was a judge. On 25 September, he and his bodyguard, Lenin Mancuso, were gunned to death in their car. One witness said that the killers wore smiles on their faces.

A journalist, a politician, a financial lawyer, a policeman and a judge. Information, democracy, honest finance, law enforcement and justice. One after another, the mafia's smiling killers had attacked five pillars of Italian society.

None of these murders, taken in isolation, was entirely without precedent for the Sicilian mafia. But coming so close together they made clear an unmistakable and chilling new trend. Sicilian *mafiosi* had never launched such a systematic assault on representatives of the state. The institutions were infiltrated and corrupted, but they were not attacked head on. Now, suddenly, the mafia had taken a terrorist turn.

Comparisons between the mafia and the threat from subversives of right and left were on many commentators' lips during the season of terrorism known as the Years of Lead. Cosa Nostra itself had given them a cue. Following both the Reina and Terranova murders, the offices of *Giornale di Sicilia* received anonymous calls claiming to be from terrorist cells. The calls were fake, and intended to mislead investigators. But the parallel between the Sicilian mafia and the Red Brigades was far from spurious. Both killed journalists, politicians, lawyers, police and magistrates. Both arrogantly assumed themselves to be above the law. Both thought the Italian state was so weak, and so discredited, that it could simply be bullied into submission. Violence was used because violence would work – by now, it was part of the language of Italian public life. The Italian people could be relied upon to sit, arms folded, and watch as their country went down.

Yet within some of those murders from 1979 the signs of resistance against the mafia threat were also visible. Cosa Nostra was killing people it feared.

The journalist Mario Francese was a relentless investigator, one of the few journalists who sensed the growing menace of Shorty Riina and his *corleonesi*; he had even dared interview Riina's wife.

Giorgio Ambrosoli had discovered that Michele Sindona had been laundering the profits of the US heroin trade.

Boris Giuliano was a born policeman who had tracked down some of Cosa Nostra's heroin refineries. He also knew how to follow the mafia's money, and the money trail had led him into collaboration with the US Drug Enforcement Administration and to a clear conclusion: 'Palermo's mafia organisations have now become pivotal in heroin trafficking, the clearing house for the United States.'

Judge Terranova had led a large-scale prosecution of the mafia following the Ciaculli bomb outrage back in the 1960s. In 1974, he consigned Luciano Liggio, the boss of Corleone, to a life behind bars. Having spent several years in parliament as an independent MP under the wing of the Communist Party, he had just returned to Palermo, and to the judicial trenches of the anti-mafia struggle, when Cosa Nostra decided to kill him.

The death of Michele Reina, the DC politician, was much more difficult to interpret at the time. Only those closest to the mafia would have been able to decode the meaning in the murder. Everyone else had to be content with the rumours and theories that filled the newspapers. We now have a good idea which of those theories was closest to the truth. Reina was an ambitious man who had had brushes with the law. He had been educated politically in the heart of Palermo's DC machine. He was a 'Young Turk' who belonged to the faction of the party headed by Salvo Lima – one of Cosa Nostra's most reliable politicians. But now that he was local party chief, Reina's ambition had led him to begin thinking independently. He formed a coalition with the Communist Party: heresy for some. He declared that he wanted to be the leader of a DC that would 'no longer live for the construction industry and off the construction industry'. Dangerous talk: Reina had already received threats. Perhaps Reina does not deserve to be called a martyr, but his assassination was a chilling challenge to the state all the same. In the new era of mafia terror, the penalty for independent thinking in the Sicilian DC was death.

The five murders of 1979 amounted to a declaration of war: Cosa Nostra, for the first time in its history, was directly confronting the state – or at least those few people working within Italy's ramshackle government apparatus who embodied what the state ought to be.

And here lay the crucial *difference* between Cosa Nostra and the Red Brigades, a difference that made the former far, far more dangerous than the latter. The Red Brigades certainly had their spies and their sympathisers. All the same, they were *outside* a state that they wanted to overthrow. Active *brigatisti* operated from clandestine hideouts deep in the most anonymous quarters of Italian cities. Cosa Nostra, by contrast, was an integral part of the state – a state it now wanted to neuter and bend entirely to its own bloodthirsty, rapacious will. Active *mafiosi* operated from the very institutions where people like Mario Francese, Michele Reina, Giorgio Ambrosoli, Boris Giuliano and Cesare Terranova worked. For that reason, standing up to Cosa Nostra required a particular kind of heroism.

The following year, 1980, the assault continued: more eminent corpses fell. And new heroes emerged.

On 6 January, Piersanti Mattarella, the Christian Democrat leader of the Sicilian regional government – the most important politician on the island, in other words – was executed just as he got into his car to go to Mass with his wife and son. Mattarella had initiated a campaign to clean up the way government contracts were awarded. His wife saw the killer approach the car, and had time to plead with him not to shoot.

Emanuele Basile was a young captain who commanded the *Carabinieri* in Monreale, a hilltop town overlooking the Conca d'Oro. The night he was killed, 4 May, the streets were crowded, brightly lit and filled with the smell of nougat emanating from street stalls: it was the local festival of the Holy Crucifix. Basile, who was holding his four-year-old daughter Barbara in his arms at the time, was making his way home through the crowds when two assassins appeared behind him. His little daughter's hand was burned by a muzzle flash; miraculously, she was not otherwise hurt. Basile only had time to breathe 'help me' to his wife before he lost consciousness. He died a few hours later on the operating table.

Basile was investigating both the *corleonesi* and the narcotics trade with the United States. The magistrate who was working closely with him on those investigations – a gregarious, chain-smoking Palermitan with slicked-back hair and a trim, sloping moustache – was called Paolo Borsellino. Borsellino was devastated when they called him to break the news about his friend Basile. At forty years old, it was the first time his wife had ever seen him cry. The murder was not just a tragedy, it was also a message – a warning directed at Borsellino himself. But, faced with grief and fear, and the Sicilian mafia's declaration of war, Borsellino responded with resolve. As his wife would later recall, 'The Basile murder made me sure: I had married a man carved out of rock.' Her husband threw himself into his work. In the next few days, he became one of the first Palermo magistrates in the era of eminent corpses to be allocated an armed escort. Paolo Borsellino would go on to become one of the two great champions of the fight against Cosa Nostra.

Three months after the Basile murder, on 6 August 1980, Gaetano Costa, the quietly spoken Chief Prosecutor of Palermo, was shot several times in the face by a single killer who pulled a pistol from inside a rolled-up newspaper. Costa bled to death by a bookstand just across the street from the Teatro Massimo, the giant theatre that is one of Palermo's most famous landmarks. A veteran of the Resistance against the Nazis, he had recently put his name to arrest warrants related to an investigation into Cosa Nostra's biggest heroin traffickers.

As fate would have it, the investigating magistrate working on that very case was a childhood friend of Paolo Borsellino's who was also just getting used to living with the constant company of armed policemen in bulletproof vests. His name was Giovanni Falcone. Falcone's large, friendly face disguised the fact that he was much less outgoing than Borsellino. But he too was a man of granite courage and a voracious appetite for hard work. His meticulous and brilliant research into the finances of heroin trafficking had already unearthed the Sicilian mafia's business dealings with Neapolitan *camorristi* for the first time. Falcone had also encountered the insidious resistance that some of his colleagues put up against anyone who was too diligent. His direct superior had been warned in no uncertain terms by another judge that Falcone was 'ruining the Palermo economy', and that he should be loaded with ordinary casework to prevent him from digging too deep. When Falcone rushed to the scene of Costa's murder, a colleague muttered confidentially to him as he gazed down at the disfigured body: 'Well I never. I was absolutely sure it was your turn.' Giovanni Falcone was on the way to becoming Cosa Nostra's greatest enemy. With Paolo Borsellino, he would become a symbol of the struggle against the mafia. The story of the fight against Cosa Nostra in the 1980s and early 1990s is, in large measure, their story.

But to begin the work of challenging Cosa Nostra in earnest, and to do so within the framework of the law, Falcone and

Borsellino would need new tools. Directly and indirectly, those tools would emerge from the campaign against terrorism. The Italian state's struggle with the death-bringing idealists of the Red Brigades during the Years of Lead had crucial consequences for the history of organised crime.

In 1980 the state acquired its decisive weapon in the fight against the Red Brigades. Subsequently, the same weapon was deployed with devastating effect against the mafias.

Law number 15 of 6 February 1980 awarded sentence reductions to members of subversive organisations who provided evidence against fellow terrorists. The first member of the Red Brigades to take advantage of the new law, a carpenter's son called Patrizio Peci, began talking in April of the same year. Peci was the commander of the Red Brigade column in Turin, and his testimony almost completely dismantled the Red Brigades in the north-west.

Peci's story introduced a new and highly controversial figure to the drama of Italian public life: the *pentito*, or 'penitent', as the newspapers insisted on calling any terrorist who informed on his associates. In Italy, lawmakers and magistrates bristle at the very mention of the term 'penitent', and for good reason. 'Penitence' is one of the most powerful identity narratives in Christian civilisation: it tells of past sins acknowledged and transcended, of a joyful new life born from remorse. But the Christian psychology of penitence fits badly with the varying motives of *pentiti*. Trading secrets for freedom is often a self-interested business – even when it does bring valuable truths to light. Cold-blooded murderers can barter their time behind bars down to just a few years. Penitents also bring an obvious risk for the legal process: a *pentito* who can convincingly fabricate more evidence than he really knows may be rewarded with greater benefits. 'Penitent', then, is a controversial term for a controversial thing. (Which perhaps helps explain why none of the unwieldy alternatives – like 'collaborator with justice', and 'caller into complicity' – has ever really caught on.)

Yet, for many *pentiti*, the decision to betray former colleagues is an agonising one. (Which is another reason why the term 'penitent' is inadequate, although inevitable.) Patrizio Peci's decision to collaborate with the state was born of a profound disillusionment with the cause he had killed for. But he contemplated suicide when, after his tip-off, *Carabinieri* got into a firefight with four *brigatisti* in Genoa, killing them all, including two of his closest friends. Peci also paid a terrible price for his repentance when the Red Brigades kidnapped his brother Roberto, subjected him to a 'proletarian trial', and murdered him. Horrifyingly, they even filmed the execution as a deterrent to others. Such inhuman cruelty was powered by the loathing that penitents inspired in those they betrayed. Penitents were more than stool pigeons: they were *infami* – vile, unholy, scum. When *mafiosi* began to turn *pentiti* as terrorists had done, the moral ambiguities, psychological tensions and vindictive violence surrounding judicial repentance were all magnified.

The Red Brigade penitents who braved the loathing of their former comrades encountered a state that was better equipped to make use of their evidence than it had ever been. Italy's police, particularly the *Carabinieri*, learned to operate in specialised, specially trained teams against the terrorists, and they emerged from the fight with a greatly enhanced reputation.

During the Years of Lead, the Italian judicial system also came of age. *In theory*, since the Constitution of the Italian Republic was promulgated in 1948, magistrates and judges had been free from political interference, subject only to their own governing body. *In practice*, genuine judicial independence took much longer to arrive. During the 1960s, the expanding education system and the selection of magistrates through public examinations made a career in the legal system an option for bright young people from many different backgrounds. As a result, the magistracy was becoming less of a caste and more of an open profession.

Some of the magistrates who went to university in the 1960s were the legal professionals who stood in the front line during the Years of Lead. Like the senior police officers, they ran terrible risks: their movements were constantly trailed by terrorist cells spying out any opportunity to strike. The successes that the state eventually won against left-wing terrorism gave the legal system a store of credibility that it could then draw on when taking the fight to Italy's bastions of illicit privilege – corrupt politicians and the mafias.

In Sicily, the conflict within Cosa Nostra that had been rumbling since 1978 exploded in the spring of 1981 when Shorty Riina launched his assault on the mafia's heroin elite. Meanwhile, on the mainland, the Nuova Camorra Organizzata and the Nuova Famiglia were scattering Campania with cadavers. The first penitents from criminal organisations would be born of the carnage.

The fatal combination

Anywhere else in the world, Pio La Torre and Carlo Alberto Dalla Chiesa would have been enemies: the one, a Sicilian Communist militant devoted to radical social change; the other, a rigorous northern military man devoted to defending society from subversives. Cosa Nostra turned them into allies. Then in 1982, Cosa Nostra killed them both.

Few people knew the Sicilian mafia more intimately than Pio La Torre. He was born in 1927 in the village of Altarello di Baida, set among the mafia-controlled lemon groves of Palermo's Conca d'Oro. Life was hard. His father kept a few animals to top up what he could earn as a farm hand. With a stubbornness that would characterise him for the rest of his life, Pio studied by candlelight, laboured to cover his living costs, and worked his way into university. There, in 1945, he joined the Communist Party, soon rising to be a local leader of the Communist agricultural workers' union. He gained his first experience of political action – and had his first set-to with the mafia – during the post-war peasant struggle for control of the land. The local boss, always on the lookout for talent, sidled up to him during an election campaign: 'You're an intelligent lad. You'll go far. You just have to come with us . . . ' Soon afterwards, the mafia made Pio an offer through his father: he could become a Member of Parliament straight away – all he had to do was change his political colours. 'We just can't stomach this party. Over there in Russia maybe . . . But in Italy, we just don't do that kind of thing.' When La Torre refused, his father woke one morning to find the cowshed door ablaze. The warnings were clear: Pio had to choose between his home and his politics. He packed his bags.

These were acutely dangerous years to be a left-wing militant in western Sicily. Dozens of trades unionists and political activists were murdered by *mafiosi* or by Salvatore Giuliano's bandit gang. In March 1948 Placido Rizzotto, a union leader from the mafia stronghold of Corleone, vanished. La Torre went to take his place. In March 1950, La Torre led several thousand peasants from nearby Bisacquino on a march to occupy part of an undercultivated estate. Along with 180 others he was arrested, and charged with violent conduct based on the false testimony of a *Carabiniere*. He would spend a terrifying eighteen months in Palermo's Ucciardone prison – confined with members of Salvatore Giuliano's gang, among others – before his case even came to trial.

Pio La Torre encapsulated a tradition of Sicilian peasant militancy, and of opposition to the mafia, that went back to the nineteenth century. Again and again, just like La Torre, the peasants had found their hunger for land and a decent living thwarted by a *de facto* alliance between the landowners, the police and the mafia. In the fight for social justice, the rule of law was a mask for repression, and the state was not an ally but an enemy.

But in those earliest years of his career as a militant, Pio La Torre also encountered another face of the Italian state, and a very different tradition of opposition to the mafia – one rooted not in the radical aspirations of the peasantry, but in the patriotic, conservative instincts of the forces of law and order. In 1949, when La Torre first went to serve the proletarian cause in Corleone, he found that a young Captain of the *Carabinieri* had been posted there too: Carlo Alberto Dalla Chiesa.

There is one vignette that captures, better than any description, the value system into which Carlo Alberto Dalla Chiesa was born – and the enormous cultural distance that separated him from Pio La Torre. In 1945, he and his brother Romolo, both of them lieutenants in the *Carabinieri*, both of them in uniform, were waiting anxiously for their father's train to pull into Milan station. The reunion was no ordinary one: General Romano Dalla

Chiesa was due to arrive home from a concentration camp. Back in September 1943, Italy had capitulated to the Allies, and the Nazis set up a puppet regime. Like many military men, the General faced a choice between enlisting on the German side or being interned: he opted for the latter, and he had not seen his family since.

At last, the train pulled in, and the two Dalla Chiesa boys saw their father's emaciated figure emerge from the crowd on the platform. Carlo Alberto clicked his heels, stood to attention, and snapped his hand to the peak of his cap. But the emotion of the occasion overcame Romolo, who threw himself into his father's arms.

The following day General Romano Dalla Chiesa sent Romolo a disciplinary notice. *Carabiniere* regulations explicitly state that an officer in uniform may not embrace anyone in public.

Carlo Alberto Dalla Chiesa was a man cut from the same military-issue serge as his father. Like his father, he had faced a stark choice in the terrible September of 1943. At the time, he was billeted in a villa on the Adriatic, charged with supervising the coastguard. When he refused to join the hunt for partisans, the SS came to arrest him. Warned just in time, Dalla Chiesa escaped from a first-floor window and out into the open country-side. He organised a partisan band, and then in the winter of 1943 passed through the battle lines to resume his duties in the liberated South.

Dalla Chiesa had a family connection with Sicily, because his father was a veteran of the Fascist campaigns against the mafia in the 1920s. Two decades later, Carlo Alberto volunteered to join the special force set up to combat banditry on the island. When he reached Corleone, he made a promise to the family of the vanished trade unionist Placido Rizzotto that he would find out who had killed their son. Rizzotto, like Dalla Chiesa, was a former fighter in the Resistance against the Nazis. Thanks to Dalla Chiesa's sleuthing, the wall of *omertà* began to crumble, parts of Rizzotto's body were recovered, and a report – naming an up-and-coming young *mafioso* called Luciano Liggio as the killer – was sent to the prosecuting authorities. Alas, the two key witnesses were intimidated into retracting their statements, and Liggio was released: a dispiriting reprise of countless mafia trials of the past, and a foreshadowing of many more still to come. All the same, Dalla Chiesa's determination would remain impressed in the memory of Corleone's peasants.

After Corleone, Pio La Torre and Carlo Alberto Dalla Chiesa would continue to cross paths. When he was released from prison, La Torre was elected to Palermo city council, where he spent the years of the Sack of Palermo denouncing the corrupt goings-on within the ruling DC. As a trade-union militant, he also campaigned against mafia influence in Palermo docks, where big companies used bosses to recruit casual labour. In 1962 he was elected to the regional leadership of the Communist Party in Sicily, and the following year he won a seat in the Sicilian Regional Assembly. At the end of the 1960s he took up a national role within his party, and in 1972 he became a Member of Parliament, where he took a particularly energetic role in the last years of the parliamentary inquiry into the Sicilian mafia.

Carlo Alberto Dalla Chiesa testified before the inquiry, by virtue of being commander of the *Carabinieri* legion in Palermo between 1966 and 1973. He provided some of the inquiry's most explosive evidence against mafia-backed politicians, and compiled reports on, among others, the 'Concrete King', Ciccio Vassallo.

In 1974 Dalla Chiesa was promoted to General, and appointed to a command in north-western Italy, where he created a specialised anti-terrorist unit to combat the Red Brigades. After the kidnap and murder of former Prime Minister Aldo Moro in 1978, Dalla Chiesa became the prime figure in the fight against left-wing terrorism nationally. Dalla Chiesa it was who convinced Patrizio Peci to become the first *brigatista* to turn penitent. The

General was number two on the Red Brigades' death list in the motor city of Turin – a list that Peci had helped draw up. (Number one was the FIAT dynast Gianni Agnelli.) He knew that Peci had tried several times to kill him, and yet dealt with his prisoner in a humane and professional fashion. Dalla Chiesa personally guaranteed the penitent's safety while he was in prison, and came to visit him after the Red Brigades tortured his brother to death. As Peci later recalled: 'His manner was severe but gentle, authoritative but kind. He never treated you with familiarity, but he didn't make you feel like a shit either . . . I came to admire him more and more: for his character, confidence, imagination and ability to command.'

Peci's information led to the dismantling of most of the Red Brigades' structure, and made Dalla Chiesa, with his salt-and-pepper moustache set over stern jowls, a famous face and a national hero. At the close of 1981 he was appointed deputy commander of the *Carabinieri* nationally. Then, in April of the following year, with a nation's plaudits still ringing in his ears, General Carlo Alberto Dalla Chiesa was sent to Sicily to break the mafia in the same way that he had broken the Red Brigades.

In Palermo, there was a bloodbath: Riina's savage mafia coup was in full swing, and the eminent corpses were continuing to fall. One of the most vocal supporters of Dalla Chiesa's appointment as Prefect of Palermo was Pio La Torre, who had also recently returned to his native city, drawn back by the mafia crisis and by the decision to allow the United States to base new Cruise missiles at an airbase in the south-east of Sicily.

La Torre was still busy lobbying in support of new anti-mafia legislation that he had proposed the previous year. The planned law was based on the Racketeer Influenced and Corrupt Organizations (RICO) Act that had done such damage to the mafia in the United States since it came into effect there in 1970. The key law enforcement tools that La Torre wanted were two: heavy sentences for anyone proved to be a member of an organisation that used intimidation and *omertà* to gain control of companies and public resources; and the power to confiscate the mafia's illegally acquired wealth. The political irony in La Torre's proposal was clear: once again, it was the Communists who were the keenest to learn lessons from Uncle Sam's experience in fighting organised crime.

A short time before taking up his post as Prefect of Palermo, Carlo Alberto Dalla Chiesa wrote to his sons about what lay ahead. His hopes were high: 'In a couple of years, La Torre and I should be able to get the most important things done.' Faced with unprecedented slaughter in Sicily, the two great but divergent traditions of resistance to mafia power were set to unite their forces after more than a century of suspicion and misunderstanding. Honest Sicilians of all political persuasions would see their champions working together.

Dalla Chiesa's first official duty as Prefect of Palermo was to attend Pio La Torre's funeral. On 30 April 1982, La Torre was trapped in his car in a machine-gun ambush. The driver, Rosario Di Salvo, managed to get off four futile shots against the attackers before dying alongside his great friend. Di Salvo was not a police bodyguard, but a Communist Party volunteer.

Pio La Torre's murder prompted what was now a horrendously familiar public ritual in Palermo. First, on the front pages of the dailies and in TV news bulletins, there would be the macabre images of the victims slumped in ungainly postures in a pool of blood or a bullet-pocked car. Then there came the formulaic condemnations by politicians momentarily distracted from the business of jostling for position and influence. Then finally the funeral, with senior statesmen – representatives of a state that was patently not doing its job – forced to risk the wrath of the mourners and public. (One leading Sicilian politician who tried to speak at La Torre's funeral was heckled with cries of 'Get lost, *mafioso!*')

To anyone with eyes to see, it was clear that Sicilian *mafiosi* were systematically decapitating that part of the state that stood in the way of their lust for power. If a shocking chain of 'eminent corpses' had been seen anywhere else in the Western world, then the most elementary laws of politics would have guaranteed that a national hero like General Carlo Alberto Dalla Chiesa would be given a unanimous and clear mandate to lead the state's fight-back. And when the first reports of his mission appeared, back in March 1982, the elementary laws of politics seemed to be in force: both the government and Communist opposition were agreed that Dalla Chiesa would be granted wide-ranging powers, not limited to Palermo or even to Sicily. 'There should be no political difficulties,' one national paper declared.

Yet, as he mourned Pio La Torre, political difficulties soon became a bigger worry to Dalla Chiesa than the mafia. Through press releases and interviews, the dealmakers of Rome began to send their coded public messages about Dalla Chiesa's appointment. Lukewarm expressions of support were mixed with polite perplexity. Fighting the Sicilian mafia was crucial, but it should not hinder the workings of the market economy, they said. Of course Dalla Chiesa's appointment was a good thing. But Italian democrats needed to be watchful, they said. The General should not be the herald of an authoritarian turn: Sicily didn't need another 'Iron Prefect'. (The reference was to Prefect Cesare Mori, who had led Fascism's clampdown on organised crime in the 1920s.)

On 2 April, Dalla Chiesa wrote to the Prime Minister to demand an explicit and formal anti-mafia mandate for his new job. 'It is certain that I am destined to be the target of local resistance, both subtle and brutal.' He pointed out that the 'most crooked "political family"' in Sicily was already making sinister noises about him.

There was little mystery about who that political family was: the Andreotti faction of the Christian Democrat Party, headed by the 'Young Turk' Salvo Lima. Dalla Chiesa knew Andreotti well. For the DC magus was Prime Minister when former premier Aldo Moro was kidnapped and murdered by the Red Brigades. Andreotti it was who conferred special powers on Carlo Alberto Dalla Chiesa to get to grips with the terrorist threat.

Dalla Chiesa was a man who believed profoundly in the values of the state – he had the *Carabinieri* insignia sewn onto his skin, as he often said. Yet he was no ingénu. He was ambitious, and he knew how liquid power was in Italy, how it often coursed through personal channels, and collected in the hands of cliques. He knew the art of modulating relations with his political masters by means of a quiet word, a letter, a leak to a journalist, or a formal newspaper interview. When the list of members of the covert Masonic lodge P2 was discovered in 1981, Dalla Chiesa's name was rumoured to be on it. He explained that he had applied to join, partly out of a desire to monitor the lodge's activities, but that his application was not accepted. The P2 affair cast a shadow over Dalla Chiesa's reputation. Nonetheless, his sense of duty made him an outsider in the Italy of factions and shady schemes. When he reached Palermo, his dealings with Andreotti – the man at the centre of many a shady scheme – showed just how vulnerable that outsider status made him.

On 6 April 1982 Dalla Chiesa was called in to see Giulio Andreotti himself. This meeting was yet another example of just how individualised influence can be in Italy: it resides not in institutions, but in men and their networks of friends. For the spring of 1982 was one of the very rare moments in post-war history when Andreotti did not hold a government post. So he had no official claim to meddle in Dalla Chiesa's Sicilian mission, or request a meeting. Dalla Chiesa answered the summons all the same. As usual, the General did not mince his words: he declared he would show no special favours to Andreotti's supporters on the island. He later told his children, 'I've been to see Andreotti; and when I told him everything I know about his people in Sicily, he blanched.'

Andreotti's typically coded and devious public reply to Dalla

Chiesa's bold statement of intent came in a newspaper column. Sending Dalla Chiesa to Sicily was a welcome initiative, he wrote. But surely the problem was more serious in Naples and Calabria than in Sicily?

This rhetorical question was both disingenuous and alarming. In raw numerical terms, Andreotti was right: at that moment, organised crime was causing more fatalities outside Sicily. But no one could fail to see the vast qualitative difference in the targets of mafia violence in Sicily. Granted, there were a few 'eminent corpses' in Campania and Calabria. In 1980, the 'ndrangheta killed two local Communist politicians. In the same year, the camorra murdered a Catholic mayor and a Communist town councillor who were trying to block the gangsters' access to the earthquake reconstruction goldmine. Lamentable as these crimes were, they did not bear comparison with the long roll of senior policemen, judges and politicians who had been cut down in Sicily. Andreotti knew this. And he knew that everyone else knew this. So he can only have been dropping a hint. The kind of hint that could bring a shiver of fear to even a brave man like Dalla Chiesa.

In the eyes of external observers of post-war Italy, the country's political life could seem confusing to the point of being comic: the same grey suits squabbling and making up, endlessly recombining to form governments that came and went like the rounds of a parlour game. Fear is one of the factors missing from this outside impression. The great string-pullers of Italian politics inspired real fear. For they had the power to take jobs and marginalise, to blackmail, to smear in the media, to initiate Kafkaesque legal proceedings or tax investigations. In Sicily in the 1970s and 1980s, violent death was added to the weaponry of influence.

(When Andreotti eventually went on trial accused of working for Cosa Nostra, the Supreme Court ruled that Andreotti's relationship with the bosses rapidly became more tenuous after 1980, when his party colleague Piersanti Mattarella was murdered. Andreotti, the court ruled, knew that Cosa Nostra was intending to kill Mattarella, but did nothing about it. However, he was cleared of any criminal responsibility in the Dalla Chiesa affair. All the same, he must bear a huge moral responsibility for helping to increase the General's exposure to danger, for increasing the impression in the public's mind – and in the mafia's – that the new Prefect of Palermo lacked support.)

Dalla Chiesa's job description remained unclear long after he took up residence in the elegant neo-Gothic villa that served as Palermo's prefecture. On 9 August 1982 – an unusually cool day by the fierce standards of the Sicilian summer – he voiced his worries to one of Italy's leading journalists. The interview became one of the most famous in the history of Italian journalism. The headline was: 'One man alone against the mafia'.

Dalla Chiesa was as forthright as he had been at every stage of his Palermo journey. Citing events over the past few days, he told how the mafia was flaunting its scorn for the authorities:

> They murder people in broad daylight. They move the bodies around, mutilate them, and leave them for us to find between Police Headquarters and the seat of the regional government. They set light to them in Palermo city centre at three o'clock in the afternoon.

The General laid out his strategic response. First, intensified police patrols to make the state visible to the citizenry. Then the mafia's money must be targeted. The mafia was no longer a problem limited to western Sicily: it invested right across the country, and those investments had to be exposed.

Dalla Chiesa was asked if it had been easier fighting terrorism. 'Yes, in a sense. Back then I had public opinion behind me. Terrorism was a priority for the people in Italy who really count.' There was a bleak truth to Dalla Chiesa's words. There may have been eminent corpses in Sicily – journalists, magistrates, politicians – but they counted for less than victims of equivalent stature in Milan or Rome.

The General also explained the subtle tactics the mafia used to undermine his credibility. The honest police who had fought the mafia since the 1870s, in the teeth of resistance from the island's VIPs, would have read his words with a bitter, knowing smile.

> I get certain invitations. A friend, someone I have worked with, will casually say: 'Why don't we go and have coffee at so-and-so's house?' So-and-so has an illustrious name. If I don't know that so-and-so's house has rivers of heroin flowing through it, and I go for coffee, I end up acting as cover. But if I go for coffee in full knowledge, that's the sign that I am endorsing what is going on by just being there.

Anyone who refused to play along would quickly acquire a reputation for being 'awkward', 'unfriendly' and 'self-important' in Palermo's influential circles. Acquiring such a reputation was often a prelude to being shot dead.

Why had Pio La Torre been killed? 'Because of his whole life. But the final, decisive reason was his proposed anti-mafia law.'

Why was the mafia now murdering so many important representatives of the state? 'I think I've grasped the new rules of the game. Someone in a powerful position can be killed when there is a fatal combination of two things: he becomes too dangerous, and he is isolated.'

From his exchanges with Andreotti, General Dalla Chiesa knew only too well that this 'fatal combination' applied to him. He was a threat, he was isolated, and his life was in very serious peril. Why, then, did he persist, when throughout its history the mafia had defeated everyone sent to fight it?

> I am pretty optimistic – as long as the specific mandate they sent me to Sicily with is confirmed as soon as possible. I trust in my own professionalism . . . And I've come to understand one thing. Something very simple, something that is perhaps decisive. Most of the things the mafia 'protects',

most of the privileges that it makes citizens pay a steep price for, are nothing other than elementary rights.

At around ten past nine on the evening of 3 September 1982, Nando Dalla Chiesa, the university lecturer son of General Carlo Alberto, was listening to music on the radio. The telephone rang. 'A normal ring,' he later recalled. It was his cousin, who told him he needed to be strong, very strong. 'What we were afraid of has happened.'

In Palermo's via Carini, General Carlo Alberto Dalla Chiesa, his new wife, and his bodyguard lay disfigured by the Sicilian mafia's Kalashnikov fire. Someone stuck up an improvised poster beside them: 'Here died the hope of all honest Sicilians'.

Back in Dalla Chiesa's apartment in the Prefect's residence, the General's safe was opened and emptied of its contents.

Even in Italy, even in the 1980s, shame could carry political weight. Days after the Dalla Chiesa murder, Italy's two houses of parliament gave an express passage to the anti-mafia legislation that Pio La Torre had been campaigning for: the Rognoni-La Torre law, as it became known.

A hundred and twenty-two years had passed since Italian unification, years when the violence of organised crime had been a constant feature of the country's history. The mafias' methods – infiltrating the state and the economy through intimidation and *omertà* – had been familiar to the police throughout. Yet only now had Italy passed legislation tailored to those methods. The delay had been exorbitant. The price in blood had been terrible. Nevertheless, Italy finally had its RICO acts.

The Rognoni-La Torre law had its limits. It explicitly applied 'to the camorra and the other associations, whatever their local names might be, that pursue aims corresponding to those of mafia-type associations'. The 'ndrangheta, typically, was not deemed worthy of name-check. More substantially, there were no measures to regulate the use of mafia penitents passed in the aftermath of the via Carini massacre. Dalla Chiesa had fought Red Brigade terror using penitents who had been incentivised by reductions in their sentences. He wanted the same incentives to apply to *mafiosi*. But, for good reasons and bad, Italy's political class remained profoundly wary of what mafia penitents might say. If the ongoing Bacchanalia of blood-letting within the world of organised crime ever generated any penitents, and if the police and magistrates wanted to use their testimony to test the Rognoni-La Torre law, then improvisation would be the only recourse.

Right on cue, barely a month after the Rognoni-La Torre law entered the statute book, the first penitent arrived. Not from Palermo, however, but from Naples.

Pasquale 'the Animal' Barra was the first initiate to the Nuova Camorra Organizzata, its second in command, and the lord high executioner of the Italian prison system. He was a childhood friend of NCO chief Raffaele Cutolo, and the Professor had dedicated a poem to his knife-fighting skills. In August 1981, on the Professor's orders, 'the Animal' murdered yet another inmate, a Milanese gangster. The victim was stabbed sixty times.

The problem was that the gangster in question also happened to be the illegitimate son of Sicilian-American Man of Honour Frank Coppola. The Professor was called to account by Cosa Nostra for the killing. Fearing an out-and-out confrontation with Palermo, he cut his childhood friend loose: he said that the Animal had murdered Frank Coppola's son on his own initiative.

The Animal was now an outcast in the prison underworld, persecuted by the affiliates of every mafia, including his own. He shunned all contact with others, always made his own food and drinks, and took to carrying a clasp-knife hidden in his anus at all times. Eventually, the pressure and his sense of betrayal overcame his blood bond to the Cutolo organisation: the Animal begged the authorities for help. He told investigators the whole story of the Nuova Camorra Organizzata, right from its foundation in Poggioreale prison.

With the NCO disintegrating after the Professor was sent to the prison island of Asinara, more defectors soon joined the Animal. On 17 June 1983, magistrates issued warrants for the arrest of no fewer than 856 individuals across Italy, ranging from prisoners and known criminals, to judicial officials, professionals and priests. They were all charged under the Rognoni-La Torre law. Italy's newest and most important piece of anti-mafia legislation, and the precious evidence of the penitents, were about to be tried out on the Nuova Camorra Organizzata.

Doilies and drugs

An exercise bike for astronauts. An alarm clock contraption that tipped persistent sleepers out of bed. A drastic cure for the Po valley fog.

A father flown home from Iran to his young family for Christmas. An agèd but picky Neapolitan spinster matched with the Spanish Flamenco dancer of her dreams.

Talented kids. Fancy dress. Comedy turns. Cheery jazz. Good causes. A set made up to look like a giant patchwork quilt. And a scruffy green parrot that resolutely refused, despite the tricks and blandishments of dozens of studio guests, to squawk its own name: 'Portobello'.

On Friday nights, between 1977 and 1983, 25 million Italian TV viewers had their cockles warmed and their tears jerked by a human-interest magazine show called, like the parrot, *Portobello*. Many thousands of ordinary people took part in the show: their phone calls were answered by a panel of lip-glossed receptionists who sat at one end of the studio floor. The host of *Portobello* skilfully deployed his patrician manners, common touch and toothy smile to hold it all together with aplomb. His name was Enzo Tortora; he had been born into a well-to-do family in the northern city of Genoa in 1928, and *Portobello* made him one of the three or four most popular TV personalities in the country. Between the cosy, warm-hearted Italy that *Portobello* constructed around the clean-living Tortora, and the savage and corrupt world of the Nuova Camorra Organizzata, the distance was astral.

Tortora's show owed its name to London's Portobello Road market for antiques and second-hand goods. The core idea was to stage a televised exchange service for curios. And the idea very quickly caught on. Although RAI, the state broadcaster, sternly told them not to, viewers sent in every conceivable bit of bric-a-brac for barter or auction. The contents of the nation's attics soon filled up the studio's huge storage facilities and spilled into the corridors.

Somewhere, lost among those piles of humble treasure, was a package dispatched from Porto Azzurro prison, on the Tuscan island of Elba; it contained eighteen silk doilies, hand-crocheted by a long-term inmate called Domenico Barbaro. Five years later, Barbaro's doilies triggered one of Italy's most notorious miscarriages of justice. Because of them, *Portobello* went off the air, and Enzo Tortora was accused of being a cocaine dealer to the stars, and a fully initiated member of Raffaele Cutolo's Nuova Camorra Organizzata. The world of *Portobello* and the world of organised crime collided. The resulting explosion inflicted grave damage on the Italian judicial system at the very moment when the power of Italy's mafias was reaching its peak. Just when the Italian state finally had the weapons it needed to combat organised crime, it suffered yet another blow to its legitimacy.

Tortora was arrested before dawn on 17 June 1983, in the luxury Roman hotel that had become a second home. As is so often the case in Italy, fragments of the evidence against him were leaked to the media while he was still being interrogated, creating a widespread assumption that he was guilty. On 21 August – long before any trial – the key testimony against Tortora was published in the current affairs magazine *L'Espresso*. His principal accuser was another prisoner and *camorrista*, Giovanni Pandico.

Pandico was that rare thing. a con who could read and write; he even had a smattering of legal knowledge, which was enough to make him a Lord Blackstone in the eyes of his fellow jailbirds. His appearance also proclaimed his intellectual gravitas: bland, waxy features hidden behind the boxy black frames of his spectacles. But Pandico was also unstable and very violent. Even as a young man, psychiatrists had defined him as paranoid, and as having an 'aggressive personality strongly influenced by delusions of grandeur'. In 1970, Pandico was released from a short sentence for theft. Someone had to be responsible for his troubles with the law, and that someone had to be important – like the local mayor. As his paranoid reasoning dictated, Pandico rampaged through the Town Hall, Beretta 9mm in hand, killing two people and wounding two others. The mayor only saved himself by tipping over his desk and sheltering behind it.

Pandico began a long stretch behind bars. There his literary and legal expertise were spotted by Raffaele 'the Professor' Cutolo, who initiated him into the NCO and used him as a secretary, a position that gave him access to a great deal of inside information. In a typically self-aggrandising fashion, Pandico would later claim that he had been nothing less than Cutolo's *consigliere*, and thus the acting boss of the NCO after the Professor was transferred to the prison island of Asinara.

Pandico was the second member of the NCO to turn penitent after the Animal. He told magistrates that *Portobello* presenter Enzo Tortora was a cocaine dealer and money launderer for the NCO. Indeed the TV star had been such a successful criminal that he had been initiated into the brotherhood in 1980. But some time after that, according to Pandico's narrative, Tortora's relationship with the NCO had broken down when he failed to pay for a large consignment of cocaine. Pandico claimed to have been entrusted by Cutolo himself with the task of getting the money back. He also said that Tortora received his drugs wholesale through Domenico Barbaro – the same Domenico Barbaro who had sent the doilies to *Portobello* back in December 1977.

Tortora was confronted with these accusations in Rome's historic Regina Coeli prison. He admitted that, yes, he had had indirect contact with Barbaro. Through 1978 and into 1979, Tortora had received a long, indignant and verbose correspondence demanding to know what had become of the doilies. He showed investigators the letters, pointing out their absurd contents: they accused Tortora of stealing the doilies and made far-fetched threats of legal action. One of the letters Tortora received contained the following passage:

> My current status as a detainee who is still bound to the healthy principles of Honour, would oblige me not to inflict damage on you, if I were to see that you forthwith intended, giving tangible proof thereof, to see to the return of the package. As a result, in agreement with my legal advisors, I have decided to suspend the planned penal action as long as you demonstrate your goodwill.

As their cod legalese, rambling logic, paranoia and scarcely suppressed violence betray, the semi-literate Barbaro was not the author of these words. They were the work of Giovanni Pandico, who was an inmate at the same Elba prison as Barbaro at the time of the doilies affair. Pandico had evidently taken charge of pressing the case for the return of the doilies with his usual obsessive persistence.

As a popular TV presenter, Tortora was meticulously protective of his public image, even when the public in question was languishing in jail. So, as he explained to his interrogators, he personally wrote a polite reply to Barbaro/Pandico's complaints, and even arranged for the RAI legal office to compensate the prisoner to the very generous tune of 800,000 lire – some £300 at the time.

> Dear Mr Domenico Barbaro,
> I am very sorry to tell you that I know nothing about the package you sent and have never seen a trace of it. What concerns me is that you are drawing conclusions from this fact that do not shed a very honourable light either on me, or on the respect that I have always shown to whoever it might be.

307

Tortora's perfectly reasonable assumption was that these documents would bolster his defence. As it turned out, passages from them would become a central part of the prosecution case. On Pandico's prompting, magistrates decided that these were coded messages: for 'package' read 'consignment of drugs'; for 'doilies' read 'cocaine'. And when 'honour' and 'respect' were mentioned, it was a signal that both parties in the deal adhered to the ethical code of the criminal underworld.

What seemed to give this airy-fairy interpretation the heft of truth was the cascade of NCO defectors, including the Animal, who backed up Pandico's story. The NCO certainly feared the penitents enough to mount violent attacks on them and their relatives in the build-up to the trial. Pandico's own mother died in an explosion only a few days after he had been cross-examined in court. Crucially, there were also two witnesses, an artist and his wife – neither of them prisoners or *camorristi* – who claimed to have seen Tortora actually swapping a small suitcase of cash for a package of white powder in a Milan TV studio.

On 17 September 1985, the huge trial against Cutolo's NCO reached its conclusion: Enzo Tortora was found guilty; he was sentenced to ten years in prison and given a fine of 50 million lire (€60,000 in 2011). For similar offences, Tortora's principal accuser, Giovanni Pandico, received a three-year sentence. The judge's ruling demolished the *Portobello* presenter's character:

> Tortora has demonstrated that he is an extremely dangerous individual who for years has managed to conceal his sinister activities and his true face – the face of a cynical merchant of death. His real identity is all the more pernicious because it has been covered by a mask which exudes nothing but courtesy and *savoir-faire*.

The verdict against Tortora seemed to confirm suspicions about the real nature of public life – suspicions that had deep roots in the country's psyche. Many of the millions of ordinary Italians who spent their Friday nights in front of *Portobello* also harboured a half-buried belief that they were witnessing a façade. Behind the televisual world of light entertainment, sport, and above all politics, lay a sordid reality of favouritism, corruption, political shenanigans, and – why not? – organised crime and drug dealing. Indeed, the more suave and convincing the façade, the more cunning and devilish was the truth it concealed. According to this pernicious calculus, Enzo Tortora stood condemned by his own affable public image. The sentimental glow that issued from *Portobello* was reflected back onto its presenter as the incriminating glare of an interrogator's lamp.

The truth of Tortora's off-screen life was anything but lurid. He was exceptionally quiet and bookish by the standards of the media milieu. A non-smoking, non-drinking vegetarian, his favourite author was Stendhal and he liked to spend his spare time reading Livy and Seneca in the original Latin. But before the trial even began, journalists had been hunting for – and finding – evidence of the double life that he *surely* must have led.

To British observers like myself, the Italian legal system's way of doing things can sometimes seem monstrous. That is to say: to anyone raised on an adversarial system that gives judges the power to abandon a trial if the press has said anything likely to prejudice the outcome of the jury's deliberations, the sheer noise that accompanies a prominent case in Italy can be disturbing. Long before the decisive hearings, much of the evidence to be cited by lawyers on both sides is widely available and widely discussed. Witnesses and defendants give lengthy interviews. Multiple media investigations run in parallel to the official legal process. Opinions divide into opposing factions of *colpevolisti* and *innocentisti* (literally 'guilty-ists' and 'innocent-ists'). The actual verdict is frequently not enough to dislodge the most hardened views on the case: it remains only one view among many.

The most important argument in the Italian system's defence is that every stage of a trial, including the preparation of evidence, must be open to public scrutiny. In other words, the axiom 'justice must be seen to be done' applies long before prosecution and defence square up in front of a judge. And this is a strong argument in a country like Italy, where all kinds of undue influences, ranging from a Fascist dictatorship to the mafia, have tilted the scales of justice over the years.

Enzo Tortora certainly had the skills and the influence to fight his corner in the media battle leading up to the trial. Seven months after being arrested, he was granted house arrest for the remainder of his time on remand. He stood for election under the Radical Party banner for the European elections of June 1984. (The Radical Party had a strong civil liberties platform.) Tortora's living room was converted into a TV studio for the campaign, and he was resoundingly elected. In Italy at the time, Members of Parliament, whether in Rome or Strasbourg, had immunity from prosecution. Tortora publicly renounced his immunity.

After being convicted, he took advantage of a period of bureaucratic formalities to visit Asinara maximum security jail as part of a Radical Party initiative highlighting the desperate conditions for inmates. In a bizarre encounter, Tortora even shook hands with Raffaele 'the Professor' Cutolo. 'Very pleased to meet you,' the NCO boss quipped. 'I'm your lieutenant, remember?'

Tortora, who knew that Cutolo had openly called Pandico a liar, accepted the joke in good spirits: 'No, look, you're the boss.'

Between Christmas and New Year 1985, Tortora resigned as a Euro MP. In front of a meeting of thousands of supporters in Milan's vast piazza Duomo, he gave himself up to the police who took him off to begin his jail sentence.

In September 1986, almost exactly a year after Tortora was first found guilty, the Appeal Court overturned his conviction and restored his reputation completely.

The Appeal Court judges' ruling made the first trial seem like *The King of Comedy* rescripted by Franz Kafka. Tortora's main accuser, Giovanni Pandico, was exposed as a vindictive, self-aggrandising fantasist. Flattered by the attention and power that turning penitent brought him, he had taken revenge on the *Portobello* star for 'snubbing' him over the doilies. The other NCO defectors, many of whom were held together in an army barracks for their own protection during the investigation, had simply brought their stories into line with Pandico's. The artist who claimed to have seen Tortora swapping cash for cocaine in a TV studio, it turned out, was a known slanderer desperate to use the publicity surrounding the case to flog a few more of his execrable paintings.

Portobello returned to the airwaves on 20 February 1987. Tortora, visibly worn down by his ordeal, nonetheless opened the show in his usual gentlemanly style: 'So then, where were we?' It is still one of the most remembered moments in Italian television history, a moment marked with indelible poignancy because Tortora died of cancer a little over a year later.

The whole Tortora story did serious damage to the public's support for the fight against organised crime. The successes of the trial against the Nuova Camorra Organizzata were completely overshadowed. The image of the *pentito* that would remain fixed in the public mind was of Giovanni Pandico in court decrying Tortora's evidence as a mere 'performance', and melodramatically demanding to undergo a lie-detector test.

Just before lunchtime on Monday 16 July 1984, with the Tortora saga still a long way from being resolved in Naples, another penitent from the world of organised crime was going through the formalities of his first interrogation in a police cell in Rome.

I am Tommaso Buscetta, son of the late Benedetto and the late Felicia Bauccio. Born in Palermo on 13 July 1928. I have not done military service. Married with children. Agricultural entrepreneur. With a criminal record.

Buscetta had once been one of the most charismatic and powerful bosses in Sicily, an international drug lord with contacts on both sides of the Atlantic that earned him the nickname 'the boss of two worlds'. Now, he was a physical wreck. His dark features, which had the noble impassivity of an Aztec prince's, were pale and blurred. Having broken parole and fled Italy in 1980, he had taken refuge on his 65,000-acre farm in Brazil. From there he had watched, impotent, as the *corleonesi* slaughtered his friends and picked off several members of his family.

When the Brazilian police caught up with him, they tortured him: they pulled his toenails out, electrocuted him, and then took him for a ride in an aeroplane over São Paolo and threatened to throw him out. All he said was, 'My name is Tommaso Buscetta.' Just before being extradited to Italy, Buscetta tried to commit suicide by swallowing strychnine. When he landed at Rome airport, he had to be helped from the plane. Soon afterwards, he asked to speak to Giovanni Falcone, who now sat across the desk from him, listening to his every word. When asked if he had anything to declare, Buscetta spoke the following words:

Before anything else, I want to point out that I am not a stoolie, in the sense that what I say is not dictated by the fact that I intend to win favours from the justice system.

And I am not a 'penitent' either, in the sense that the revelations I will make are not motivated by wretched calculations of what is in it for me.

I was a *mafioso*, and I made mistakes for which I am ready to pay my debt to justice completely.

Rather, in the interests of society, of my children and of young people generally, I intend to reveal everything I know about that cancer that is the mafia, so that the new generations can live in a worthier and more human way.

The history of the Sicilian mafia was about to move into unknown territory. Unknown, and yet very familiar.

Walking cadavers

In his last interview, General Carlo Alberto Dalla Chiesa had spoken about the 'fatal combination' of being a danger to the mafia, and of being isolated. The same sense of isolation was articulated very clearly by one young magistrate based in Trapani, on the very western tip of Sicily. In 1982 a TV journalist provocatively asked him whether he was mounting a 'private war' against the mafia. The magistrate calmly explained that only certain magistrates would deal with mafia crime, and build up what he called a 'historical memory' about it. For that reason, what those few magistrates were doing in the public interest ended up looking like a private crusade 'Everything conspires to individualise the struggle against the mafia.' And that, of course, is precisely how *mafiosi* themselves viewed the struggle: as a confrontation between Men of Honour and a few ball-breakers in the police and judiciary. For the *mafiosi*, the lines between private business and the public interest are simply invisible.

The young Trapani magistrate who made this point was a brusque, bespectacled classical music-lover called Gian Giacomo Ciaccio Montalto. One evening, only a few months after the interview, he and his white VW Golf were hosed with bullets. The street where he lay bleeding to death was a narrow one, and tens of people in the overlooking apartments must have heard the gunfire. Yet no one reported the incident until the following morning. Right up to its tragic conclusion, Ciaccio Montalto's battle was an individualised one indeed.

As each 'eminent corpse' fell, seeming to confirm the mafia's barbaric supremacy over Sicily, the tightly knit but isolated group of police and magistrates who were fighting Cosa Nostra somehow found the will to carry on. One of the worst blows came in the summer of 1983 with the death of Falcone and Borsellino's boss, the chief of the investigating magistrates' office, Rocco Chinnici. Chinnici was murdered by a huge car bomb outside his house; two bodyguards and the janitor at the apartment block were also killed in the explosion. This was the most spectacular escalation yet of the Cosa Nostra's terror campaign. Chinnici was one of the first magistrates to understand the importance of winning public support for the anti-mafia cause, of leaving the Palace of Justice to speak in public meetings and schools. His shocking death was intended to intimidate the whole island.

As one hero was cut down, another stepped in to take his place – a volunteer. Antonino Caponnetto was a quiet man, close to retirement, who gave up a prestigious job in Florence to return to his native Sicily. Before he even moved into the barracks that would be his Palermo home, Caponnetto knew what he wanted to do: adopt another lesson from the battle against terrorism in northern Italy. Faced with the daily threat of the Red Brigades, investigating magistrates had decided to work in small groups, or 'pools' (the English word was used), so that the elimination of one magistrate would not cripple a whole investigation. Caponnetto wanted to use the same method against the mafia. The Palermo anti-mafia pool – Giovanni Falcone and Paolo Borsellino, along with Giuseppe Di Lello and Leonardo Guarnotta – would share the knowledge and the risks, uniting the different cases into a single great inquiry. The pool system was the magistrates' response to the 'fatal combination'.

The Palermo pool made steady progress. For example, Gaspare 'Mr Champagne' Mutolo's phone was tapped, and the passages of his heroin trade with the Far East reconstructed. Mutolo's supplier, Ko Bak Kin, was arrested in Thailand and subsequently agreed to come back to Italy to testify. Ballistic analysis had revealed that the same Kalashnikov machine gun was used in a whole series of mafia murders – from that of

Stefano Bontate to General Carlo Alberto Dalla Chiesa's. The weapon was a common signature that began to make patterns discernible in the gore. Most importantly, the Flying Squad produced a report on 162 *mafiosi* that included a rough sketch of the battle lines in the war that had led to the extermination of Stefano Bontate, Salvatore Inzerillo and their followers. But as yet, investigators were reliant on secret internal sources from the world of the mafia – men who were far too afraid, and far too mistrustful of the authorities, to give their names, let alone give evidence that could be used in court.

Then, in the summer of 1984, came Tommaso Buscetta, the boss of two worlds. The new penitent's evidence marked a huge leap forward. Buscetta began from scratch by revealing the name that *mafiosi* used for their brotherhood. 'The word mafia is a literary invention,' Buscetta told Falcone. 'This organisation is called "Cosa Nostra", like in the United States.'

Buscetta's interviews with Falcone carried on, almost without interruption, until January 1985. He revealed Cosa Nostra's entire structure, naming everyone he could remember – from the soldiers at the bottom of the organisational pyramid, to the bosses of the Palermo Commission at the top. Drawing on nearly four decades of experience as a Man of Honour (he was initiated into the Porta Nuova Family in 1945), Buscetta taught Falcone about the exotic inner workings of the mafia world, its rituals, rules and mind-set. He identified culprits responsible for a host of murders. Still more importantly, he explained how those murders fitted into the strategic thinking of the bosses who had commissioned them. At last, the entire story of Shorty Riina's rise to power in the Sicilian underworld made sense. The Sicilian mafia was not an unruly ensemble of separate gangs. It was Cosa Nostra: a unified, hierarchical organisation that had undergone a ferocious internal conflict.

Until now, Falcone and his colleagues had been examining the Sicilian mafia from the outside. It was as if they were trying to draw a floor plan of a building by peering in through the keyhole. Buscetta changed everything 'by opening the door for us from the inside', as Caponnetto would later recall. Falcone thought that Buscetta 'was like a language professor who allows you to go to Turkey without having to communicate with your hands'. Following Buscetta's example, more penitents would begin to talk. The most important of them was Totuccio Contorno, the soldier from Stefano Bontate's Family who had narrowly survived a Kalashnikov attack in Brancaccio.

The pool managed to keep Buscetta's collaboration a secret for months. Finally, on 29 September 1984, the secret could be kept no longer. Arrest warrants for 366 *mafiosi* were put into effect at dawn: the operation became known as the St Michael's Day blitz. The police ran out of handcuffs. And when the police's work was done for the day, the pool held a press conference to proclaim to the world that the Sicilian mafia *as such* was to be brought before justice. Borrowing a word used to describe the massive prosecution of the Nuova Camorra Organizzata in Naples, the press began to talk about the forthcoming 'maxi-trial' in Palermo. In the streets where dialect was spoken, the trial became simply *'u maxi*. And the central issue in 'the maxi' would be Buscetta's allegation – the 'Buscetta theorem', it was dismissively labelled – that Cosa Nostra was a single, unified, hierarchical organisation.

The boss of two worlds was perfectly well aware of the historic scale of the trial that was being prepared around his testimony. Indeed a sense of his own historical mission was probably part of the mix of motives that led him to turn to Giovanni Falcone.

When the news first broke that Tommaso Buscetta was helping investigators, many commentators assumed that he was the first Sicilian *mafioso* to break the code of *omertà*. We now know more than enough about mafia history to be certain that Sicilian *mafiosi* have always talked. Both the winners and losers in the Sicilian underworld's constant struggle for supremacy have broken *omertà* over the decades.

The winners talked in order to make a partnership with the police: in exchange for passing on information on their criminal competitors, they would be granted immunity from harassment. At a grass-roots level, for the police or *Carabinieri* who demonstratively walked arm-in-arm around the piazza with the local boss, this arrangement guaranteed a quiet life. The Sicilian mafia specialised in a higher level of partnership with authority: when the mafia threatened to make Sicily ungovernable, 'co-managing crime' (as Italian mafiologists call it) could become a cynical and covert official policy.

The mafias' losers have broken *omertà* for a reason every bit as sordid: revenge. Abandoned by their powerful friends, outfought and out-thought by their mafia rivals, they turned to the police as the instrument of vendetta, when no other instrument remained.

Tommaso Buscetta, like generations of *mafiosi* who broke the code of *omertà* before him, was a loser. He was part of the Transatlantic Syndicate that brokered narcotics between Sicily and the United States. As such, he felt the wrath of the *corleonesi* both before and after he decided to speak to Giovanni Falcone: between 1982 and 1984, no fewer than nine members of his family were killed, including two sons and a brother. The boss of two worlds, like many of the mafia's losers before him, had many reasons to seek vengeance through the law. He was also like many mafia witnesses before him in that he told only a part of what he knew: his drug-trafficking friends were barely touched by his revelations.

Buscetta's testimony also followed a script, a narrative about his personal journey that many other defeated *mafiosi* before him had recited. Once upon a time there was a good mafia, he claimed, a Cosa Nostra that adhered to the organisation's true, noble ideals. Now Cosa Nostra had changed. Honour was dead and greed and brutality held sway. Now the mafia killed women and children – and so he, Tommaso Buscetta, as a true Man of Honour, would have nothing more to do with it. A misleading and self-interested tale, of course.

But if *mafiosi* have always talked, and Tommaso Buscetta was like the many *mafiosi* that had talked before him, why was he so important? Why is he always defined as the 'history-making' penitent? The main reason is that, whether the mafia reabsorbed them, intimidated them or simply killed them, mafia defectors rarely got to repeat their testimonies where it really counted: before a judge. What the prosecutors knew, they could not prove. When the mafia's losers spoke, Italy refused to believe them. And a Sicilian elite that had been profoundly implicated with the killers of the mafia since Italy was unified needed no further invitation to bury what the mafia's defectors said in waffle: the mafia did not exist, they said; it was all a question of the Sicilian mentality, they said; all those rumours about a secret criminal association were the result of northern prejudices and paranoia; it was all the fault of Arab invaders, centuries ago.

Between talking to the police and testifying to a court, there was a long and difficult journey. For Falcone and the Palermo anti-mafia pool, the challenge was to help the boss of two worlds make it to the end of his journey. Only then could he really be said to have changed the course of history.

Falcone and Borsellino received crucial help in that task from the United States. The investigations into drug trafficking that had first drawn Falcone into the fight against the mafia had taught him just how profoundly linked, by both kinship and business ties, were *mafiosi* on both sides of the Atlantic. Falcone was a pioneer in grasping that anti-mafia investigators had to have the same, international outlook as their foe. Sicilian magistrates and police could make themselves twice as effective by seeking the help of their American counterparts. Buscetta, the boss of two worlds, was almost as precious a witness in the United States as he was in Italy. And the United States, unlike Italy, had a proper witness-protection programme to which Buscetta could be entrusted.

Many dark days passed between the day when Tommaso Buscetta first sat down to speak to Giovanni Falcone and his date with the judge. The darkest days of all came in late July and early August 1985.

Beppe Montana was one of the members of the Flying Squad that had been working closely with the pool – his specialism was hunting down the many *mafiosi* who had dodged arrest warrants by going on the run. When interviewed by the press, Montana had summed up the mood of determined fatalism in his unit: 'In Palermo there are about ten of us who are a real danger for the mafia. And their killers know us all. Unfortunately, we are easy targets. If the *mafiosi* decide to kill us they can do it easily.'

On 25 July, two killers surprised Montana as he reached shore after a boating trip with his girlfriend; he died in his swimming trunks, aged just thirty-three. The fatal combination had struck again.

Paolo Borsellino recalled giving Ninni Cassarà, the deputy commander of the Flying Squad, a lift back from the scene of Montana's murder. Cassarà too was working closely with the pool, and Montana was much more than a colleague to him. After a silent journey ashen-faced, Cassarà could only mutter: 'We'd better resign ourselves to being walking cadavers.' A couple of days later, Cassarà found the composure to give a lucid interview on the political context of Montana's death. By this time, the huge trial against the Nuova Camorra Organizzata was generating a fierce row over *Portobello* star Enzo Tortora's conviction:

> We keep a very close eye on the worrying events surrounding *both* the build-up to the Palermo maxi-trial, *and* the maxi-trial against the camorra. In Naples we can see exactly what is happening both inside and outside the courtroom. There is a frontal assault on the value of evidence from penitents. We don't know how our Neapolitan colleagues have behaved. What we do know very well is that here we have proceeded

by seeking out meticulous, rigorous and even wearying proof
to confirm every detail of the penitents' accusations.

What Cassarà did not point out was that, in Naples, it was a
criminal organisation in terminal decline that was in the dock.
The Palermo maxi-trial set out to prosecute a mafia in its pomp,
with most of its leaders still at large. In a more private moment
at the end of the interview, Cassarà added a chilling final note.
'Sooner or later all the investigators who really take their job
seriously end up getting killed.'

Montana's cruel death pitched the men under Cassarà's
command from determined fatalism into desperate rage. Five
days later, a young fisherman and amateur footballer called
Salvatore Marino was brought in for questioning. Witnesses
placed Marino at the scene of the crime; at his home the police
found a bloodied shirt and 34 million lire (about €40,000 today)
in cash, part of it wrapped in a piece of newspaper bearing the
story of Montana's assassination. (Mafia penitents have since
claimed that Marino, although not a mafia affiliate, was indeed
the lookout for the murderers.)

None of that excuses what happened to him. While in custody,
he was punched, beaten and even bitten. Face up and head leaning
back, he was then tied to a desk; a hood was placed over his
head, and a hose leading into a bucket of seawater was shoved
into his mouth. With a policeman sitting on his stomach, Marino
was forced to drink litres and litres. This was a torture known
as the *cassetta* ('box'), and it was a relic of Fascist police brutality.
Like many victims of the *cassetta* before him, Marino died under
torture.

In a panic, the men responsible for his death faked a drowning.
Ninni Cassarà found out what had happened, and decided to
support the ham-fisted cover-up that his beleaguered men were
trying to stage. He went to Falcone's house in the middle of the
night to ask for support. The two men had by now been working
together for several years, and had become the closest of friends.

They paced the room in anguish for hours. Before morning, the investigating authorities were alerted to what had really happened to Salvatore Marino.

On 5 August Salvatore Marino's white coffin, draped in his blue football shirt, was taken on a tour of the city to the cry of 'police murderers'. At his funeral, a Carmelite priest gave an angry homily directed at the police. The same Radical Party leader who had offered TV presenter Enzo Tortora a parliamentary seat and a platform for his fight for justice came down to Palermo to decry Marino's killers. There were rumours that the young suspect's death was no accident, and that the Flying Squad had a deliberate policy of 'taking out' mafia captives. Newspaper opinion-formers across the country began to draft well-rehearsed reflections on whether the fight against Cosa Nostra was imperilling citizens' rights. That very evening, before the results of Salvatore Marino's autopsy had even been issued, the Minister of the Interior had the chief of the Palermo Flying Squad and two other senior law-enforcement officers removed from their jobs. The same ministry that had been umming and ahhing for months over whether to replace the Palermo anti-mafia pool's outdated computers had been shaken into absurdly precipitant action by the outrage over Marino's death.

The following afternoon, Ninni Cassarà left work early to find a platoon of mafia killers waiting in two separate firing positions in the apartment block across the road from his house. Three Kalashnikovs and assorted other weapons unleashed 200 rounds. Cassarà's wife, waiting at home with their three young children, saw the whole ambush from a window. Alongside Cassarà died Roberto Antiochia, a twenty-three-year-old Roman boy who had come back early from his holidays after the Montana murder to watch his commander's back.

Between them, the mafia and the politicians had utterly incapacitated the Flying Squad, cutting off the anti-mafia pool's right arm. The rage among the surviving members of the Flying Squad was barely contained. Refusing to let Antiochia lie in state in police headquarters, they kidnapped his coffin, along with the brass posts and cordon that had been positioned around it, and carried them off to the atrium of Flying Squad HQ fifty metres away. The Interior Minister had to be protected from the dead men's colleagues when he came to Palermo for their funeral. There was fighting in the street with men from other forces. Once again, the government was panicked into inappropriate action, sending 800 police and *Carabinieri* to the island to man largely symbolic roadblocks.

The Flying Squad, like the anti-mafia magistrates of the pool, had good reason to feel not only isolated, but misrepresented. In the national and local media, the mafia's friends, or just lazy journalists in search of a polemical angle, could easily shape the frightening isolation in which they worked into a very different story: the men and women in the front line of the anti-mafia struggle were egotists, lone obsessives, loose cannons, self-appointed sheriffs. After Cassarà's death Vittorio Nisticò, a veteran of campaigning anti-mafia journalism in Sicily, rounded on a number of irresponsible crime correspondents:

> You knew Cassarà. And you understood. The mistake you made was that, when he was alive, you didn't show him for what he was: a modern hero. It would have been a way to protect him. Now, it's too late to tell his story.

While all this was going on, two more modern heroes, Giovanni Falcone and Paolo Borsellino, were hard at work preparing the prosecution case for the maxi-trial – a document that, in the end, would amount to 8,607 lucidly argued pages. (As was normal in the Italian legal system at the time, the investigating magistrates would leave to others the task of standing up before the court and arguing this case to a judge.) Two weeks after the Cassarà atrocity, both Falcone and Borsellino were transferred with their families to an offshore prison so that they could conclude their mammoth labour. Ironically, the island chosen to host them was Asinara, off the north coast of Sardinia, the very same maximum security facility where Raffaele 'the Professor' Cutolo was now being held. For once, the anti-mafia magistrates' isolation was keeping them safe.

The capital of the anti-mafia

Palermo's Ucciardone prison is a monument to shattered dreams of reform. Rising in what was once open countryside near the port, it is a Victorian brick polygon with fat towers at each corner. But its forbidding appearance gives no clue to the enlightened hopes that inspired its construction. It was designed in the 1830s along the lines suggested by the great British philosopher Jeremy Bentham. No longer would men and women, adults and children, the guilty and those awaiting trial, murderers and mere petty thieves, be thrown together in the verminous promiscuity of great dungeons. In the new jail prisoners would be held in separate cells where their God-given consciences would have a chance at last to work on their souls. Rehabilitation would be born from within.

Bad planning, poor resources and a lack of political will soon buried these far-fetched dreams, and transformed the Ucciardone into a filthy, overcrowded mockery of the rule of law. For the police, it became an instrument of blackmail into which suspects would disappear, without due process, for months on end. For the underworld, as one parliamentary inquiry heard in the 1860s, the Ucciardone was 'a kind of government' whence orders were issued in times of political turbulence.

A century later, Palermo prison earned the nickname, the 'Grand Hotel Ucciardone': mafia bosses came and went from their cells in silk dressing gowns, ate lobster and drank champagne, and gave orders for murders and consignments of narcotics. Much of what Tommaso Buscetta told Giovanni Falcone about the personnel of Cosa Nostra was learned in prison. As he explained during their first interviews in the summer of 1984: 'The presence of so many Men of Honour in the Ucciardone at the same time further reinforces the links between them, allowing them to help and encourage one another.' The Ucciardone was what it had been since the nineteenth century: *the* great meeting place for Men of Honour from different Families, a hub of criminal power.

During the course of 1985, a vast new annexe to the prison was built – a courthouse with space for up to a thousand lawyers and witnesses, and as many journalists. Trees were cut down. Buildings requisitioned. Well over 30 billion lire (€36 million in 2011 values) were spent on creating what looked like a gargantuan bomb shelter. A three-metre-high steel fence was erected, just in case the reinforced concrete walls were not enough to protect the court's proceedings from a missile attack or an armed assault. Underground passages connected the Ucciardone's cells directly to the cages arranged in a semicircle around the edges of the courtroom.

Unlike so many other shambolic public works projects of the 1980s, it was all completed in months. Contractors were rigorously checked to exclude anyone tied to the mafia. The 'bunker courtroom', as it is known, was built for one trial: the maxi-trial, in which 475 men were due to stand accused of being members and leaders of Cosa Nostra, and the Buscetta theorem would be put to the test.

Like the maxi-trial for which it was built, the bunker courtroom divided the city of Palermo. For some, despite its forbidding aspect, it was a symbol of hopes far more down-to-earth than those that had inspired the construction of the Ucciardone 150 years earlier: hopes for justice.

The bunker courtroom certainly showed that the national government, or at least parts of it, had found the political will to fight Cosa Nostra. In Rome, ministerial support had swung temporarily behind the anti-mafia pool: funds were provided not only for the bunker courtroom, but also for improved security and information technology for the investigating magistrates.

In Palermo too, there were many who shared the hopes made concrete in the new wing of the Ucciardone. In 1985 the city elected a new mayor, Leoluca Orlando, whose political mentor was Piersanti Mattarella, the reforming Christian Democrat who was murdered at his own front door in 1980. Orlando made sure that any planning issues related to the construction of the bunker courtroom were addressed in record time. He also announced that the city council would be a civil complainant in the maxi-trial: in effect, he was announcing his administration's intention to sue the bosses. Where countless mayors had played the usual game of denying the existence of the mafia, or pretending that it was just organised crime of a kind that could be found anywhere, the new first citizen did not mince words. 'Palermo has always been the mafia's capital city. But I want to express my pride in its ability to be the capital of the anti-mafia too.'

This was not an empty boast. Compared to the other heartlands of criminal power on the southern Italian mainland, Sicily did have a much greater depth and variety of experience when it came to resistance against the mafia. We have already encountered the traditions embodied by Communist leader Pio La Torre and General Carlo Alberto Dalla Chiesa. The investigating magistrates Giovanni Falcone and Paolo Borsellino were themselves, in some senses, the inheritors of those divergent traditions of resistance to the mafia: Falcone was a man of the left, and Borsellino had right-wing sympathies.

The post-war years had seen other, perhaps more sporadic examples of anti-mafia activity. Like the 'Sicilian Gandhi', Danilo Dolci, whose campaign against poverty in the 1950s soon brought him up against one of that poverty's underlying causes. Or the courageous investigative journalists of *L'Ora*, who were denouncing the mafia in the general silence of the late 1950s. Or the vast public demonstration that accompanied the funerals of the four *Carabinieri*, two military engineers and a policeman killed by the Ciaculli car bomb in 1963. The new dissident left groups that emerged after 1968 also had a strong anti-mafia tendency. In 1977 a small group of militants founded a study centre in Palermo that was destined to be a constant presence in anti-mafia campaigns Peppino Impastato, the left-wing journalist son of a *mafioso* from Cinisi, near Palermo's airport, for years harangued the local boss Tano Badalamenti – the boss of all bosses in the mid-1970s. Impastato paid with his life for his devotion to the cause: in 1978 he was tied to a railway line and blown up. For a long time, the authorities dismissed his death as a bungled terrorist attack.

The bloody years of mafia conflict after 1979 saw the flowering of new and much more insistent forms of resistance. An estimated 100,000 people packed themselves into Palermo's piazza Politeama for Pio La Torre's funeral in 1982. A mass torch-lit parade followed Rocco Chinnici's death in 1983. Victims' families and their supporters formed support groups and campaigning organisations. Students staged rallies in support of the police. The anniversaries of the worst atrocities, notably the death of General Carlo Alberto Dalla Chiesa, became the occasion for demonstrations and other initiatives. Back in 1972, a Sicilian Communist leader had complained, 'Why are we [i.e. Communists] the only ones who talk about the mafia?' By the time the bunker courtroom was built, his lament was no longer justified.

Mayor Orlando's own story – he was a lawyer close to the Jesuits – spoke of an increasingly vocal strain of Catholic anti-mafia feeling. Priests were beginning to talk about the mafia in their sermons. Groups of Catholic activists embraced the anti-mafia cause. Moreover, extraordinarily, bloodstained Palermo was witnessing the first hints of a truly epoch-making shift in the attitude of the Church hierarchy.

The Church had rubbed along pretty well with Sicily's Honoured Society for more than a century. As ever, the reasons were political. The Papacy was one of the losers in the process that had made Italy one country with its capital in Rome: the Pope lost all of his earthly territory apart from Vatican City.

Thereafter, the Pope banned Catholics from voting or standing for elections in Italy. Alienated from the state, and true to their profoundly conservative instincts, bishops and prie ts sought out alternative sources of authority in the society around them. And *mafiosi* proved adept at posing as a traditional source of authority. In Sicily, as in Campania and Calabria, local saints' days and processions gave the men of violence the chance to parade their power, while seeming to soften its brutal edges.

By the Second World War's end, Church and state had been reconciled. During the Cold War, Catholicism ceased to be marginal to Italy's political system, and became central. A Catholic party, the Christian Democrats, dominated the political scene and formed a shield against the satanic forces of Communism. The mafia sheltered behind that shield, and found succour in the Cold War fervour of leading clerics. One notorious case was Ernesto Ruffini, the Cardinal Archbishop of Palermo for two decades: he repeatedly denounced any talk of the 'so-called mafia' as a left-wing plot to do Sicily down.

As the violence grew in 1980s Palermo, Ruffini's successor, Cardinal Archbishop Salvatore Pappalardo, started to send out very different signals. In November 1981, the mafia-backed politicians who were assembled in Palermo Cathedral for the feast of Christ the King squirmed in discomfort as they heard him outline their complicity in murder:

> Street crime, operating in the open, is almost inextricably tied in a complex web with occult manipulators who perform shady business dealings under the cover of cunning protectors. The manual labourers of murder are tied to the men who instigate their crimes. The bullies on every street corner and in every quarter of the city are tied to *mafiosi* whose range and dominion is much more vast.

At General Carlo Alberto Dalla Chiesa's funeral in September 1982, Cardinal Pappalardo's angry denunciation of the government's failure to come to Palermo's aid made headlines even in the Communist daily, *L'Unità*.

At that point, the mafia found its own way to tell the Cardinal what it thought of his anti-mafia turn. At Easter the following year, Pappalardo respected a long-standing custom by going to the Ucciardone to celebrate Mass with the inmates. But when he reached the prison chapel he found that every single seat was empty. A journalist observed the scene:

> For almost an hour the Cardinal waited in vain for the prisoners to leave their cells. In the end, he came to the bitter realisation that they were absent because they wanted to send him a clear, hostile signal. At that point he got into his little Renault and was driven back to the curia by his assistant.

Yet within the Church, as across Palermo, the sight of the bunker courtroom and the impending spectacle of the maxi-trial provoked unease rather than hope in many. Perhaps because he was unnerved by his experiences in the Ucciardone, or perhaps because someone in the Vatican had a quiet word, Cardinal Pappalardo made a shuffling retreat from his explicit pronouncements against the mafia. Interviewed before the maxi-trial, he blamed the media for sensationalising mafia violence and said: 'the Church is worried that holding such a big trial might attract too much concentrated attention on Sicily. I am anxious about it, and in some ways alarmed. Palermo is no different to other cities.'

The Catholic Church in Italy has always tended to regard the public performance of earthly justice as if it were a distasteful parade of crude state power. As if the courthouse was somehow a sinister rival to the cathedral. Cardinal Pappalardo, like all too many clerics before him, now seemed to have retreated behind the cover-all language of evil, suffering and forgiveness: *mafiosi* were just sinners like the rest of us. Despite all the bloodshed, and despite the heroic sacrifices made so far, the Church was not yet ready to take an explicit stand against Cosa Nostra and in favour of the rule of law.

There were still more insidious voices of doubt in Palermo in the run-up to the maxi-trial. Some said that it was going to ruin the city's image. One politician hoped that it would all be over and forgotten soon, so that the bunker courtroom could be turned into something useful, like a conference centre. Sicily's most influential daily, the *Giornale di Sicilia*, was distinctly lukewarm about the whole judicial enterprise, and its editor explicitly sceptical about the key issue of the relationship between the mafia and the institutions of the state:

> Today the mafia is fundamentally unconnected to power. I don't believe it can be said that there are organic links between power and the mafia; just as it can't be said that every corrupt man in public life is necessarily a *mafioso*.

As if to prove this assertion, on the eve of the maxi-trial, the *Giornale di Sicilia* sacked a crime correspondent who had been particularly diligent in his work on mafia issues.

Silently watching the evolving spectacle was a nervous, amorphous, and far from entirely innocent majority of the city's population. Some voices blamed the anti-mafia magistrates for creating unemployment in the city. The argument was groundless, of course: mafia influence had caused scandalous waste and inefficiency for generations. But that did not deaden the ring of truth it had for the architects and civil engineers who profited nicely from the corrupt construction system; for the bankers who did not care where their customers' money came from; for the owners of swanky boutiques and restaurants on via Libertà whose businesses floated high on the trickle-down profits of narcotics; for the idlers who had pulled in favours to get a public-sector job, or for the worker bees of the drugs and contraband tobacco industries.

Palermo remained hard to decipher in the 1980s. Every pronouncement by a public figure was scrutinised for a coded comment on the work of the anti-mafia pool. Giovanni Falcone gave a resolutely optimistic reading of the public mood in the city of his birth. He talked about the numerous letters of support and admiration that he and his colleagues received. And of how the young people who staged demonstrations in favour of the investigating magistrates were showing great maturity: 'They have shown that, in the struggle against the mafia, party political labels are irrelevant.' The journalists interviewing him probed him further about his increasing fame, and the conflicting views of what he was doing.

> You certainly don't have an easy relationship with this city.
> There are those who say that you tend to overdo things,
> that you want to ruin Sicily. Then there are people who,
> albeit in a whisper, say, 'What we need is a thousand
> Falcones.' What is your reply?

Falcone gave a typically unassuming response, one designed to play down the familiar and potentially dangerous idea that the anti-mafia cause was a personal crusade. 'I would like to say to this city: men come and go. But afterwards their ideas and the things they strive for morally remain, and will continue to walk on the legs of others.'

The maxi-trial began on 10 February 1986. As it did, Cosa Nostra's guns fell silent while the bosses waited for the curtain to lift on the trial drama.

Meanwhile, as if to remind Italians just how high were the stakes in Palermo's bunker courtroom, the slaughter continued unabated elsewhere – and with it organised crime's insidious hold over the state machinery and the democratic process designed to

run it. Palermo may have been living through an optimistic interlude in the run-up to the maxi-trial, but across the country the
political system was becoming yet more dysfunctional: a 'rule of
non-law'.

The rule of non-law

In Campania, the military and judicial defeat of the Professor's Nuova Camorra Organizzata meant that the coalition formed to oppose him, the Nuova Famiglia, had the region to itself. Once victory was assured, the NF immediately descended into a bloody internecine struggle to control the post-earthquake economy. The first signs of that war came in Marano, the town just to the north of Naples where the Nuvoletta clan – Cosa Nostra's viceroys in Campania – had their notorious farmhouse.

On 10 June 1984 four cars screeched through the centre of Marano, firing wildly at one another with machine guns and pistols. A bystander, Salvatore Squillace, aged twenty-eight, was hit in the head: yet another innocent victim of camorra violence. The *Carabinieri* investigating his death traced the cars' route back up to a place they knew well, because they had searched it several times: the farmhouse shrouded by trees that was the operational base of the Nuvoletta crime family. There they found the aftermath of a huge gun battle. The front of the house was pockmarked by bullets, and shellcases were strewn all around. Searching further, down an avenue leading away from the house they found the body of a man, his forehead flattened by a pistol shot fired at close range: it was one of the younger Nuvoletta brothers, Ciro. Extraordinarily, someone had staged a frontal assault on the most powerful *camorristi* of all.

The first journalists to report on the incident, well aware of the Nuvolettas' leading role in the resistance to the Nuova Camorra Organizzata, speculated that the Professor's men were responsible. Was this the sign of an NCO resurgence? The true significance of the gun battle in Marano only emerged later. The geography of camorra power was shifting. With the NCO on its way to defeat, the victorious alliance, the Nuova Famiglia, had begun to splinter. The Nuvolettas, the oldest camorra dynasty, the pillar around which Cosa Nostra had built its Campanian protectorate, stood to be eclipsed. And as they were, the Sicilian mafia's influence in Campania came to an end, the camorra came of age, and the face of much of the region was transformed.

The man who staged the spectacular, demonstrative attack on the Nuvoletta farmhouse was Antonio Bardellino. Bardellino was born in San Cipriano D'Aversa, one of three contiguous agricultural towns (the others are Casapesenna and Casal di Principe) to the north of the Nuvolettas' base. Generations of illegal building turned these towns into a two-storey maze of unmapped alleys. The area, known for its fruit trees and its buffalo-milk mozzarella industry, had been notorious for more than a century: Mussolini's repressive drive against the rural camorra in the 1920s was concentrated here.

Although he came from a very traditional camorra territory, Bardellino was something of an upstart compared to the Nuvolettas: he began his career holding up trucks. He was formally a part of the Nuvoletta organisation, and had been put through Cosa Nostra's finger-pricking initiation in the Marano farmhouse. However, the war between the NCO and the NF quickly created tensions between Bardellino and his masters. As we have seen, both Lorenzo Nuvoletta and Michele 'Mad Mike' Zaza were reluctant to commit themselves to the campaign against the Professor. Bardellino, by contrast, opted for a much more aggressive stance. He commanded a committed team of young killers who were one of the Nuova Famiglia's most efficient fighting forces – and more than a match for the numerically superior NCO. One of Bardellino's allies at the time recalled that 'we felt like the Israelis facing up to the Arabs'.

As the war dragged on, further differences between the Nuvolettas and Bardellino surfaced. The Nuvoletta brothers were closely linked to Shorty Riina and the *corleonesi*. Bardellino, on the other hand, was a business partner of some of Shorty's enemies in the Transatlantic Syndicate, and spent increasing amounts of his time with them, away from Campania, on the narcotics route from South America. Thus the same battle lines that were mapped across Sicily during the Second Mafia War in 1981–3 were now being redrawn across Cosa Nostra's Campanian territories.

By 1984, the *corleonesi* knew that Bardellino had been continuing to network with surviving Men of Honour from the losing side in Sicily, thus flouting Shorty Riina's newly established hegemony over Cosa Nostra. Bardellino and his allies, by contrast, were now certain that the Nuvolettas had adopted a duplicitous waiting strategy during the war against the Nuova Camorra Organizzata. On instructions from Corleone, the Nuvolettas had kept their Family out of the conflict, while Bardellino and his killers bore the brunt of the fighting. The Nuvolettas' intention was to wait until the Professor and Bardellino had fought one another to a standstill, leaving them free to mop up.

When Bardellino realised that war with the Nuvolettas was inevitable, he came home from his drug-trafficking base in Mexico especially to lead his men against the Marano farmhouse. Later confessions would make it clear that Bardellino's assault could have been absolutely devastating for the Nuvolettas: the *capo*, Lorenzo Nuvoletta, was due to hold two meetings in his farmhouse at that time, one with his senior commanders and one with the Professor's sister: a last-minute change of plans saved his life.

Thus the Bardellino–Nuvoletta conflict of 1984 was a restaging of the Sicilian war of 1981–3, only on Neapolitan soil. This time, however, the outcome was different.

After the success of the assault on the Nuvoletta farmhouse, Antonio Bardellino returned to his drug trafficking in South America, leaving the campaign against the Nuvolettas in the hands of his main ally, Carmine Alfieri, known simply as 'o 'Ntufato – 'Mr Angry'. Alfieri came from another historic stronghold of organised crime in Campania, the cattle-market town of Nola, birthplace of the Italian-American gangster Vito Genovese. 'Mr Angry' was a meat trader and loan shark who had grown up amid the middle-class ferocity that characterises the towns of the Neapolitan hinterland: his father was murdered when he was young. He met Raffaele 'the Professor' Cutolo in jail, and was later invited to join the Nuova Camorra Organizzata. When he refused, the Professor killed his brother. 'Mr Angry' joined forces with the Nuova Famiglia.

'Mr Angry' Alfieri proved to be even more spectacularly ruthless than Bardellino. His first major attack on Nuvoletta allies was one of the worst massacres in Italian gangland history. Late on the morning of 26 August, a battered tourist coach pulled up on the main thoroughfare of Torre Annunziata, just outside a fishermen's club. The streets were crowded with people strolling, or taking coffee, or leaving church. Nobody took any notice of the bus – after all, Torre Annunziata, which lies between Mount Vesuvius, Pompeii and the Sorrento peninsula, was a frequent watering hole for tourist parties. Fourteen killers, carrying a mixture of machine guns, shotguns and pistols, calmly descended the steps of the bus and started shooting at the men playing cards and chatting in the fishermen's club. Eight people were killed. The club, it turned out, was a regular meeting place for the Nuvolettas' local allies, the Gionta clan, whose leader was yet another *camorrista* initiated into Cosa Nostra at the Marano farmhouse.

For Carmine 'Mr Angry' Alfieri, the massacre was a military triumph. Intended to damage the Nuvolettas' prestige as loudly and visibly as possible, it succeeded in its aim. The Nuvoletta clan, who were also reeling from heavy blows inflicted by the police, sued for peace. Cosa Nostra's authority in Campania crumpled. Many Sicilian construction companies operating in Campania immediately abandoned the region, some without even waiting to finish the projects they were working on.

Founder of the Nuova Camorra Organizzata. Raffaele 'the Professor' Cutolo was the most influential Italian criminal of the twentieth century.

Prison assassin. Pasquale 'the Animal' Barra was the Nuova Camorra Organizzata's principal enforcer within the prison system.

...ath blow. The car-bomb that led to the defeat of the Nuova Camorra Organizzata. ...zo Casillo, the Professor's military chief, was murdered in Rome in January 1983.

Unlikely allies, and anti-mafia martyrs: Pío La Torre of the Italian Communist Party and Carlo Alberto Dalla Chiesa of the *Carabinieri*.

La Torre addresses a local Communist rally in Palermo, 1968.

The future General Dall Chiesa during his time i Corleone, *c.* 195

La Torre and his bodyguard were murdered in April 1982. His legacy was the law that underpins the anti-mafia struggle to this day.

'Here died the hope of all honest Sicilians'. Dalla Chiesa, his wife and bodyguard were machine-gunned to death in September 1982.

The 'Treasurer of Cosa Nostra'. Pippo Calò's worst crime was the bomb that killed seventeen on a train between Florence and Bologna in 1984. His confrontation with Tommaso Buscetta was one of the highlights of the maxi-trial in 1986.

The most important supergrass in Italian underworld history. Cosa Nostra's Tommaso Buscetta is brought back to Italy in 1984 after surviving a suicide attempt.

Caged defendants look out at proceedings in the history-making maxi-trial against Cosa Nostra, Palermo, 1986–7.

Giovanni Falcone and Paolo Borsellino photographed in March 1992, on one of the last occasions when the two heroic magistrates were seen in public together. Photographer Tony Gentile's image is now an icon of the anti-mafia movement.

The Capaci massacre, 23 May 1992. Falcone, his wife and three of their bodyguards were murdered by a bomb placed under the motorway leading back to Palermo from the airport.

The via d'Amelio massacre, 19 July 1992. Paolo Borsellino and five police bodyguards were blown apart by a car bomb in Palermo.

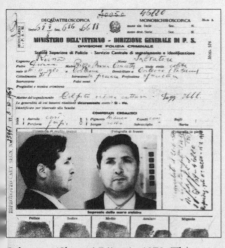

Salvatore 'Shorty' Riina in 1970. The man destined to exercise a dictatorial power over Cosa Nostra would be on the run from the law for the next twenty-three years.

After his capture in 1993, Riina is made to pose before a picture of one of his most illustrious victims, General Carlo Alberto Dalla Chiesa.

Bernardo 'the Tractor' Provenzano. Riina's sidekick tried to repair the damage caused to Cosa Nostra by Riina's war on the state. Provenzano was captured in 2006 after a record forty-three years on the run.

CCTV footage shows a camorra killer calmly finishing-off his victim, Naples, 2009.

The worst housing project in Europe. The camorra turned the triangular tower blocks of Le Vele ('The Sails') into a narcotics shopping mall in the 2000s.

Cash from trash. Shocking mismanagement of the rubbish system created lucrative opportunities for the camorra, Naples, 2008.

Cocaine containers. The colossal transhipment port at Gioia Tauro in Calabria is a major entry point for the 'ndrangheta's narcotics.

Rebirth of the Commission. Benedetto Capizzi was at the centre of Cosa Nostra's efforts to reconstruct its governing body, the Palermo Commission. Would-be boss of all bosses Capizzi was arrested in 2008.

Camorra *capo* Michele Zagaria was captured in an underground bunker in his home town of Casapesenna, 2011. His organisation, the *casalesi*, became the most powerful in the Campania underworld in the 1990s.

Head of the Great Crime? Domenico Oppedisano, arrested in 2010, is alleged to have been elected to the highest office in the 'ndrangheta.

The war against the Nuvolettas left Carmine 'Mr Angry' Alfieri as the most powerful *camorrista* in Campania. But Mr Angry had learned the lessons of Cosa Nostra's colonialism, and of the Professor's megalomania, and he did not try to impose central control. Alfieri's camorra was a confederation, as his lieutenant would later explain. 'Everyone remained autonomous. We weren't like the Sicilian mafia . . . Every group had its boss, with men loyal to him who were the sharpest and most enterprising.'

Alfieri's presiding authority finally guaranteed a measure of equilibrium in Campania's volatile gangland, albeit that the map of organised crime in the region was much more fragmented than it had been at the height of the Professor's power. In 1983, at the conclusion of the war between the Nuova Camorra Organizzata and the Nuova Famiglia, there were a dozen camorra organisations in Campania. Five years later, in 1988, there were thirty-two, many of them the splinters of the NCO and the NF.

One distinguished victim of the upheaval in the camorra was Mr Angry's ally, Antonio Bardellino, who did not live long to enjoy the fruits of victory over the Nuvolettas. In Rio de Janeiro, in 1988, he paid the price for abandoning hands-on management of his territory when one of his underlings battered him to death with a hammer. His successors – the young 'Israelis' who had been in the vanguard of the Nuova Famiglia during the war against the Professor – would no longer have their boss's taste for Cosa Nostra-style rituals. The last trace of Sicilian influence over the Campanian underworld was gone. From now on, the camorra had to stand up for itself.

The fragmentation of some camorra clans in the mid-1980s did not mean that the camorra as a whole was less powerful. Quite the contrary. Cutolo's cultish Nuova Camorra Organizzata, and the fractious Nuova Famiglia that opposed it, certainly had thousands of soldiers and ruled broad expanses of Campanian territory. But because they were only in at the beginning of the post-earthquake construction bonanza, they never achieved as deep a penetration of the economy and political system as did the more territorially circumscribed clans that came in their wake.

The new camorra groups of the mid- and late 1980s were also the beneficiaries of a whole new phase in the blend of economic growth and political failure that has characterised recent Italian history. The Italian economy returned to growth in the early 1980s. Inflation dropped, and there was a stock-market boom between 1982 and 1987. The big success story of the decade was the north-east and centre of the country where small, often family-run businesses produced specialist manu-factures for export: luxury fabrics, high-specification machinery, spectacles, ski boots and so on. By 1987, the Treasury Minister could claim that Italy had overtaken the United Kingdom to become the fifth biggest economy in the world. Italy entered the age of remorseless consumerism, driven by a huge growth in advertising on new private TV stations that offered a boun-tiful diet of soap operas, game shows, Hollywood movies, sport and stripping housewives.

Beneath the glitzy surface, all was not well with the Italian economy. Tax dodging was widespread. The South retained its chronic problems of administrative inefficiency, poor skills and education, and a lack of inward investment. Submerged, unreg-ulated, untaxed businesses were everywhere. Southerners bought their fair share of Levi's jeans and Timberland shoes in the consumerist boom. But what they spent tended to come from public funds rather than productive economic activity. Not coincidentally, Italy's public debt grew inexorably during the 1980s, although the South was by no means the only region responsible for the unrestrained borrowing.

The chief culprits for the debt were the usual suspects: the state and the political system that was supposed to manage it. The old vices of pork-barrel politics, nepotism and clientele-building grew worse in the 1980s – in part because there were fewer restraints. The Communist Party had reached its highest ever percentage of the vote in the 1976 general election. Thereafter, it went into decline, beached by the final retreat of the tide of labour militancy in the early 1980s. The PCI could now only look on from the margins, its leaders bewildered by change.

The decade was dominated by a five-party coalition, centred on the DC and the Socialist Party, which seemed to spend most of its time squabbling over the spoils of office. Endless bargaining, and endless jockeying for position and influence, robbed the executive of its ability to make reforms, plan for the future, or put a brake on public spending. The extension of local democracy (Italy's regional governments began in 1970) only spread the same methods deeper down into society. The parties, and party factions, moved in to place their men in every possible position of influence: from government ministries, national TV stations and nationalised banks to local health authorities. This 'party-ocracy', as it was termed, became entirely self-serving, cutting politics and the state off from the ordinary job of reflecting the people's will and administering collective services. A new breed of 'business politician' emerged: a party functionary or state administrator devoted to systematically taking bribes on public contracts. The business politicians then embezzled those bribes or, much more often, reinvested them in the sources of personal power: a party or party faction, a clique of friends or fellow Masons. Some money went on conspicuous consumption to advertise political traction and lack of scruple: a big car, a flash suit or a daughter's lavish wedding. When the occasional corruption investigation hit the headlines, the governing classes united in denouncing the magistrates for political bias.

In the South, but not just in the South, this newly degraded political system was easy prey to the threats and wiles of organised crime. In the ethics-free world of the party-ocracy, criminal organisations became just one more lobby group to buy off. For any given political coterie, as for any given company looking to do business with the public sector, having *camorristi, 'ndranghetisti* or *mafiosi* as friends became a competitive advantage in the struggle to corner public resources. Even as they became more violent than ever before, more hooked on the profits of narcotics trafficking, the mafia, camorra and 'ndrangheta became more deeply entwined with the state – a state which had occupied more of society and the economy than ever before.

Organised crime had made itself indispensable. Looking back on the growth of the camorra in the 1980s, a parliamentary inquiry into the camorra put it this way in 1993:

> In areas dominated by the camorra, society, companies and public bodies tend to become dependent on the camorra organisation. The camorra becomes the great mediator, the essential junction box linking society to the state, linking the market to the state, and linking society to the market. Services, financial resources, votes, or the buying and selling of goods: all are subject to camorra mediation. The camorra's activities create a generalised 'rule of non-law'.

The line between criminal business and legal business had never been as blurred. In the construction sector, it was difficult to discern any line at all. *Camorristi* were newcomers to the building game, but by the early 1980s every major clan could boast its own cement works. Paying kickbacks became routine, as did hiving off fat subcontracts.

Naples and the towns of Campania were rebuilt in organised crime's ghastly image. An entire neighbourhood of 60,000 inhabitants, Pianura near the Nuvoletta capital Marano, was built using mob money and without a single building licence. The whole of greater Naples, in the words of the parliamentary inquiry's report, has been transformed into a conurbation that can only be compared to some of the metropolises that have grown up rapidly and chaotically in South America or South-East Asia: it is uninhabitable, and impossible to travel across. This level of disorder helps the camorra prosper and grow vigorous.

Illegal building has corrosive long-term effects. People who live in houses put up without planning permission, or businesses based in illegally built real estate, make up a vast and vulnerable constituency for the most unscrupulous power brokers. They are dependent on favours from on high to have their properties linked up to the electricity grid, to the road network or to water supplies. They need to be protected from any politician or administrator who might take it upon himself to enforce the law and begin demolition procedures. And they seek the help of any politician or administrator above to give them planning approval retrospectively. Such people are the *camorrista*-politician's perfect constituents.

The camorra (and the same could be said for Cosa Nostra and the 'ndrangheta) exploited Italy's political and social weaknesses with cool entrepreneurial rationality. Antonio Bardellino's business manager later explained his clan's strategic thinking:

In the 1980s we realised that we had to 'industrialise mafia activities' in the way that the Nuvolettas had already done. We needed to do this for several reasons: so as to have capital constantly available; so that we could plan the organisation's future activities; and so that we didn't end up like Cutolo's Nuova Camorra Organizzata, which no longer had the money to pay what was due to its affiliates behind bars. That's the time when [our people] set up CONVIN, an aggregates consortium. In 1982 Antonio Bardellino and I also set up CEDIC, a concrete supply consortium. We entrusted the running of CEDIC to a qualified surveyor, Giovanni Mincione.

Before being nominated chairman, Mincione was ritually affiliated to Antonio Bardellino's organisation by having his finger pricked while an image of the patron saint of our village was burned.

Force of arms, and through it the establishment of territorial control, was of course integral to this business plan. After the Torre Annunziata massacre, Antonio Bardellino's victorious troops ousted the Nuvolettas from the pits that supplied sand and gravel for the building industry.

Carmine 'Mr Angry' Alfieri's territorial control around his home town of Nola was so undisputed that no one would have dreamed of awarding a contract except through his good offices. All the commodities of the modern mob imperium flowed through Alfieri's hands: bribes and votes, narcotics and concrete, contracts and weapons. In just one operation against one of Alfieri's lieutenants in the Sarno and Scafati area to the south-east of Mount Vesuvius, the police arrested a former mayor, a chief of a local health authority and three bank managers.

The Torre Annunziata bus massacre that confirmed 'Mr Angry' Alfieri's pre-eminent position in the camorra in 1984, happening as it did in a tourist hotspot, was the cause for renewed chest-beating by politicians and the media. The Italian state seemed to have lost control of the streets, its right to rule usurped by gangsters who were dragging much of the South and Sicily into a slough of gore. Once the question had been, 'When will it all end?' Now the press was asking, 'When will we even reach the bottom?'

The answer was not yet. Across Calabria, *'ndranghetisti* fought one another throughout the 1980s in a seemingly interminable sequence of feuds over local turf. Then in 1985, yet another major conflagration broke out in Reggio Calabria over control of narcotics trafficking and construction. The so-called Second 'Ndrangheta War began with a bang: on 11 October 1985, in Villa San Giovanni, an ugly ferry port north of Reggio, a FIAT Cinquecento stuffed with dynamite exploded, killing three people. The intended target, the local boss Antonio 'Ferocious Dwarf' Imerti, survived. But the criminal balance of power in place since the end of the previous war in 1976 was blown apart.

The First 'Ndrangheta War had left Paolo De Stefano as the dominant boss in the city of Reggio Calabria and its environs. De Stefano's authority in the city had the blessing of the 'ndrangheta's regional institutions. He boasted to one of his lieutenants that, 'He lived to do justice because he was the armed emissary of the Madonna of Polsi, which used him to kill and eliminate all the dishonoured scum and schemers in the 'ndrangheta.'

De Stefano it was who had tried to kill Ferocious Dwarf. Two days later he was cruising on his motorbike round Archi, the ramshackle new quarter of Reggio Calabria that was his fortress, when the assassins caught up with him.

After Paolo De Stefano's death, the underworld in Reggio Calabria again split into two factions, and descended into a seemingly endless slogging match. Canadian 'ndrangheta bosses tried to intervene to stop the blood-letting, but to no avail. Six years passed, and six hundred lives were lost before a compromise was reached. When judges came to reconstruct the events of the Second 'Ndrangheta War, their narrative of how it all began was tinged with justified fury: 'Great fluctuations in power. Marriages to seal pacts. Secret alliances. These were the warning signs of the conflict – a conflict between opposed criminal personalities who were all just as cunning as they were stupidly determined to carry on with a futile massacre.' By the end, according to the same investigating magistrates, 'the war's protagonists, who had by now been decimated, were irrationally hitting victims chosen at random just so that they could demonstrate – perhaps more to themselves than to their adversaries – that they still existed.'

Mafia war had become its own reason. Sicily, Campania and Calabria stood at risk of becoming narco-regions, swollen empires of graft, nightmarish mockeries of the civilised Europe to which they purported to belong.

'U maxi

The Palermo maxi-trial opened on 10 February 1986 amid barely concealed scepticism in the international press. Foreign correspondents were uniformly puzzled by the sheer scale of the undertaking: 3,000 police occupying the area of the bunker courtroom; an entire spare team of judges and jurors, just in case anything should happen to the first lot; 475 defendants, a quarter of whom were being tried *in absentia* – including, of course, Shorty Riina himself. The *New York Times* summarised the 'Buscetta theorem' in terms that made it sound as if Falcone and Borsellino were tilting at windmills: 'The prosecution will try to prove how individual acts were part of a vast criminal conspiracy born centuries ago and now able to reach from Bangkok to Brooklyn.'

Across the pond, the *Economist* referred to the Palermo Commission, Cosa Nostra's ruling body, as 'semi-mythical'. The *Observer* called the maxi a 'show trial' whose only precedents dated back to the Fascist era. The *Guardian* was more disparaging still, saying that the whole affair had 'overtones of a Barnum and Bailey production' – a circus or a freak show, that is.

There were barely concealed stereotypes at work in these views: the anti-mafia pool's work, like the Fascist campaign against the mafia that it inevitably called to mind, was a typically Italian mixture of the sinister, the melodramatic and the farcical.

It was not only the foreign media who dealt in stereotypes. In Italy, as abroad, Mussolini's anti-mafia drive was frequently evoked as a parallel for Falcone and Borsellino's maxi-trial. But what people meant by 'Fascism' was rarely more than a crude metaphor – the image of a demonic alliance between propaganda and state brutality. In other words, the Fascism of popular

345

memory bore little relationship to the contradictory reality of what had actually happened in the 1920s and 1930s. Mussolini's crackdown in western Sicily certainly had its brutal side. But it was also surprisingly weak. In 1932, just to give one example, many recently convicted *mafiosi* were released in an amnesty granted to celebrate the tenth anniversary of the Duce's rise to power. The truth was that the maxi-trial bore comparison with Fascism only in the minds of its enemies.

Nevertheless, the doubters seemed to have their prejudices confirmed by the inordinately slow opening to proceedings. It took three hours for the judge just to read out the charges; and two days for him to check that all the defendants had lawyers to call on. As they were trained to do, *mafiosi* did their part in trying to discredit the court: some feigned insanity or illness; others brought up endless procedural quibbles, or complained loudly about prison conditions. The presiding judge, Alfonso Giordano, refused to be thrown off course, but also listened to any sensible requests from the defendants and their lawyers. In the coming months, he would show reserves of patience and good sense that would earn him deserved plaudits. The maxi-trial would be many things, but it would not be a farce.

Falcone, Borsellino and Caponnetto responded to the many critics and doubters in a series of interviews. They vehemently denied that their case was founded only on finger-pointing by former crooks. A mountain of evidence had been gathered to back up what Tommaso Buscetta, Totuccio Contorno and the other penitents alleged. Falcone and Borsellino took justifiable pride in claiming that the maxi-trial also included the largest investigation of bank records in Italian history. They also denied that they were trying to deliver herd justice, trampling over the specific circumstances of each individual defendant. As the two magistrates argued, none of the individual crimes made sense outside of the bigger picture of a struggle for power within the whole of Cosa Nostra; these crimes were local battles conducted in the context of a war-fighting strategy. Above all, the magistrates insisted that the maxi was not a gargantuan show. The unitary nature of Cosa Nostra could not be proved without putting a large number of *mafiosi* on trial at the same time.

Falcone and Borsellino were, of course, absolutely correct to say what they said. They were also politically smart to say what they said. Any concession to the idea that they had written the script for a judicial extravaganza would open them up to their enemies' charge that they were merely ambitious showboaters. Nevertheless in Sicily, where the Honoured Society's power had hitherto been as fearsome as it was invisible, the sight of *mafiosi* undergoing cross-examination helped puncture the mafia's aura of invincibility. So it was inevitable that the maxi-trial would be a spectacle.

The spectacle really began on 3 April 1986, when the constant backdrop of argument and chatter from the defendants' cages was finally silenced by Judge Giordano's declaration that Tommaso Buscetta was ready to give evidence. The boss of two worlds was about to live up to his epoch-making promise not to retract his confessions. The accused were rapt as he spoke – first from behind a hedge of policemen, and subsequently from behind a portable bulletproof shield that had been brought in at the insistence of the United States authorities. Over the course of a week, Buscetta confirmed the structure of Cosa Nostra as he had first explained it to Giovanni Falcone, and told the story of the rise of the *corleonesi*. Although this was the prosecution's central contention, it was not news to the watching public: diagrams of the mafia's pyramidal structure had appeared in every newspaper since the pool went public with the news that Buscetta had 'repented'.

Remarkably, one of the defendants asked for the chance to question Buscetta face to face. Pippo Calò was no run-of-the-mill *mafioso*. Initiated into the Porta Nuova Family of Cosa Nostra by none other than Buscetta, Calò had risen to become the Family's representative, and had allied himself with Shorty Riina. In the early 1970s, Calò had transferred to Rome, where he worked closely with the Banda della Magliana, sharing their contacts with right-wing terrorists. The investments he managed on behalf of the Palermo bosses earned him the press nickname of the 'Treasurer of Cosa Nostra'. Calò stood accused of no fewer than sixty-four murders. In a separate case, he had also been charged with planting a bomb on a Naples–Milan train. (The charge was, in the end, confirmed.) On 23 December 1984 the bomb detonated in a mountain tunnel between Florence and Bologna; seventeen people were killed, including Federica Taglialatela (aged twelve), and the entire De Simone family, comprising Anna and Giovanni (aged nine and four) and their parents. Calò's aim in planning this slaughter of innocent people was to turn the government's attention away from Cosa Nostra and back towards terrorism. Police investigating the 'Christmas train bomb' (as it was called) found an arsenal in Calò's house that included anti-tank mines.

Now Calò loped across the green floor of the bunker court-room in a yellow shirt and fawn flared slacks, his grey hair combed back over his ears and collar from a bald pate. His insolent smirk betrayed a supreme confidence that one hundred and fifty years of Sicilian mafia impunity was not about to end. Buscetta was 'ten times a liar', Calò declared; he had cribbed his evidence from *The Godfather*, and he could not be trusted because of his immoral private life. (The history-making penitent had been married three times.)

Buscetta's retaliation was withering. On the subject of family values, Calò had taken part in the Commission meetings that had sentenced Buscetta's own brother and nephew to death: their only 'crime' was being related to the boss of two worlds. Buscetta went on to accuse Calò of strangling another member of the Porta Nuova Family with his own hands.

In response, Calò wavered visibly. Having denied ever meeting the strangling victim, he was forced to admit that he had known him in prison. After this encounter, no other defendant dared challenge Buscetta directly.

More and more evidence of Cosa Nostra's barbarity emerged. Particularly shocking was the testimony of a petty criminal from the slums of Palermo called Vincenzo Sinagra, who gave evidence in an almost impenetrable dialect. Sinagra's relationship with the mafia had begun when he made the terrible mistake of robbing someone with mafia connections – a capital offence in Cosa Nostra's value system. But because he had a cousin who was a Man of Honour, Sinagra was offered the chance to work for the mob during its murder campaign of 1981–3. Arrested after he botched an assassination, Sinagra made an unconvincing attempt to feign insanity. Largely thanks to Paolo Borsellino's extraordinary powers of empathy, this pitiful figure was then persuaded to put his trust in the state, and to confess his every murder. He explained that he had been paid the equivalent of two or three hundred dollars a month to help one of Riina's most ruthless killers torture and strangle his victims, and then dissolve their bodies in acid – a process he described to the court with unassuming clarity and in horrific detail.

Played against the background of evidence like Sinagra's, the words of the bosses seemed grotesquely mannered, separated by an almost ludicrous distance from the realities of their calling. The *capo* whose performance would remain longest in the memory was Michele 'the Pope' Greco, nominally the head of the Commission at the time of the Second Mafia War, but in reality a mere patsy of Shorty Riina's. Greco's Favarella estate in Ciaculli had been the theatre of much of the action in the early 1980s. It had hosted a heroin refinery, and its large cellars were a reliable refuge for killers on the run. Many of the Commission's meetings were held there. Late in 1982, the Pope had hosted the banquet after which Saro Riccobono, the boss of Gaspare 'Mr Champagne' Mutolo's Family, was garrotted in his chair while his men were hunted down amid the fruit trees.

Sitting in a midnight-blue suit before a microphone in the vast space of the bunker courtroom, Greco insisted on prefacing his cross-examination with a lapidary declaration: 'Violence is not part of my dignity Let me repeat that for you: violence is not part of my dignity.' Greco uttered these words, carefully framed by pregnant pauses, as if he had just enunciated one of the fundamental laws of physics for the first time in history. He gave every indication of thinking that a mere reassurance about his own good character would be sufficient in itself to guarantee an acquittal. He went on to blame the cinema for putting ideas into the penitents' heads. 'It's certain films that are the ruin of human kind. Violent films. Pornographic films. They are the ruin of human kind. Because if [Totuccio] Contorno, instead of watching *The Godfather*, had seen *Moses*, for example, then he would not have uttered such slanders.'

The least spectacular cross-examination in the maxi-trial was among the most revealing and intriguing. On 20 June 1986, Ignazio Salvo entered the bunker courtroom in an elegant light blue suit, carrying a briefcase. For thirty years, before he was brought blinking into the light of publicity and justice by the anti-mafia pool, Ignazio had controlled tax-collecting franchises across much of Sicily with his cousin Nino. The inflated profits of their licensed robbery were reinvested in agribusiness, tourism, property, and in buying the political leverage within the DC that was essential to the whole operation. Nino Salvo, who had died of a tumour just before coming to trial, was a more abrasive man than his cousin. When he was called to the Palace of Justice, his growling voice had uttered an admission (and a veiled threat) that had echoed through the building's marble and glass atrium: 'The Salvos paid all the political parties. Money to all of them: no exceptions.'

Unlike most of the other defendants at the maxi-trial, Ignazio Salvo had not been held in the Ucciardone, but under house arrest. Now, with his reading glasses halfway down his long nose, he addressed the presiding judge with relaxed precision. He began by giving a point-by-point response to Buscetta's allegations, and then embarked on a long and monotonous explanation of the reams of documentary evidence he had in his briefcase. 'You seem bored,' he said at one point to the judge, through a thin smile of contempt. It was as if, by sheer grinding force of tedium, the richest and most powerful man in Sicily hoped to vanish slowly into the background once more.

The Salvos were particularly close to Stefano Bontate, the 'Prince of Villagrazia', and other members of Cosa Nostra's drug-trafficking elite. That friendship had cost the cousins dear, when in 1975 Nino Salvo's father-in-law was kidnapped by the *corleonesi* and never returned. The Salvos were understandably terrified in 1981, when Shorty Riina began slaughtering Bontate and his allies. For safety's sake, Nino went for a long cruise on his yacht. Meanwhile Ignazio stayed in Palermo frantically trying to contact Tommaso Buscetta to find out what was going on and organise resistance to Shorty Riina's coup. It was to be the beginning of the end of the Salvos' power.

Ignazio Salvo's response to the prosecution's narrative, apart from trying to bore the court to a standstill, was an argument of devilish subtlety:

For many a long year the state was practically absent from the struggle against the mafia. Connivance and complicity were so widespread that citizens were left defenceless before the power of mafia organisations. The only thing for us to do was to try and survive by avoiding threats, especially to family members, and especially when our activity as businessmen necessarily put us in touch with those organisations. I have never been a *mafioso*. But I am one of the many entrepreneurs who, in order just to survive, has had to strike a deal with these *enemies of society*.

'What could we do?' Ignazio Salvo was saying. We thought we made just enough concessions to the men of violence to be left alone. Alas, we were wrong, and we ended up on the receiving end of a kidnapping. We are not culprits, but victims.

This defence was part admission and part excuse – and all completely disingenuous. Generations of Sicilian landowners and entrepreneurs had produced *exactly* the same argument when their links to *mafiosi* were discovered.

Buscetta and other penitents knew that Ignazio Salvo was a Man of Honour from the Salemi Family of Cosa Nostra – the underboss, indeed. As early as 1971, the then colonel of the *Carabinieri* Carlo Alberto Dalla Chiesa had filed a report stating that Ignazio was a *mafioso* and that his father Luigi had been the town's boss. Falcone and Borsellino's work on bank records showed that the Salvos had been illegally exporting capital – the mafia's profits, likely as not. But the cousins' real sphere of influence lay *outside* the criminal brotherhood. On that score, Buscetta's analysis of the Salvos was a lesson in the subtle relationships between the mafia and Sicily's economic and political system.

> The Salvos' role in Cosa Nostra is modest. Yet their political importance is huge, because I know about their direct relationships with extremely well-known Members of Parliament, some of whom are from Palermo, and whose names I will not give.

'Whose names I will not give' – Buscetta was saying that the Salvos were the link between Cosa Nostra and politics. But he would not say *which* politicians. He had warned Falcone at the very beginning of their discussions that he did not think Italy was yet ready for such revelations, which would have been more controversial, harder to prove, and more dangerous. Ignazio Salvo was as close as the maxi-trial was going to get to the explosive subject of the mafia's 'untouchable' friends inside the institutions of government. Yet the message in Ignazio Salvo's presence at the maxi was clear all the same: there were more revelations of political scandal to come.

Just before 9 p.m. on 7 October 1986, there was a brief and hideously cruel interruption to the mafia truce that had accompanied the maxi-trial. Claudio Domino was an eleven-year-old boy from San Lorenzo in the Piana dei Colli, the strip of land to Palermo's north where the mafia-backed construction boom had haphazardly planted concrete blocks amid the lemon groves and cowsheds. Claudio was on his way to fetch bread for the family's dinner when a leather-clad motorcyclist on a throbbing Kawasaki called him over. As Claudio gazed in wonder at the machine, the man pulled out a pistol and shot him in the forehead from less than a metre away.

Across the country, sorrow and anger competed with speculation in the media. Did Claudio's death have anything to do with the fact that his father had a contract to clean the bunker courtroom? Had the boy seen something he shouldn't have? Thousands came to the funeral. The newspapers reported Claudio's brother's anguished cry: 'And they call themselves Men of Honour!'

On the day of the funeral, from cage number fifteen of the bunker courtroom, Giovanni Bontate asked to read a prepared statement. Articulating his words methodically, the *mafioso* who had betrayed his brother to the *corleonesi* addressed the court:

We join the Domino family in their grief. We refute the idea that such a barbaric act could have anything to do with us. We reject the attacks and indiscriminate accusations that the press is making against the defendants. We are moved. We have children too. We ask that there be a minute's silence.

The hypocrisy of this moral posturing is not diminished by the fact that we now know what really happened to Claudio. A band of drug dealers to whom Cosa Nostra had subcontracted distribution in the San Lorenzo area killed him because they suspected he had given information to the police. On the orders of the Commission, Claudio's killer subsequently vanished. Unconfirmed rumours said that Claudio's father had been loaded into the boot of a car and taken to an isolated garage; there he was shown what had happened to his son's murderer, and warned not to make any more noise.

Giovanni Bontate's declaration was an attempt to make the mafia appear to be what its defenders through history had often claimed that it was: a bringer of order, an informal police force rooted in the community. In other words, the fictional mafia boss Turi Passalacqua from the movie *In the Name of the Law* was raising his head once more. But this time, the propaganda backfired. Bontate used one extraordinarily significant word in his statement: 'we'. 'We, Cosa Nostra', that is. In trying to distance his organisation from Claudio Domino's murder, Giovanni Bontate had implicitly admitted what the prosecution was trying to prove: that the Sicilian mafia existed. It was a catastrophic mistake that cost Bontate dear when the maxi was over. After being convicted, and while waiting for the appeal, he was granted house arrest due to a slipped disc (of all things). One morning, still in his dressing gown, he opened the door to greet two friends. Coffee was offered and accepted. When the chatting was finished and the friends got up to leave, they shot both Giovanni Bontate and his wife dead.

When the major bosses had finished giving evidence, the maxi still had over a year left to run. Vast quantities of bank data and other evidence needed to be aired. The relatives of mafia victims were given the chance to speak too. It was difficult to tell which of them made the more harrowing sight: those who pleaded tearfully for news of where their loved ones were buried; or those who, evidently petrified, recited the familiar refrain of 'I didn't see anything. I don't know anything.'

In April 1987, the prosecution summed up: a process that took more than two weeks. When one of the two prosecuting advocates finally sat down after eight long days of oratory, he found himself unable to get to his feet again and had to wait for the closure of the day's proceedings so he could be carried bodily out of the courtroom by the *Carabinieri*.

One by one, the squadron of nearly two hundred defence lawyers then took the floor to give their final remarks, a process that took months.

Finally, on 11 November 1987, the judges and jury retired to consider their verdict. But just before they did, Michele 'the Pope' Greco made it known that he wanted to address them. His short speech would become the most famous of the whole maxi.

I wish you peace, Your Honour. I wish you all peace. Because peace, and tranquillity, and serenity of mind and conscience . . . It's for the task that awaits you. Serenity is the fundamental basis for standing in judgement. These are not my words: they are the words of Our Lord, his advice to Moses. May there be the utmost serenity when it comes to passing judgement. It's the fundamental basis. What is more, Your Honour, may this peace accompany you for the rest of your life.

A threat, of course. But one draped in the cloying language that had characterised the Pope's defence throughout: he was a family man, a citrus-fruit farmer, a devout Christian who knew nothing of the mafia and narcotics.

True to his imperturbable self, Judge Giordano replied only, 'That's what we wish for too.'

Five weeks later, some twenty-two months after the opening of proceedings, came the verdict. Life imprisonment for nineteen men, including Shorty Riina, Michele 'the Pope' Greco, and three bosses who, unknown to the rest of the world, had already been dealt a swifter form of justice by Cosa Nostra itself. Pippo Calò was sentenced to twenty-three years. The tax farmer Ignazio Salvo was given six years for being a fully fledged member of Cosa Nostra – an 'enemy of society', to use his own words.

Just as striking as these heavy sentences were the acquittals: fully 114 of them. Even Shorty Riina's *corleonese* mentor Luciano Liggio was acquitted, because the court found that there was not sufficient proof that he had been giving orders from behind bars since the mid-1970s. The 2,665 years of jail handed down to the guilty were 2,002 fewer than the prosecution had asked for in its summing up. Even those who had been sceptical about the maxi-trial now had to admit that it had manifestly *not* delivered summary justice in bulk.

The outcome was a cause for celebration. It was widely viewed as a victory for justice. The penitents had been believed. Buscetta's account of Cosa Nostra and its structure had been confirmed. The Sicilian mafia existed, in other words.

Or at least it did for now. Falcone and Borsellino had always warned that the maxi-trial was just the beginning. An appeal was bound to follow. And the Supreme Court after that. There was still plenty of time for Cosa Nostra to strike back, and then to vanish once more into the mists of history.

One step forward, three steps back

Early in his first interviews with Giovanni Falcone in 1984, Tommaso 'the boss of two worlds' Buscetta put the magistrate on notice.

> I warn you, judge. After this interrogation, you will become a celebrity. But they will try and destroy you physically and professionally. They will do the same with me. Do not forget that Cosa Nostra will always have an account to settle with you for as long as you live.

Buscetta's prophecy began to come true in the months and years following the conclusion of the maxi-trial in 1987. What faced Falcone was not just the renewed threat of violence. (As would later become clear, Cosa Nostra's plans to kill him reached an advanced stage at various moments between 1983 and 1986; Shorty Riina had even ordered bazooka tests.) Nor was the danger just the Sicilian mafia's well-practised tactics of spying, intrigue and misinformation. For, in addition, Falcone ran into resistance at the very heart of the judicial system. The outcome was an ordeal both humiliating and terrifying.

Today, Giovanni Falcone is remembered as a national icon. Any nation would have been lucky to have him. But the bland hero-worship to which he is inevitably now subjected, and the hollow tributes paid to him even by the shadiest politicians, still provoke a gritty resentment among those who supported him during his darkest days. They are determined, quite rightly, that both Falcone and Borsellino should remain controversial figures in death as they were in life. For as long as Italy's mafias still exist, and for as long as there is institutional collusion with the mafias, Falcone and Borsellino should retain their divisive charge.

In the late 1980s, Falcone in particular was sucked into a series of nerve-shredding institutional squabbles that would have destroyed a weaker man. The anti-mafia pool and the maxi-trial offended some deeply rooted conservative instincts among judges. The pool system challenged a cherished vision of the magistrate as a solitary figure, answerable only to his conscience and to the law. So some of the resistance to Falcone was well intentioned: the very nature of the magistrate's calling was at stake. But if conservatism had been all Falcone had had to put up with, he would not have been put through such tribulation. Sleazier forces combined to create a quagmire of opposition: professional jealousy; territorial conflicts between factions; a jobsworth attitude; and the engrained fear of talent within all Italian institutions. All in all, at the very least, Falcone's enemies were guilty of a complete failure to appreciate the dangers that lay ahead for Falcone and his work once the maxi-trial had concluded. They could not grasp just what a threat Cosa Nostra represented, and how insidious were its efforts to marginalise Falcone and dismantle what had been achieved so far, at such an appalling cost in blood. Nor did Falcone's enemies see how vulnerable he was to the 'fatal combination' that General Carlo Alberto Dalla Chiesa spoke of before his assassination in 1982: the magistrate who posed the biggest danger to Cosa Nostra would be pitilessly exposed by any hint that he was on his own.

Many of Falcone and Borsellino's enemies took their cue from Sicily's most celebrated writer. On 10 January 1987, with the maxi-trial still going on, Leonardo Sciascia published a book review in the establishment daily *Corriere della Sera*. The volume in question was a study of Fascism and the Sicilian mafia by a young British historian, Christopher Duggan, who put forward a highly controversial thesis: the mafia did not exist, but Mussolini had puffed up reports of a secret criminal organisation in order to strike at his political enemies on the island. Far more controversial were the parallels that Sciascia drew with the present day: the anti-mafia had once more become an 'instrument of power', he claimed. The novelist cited two examples. One was Mayor Orlando in Palermo, who spent so much time posing as an anti-mafia figurehead that he neglected the most basic duties of running the city, said Sciascia. No one dared oppose him for fear of being branded a *mafioso*. The other example was none other than Paolo Borsellino, who had just been made chief prosecutor in Marsala despite having served much less time in the judiciary than other candidates for the job. As Sciascia concluded, in the snide conclusion to his article, 'If you want to get ahead in the magistracy in Sicily, there's no better way to do it than to take part in mafia trials.'

Borsellino, in other words, was a mere careerist. Sciascia's review predictably detonated an enormous row.

The facts spoke out resoundingly against Sciascia's contrarian griping. It would have been more accurate to say that there was no better way for a magistrate to end up in a box than to take part in mafia trials. Since 1979, four frontline magistrates had been murdered by Cosa Nostra, and a fifth by the 'ndrangheta. Others had been lucky to survive assassination attempts. Yet more would die soon. What drove Borsellino to move to Marsala, in Sicily's most westerly province of Trapani, was certainly not ambition. He knew that Trapani province was a key power base for the *corleonesi*. In 1985, the biggest heroin refinery ever discovered in Italy was unearthed there. Borsellino's promotion was, unusually for Italy, based on merit and not seniority – on his 'specific and very particular professional expertise in the sector of organised crime', as the official explanation of his promotion put it. Yet Sciascia had cited this passage in his review as if it were self-evidently a reason for casting doubt on the legitimacy of Borsellino's transfer.

Sciascia would later come to regret his review, which was a tragically misjudged coda to his career as a voice of intellectual dissent. He deserves to be remembered for the incisive pages he wrote about the mafia back in the 1960s when most other writers refused to tackle the subject. But the regrets came too late. Sciascia had given voice to old Sicilian suspicions about the state; and the title of his review – '*Professionisti dell'antimafia*' or 'Professional anti-mafia crusaders' – had given Falcone and Borsellino's enemies their slogan.

The next blow against Falcone and Borsellino's cause was perhaps the most devastating of all. The Sciascia slogan could be heard being muttered in the Roman corridors of the Consiglio Superiore della Magistratura (High Council of the Magistracy), the body that guarded the judiciary's independence from the government, ruled on appointments and administered discipline within the judicial system. Late in 1987, Antonino Caponnetto, who was Falcone and Borsellino's boss and the man who had overseen the birth of the anti-mafia pool, went into retirement. There was still much work to be done. Two more maxi-trials were in preparation. Since the spring of '87, Falcone had been taking weekly flights to Marseille where an important new penitent, Antonino Calderone, was confessing all. Falcone was the obvious man to replace Caponnetto, and thereby guarantee continuity in the anti-mafia magistrates' work.

That was not how the High Council of the Magistracy saw it. On 19 January 1988, by a small majority, it voted *not* to give Caponnetto's job to Falcone. The post went instead to Antonino Meli, a magistrate twenty years Falcone's senior who had far less experience of mafia cases and no sympathy for the anti-mafia pool's methods. Explaining their decision in opaque legalese, the members of the Council made reference to Falcone's 'distorted protagonism' and the 'personality culture' surrounding him.

Shortly afterwards, the High Council of the Magistracy slapped Falcone down again when he applied to become High Commissioner for the Fight Against the Mafia. The role, created in a political panic after the murder of General Carlo Alberto Dalla Chiesa, was that of a supervisory super-investigator. Falcone knew that the job entailed being a lightning conductor for public criticism of the government's inactivity on mafia issues. Nonetheless, he thought he could achieve something with the powers available. His application was rejected – despite (or perhaps because of) the fact that he was the most qualified candidate by far.

Back in Palermo, the appointment of Antonino Meli proved more destructive than Falcone and his friends had feared. Once in charge, Meli began to override the anti-mafia pool. Mafia cases were entrusted to magistrates with no experience and no formalised links to other magistrates working on the mob. Falcone and his colleagues were loaded with ordinary criminal investigations. All the crucial advantages that the pool had brought – the accumulation and sharing of expertise, the panoramic view of the Sicilian criminal landscape, the mitigation of risk – were being frittered away. In the practical workings of the Palermo prosecutors, Cosa Nostra had already ceased to exist as a single organisation.

In the summer of 1988, Borsellino took his career in his hands by complaining publicly from Marsala about Meli's management of the Palermo investigating magistrates. 'I get the impression that there is a great manoeuvre under way aimed at dismantling the anti-mafia pool for good.' The President of the Republic ordered the High Council of the Magistracy to investigate. Meli demanded Borsellino's head. Falcone confirmed Borsellino's complaints and asked to be transferred. During a drawn-out and exhausting Supreme Council hearing, there were more Sciascia-type noises about Falcone: 'No one is irreplaceable . . . there is no such thing as a demi-god.' In the end, there was a messy compromise: Borsellino received only a slap on the wrist, and Falcone withdrew his transfer request.

On both sides of the Atlantic, Cosa Nostra kept close tabs on the arcane shenanigans within the High Council of the Magistracy. Joe Gambino, one of the Cherry Hill Gambinos, telephoned a friend in Palermo and asked for an update on Falcone:

– Has he resigned?

– Things in Palermo are still trouble. He's withdrawn his resignation and gone back to where he was before, to do the same things he was doing before.

– Shit.

But the mafia had reasons to be optimistic too: Antonino Meli stayed where he was and continued to dismantle the pool. He simply did not believe that Cosa Nostra was a single, unified organisation, and the way he shared out mafia cases reflected his atomised view of it – a view that was already outdated in the 1870s, never mind the 1980s. Cosa Nostra was taking its own precautions, nonetheless. In September 1988, Antonino Saetta, a judge who looked likely to take charge of the maxi-trial appeal, was shot dead along with his son.

In June 1989, the campaign against Falcone took a far more sinister turn. Anonymous letters falsely accused him of using a mafia penitent to kill some of the *corleonesi*. The mysterious source of the letters, dubbed 'the Crow' by the press, was clearly inside the Palermo Palace of Justice because there was just enough circumstantial detail in the accusations to give the slander a vague ring of plausibility. Falcone was again hauled before the High Council of the Magistracy.

Then on 21 June 1989, with the furore about the Crow letters still in the air, a sports bag containing fifty-eight sticks of dynamite was found on the rocks below Falcone's holiday home at Addaura just along the coast from Palermo. Riina and other *mafiosi* were later convicted of planting the bomb, but several aspects of the Addaura attack remain mysterious to this day. Two policemen who were at the scene, and who may have been secret agents involved in saving the magistrate's life, were both murdered within months. Some rumours say that deviant elements within the secret services were to blame. Falcone was not a man given to conspiracy theories. But he was convinced that 'extremely refined minds' were behind the attack, and that the Crow letters had been part of the plan. His logic had an impeccable grounding in patterns of mafia behaviour over a century and a half: first they discredit you, and then they kill you. The magistrate's enemies aired a simpler explanation. They claimed that the attack was a fake and Falcone had orchestrated it himself to further his career.

These were the bleakest and most anxious days of Falcone's life. Over the past eighteen months, he had discovered how many fair-weather friends he had. In May 1986 he married the love of his life – an academically outstanding magistrate called Francesca Morvillo. The couple had already decided not to have children: 'I don't want to bring any orphans into the world,' Falcone said. But after the Addaura attack, he seriously entertained the idea of separating from Francesca so that she would not have to share his inevitable fate. He told his sister, 'I am a walking corpse.'

Falcone's mood improved slightly over the coming months. The prosecutor's office was restructured as part of a far-reaching reform of the judicial system. Falcone was promoted. But he soon found himself at loggerheads with his new boss. As he confided in an off-the-record briefing to a journalist: 'Working here is impossible. One step forward, three steps back: that's how the fight against the mafia goes.'

Falcone continued to be buffeted in the media too. In May 1990, the anti-mafia Mayor Leoluca Orlando used a politics chat show as a platform to accuse Falcone of protecting mafia-backed politicians from prosecution – of keeping sensitive cases 'hidden in his desk drawer'. Here was yet another insidious slur. There was a widespread conviction that the law only ever caught the underworld's lower ranks; that the 'big fish', or the 'real mafia', or the so-called 'third level' were never touched. Such a conviction is impossible to disprove, and plays to a disgust with politics that is dyed into the fabric of Italian public opinion.

Falcone angrily demanded that Orlando prove his allegations, and stated that if he had not charged anyone with having links to the mafia it was for the elementary legal reason that he did not have enough evidence. As Falcone appreciated, Orlando was cynically trying to make himself seem more anti-mafia than the champion of the anti-mafia cause. The episode was also personally hurtful because Falcone had considered Orlando a friend: the mayor had conducted the magistrate's wedding ceremony in 1986. Nevertheless, Orlando would persist in his accusations for months, accusing Falcone of cosying up to the corrupt establishment in Rome.

More serious than all of these personal attacks was the gradual erosion of Falcone and Borsellino's work in the maxi-trial. By early 1989, only 60 of the 342 men who had been convicted at the maxi were still in jail. Many were released because the Italian legal system did not consider anyone guilty until their case had been through all possible stages of the trial process, right up to the Supreme Court. Even those who were still behind bars had managed to find a way to make themselves comfortable. Pippo Calò, the train bomber who confronted Buscetta in the bunker courtroom, had arranged an asthma diagnosis and was now living comfortably in a Palermo hospital.

Worse was to come. In December 1990, the Appeal Court ruled on the maxi-trial verdicts. Seven of nineteen life sentences were overturned, as were Falcone and Borsellino's explanations of a number of high-profile murders, including that of General Carlo Alberto Dalla Chiesa. Doubt was cast on the whole 'Buscetta theorem' and the value of penitents' evidence. The case would soon be passed on to the Supreme Court, which had already demonstrated its deep suspicion of the Palermo magistrates' methods and the theory that the Sicilian mafia was a single organisation. Having been revealed in all its ferocious complexity by the maxi-trial, the mafia was rapidly becoming as legally diaphanous as it had been for the previous century and more.

Falcone goes to Rome

Deep down, below the surface heat of its terrorist violence, its constant crises and unstable coalition governments, post-war Italy was a country immobilised by the Cold War. In eternal opposition, the Italian Communist Party received funding from Moscow; in eternal government, the Christian Democrats banked money from the CIA. Rot spread in the stagnant political air: in every corner of the state, factions and secret cabals fought over the spoils of power. In a very Italian paradox, ties between the palaces of power and the country 'out there' became both utterly remote and stiflingly intimate. *Remote*, because the obsession with promoting allies and friends, with occupying 'centres of power', made reform close to impossible. The real rights and needs of the Italian people – among them the rule of law – went unserved. Yet also *intimate*, because as the state gradually occupied more and more of society, citizens had to make political allies and friends to get a job, or get anything done. Here was a people that loathed politicians, and yet was more addicted to politics than any other nation in Europe. Here was a state that the mafias were perfectly adapted to infect, and a governing party that had few antibodies to the mafia infection. Here was a society where anyone doing their job properly, anyone taking the initiative, risked being looked on with suspicion, if not outright hostility. The tale of Giovanni Falcone's woes in the late 1980s was a metaphor for the experience of countless other honest citizens.

The fall of the Berlin Wall in November 1989, and the end of forty-two years of Cold War, would profoundly destabilise the system. Its most immediate effect was to provoke the Italian Communist Party into changing its name, and tip it into an identity crisis that rendered it virtually inoperative. The great bugbear of Italian politics was no more. At first, the Christian Democrats and their allies seemed unscathed, victorious. But their system had now lost its chief *raison d'être*: keeping the reds out. The DC was living on borrowed time.

The man who embodied the most cynical and slippery aspects of Christian Democrat rule, Giulio Andreotti, was Prime Minister between 1989 and the spring of 1992. Even Andreotti and the other grandees of the old system could see that the government now had to take the initiative. The hunger for reform, and the pent-up public disgust at the Italian political class, was seeking outlets. In the Christian Democrat strongholds of the north-east, the Northern League, heaping racist abuse on southerners and spraying vulgar invective against 'robber Rome', began to rake in votes. Fighting crime was a handy way for the politicians who had governed Italy for so long to win fresh legitimacy.

In February 1991, Giovanni Falcone accepted the offer of a senior post in the Ministry of Justice: his brief was to overhaul Italy's entire approach to organised crime. On the government's part, this was a jaw-slackening volte-face. As everyone knew even then, Andreotti had garnered political support from Salvo Lima and the island's 'most crooked "political family"' since the late 1960s. As everyone knows now, Andreotti was on intimate terms with Cosa Nostra until 1980. Yet here he was handing power over key aspects of the justice system to Cosa Nostra's greatest foe. Falcone's appointment was both extraordinarily welcome, and cynically expedient.

Many in Palermo, from *mafiosi* to some of Falcone's supporters, were convinced that the anti-mafia's champion had traded in his cause for a fat armchair in a grand Roman office. By sheer attrition, the scandals and disappointments of the years since the maxi-trial had neutralised him. Andreotti had ensnared yet another victim.

On the eve of his departure for Rome, Falcone responded to these accusations in a revealing interview in a restaurant in

Catania. He used a humble metaphor for his past achievements and future plans in the fight against the mafia. In Palermo he had built a room, he said. Now the time had come to construct a whole building. And to do that he had to go to Rome.

As the interview progressed, Falcone could not conceal the hurt he felt at being forced to leave Palermo. Most hurtful of all was the insinuation that the Addaura bomb attack had broken his nerve and that, by going to Rome, he was running away. Falcone's response was an uncharacteristic display of anger. 'I am not afraid to die. I am Sicilian,' he said. Grabbing the button of his jacket so hard that he almost ripped it off, he continued: 'Yes, I am Sicilian. And for me, life is worth less than this button.'

Once in Rome, Falcone set to work with his habitual dynamism. The result was an astonishing rebuttal to anyone who thought he had been rendered harmless. He designed a whole series of laws to gear up the fight against all the mafias, nationwide. There were measures to check money laundering and keep the defendants in mafia trials behind bars during the long unfolding of their cases. The government was given the power to dissolve local councils that had become infiltrated by organised crime. A new fund was set up to support the victims of extortion rackets. Politicians and bureaucrats convicted of mafia-related crimes were banned from public office. And, at long last, a law was passed to regulate the incentives that could be offered to penitents in return for reliable information.

Far more important even than any of these laws were Falcone's plans for entirely new structures to investigate and prosecute Cosa Nostra, the camorra, the 'ndrangheta and Italy's other mafia organisations. The Direzione Investigativa Antimafia (Antimafia Investigative Directorate), or DIA, was a kind of Italian equivalent of the FBI: it would marshal Italy's various police forces in their war on gangland. For the judiciary, Falcone also took the model of Palermo's anti-mafia pool and proposed replicating it. Specialised teams of magistrates devoting their efforts entirely to the fight against the mafias would be set up in all the prosecutors' offices in the country. These were to be known as the Direzioni Distrettuali Antimafia (District Anti-mafia Directorates), or DDAs. The pool system dismantled in Palermo had now become the template nationwide. The DDAs would be coordinated by a Direzione Nazionale Antimafia (National Anti-mafia Directorate), or DNA, headed by a senior magistrate whom the press soon dubbed the 'Super-prosecutor'. Huge new databases would keep track of the myriad names, faces and connections in Italy's mafia networks.

Falcone had been marginalised in Palermo, and the pioneering efforts of the anti-mafia pool, carried out in the teeth of horrific violence, had gradually been hobbled. Yet with extraordinary lucidity and daring, Falcone had grasped a fleeting moment of political opportunity to apply the lessons of his bitter Palermo experience and utterly transform the fight against the mafias nationwide. It was to be his crowning achievement, his legacy to the country that never embraced him as it should.

For one hundred and thirty years, Italy's response to the mafias had been half-hearted and sporadic at best. No one in power had seen fit to view the three historic gangster organisations – Cosa Nostra, camorra and 'ndrangheta – as a *national* issue, as three faces of the same fundamental set of problems. Most disturbingly of all, Italy had been forgetful. Each new generation of police, magistrates, politicians and citizens had had to rediscover the mafias for itself. Falcone's plans for the DIA, the DNA and the DDAs brought huge improvements, and a new continuity in the anti-mafia drive. From now on, when Italy investigated the crimes of Cosa Nostra, the camorra and the 'ndrangheta, it would do so using Falcone's method. For the first time in its life as a unified state, Italy had been endowed with an institutional memory when it came to mafia crime.

Falcone had finally lifted the curse of amnesia, and enabled his country to begin to learn.

While they watched developments in Rome in horror, Sicilian *mafiosi* knew that the Supreme Court verdict on the maxi-trial, due early in 1992, would be crucial to their fortunes. A verdict confirming the Buscetta theorem would set a momentous legal precedent by finally confirming the existence of Cosa Nostra as a single criminal organisation. The bosses of the Palermo Commission also had strong personal reasons to follow the Supreme Court's deliberations closely: most of them risked irreversible life sentences. The wrong outcome of the maxi-trial, from the Sicilian mafia's point of view, would also be a catastrophic judgement on Shorty Riina's dictatorial rule of the Honoured Society. Ten years of unprecedented slaughter had exposed Cosa Nostra to the risk of its worst-ever legal defeat. Countermeasures were in order.

On 9 August 1991, the Calabrian magistrate Nino Scopelliti was on his way home from the beach when he was ambushed on a road overlooking the Straits of Messina. Scopelliti was due to present the prosecution's case in the maxi-trial to the Supreme Court. To this day, his murder remains unsolved, although the most likely scenario is that Cosa Nostra asked the 'ndrangheta to kill him as a favour. It is thought that the peace that finally put an end to the Second 'Ndrangheta War at around this time was brokered by Cosa Nostra as part of the deal. Today, a monument marks the spot where Scopelliti's BMW crashed to a halt: it shows a winged angel on her knees, holding the scales of justice.

Shorty Riina made his men promises. He told them that Cosa Nostra's tame politicians, notably 'Young Turk' Salvo Lima, would pull strings to ensure that the final stage of the maxi-trial would go their way. He claimed that the case would be entrusted to a section of the Supreme Court presided over by Judge Corrado

Carnevale, whose tendency to overturn mafia convictions on hair-splitting legal technicalities had earned him newspaper notoriety as the 'Verdict Killer'. Judge Carnevale made no secret of his disdain for the Buscetta theorem.

Despite these promises, by the end of 1991 Cosa Nostra knew that the battle over the maxi-trial was likely to be lost. In October Falcone managed to arrange for the maxi-trial hearing to be rotated away from the Verdict Killer's section of the Supreme Court. Shorty called his men from across Sicily to a meeting near Enna, in the centre of the island, to prepare the organisation's response to the Supreme Court ruling. The time had come to take up their weapons, he said. The plan was to 'wage war on the state first, so as to mould the peace afterwards'. The mafia's dormant death sentences against Giovanni Falcone and Paolo Borsellino were reactivated. As it had always done, Cosa Nostra was going to negotiate with the state with a gun in its hand. But this time, the stakes would be higher than ever.

On 30 January 1992, the Supreme Court issued its ruling and re-established the maxi-trial's original verdict. The Buscetta theorem had become fact. Cosa Nostra existed in the eyes of the Italian law. When the news broke, Giovanni Falcone was in a meeting in the Ministry of Justice with a magistrate who had come all the way from Japan to seek his advice. Falcone smiled and told him what the maxi-trial's final outcome meant: 'My country has not yet grasped what has happened. This is something historic: this result has shattered the myth that the mafia cannot be punished.'

It was equally evident to Falcone's enemies how significant the Supreme Court verdict was. Shorty Riina's brutality had cut Cosa Nostra off from its political protectors. His leadership would be called into question, and his life was inevitably forfeit. The boss of all bosses declared that Cosa Nostra had been betrayed, and was entitled to take vengeance. His leading killer has since told judges that Cosa Nostra set out to 'destroy Giulio Andreotti's political faction led [in Sicily] by Salvo Lima'. Without Lima and

Sicily, Andreotti would lose much of his influence within the DC. Thus, less than six weeks after the Supreme Court's ruling on the Buscetta theorem, Salvo Lima received his reward for forty years of service to Cosa Nostra when he was gunned down in the Palermo beach suburb of Mondello by two men on a motorbike.

Falcone understood the ground-shaking implications of Lima's execution. As he said to a magistrate who was with him when the news broke: 'Don't you understand? You must realise that an equilibrium has been broken, and the entire building could collapse. From now, we don't know what will happen, in the sense that anything may happen.'

With the establishment of the DIA, the DNA and the DDAs, the confirmation of the Buscetta theorem, the political orphaning of Cosa Nostra, and finally the murder of Salvo Lima, Falcone's brief months in the Ministry of Justice saw the dawn of an entirely new epoch in the long history of Italy's relationship with the mafias. An epoch we are still living in. An epoch born to the sound of bombs.

6

THE FALL OF THE FIRST REPUBLIC

Sacrifice

At 17.56 and forty-eight seconds on 23 May 1992, at the geological observatory at Monte Cammarata near Agrigento in southern Sicily, seismograph needles jumped in unison. Sixteen seconds earlier, and sixty-five kilometres away, a stretch of motorway leading back to Palermo from the city's airport had been torn asunder by a colossal explosion.

At the scene of the explosion, three policemen, Angelo Corbo, Gaspare Cervello and Paolo Capuzza, felt a pressure wave and a flash of heat, and were thrown forwards as their car juddered to a halt under a cascade of debris. They were in the third vehicle of a three-car convoy escorting Giovanni Falcone and his wife back home to Palermo for the weekend. Groggy from the impact, they peered in horror at the devastation. Then it dawned on them that there could be a secondary assault, a death squad moving in to finish off the man under their protection. Capuzza tried to grab his M12 submachine gun, but his hands were shaking too much to pick it up. So, like the others, he opted for his service pistol. The three stumbled onto the tarmac. Falcone's white FIAT Croma lay a few metres away, pitched forwards, on the edge of a four-metre-deep crater. Falcone sat in the driver's seat behind a bulletproof door that refused to budge. Gaspare Cervello later recounted the scene: 'The only thing I could do was to call Judge Falcone. "Giovanni, Giovanni". He turned towards me, but he had a blank, abandoned look in his eyes.'

Giovanni Falcone and Francesca Morvillo died on the operating table that evening. Three of their bodyguards, Vito Schifani, Rocco Dicillo and Antonio Montinaro, were already dead: they were in the lead car of the convoy that took the full force of the detonation.

What makes a hero? Where did Falcone get his courage? After so many setbacks, so much terror? The Italian state was viewed with scorn by many of its citizens; its human and material resources were treated by all too many politicians as mere patronage fodder. Yet it was in the name of that very state that Falcone chose to give his life.

The definitive answer to those questions lies hidden in psychological depths into which no historian will ever be able to reach. All the same, the question is far from being an idle one. Indeed it is extremely historically important. Because Falcone was not alone. His cause was shared by many others – beginning with his wife and his bodyguards. After Falcone, many others would be inspired by his story, just as he had been inspired by the example of those who died before him.

When Falcone's friends and family were asked about what drove him, they spoke of his upbringing, and the patriotism and sense of duty that were instilled in him from a young age. Such factors are undoubtedly important. But the most insightful account of Falcone's motives came from the man who shared his destiny.

On the evening of 23 June 1992, exactly a month after Giovanni Falcone passed away in his arms, Paolo Borsellino stood up in his local church, Santa Luisa di Marillac, to remember his great friend. As he made his way to the pulpit, the hundreds who had crowded into the candle-lit nave spontaneously got up to applaud him. Hundreds more could be heard clapping outside. Seven minutes later, his voice unsteady, Borsellino began one of the most moving speeches in Italian history:

> While he carried out his work, Giovanni Falcone was perfectly well aware that one day the power of evil, the

mafia, would kill him. As she stood by her man, Francesca Morvillo was perfectly well aware that she would share his lot. As they protected Falcone, his bodyguards were perfectly well aware that they too would meet the same fate. Giovanni Falcone could not be oblivious, and was not oblivious, to the extreme danger he faced – for the reason that too many colleagues and friends of his, who had followed the same path that he was now imposing on himself, had already had their lives cut short. Why did he not run away? Why did he accept this terrifying situation? Why was he not troubled? . . .

Because of love. His life was an act of love towards this city of his, towards the land where he was born. Love essentially, and above all else, means giving. Thus loving Palermo and its people meant, and still means, giving something to this land, giving everything that our moral, intellectual and professional powers allow us to give, so as to make both the city, and the nation to which it belongs, better.

Falcone began working in a new way here. By that I don't just mean his investigative techniques. For he was also aware that the efforts made by magistrates and investigators had to be on the same wavelength as the way everyone felt. Falcone believed that the fight against the mafia was the first problem that has to be solved in our beautiful and wretched land. But that fight could not just be a detached, repressive undertaking: it also had to be a cultural, moral and even religious movement. Everyone had to be involved, and everyone had to get used to how beautiful the fresh smell of freedom is when compared to the stench of moral compromise, of indifference – of living alongside the mafia, and therefore of being complicit with it.

Nobody has lost the right, or rather the sacrosanct duty, to carry on that fight. Falcone may be dead in the flesh, but he is alive in spirit, just as our faith teaches us. If our consciences have not already woken, then they must awake.

Hope has been given new life by his sacrifice, by his woman's sacrifice, by his bodyguards' sacrifice . . . They died for all of us, for the unjust. We have a great debt towards them and we must pay that debt joyfully by continuing their work, by doing our duty, by respecting the law – even when the law demands sacrifices of us. We must refuse to glean any benefits that we may be able to glean from the mafia system (including favours, a word in someone's ear, a job). We must collaborate with justice, bearing witness to the values that we believe in – in which we are obliged to believe – even when we are in court. We must immediately sever any business or monetary links – even those that may seem innocuous – to anyone who is the bearer of mafia interests, whether large or small. We must fully accept this burdensome but beautiful spiritual inheritance. That way, we can show ourselves and the world that Falcone lives.

As he spoke these words, Borsellino knew he was next. He knew that Falcone was his shield against Cosa Nostra. His family often heard him say, 'It will be him first, then they will kill me.' When Falcone went to work at the Ministry of Justice in Rome, Borsellino returned from Marsala to Palermo to pick up where his friend left off. Now Borsellino was widely rumoured to be the leading candidate for the job Falcone had designed: 'Super-prosecutor', in charge of the National Anti-mafia Directorate, coordinating organised crime investigations at a national level. Borsellino had prepared the maxi-trial with Falcone. Sicily had chosen him, willing or not, to be Falcone's heir as the symbol of the struggle against Cosa Nostra. He had been informed that the explosive meant for him was already in Palermo.

All of which makes his courage all the more astonishing, and the Italian state's failure to protect him all the more appalling.

On 19 July 1992, a FIAT 126 stuffed with explosives was detonated outside Paolo Borsellino's mother's house in via Mariano d'Amelio. The magistrate had just rung the doorbell when he was torn limb from limb.

With Borsellino died his five bodyguards, volunteers all: Agostino Catalano, Vincenzo Li Muli, Walter Eddie Cosina, Claudio Traina, and a twenty-four-year-old female officer from Sardinia called Emanuela Loi. Several times during the previous fifty-six days, Borsellino had gone out alone to buy cigarettes in the hope that he would be shot, thus sparing anyone else from sharing his end.

At his wife's insistence, Borsellino's funeral was private, held in the very church where he had pronounced his own epitaph on 23 June.

The state funeral of his five bodyguards took place in Palermo Cathedral. It turned into a near riot. The streets around were closed off, and a police cordon tried to deny access – for reasons that nobody could understand. Among the vast crowd of grief-stricken citizens shut outside were members of the dead officers' families. There was screaming, spitting, pushing and shoving. Police fought police, to cries of 'they won't let us sit with our dead'. As one eyewitness commented:

> The state seemed like a punch-drunk boxer throwing his fists in the wrong direction, at the people. The tens and tens of thousands of Palermitans who had shown up in the piazza to protest against the mafia were being treated as if they were a gigantic public order issue.

Eventually, the cordon broke, and the crowd flooded into the cathedral. The coffins of Borsellino's bodyguards were greeted with a chorus of '*GIUS-TIZ-IA, GIUS-TIZ-IA.*' Justice. Justice. Justice.

The collapse of the old order

The summer of 1992 in Palermo was a time of rage, despair and disbelief. It was also a time of enormous cultural and political energy as the healthy part of the city sought to broadcast its feelings. There were demonstrations, torch-lit parades, human chains . . . The tree outside Falcone's house in via Notarbartolo became a shrine to the heroes' memory. Balconies across the city were hung with sheets bearing anti-mafia slogans: 'FALCONE LIVES!'; 'GET THE MAFIA OUT OF THE STATE'; 'PALERMO DEMANDS JUSTICE'; 'ANGER & PAIN – WHEN WILL IT END?'

The echoes from Palermo reverberated across a national political landscape that was in the throes of an earthquake. A many-layered crisis was in the process of utterly discrediting the system that had been in force since 1946. The end of the Cold War was working its delayed effects.

Falcone died on 23 May 1992 in the middle of a power vacuum in Rome. Recent general elections had witnessed a slump in the DC vote. 'Collapse of the DC wall', ran one newspaper headline. Following the elections, the beginning of a new five-year parliamentary cycle coincided with the beginning of a new seven-year term for the President of the Republic. A governing coalition had yet to be formed, and newly elected Members of Parliament and the Senate were still busy haggling over who would be the next President of the Republic. Giulio Andreotti was playing a canny game as ever, waiting for other candidates to be eliminated before putting himself forward. The keys to the Quirinale, the Head of State's palace in Rome, were to be the crowning glory of his long career.

The shame and horror surrounding Falcone's death made Andreotti's candidature unthinkable. In the coming months, the most powerful politician in post-war Italy would be increasingly marginalised. Oscar Luigi Scalfaro, a respected Christian Democrat senior statesman with no 'odour of mafia' around him, was rapidly elected President.

However, Italy was not allowed to regain its equilibrium after 23 May. On the evening of Borsellino's assassination, 28 million people followed the news special on the state broadcaster RAI, and a further 12 million watched the horror unfold on the private channels. 'The mafia declares war on the state', ran one national headline the next day. The war, in actual fact, had been declared more than a decade earlier. It now looked as if the state was about to *lose* that war. Not only that, but the country itself seemed to be falling apart.

On 16 September 1992, after months of pressure on international currency markets, the lira was forced out of the Exchange Rate Mechanism – the forerunner of the planned single European currency. The debts racked up by the party-ocracy had destroyed Italy's financial credibility.

The day after the lira's exit from the ERM, Cosa Nostra killed another key component of what had once been the DC machine in Sicily: Ignazio Salvo, the tax collector brought down by the maxi-trial, was shot dead at the door of his villa. Like Salvo Lima, Ignazio Salvo paid the price for failing to protect Cosa Nostra from Falcone and Borsellino.

Meanwhile, a huge corruption scandal had begun, with investigations into the Socialist Party in Milan. The summer and autumn months witnessed more and more politicians and party functionaries targeted by investigations grouped under the name 'Operation Clean Hands'. The scandal continued to gain momentum until it engulfed the weakened 'party-ocracy'. By the end of 1993, some 200 Members of Parliament were under investigation. In January 1994, the Christian Democrat Party was formally dissolved. The First Republic, as it is now known, was dead. Cosa Nostra had helped finish it off.

Yet precisely because the old regime was toppling, Italy found the will to respond to public dismay and fight back. By murdering Falcone and Borsellino, Shorty Riina and his entourage brought down the state's retribution not just on themselves, but on the whole Italian underworld. For a brief and extraordinary season, between Borsellino's death in July 1992 and the spring of 1994, Italy's institutions finally called the mafias to account for more than a decade of slaughter. Even crude numbers registered the transformation. Between 1992 and 1994, 5,343 people were arrested under the Rognoni-La Torre anti-mafia law. In 1991 there were 679 mafia-related homicides in Italy; by 1994 the figure had fallen to 202.

Immediately after Borsellino's murder, 7,000 troops were sent to Sicily to relieve the police of more mundane duties. New anti-mafia legislation was rushed through parliament – legislation that arrived more than a century late, but which was welcome nonetheless. A witness-protection programme was set up. Just as importantly, a tough new prison regime was imposed on underworld bosses. At long last, Italy had the means to stop jails like the Ucciardone becoming command centres for organised crime.

The fight against the mafia was also stepped up on the international front. In September 1992, the Cuntrera-Caruana clan, key members of the heroin-dealing Transatlantic Syndicate, suffered a serious blow: three Cuntrera brothers, Pasquale, Paolo and Gaspare, were extradited from Venezuela.

A new Chief Prosecutor from Turin, Gian Carlo Caselli, volunteered to enter the Palermo war zone. Caselli's bravery and absolute professional integrity were not the only things that made him the perfect man for the job. He had a highly distinguished record investigating the Red Brigades in the late 1970s and early 1980s. He had experience of handling penitents, and of the rigours of life under armed escort. He had also supported Falcone at every stage of his battles with the High Council of the Magistracy. Palermo prosecutors were galvanised as never before.

In January 1993, the very day of Caselli's arrival in Sicily,

Shorty Riina was captured as he and his driver circled a round-about on the Palermo ring road. He had been on the run since 1970. But as with all the many fugitives from justice in Cosa Nostra, 'on the run' was an entirely inappropriate metaphor. In all his twenty-three years of evading capture, Riina had not only masterminded his *coup d'état* within Cosa Nostra, managed his economic empire and murdered countless heroic representatives of the law, he had also married in church, fathered and schooled four children, and obtained the best medical care money could buy.

Riina's arrest resulted from inside information from his former driver. Since Borsellino's death, magistrates had been offered a flood of such tip-offs. The number of penitents grew exponentially too. Some were encouraged by the new measures to protect them; others were afraid of the new prison regime; and some were just shocked to their human core by what happened to Falcone and Borsellino. Gaspare 'Mr Champagne' Mutolo, the Ferrari-driving heroin broker, turned state's evidence in May 1992 after months of gentle encouragement by Giovanni Falcone. He was the last man to be interrogated by Borsellino. The via d'Amelio bomb removed the residues of Mutolo's reticence, and from then on he held nothing back. Having been in prison with bosses close to Riina until the spring of 1992, he was able to supply the first insider account of Cosa Nostra's strategy following the Supreme Court's ruling on the maxi-trial. He also provided evidence that led to the arrest, on Christmas Eve 1992, of Bruno Contrada, former Chief of Police of Palermo and Deputy Head of Italy's internal intelligence service. Contrada would ultimately be convicted of collusion with Cosa Nostra.

Most sensationally of all, Mutolo's evidence was also used against seven-times Prime Minister Giulio Andreotti. When Tommaso Buscetta first met Falcone in 1984, he had warned that Italy was not ready for him to talk about Cosa Nostra's links to politics. The tragic events of 1992 convinced Buscetta that the time was now right: he too implicated Andreotti.

Another penitent, the heroin refiner Francesco 'Mozzarella' Marino Mannoia, told prosecutors that he had seen Andreotti come to a meeting in the early days of 1980 with Stefano Bontate, the Prince of Villagrazia. On the agenda of the meeting was Cosa Nostra's plan to kill the President of the Sicilian Region, Piersanti Mattarella. Andreotti objected to the plan, according to Marino Mannoia. But Bontate overruled him, went ahead and killed Mattarella. Judges would later declare that this meeting marked the point at which Andreotti would increasingly distance himself from Cosa Nostra. Yet it remains a chilling episode. Andreotti knew in advance that the mafia was planning to kill his party colleague Mattarella, yet he did nothing to save him.

Cosa Nostra tried to terrorise the penitents into silence. Santino Di Matteo, captured a few weeks after Riina, was one of the first men from within the group that had planned and executed the bomb attack on Giovanni Falcone to confess. As a result, Di Matteo's eleven-year-old son Giuseppe was kidnapped and kept in a cellar for more than two years before being strangled and dissolved in acid.

Nonetheless, more penitents followed – including from Shorty's inner circle. In September 1992 a young drug dealer called Vincenzo Scarantino was arrested and charged with planting the bomb that killed Paolo Borsellino and his bodyguards. He too would confess.

Sicily was breathing revolutionary air. The Catholic Church has always been the institution most resistant to change in Italy. Moreover, when it came to the subject of organised crime, it had long been unworthy of the faith shown by believers like Paolo Borsellino, not to mention the priests who have paid with their lives for resisting the mafia over the decades. But even the Pope could not fail to be moved by the mood radiating out from Palermo in 1992–3.

In May 1993, John Paul II came to Sicily for the first time in a decade. In Agrigento football stadium, shortly after meeting the family of a young magistrate called Rosario Livatino who was murdered in 1990, the pontiff deviated from his prepared speech to deliver a jeremiad against the mafia and its 'culture of death'. 'Convert! Because one day the judgement of God will come!' The Vatican had abandoned its traditional misgivings about the anti-mafia cause. Cosa Nostra, finally, was anathema.

The camorra suffered almost as much as Cosa Nostra from the bombs in Sicily and the collapse of what was beginning to be called the First Republic.

Camorra boss Pasquale Galasso was a prime example of what it can mean to be bourgeois in southern Italy's organised crime hotspots. He was the son of a 'man of respect' from a small town between Naples and Salerno. His father owned land, traded agricultural produce, ran a dealership selling tractors and diggers, and farmed votes for the local Christian Democrat potentates. Pasquale had a Ferrari when he was barely out of his teens, and enrolled at university to study medicine. In 1975, at age twenty, he shot two men dead. With the help of his father's lawyers, Galasso would eventually be acquitted on the grounds of self-defence. But in the meantime he was sent to Poggioreale prison. There he was taken under the wing of Raffaele 'the Professor' Cutolo.

When the war with the Nuova Famiglia broke out at the end of the 1970s, Galasso received a visit at home from the Professor, who asked him to join the Nuova Camorra Organizzata. Galasso refused, and Cutolo had one of his brothers killed in revenge. Instead of the NCO, Galasso teamed up with the Nuova Famiglia, and in particular with someone else he had met in prison: Carmine 'Mr Angry' Alfieri. The former medical student would be Mr Angry's right arm through the rest of the war; together, the two of them would rise to the top of the Campanian underworld. When the Galasso family villa was finally raided in October 1991, the *Carabinieri* found a hoard of stolen art treasures, including the gilded throne that had once belonged to the last Bourbon King of Naples.

In May 1992 Galasso was captured while chairing a meeting between construction entrepreneurs and members of his clan. Suspecting that he was about to be betrayed by his political friends, he 'repented' later that year and confessed to forty murders. His testimony allowed the police to reconstruct the whole history of the Nuova Famiglia, from its first emergence to its break-up in the wake of the victory over the Nuova Camorra Organizzata.

Galasso's tip-off also led to the arrest of Mr Angry himself, after nine years on the run. Investigators estimated that his wealth amounted to 1,500 billion lire – the biggest patrimony in Italian criminal history, equal to roughly €1,200 million in 2011. The newspapers made much play of the fact that there were heavily annotated copies of Dante and Goethe on Mr Angry's book-shelves, and that he liked to listen to Bach while he was accepting bribes and ordering murders. This most serenely powerful of *camorristi* was sent to the formidable island prison of Pianosa, off the coast of Tuscany. There, after watching the Pope's denunciation of the Sicilian mafia on television, he too resolved to tell all. As a result, the dominant camorra organisation in Campania fell to pieces.

Together Carmine Alfieri and his lieutenant Pasquale Galasso would also do their bit to destroy the DC system of which they had formed an integral part: they named a slew of politicians with whom they claimed to have done business. Many of those politicians belonged to the political machine of Antonio Gava, a former Finance and Interior Minister for the DC.

Like Cosa Nostra, the camorra reacted with ferocity to the threat from the penitents. On the day Mr Angry made his first court appearance, 8 April 1994, killers went looking for his twenty-five-year-old son Antonio. They were told he was staying at a friend's parents' house. They burst into the living room, pointing guns and demanding to know where the Alfieri boy was.

In frustration, one of the killers sprayed a darkened bedroom with machine-gun fire. When they were at last convinced that the family did not know their target's whereabouts, they left, but not before kneecapping one of Mr Angry's distant relatives who was there. Only later was it discovered that there had been an innocent victim of the raid. Maria Grazia Cuomo was asleep in the bedroom that had been sprayed with machine-gun fire. She was fifty-five, unmarried, and rarely went out of the house because she was so ashamed of the purple birthmark that covered much of her face.

Mr Angry's son would eventually be killed in September 2002. His brother was shot dead in December 2004.

The increased pressure from the authorities was also felt by the 'ndrangheta. Here too, there was a new batch of penitents whose testimonies launched important new trials, whose memories cast a light backwards into history of the 'ndrangheta, and whose life stories illustrated the deathly psychological grip of the Calabrian mafia. Here are two examples.

Giacomo Lauro was the son of a sculptor, who carved statues and reliefs for graves in Brancaleone. He was initiated into the 'ndrangheta at eighteen years old in 1960, back in the days when the Honoured Society held its meetings at night, by candlelight, and when triumvir don 'Ntoni Macrì was the dominant figure on the Ionian coast. After fighting in the First 'Ndrangheta War from 1974 to 1977, Lauro was imprisoned and then sent to internal exile in – of all places – northern Campania. There Lauro hooked up with Nuova Famiglia chiefs Antonio Bardellino and Carmine 'Mr Angry' Alfieri and became one of the link-men between the 'ndrangheta and the camorra. He was a close adviser of Antonio 'Ferocious Dwarf' Imerti during the Second 'Ndrangheta War of 1985–91. He was arrested in Holland, where he had gone to receive payment for a cocaine shipment. In his pocket was found a plane ticket for Colombia. When Falcone and Borsellino were killed, he contacted the Italian Embassy and told them he wanted to talk. Lauro's evidence would be crucial in reconstructing the whole history of the Calabrian mafia since the 'mushroom-picking' summit on Montalto in 1969. Lauro's evidence also shed light on the 'ndrangheta's most prominent political murder – that of corrupt Christian Democrat politician Ludovico Ligato in 1989.

Giovanni Riggio came from the southern outskirts of Reggio Calabria. His father was a humble builder. In 1981, when he was eleven years old, his six-year-old brother was killed in a hit-and-run motor accident. Riggio saw the driver. Everyone else in the quarter knew who it was too. But nobody spoke. Riggio's grief-stricken father turned to the authorities, but received no help. One day he asked the local *Carabiniere* officer if he could help. The man just shrugged his uniformed shoulders and said, in so many words, that only the local boss could sort things out. Riggio's father cried in desperation. Henceforth, his surviving son would have a burning resentment against the police, and a powerful fascination for the cocksure criminals who hung around in the local bar.

As a teenager, Riggio began to hang around in the bar too. After several petty crimes, the poisonous language of 'respect' and 'honour' entered his bloodstream. In September 1987, he was initiated with the rite of Osso, Mastrosso and Carcagnosso. The following spring, when Riggio bumped into the man who had run over his little brother, he shot him dead on the spur of the moment. 'Everyone saw me, and I immediately thought: now they're going to arrest me. But they didn't. No one said anything. No one talked. On the contrary: the day after, people were smiling at me, letting me know that I had done the right thing.'

By this time, Riggio's Local had been drawn into a territorial conflict. By the end of it, he had committed four murders himself and helped out in another ten. He was twenty-one years old.

Riggio turned state's evidence in September 1993, after falling in love with a girl from Rovigo who would subsequently become his wife. His evidence put his former boss and most of the Local behind bars. Asked what he thinks about the police now, he said, 'Today I feel as if I am completely one of them, because when it comes down to it we're all running the same risks and fighting for the same cause.'

These penitents, as well as the increased police pressure, undoubtedly had their effects. For it was at this time that the 'ndrangheta finally decided that kidnapping attracted too many police into the wooded folds of the Aspromonte massif. The determination of one woman played a part in their decision too. Angela Casella's son Cesare was kidnapped by the 'ndrangheta in January 1988. Several times during his 743-day-long captivity, she made the journey down to Calabria from the family's home in Pavia, near Milan. She earned the press nickname 'Mother Courage' by appealing for help from the people on Aspromonte; she even chained herself to railings in several village squares. By the time her son was eventually released in January 1990, his case had become as well known as the Getty kidnapping. In the early 1990s, Calabrian gangsters duly abandoned the traffic in captives in which they had been the leading force among Italian criminal organisations – the business that had helped launch them into narcotics and construction.

An important phase in the 'ndrangheta's history was over. But of all the three mafias, the Calabrians were the least damaged by the crackdown in the early 1990s. One measure is the number of penitents. In 1995, 381 members of Cosa Nostra were recorded as state's witnesses. There were markedly fewer penitents from the camorra in the same year: 192. But then former bosses like Carmine 'Mr Angry' Alfieri inflicted disproportionate damage. The total of 133 'ndrangheta defectors was the lowest of all the three historic criminal organisations.

Relatively unscathed, the 'ndrangheta could now harvest the rewards of the long history of invisibility that distinguished it from the camorra and Cosa Nostra. Its decision to refuse Shorty

Riina's invitation to join Cosa Nostra in his war on the state also paid dividends. After 1992, only the 'ndrangheta among criminal organisations would remain mysterious, its internal structure still only partially understood, its existence as a single criminal organisation – rather than a loose ensemble of local clans – as yet unconfirmed.

Negotiating by bomb:
Birth of the Second Republic

The shock from the murders of Falcone and Borsellino was most intensely felt among the magistracy: by their colleagues, obviously, but also by young magistrates who could only admire the two heroes from a distance, and try to live up to the spirit of self-sacrifice that they embodied. One such young magistrate summed up the feelings of a generation of his peers: 'After the second bomb we were genuinely all ready to be killed. But we certainly had not resigned ourselves to mafia rule.' The bombs of 1992 blasted out a deep trench between the representatives of the rule of law on the one side, and the criminal power system on the other. The era of dialogue, and compromise, and collusion between the state and the mafia that produced magistrates like Giuseppe Guido Lo Schiavo, the inspiration for the film *In the Name of the Law*, was over for good.

Or at least it should have been. In the years since 1992, magistrates in Sicily and elsewhere have been haunted by questions that refuse to go away. Shorty Riina had set out clear aims for his organisation when the Supreme Court's ruling on the maxi-trial went against him: 'Wage war on the state first, so as to mould the peace afterwards.' Cosa Nostra was trying to negotiate by bomb. But who was it negotiating with? Did anyone try to appease Falcone and Borsellino's murderers? Was a deal ever struck? Today, twenty years on, investigating magistrates believe they can now glimpse the answers to those questions.

Cosa Nostra's war on the state did not stop with the murders of Giovanni Falcone and Paolo Borsellino in 1992. Nor did the arrest of Shorty Riina in January 1993 bring a halt to the bombing. Indeed later that year, Riina loyalists within Cosa Nostra – bosses who became known as the organisation's 'pro-massacre wing' – launched a series of terrorist attacks aimed at high-profile targets on the Italian mainland.

On 14 May 1993 a car bomb detonated in via Fauro, Rome. The intended victim was Maurizio Costanzo, a leading chat-show host who had been very vocal in his disgust at Cosa Nostra's crimes. Luckily, although many people were wounded, Costanzo's car avoided the explosion and nobody was killed: a massacre had been narrowly averted.

Thirteen days later there was no such luck when a FIAT minivan stuffed with explosives blew up without warning in the shadow of the Uffizi Gallery in Florence. Five people died, including a nine-year-old girl. The van's engine was found embedded in a wall on the other side of the river Arno, and three paintings in the Uffizi were damaged beyond all hope of restoration.

There were five more fatalities in Milan's via Palestro on 27 July. At just after 11 p.m., three firefighters, a police officer and a man who happened to be sleeping on a bench nearby were all caught in the blast from another car bomb.

Barely an hour later, Rome became the next city to be targeted by Cosa Nostra's car bombs. The Catholic Church was made to pay a price for the Pope's denunciation of Cosa Nostra earlier in the year. One device damaged the façade of the Pope's official seat in the city, the Basilica of San Giovanni in Laterano – the huge piazza before it hosts many political rallies. A second explosion destroyed the portico of the Church of San Giorgio in Velabro. There were no victims in either incident.

Rome was also scheduled to be the venue for the worst slaughter of the whole campaign. On 31 October 1993, a Lancia Thema filled with dynamite was parked outside the Olympic Stadium where a football match between Lazio and Udinese was taking place. Activated by a remote control, the bomb was directed at supporters leaving the ground, and at the *Carabinieri* supervising the crowds. The device, which could have killed dozens, failed to detonate.

The annals of Italian organised crime contain no precedent for the outrages of 1992–3. Throughout those two terrible years, the pro-massacre wing's intentions remained consistent: 'Wage war on the state first, so as to mould the peace afterwards.' Riina's demands were high: he wanted both to blunt the state's most effective weapons against organised crime (the penitents, the Rognoni-La Torre law), and also to reverse the judicial results that those weapons had obtained (Falcone and Borsellino's maxi-trial).

As the massacres followed one another, Cosa Nostra's need to negotiate grew ever more urgent, and the list of demands longer. In response to Falcone's death, the government imposed a new prison regime, universally known as 41-*bis* ('Clause 41a'), that aimed to prevent leading *mafiosi* communicating with the outside world, and therefore running their empires. (This was yet another of Falcone's ideas.) In the middle of the night of 19–20 July, just hours after Paolo Borsellino's murder, Clause 41a came into effect when military aircraft took fifty-five bosses from the Ucciardone to join 101 other top criminals in the bleak penal colony on the island of Pianosa off the Tuscan coast. The abolition of the new prison regime was quickly added to Cosa Nostra's war aims.

The whole narrative of the season of mafia massacres in 1992–3 remains worryingly open-ended in a number of crucial respects. For example, some suspect that negligence was not the only factor in play when Paolo Borsellino was left so shamefully underprotected after Falcone's murder.

In the immediate aftermath of Borsellino's own death, his red diary, containing some of his most secret notes, disappeared from the scene of the massacre. (Borsellino's younger brother Salvatore has adopted the red diary as a symbol of his quest for the truth.)

When Shorty Riina was captured in 1993, his villa was left unguarded long enough thereafter for *mafiosi* to enter it, remove property and compromising documents, and even redecorate. Quite how this was allowed to happen has never been satisfactorily ascertained. The episode has led many to suspect that someone within Cosa Nostra betrayed Shorty to the authorities in exchange for favours.

Crucial insights into Cosa Nostra's negotiations with the state came in 2008 when Gaspare Spatuzza began to talk. Spatuzza, known by the nickname of 'Baldy', was a Man of Honour from the Brancaccio Family of Cosa Nostra, who was already serving life sentences for his role in Cosa Nostra's bombing campaign on the Italian mainland. Baldy explained that Vincenzo Scarantino, the young drug dealer who had already spent a decade and a half in prison for planting the car bomb that killed Borsellino, could not be guilty – for the simple reason that he, Spatuzza, was responsible. So convincing was the corroboration that Baldy provided to back up his revelation, that Scarantino has since been released and his innocence confirmed. (He had long maintained that he was not guilty, claiming that he was tortured until he confessed.)

Another new mystery about the massacres of 1992–3 was thereby exposed. Was Scarantino framed by overenthusiastic policemen who were desperate to get any kind of result in the climate of emergency following the deaths of Falcone and Borsellino? Or was the shocking injustice he suffered part of a bigger and much more devious plan?

Baldy Spatuzza's evidence has brought new energy to the search for the truth about the negotiations between Cosa Nostra and the state in the early 1990s. Still more worrying fragments of evidence have emerged. Some *Carabinieri* have confirmed that they tried to make contact with Cosa Nostra in the summer of 1992 to try and stop the massacres, but they deny that there were any negotiations.

In the summer and autumn of 1993, while Baldy was placing

car bombs in Florence, Milan and Rome, no fewer than 480 *mafiosi* were released from the Clause 41a prison regime by the Minister of Justice Giovanni Conso. Conso has recently offered the explanation that this act of clemency was a purely personal initiative, aimed at sending out an accommodating signal.

Most troubling of all, it has now been confirmed that Paolo Borsellino found out that overtures were being made to Cosa Nostra in the days following Falcone's death – overtures that he vigorously opposed. Shorty Riina's top killer has claimed that Cosa Nostra brought forward its plan to kill Borsellino precisely in order to stop him interfering with the deal-making: 'The ongoing negotiations were the main reason why the plan to eliminate Borsellino was accelerated.'

One of the two most important murders in the entire history of Italian organised crime therefore remains substantially unsolved. Testimonies from Spatuzza and others raise the chilling possibility that Paolo Borsellino was deliberately sacrificed. Some witnesses speak of secret service involvement both in the negotiations between the mafia and the state, and in the murder of Paolo Borsellino.

As I write, several mafia bosses, including Shorty Riina, stand accused for their part in trying to blackmail the state in 1992–3. Three senior *Carabinieri* and two politicians face related charges. A former Minister of the Interior has been accused of giving false evidence about the negotiations. Their trial has only just begun, and the presumption of innocence can be no mere formality in such an intricate and controversial case.

The charges filed by the investigating magistrates paint a picture of a negotiation that developed over several stages, and involved links between Cosa Nostra and a number of functionaries and politicians, by no means all of them among the accused in the new trial. What the magistrates believe is that, in order to achieve its aims in 1992–3. Cosa Nostra needed to find new political partners – just when Italy's Cold War political parties were breaking up, and the country was negotiating the tumultuous passage between the First Republic and the Second Republic (as we now call them). Among the protagonists of the negotiations on the state's side were politicians of three kinds, according to the as yet untested charges. First, there were those from the First Republic, previously close to Cosa Nostra, who felt threatened by Riina's rage. Second, there were statesmen trying to pilot Italy through its economic and political crisis who were not friendly with the Sicilian mafia, but who may have made or approved misguided attempts to appease the pro-massacre wing. And finally there were the new men trying to assert themselves politically in the chaos of the First Republic's collapse. Men like Marcello Dell'Utri, the Sicilian right-hand man of a media entrepreneur who went on to become the dominant and most controversial figure of the Second Republic, Silvio Berlusconi.

Berlusconi did well out of the close political friendships he made during the First Republic: the Socialist Party leader and sometime Prime Minister, Bettino Craxi, was the best man at his second wedding. The collapse of the old political order was a serious threat to his business interests. It is thought that as early as June 1992 (between the murders of Falcone and Borsellino, that is), Berlusconi's people were taking soundings about founding a new political party. The magistrates contend that, as Berlusconi's political plans took shape, Dell'Utri offered himself to Cosa Nostra as a negotiating partner, promising to grant some of its wishes in return for support. The Second Republic began in March 1994, when Berlusconi led his new party, Forza Italia, to election victory. That was the point in time, according to the magistrates, when 'the new pact of co-habitation between the state and the mafia was finally sealed'.

Marcello Dell'Utri is an old acquaintance to readers of these pages. It was he who hired the *mafioso* Vittorio Mangano in 1974 to protect Berlusconi and his family from kidnappers. Since 1996, Dell'Utri has been the subject of a seemingly endless mafia trial. He currently has an outstanding conviction for helping Cosa Nostra, and a sentence of nine years in prison to serve. But Dell'Utri is still a free man because the verdict remains provisional until the Supreme Court rules. So far, the judges have explicitly rejected the argument that Dell'Utri's relationship with Cosa Nostra was still operative in the early 1990s when the mafia–state negotiations are thought to have taken place. But that too may change. It should also be stressed that an investigation based on the theory that Berlusconi and Dell'Utri had a role in commissioning Cosa Nostra's bombing campaign was shelved because of a lack of evidence in 2002. Berlusconi has never been charged with any crime in relation to Cosa Nostra's bombs. Nor does he appear in the latest trial, except as the victim of an alleged extortion by his friend Marcello Dell'Utri, who is one of the two politicians who face charges that they helped Cosa Nostra with its negotiating strategy.

No period in Italian mafia history is without its lingering uncertainties. Historians live with the constant risk that their work will be unmade when some new document surfaces from the archives, or a new penitent unlocks his memory. The transitional years of 1992–4 are more than usually dogged by doubt. Only time – the glacier-slow time of the Italian judicial system – will reveal what truth, if any, there is in all the accusations about Cosa Nostra's plan to negotiate by bomb.

Even if the worst suspicions about the mafia–state negotiations turned out to be true, it would be very rash indeed to conclude either that Silvio Berlusconi's main aim in government was to do Cosa Nostra's bidding, or indeed that a pact with Cosa Nostra explained his political success. There is much, much more to the whole Berlusconi phenomenon than his alleged links to Cosa Nostra.

That said, Berlusconi's priority while in power was to protect his business interests from what he deemed to be a judicial conspiracy. In the process of defending himself, he damaged the anti-mafia cause. In Berlusconi's view, popularity and electoral success exempted him from the rule of law. Many of the measures he introduced, or tried to introduce, displayed a categorical failure to perceive the boundary between his own personal concerns on the one hand, and those of the state and the Italian people on the other. He repeatedly tried to make himself immune from prosecution. He introduced amnesties for people seeking to reimport money that had been exported illegally to foreign or offshore bank accounts (usually to avoid the attentions of the law or the tax authorities). He decriminalised false accounting, and made it harder for magistrates to obtain evidence from financial institutions in other countries. He introduced a law specifically targeted at Gian Carlo Caselli, the Chief Prosecutor who had gone to Palermo after the deaths of Falcone and Borsellino and achieved such extraordinary results. The law tweaked the age qualifications for the job of National Chief Anti-mafia Prosecutor, and was aimed at stopping Caselli getting the job for which he was the outstanding candidate. *Mafiosi, camorristi* and *'ndranghetisti* were not the intended beneficiaries of these and other changes, but they will have greeted them with a broad smile nonetheless.

Berlusconi's rhetoric on the issue of organised crime was frequently irresponsible. To one British journalist, he said that he thought that anti-mafia magistrates were 'mad'. 'To do that job you need to be mentally disturbed, you need psychic disturbances,' he asserted. Berlusconi's party attracted electoral support from the mafias. In open court in 1994, 'ndrangheta boss Giuseppe Piromalli said, 'We'll all vote for Berlusconi.' In a sense, that fact is not scandalous: the mafias are attracted by power, whoever holds it. But Berlusconi did little to disown or discourage such supporters.

Whether he was in opposition or in government (which he was in 1994–5, 2001–6, and 2008–11) Silvio Berlusconi was impossible to ignore, inspiring both adulation and loathing. Viewed from abroad, his dominance gave the Italian political scene during the years 1994–2011 an appearance of clarity that was deceptive. If one looks beyond those appearances, one finds a dispiritingly familiar picture of political confusion and paralysis of a kind that has always prevented Italy introducing the reforms it needs, and made the state weak in the face of the threat from organised crime.

The end of the Cold War inaugurated a new series of opportunities and threats for Italy, as for its neighbours and the other developed countries. There was the expansion and deepening of the European Union, with the creation of the Euro and its subsequent crisis. Globalisation introduced Italy for the first time to mass inward migration and the tide of cheap Chinese manufactures. The rise of the information society forced economies worldwide to recalibrate. The end of the Cold War ideologies left many political systems looking for new ways to engage with distracted electors. Old problems – like the balance between social solidarity and economic individualism – were posed in novel forms.

Italy, in particular, had a long and urgent to-do list that it had inherited from the First Republic: its poor education system; the lamentable state of its public finances; one of the worst records for youth unemployment and tax avoidance on the continent; the chronic imbalance between North and South; a serious lack of investment in research and development; a pensions time-bomb; and last but not least, the control that criminal organisations exercised over a good quarter of the national territory. The fall of the First Republic gave Italian politics of all colours a chance to make a fresh start in the task of offering collective solutions to challenges new and old, global and local. On most measures, after two decades of the Second Republic, few observers would view the results as being other than lamentable – left, right and centre.

In the First Republic, parliament and the Senate had been dominated from the centre ground by the vast, formless and irremovable 'white whale' of the DC. The extremes of left (Communist Party) and right (the neo-Fascists) were perpetually excluded from power. Now the white whale was gone. Italy's Catholics, who had once been united in the DC, were scattered across much of the political spectrum. The Communists (mostly) converted to some form of social democracy, and the neo-Fascists (mostly) restyled themselves as a conventional European party of the centre-right. No one was excluded *a priori* from the game of forming governing coalitions. Even the Northern League – a raucous movement that wanted independence for a fictional country called 'Padania', and which was given to racist outbursts unacceptable in any other European polity – was now a sought-after ally.

What many people hoped for at the birth of the Second Republic was that a new clarity would reign. To give Italy effective government, a consensus formed around so-called 'bipolarism': the idea that two opposing forces of centre-right and centre-left should compete for the voters' loyalties, and form a government or an opposition according to who came out on top. Italian politicians, in other words, would have to get used to winning *and* losing elections. Governments would rule with the knowledge that they would be thrown out by the electorate if they did not perform. Nobody would be able to occupy power in the way that the DC had done for the best part of half a century. No longer would the left have a monopoly on trying to make political capital out of accusations of corruption or complicity with organised crime.

The theory was good. The practice, however, was confusion: partly because of the badly drafted electoral laws designed to promote bipolarism, but mostly because of the familiar Italian spectacle of factional infighting. Minor parties, able to blackmail larger ones by threatening to withdraw their support, continued to proliferate. Catholics and ex-Communists continued to search, in vain, for a political identity. The interests of North and South, lay values and Catholicism, region and nation continued to divide each electoral alliance from within – to say nothing of the more conventional sources of political disagreement over economic and social policy, or indeed of the instability brought by overweening personal ambition. Shamelessly expedient deals were struck between politicians who had previously traded vicious insults. In 1998, Northern League leader Umberto Bossi said there could be 'no agreement with the *mafioso*'. He meant Berlusconi, whom he would subsequently go on to support staunchly throughout their time as coalition allies.

Each election saw a confusing array of new acronyms and symbols, shallow political 'brands' for hastily formed parties and coalitions. Each coalition of parties of centre-right or centre-left that presented itself at the polls started to fall apart almost as soon as it was elected, cripplingly divided as it was. Politicians predictably abandoned governing coalitions as soon as the going got tough. Governments continued to hand out appointments to their political friends. Most obviously, the state television networks, lacking any tradition of independence, continued to be distributed on party lines, and continued to produce boring and biased news coverage that seemed designed to put young people off democracy for life.

The end of the old ideologies killed off some of Italy's few antibodies to the old political maladies of patronage, clientelism and corruption. The country's elected representatives seemed more and more to fit to their caricature: they were a self-interested 'caste', cut off from the population behind the tinted windows of their blue, state-funded, luxury limousines. Meanwhile, the nation's problems went unsolved.

Under the Second Republic, the battle against the mafias has been carried on largely in spite of the political system, rather than because of it. The strange thing is that some quite extraordinary successes have been recorded all the same. And the most extraordinary of these have been in Sicily. If a deal *was* struck between Cosa Nostra and the state between 1992 and 1994, then almost all of the bosses who negotiated that deal are now buried in maximum-security prisons. Since the arrest of Shorty Riina, Cosa Nostra has sunk steadily into the worst crisis in its entire history.

7

THE SECOND REPUBLIC AND THE MAFIAS

Cosa Nostra: **The head of the Medusa**

Since the capture of Totò 'Shorty' Riina in 1993, Sicily's anti-mafia magistrates, police *Carabinieri*, and *Guardia di Finanza* (Tax Police) have scored a series of victories over Cosa Nostra that have absolutely no historical precedent. By comparison, the Fascist campaigns against the Sicilian mafia in the 1920s and 1930s were clumsy, superficial and fitful. Cosa Nostra continues to pay a very heavy price for its war on the state between 1979 and 1993.

Every *mafioso* accepts a certain amount of prison time as an occupational hazard. Yet he will do everything he can to avoid being convicted: from intimidating witnesses to pulling strings so that judges make 'anomalous' rulings. If he is unlucky enough to be on the receiving end of a guilty verdict, a *mafioso* still has the option of becoming a fugitive. But as we have seen, few Sicilian mafia fugitives from justice actually run away. Most just go to ground in their own fiefdom, take on an assumed identity and carry on running their criminal affairs just as before. There were hundreds of such renegades in Sicily at the start of the 1990s; among them were the bosses responsible for Cosa Nostra's worst crimes. Their charisma seemed magnified by their invisibility: an aura grew up around them – both among *mafiosi* and in the general population. They were a living proclamation of the Italian state's failure to enforce the law, to turn the sentences issued by the courts into years actually served behind bars.

Even before the maxi-trial, Cosa Nostra knew exactly how grave a challenge to its authority any serious attempt to round up fugitives would be. That is why the bosses killed Flying

Squad officer Beppe Montana in 1985. His murder – he was shot dead in his swimming trunks when he was using his own free time to follow up leads on mafia fugitives – encapsulates both the dedication and the vulnerability of the forces ranged against Cosa Nostra in the bloody 1980s.

Gian Carlo Caselli was the Piedmontese Chief Prosecutor who stepped into the Palermo hot seat after the murder of Paolo Borsellino in 1993. Caselli would continue in his role until 1999. He immediately made the capture of Cosa Nostra's fugitives from justice a priority. He kept a list of them in his desk drawer, and when one was taken, he would cross the name off in green ink. By the end of Caselli's Palermo stint, over three hundred names had been cancelled out. Penitents gave information that led to the capture of bosses in hiding, some of whom turned penitent in their turn, supplying more precious leads.

The chain of defections was not the only weapon in the authorities' armoury. In the 1990s, the pursuit of Cosa Nostra's fugitives became increasingly technologically advanced: bugging and tracking devices came into play, and the police and *Carabinieri* acquired ever more expertise in their use. Before Giovanni Falcone died, he turned his experience in the Palermo pool of magistrates into a template for Italy's new national organisations for investigating and prosecuting organised crime. After Falcone's death, Palermo continued to be the model for the rest of the country: it became an elite school for teams of *mafioso* hunters.

Among the many leading fugitives to be rounded up was Leoluca Bagarella, 'Shorty' Riina's brother-in-law. Bagarella was the first boss to step into the huge leadership vacuum created by the arrest of the dictatorial Riina. Bagarella's power was primarily military: he inherited command of Cosa Nostra's specialised death squads. He also inherited Riina's war on the Italian state, a war which Bagarella continued by orchestrating Cosa Nostra's terrorist attacks on the Italian mainland in 1993.

Tracking down a fugitive *mafioso* like Bagarella meant learning everything there was to find out about his territory and his network of contacts, piecing together fragments of information on his personal life and psychology. Once the fugitives were captured, their life stories gave sociologists and psychologists rich insights into the world-within-a-world that is Cosa Nostra. The Sicilian mafia's interior culture seemed utterly distant from our own experience, rendered alien by a constant fear of betrayal and a casual familiarity with violent death. Yet at the same time, mafia life was eerily ordinary, filled with day-to-day stories of love and loss. As so often, Giovanni Falcone's insights into the mafia mentality were proving correct. *Mafiosi* were not monsters, Falcone once pointed out:

> Getting to know *mafiosi* has profoundly influenced my way of relating to other people, and also my convictions. I have learned to recognise the humanity even in those who are apparently the worst of beings. I have learned to have a respect for other people's opinions that is real and not just a question of form.

Bagarella's story was a case in point. He married his wife, Vincenzina Marchese, in 1991. Her menfolk were members of the Corso dei Mille Family of Cosa Nostra. So this was a classic union of mafia dynasties, celebrated sumptuously with hundreds of guests. Bagarella had the *Godfather* theme tune recorded over the wedding videos. Yet at the same time, the marriage was unquestionably a love match, and the two were devoted companions. Penitents have since related that, if Vincenzina called to tell Bagarella that his dinner was nearly ready, he would even break off from strangling someone to join her at table.

However the Bagarellas had a secret anguish. Vincenzina struggled to bear the child that she yearned for. She became convinced that this was a divine punishment for what Cosa Nostra had done to Giuseppe Di Matteo – the penitent's young son who was held captive for more than two years and who would eventually be strangled and dissolved in acid. She constantly asked her husband what had happened to the boy, and received repeated reassurances (which were truthful at the time) that he was still alive. But Vincenzina could not be convinced. So, on the night of 12 May 1995, she hanged herself in the couple's hideout. Because he was on the run from the law, Bagarella could not give her a decent burial. He even had to move her from one shallow grave to another. Her body has never been found. During a month of mourning, Bagarella refused to take part in any murders out of respect for his beloved. When he was captured on 24 June 1995, six weeks after his wife's death, he was just planning a return to action. He had her wedding ring on a chain round his neck.

More fugitive members of Cosa Nostra's Palermo Commission fell into the dragnet. On 20 May 1996 came the turn of the man who killed Falcone. Giovanni Brusca was known in mafia circles as 'the Man who Cuts Christians' Throats' or, more simply, as *'U Verru* – 'the Pig'. He came up with the idea of lying on his stomach on a skateboard to push the barrels of explosive meant for Falcone into a drainage tunnel under the motorway. On 23 May 1992, it was Brusca who pressed the detonator. 'The Pig' had committed so many murders that he had lost count: somewhere between a hundred and two hundred was his disturbingly vague estimate. When he eventually turned state's evidence, magistrates had to bring him a list of all the suspicious deaths and disappearances in western Sicily in the previous twenty years so that he could tick off the ones that were his handiwork.

As the police closed in on Brusca, he was forced to move from one safe house to another. In February 1996, investigators unearthed the bunker that the boss had had built by a construction entrepreneur friend. From the outside, it looked like a peasant's dilapidated homestead. But inside, in the marble floor of the expensively appointed kitchen, there was a concealed entrance worthy of a James Bond villain. When Brusca pressed a remote control, a section of floor would descend like a lift five metres underground into a two-room apartment. One of the two rooms had a metal door with a spyhole, just like a prison cell. This was where Giuseppe Di Matteo, the penitent's son, was held captive, and where Brusca eventually had him strangled and dropped into an acid bath. Branching off from the apartment was a further secret tunnel that led to a large metal tank where investigators discovered the biggest arms cache in Italian history. A human chain of *Carabinieri* spent hours passing out more than four hundred pistols, dozens and dozens of pump-action shotguns and machine guns, explosives of all kinds (including Semtex), several bazookas, boxes and boxes of grenades, and ten RPG 18s – the shoulder-launched antitank missiles that were known as 'Allah's hammer' because the Taliban used them against Russian helicopters in Afghanistan. There were even some collector's pieces, such as a Thompson machine gun with a circular magazine, just like the ones in the Al Capone-era gangster films. Brusca's arsenal was only one of many taken out of commission in these years.

Brusca's last hideout was far from his territory, in the province of Agrigento in southern Sicily. He was eventually betrayed by his nostalgia for home. He made regular calls to order sausages and meat from the butcher in the town of his birth, San Giuseppe Jato – calls that the *Carabinieri* tapped. Brusca was watching a television programme about Giovanni Falcone when the thunder flashes went off and the police burst in on him.

The capture of bosses like Bagarella and Brusca marked the end of the most dangerous phase in the Sicilian mafia's history. Like the entire leadership of Cosa Nostra, these men had approved Shorty Riina's policy of waging war on the state. They had also been part of a smaller group of bosses (the 'pro-massacre wing' of Cosa Nostra) that favoured carrying on with that war once Riina was captured in 1993. But as the roundup continued, the pro-massacre wing lost control of the organisation, and Cosa Nostra entered an even deeper leadership crisis. A new strategy of 'submersion' was implemented in response to that crisis.

The boss responsible for the submersion strategy was Bernardo Provenzano. Provenzano was scarcely a peacemaker by vocation. For most of his criminal career, he formed a solid partnership with Shorty Riina in any question relating to Cosa Nostra's internal politics. Both were *corleonesi*, and both pupils of Luciano Liggio. Provenzano's relentless pursuit of his enemies had long ago earned him the nickname 'the Tractor'. He bore just as much responsibility for the horrors of the 1980s, and for the murders of Falcone and Borsellino, as did any other member of the Palermo Commission. Yet Provenzano also had another nickname that spoke of different skills: 'the Accountant'. To his partnership with Riina he brought greater business acumen, and a more refined aptitude for weaving ties with politicians.

Mafia penitents tell us that when the pro-massacre wing of Cosa Nostra sought to step up their terrorist campaign in 1993 (they even planned to blow up the Leaning Tower of Pisa), Provenzano began to go quiet. Internal divisions that had been kept in check by Riina began to surface once more. The centralisation process that Cosa Nostra had undergone when the *corleonesi* mounted their coup was thrown into reverse. Precinct bosses acquired more autonomy – and more power to create trouble. Try as he might to appear as if he was above the fray, the Tractor was viewed with suspicion by the pro-massacre wing. In 1995, he fought a proxy war with Riina's brother-in-law, Leoluca Bagarella, for control of the town of Villabate at the edge of Palermo. Rightly or wrongly, many within Cosa Nostra were also convinced that Provenzano had betrayed Shorty Riina to the authorities in 1993.

Provenzano was the most experienced fugitive from justice in Sicilian mafia history, having been on the run since 1963. For much of that time, he had even been rumoured to be dead. Once he was in charge, he abandoned Riina's direct challenge to the Italian state, and tried to repair the damage Cosa Nostra was suffering as a result of the reaction to the massacres of 1992 and 1993. His submersion strategy – 'walking with padded shoes', as he termed it – aimed to keep Cosa Nostra out of the headlines. Accordingly, the number of murders fell dramatically. The Tractor brought an end to the atrocities committed against penitents and their families. Instead, Cosa Nostra gave renewed support to imprisoned *mafiosi* and their families in the hope that the penitents would retract their evidence. The flood of penitents from Cosa Nostra, which had peaked at 424 in 1996, was reduced to a trickle. One effect of this was that the Tractor's support network proved much harder to disrupt than had been the case with bosses like Bagarella and Brusca.

Provenzano placed a renewed emphasis on cultivating the Sicilian mafia's traditional, covert friendships with corrupt elements in the state and business. Extortion rackets were absolutely central to the submersion strategy. Extortion is the Sicilian mafia's least visible and yet most important crime. Each entrepreneur or criminal who gives in to the local boss's demand for a percentage of takings is not only providing the mafia with its staple income; he or she is also recognising the mafia's sovereignty, its right to intervene. Extortion is how a boss gathers information about his territory, and how he gets his foot in the door of lawful businesses. What the tax system is for a democratic state, extortion rackets are for the mafias – southern Italy's shadow state.

The submersion strategy certainly managed to buy time. But Provenzano faced perhaps insuperable challenges. For one thing, an old problem for the Sicilian mafia was rearing its head once more: the tendency of politicians to break their promises. The laughably bad Italian that Provenzano used in his typed messages to his network is impossible to render properly in English. But I hope the following extract from a 1997 message gives some idea of the Tractor's concerns when it came to making friends in politics:

> Now you tell me that you've got a good level political contact, whod allow you to manage lots of big works, and before going ahead you wanna know what I fink? If I don't no him I can't tell you nothing. You'd need to no the names? And no how they are set up? Coz today you can't trust no one. Could they be swindlers? Could they be cops? Could they be infiltrators? Could they be time wasters? Could they be massive schemers? If you don't no the road you gotta travel, you can't set off – so I can't tell you nothing.

In this case, as in many others, Provenzano failed to make a clear decision. Truth be told, his power to make policy had severe limits. For one thing, his authority still depended to a great extent on Riina's prestige. The Tractor never sat at the head of the Commission, which had not been convened since Shorty was captured. As Sicilian investigating magistrates have put it:

> Provenzano never underwent a formal investiture by the other precinct bosses. So he exercised his supremacy in substance, but not officially, and he did so only by virtue of the fact that he was considered to be 'the same thing' as Riina.

In other words, the Tractor was a first among equals, and not a *capo di tutti i capi*. He had the authority to *advise*, but not to *order*. In the end, mere advice would not be enough to save Cosa Nostra's leadership – either from the persistent divisions within the organisation, or from the mafia hunters.

The first of Provenzano's inner circle to be caught was his number two, Pietro Aglieri, the boss of Santa Maria di Gesù. Aglieri's story revealed yet more about the strange world of Cosa Nostra, and in particular about the religious beliefs that historically have helped *mafiosi* cloak the real nature of their power. In his youth, Aglieri had studied theology in a seminary. Investigators tracked him down by following a Carmelite priest, Father Mario Frittitta. (He was the same Carmelite who had spoken the homily at the funeral of the footballer-fisherman suspected of being the mafia's lookout when Flying Squad officer Beppe Montana was killed in 1985.) Father Frittitta, it turned out, was Aglieri's confessor. In the boss's farmhouse hideout, as well as the usual gangland paraphernalia like weapons and a radio for listening to police communications, was a chapel complete with an altar, crucifix, incense-burner, pews, and cushions for kneeling on during prayer.

Was Aglieri's faith genuine? Ultimately, only the Almighty himself can give us the answer to that question. Clearly, what Aglieri believed in was a twisted version of Christianity that he somehow thought was compatible with his vocation as a professional criminal. He may have found in it some kind of justification for the evil he did.

What *is* certain about Aglieri's religion is that it was strategically useful to him at that moment in Cosa Nostra's history. Aglieri, like his mentor Provenzano, was seeking ways to repair the damage to Cosa Nostra's legitimacy caused by the deaths of Falcone and Borsellino, and by the Pope's long overdue condemnation of mafia culture. Making religious noises – of humility and piety – could feasibly help the bosses mend the bonds with the organisation's members and friends that were broken by episodes like the horrific murder of the young penitent's son, Giuseppe Di Matteo. The typed notes through which Provenzano communicated with other bosses, and with his business friends, are full of religious phrases: 'Thanks be to God', 'God willing, I am at your complete disposal'. Whether it expressed any form of devotion, Provenzano's language revealed a political style that contrasted markedly with his old friend Riina's.

In the spring of 2000, the 'devout' boss Pietro Aglieri – now in prison – was one of a group from Provenzano's wing of Cosa

Nostra who proposed to dissociate themselves from the organisation. The idea was that they would confess their crimes and repudiate the mafia, but without turning state's evidence and ratting on former comrades-in-arms. In short, Aglieri and his allies would repent in the eyes of God; but they would not turn penitent in the eyes of the state.

The Sicilian mafia being what it is, there was a catch: dissociation would only happen if prison conditions were relaxed and some of Italy's new anti-mafia legislation repealed. Not long afterwards, it became clear that members of the 'ndrangheta and camorra also supported such a bargain. Life behind bars had created a common front between some of southern Italy's most feared mob bosses.

Investigating magistrates immediately realised that accepting 'dissociation' would be a very bad deal indeed for the state. Moreover, they suspected it was part of a plan to engineer a negotiated settlement to the war between the state and Cosa Nostra – a settlement that would leave Cosa Nostra intact, and pave the way for a return to the traditional partnership between the authorities and the Sicilian mafia's shadow state. The dissociation offer fitted perfectly with the Tractor's submersion strategy, in other words. Worryingly, the proposal received a warm welcome in a newspaper article published in Silvio Berlusconi's newspaper *Il Giornale*. More worrying still, in 2001, the magistrate who did most to oppose the dissociation deal was suddenly removed from his job by Berlusconi's Minister of Justice.

In the end, Aglieri's dissociation proposal never came to anything, thanks to incisive coverage by investigative journalists and political lobbying by anti-mafia magistrates. Nevertheless, it resurfaced now and again over the coming years, as a reminder of Cosa Nostra's ability to strike up an insidious dialogue with elements of the Italian state.

The pursuit of the mafia fugitives continued, meanwhile. In April 2002, the police captured Antonino Giuffrè, known as *Manuzza* ('Little Hand') because his right hand was mangled in a hunting accident. Unlike the devout Pietro Aglieri, Little Hand quickly turned penitent, giving investigators important new insights into the way Bernardo 'the Tractor' Provenzano was restructuring Cosa Nostra and rebuilding its links to business. When he was captured, Little Hand was found with a shopping bag full of letters to Provenzano from *mafiosi* and entrepreneurs in his network.

But it would take another four long years of sleuthing for the Tractor's logistical system to be dismantled and for Provenzano himself to be unearthed. In April 2006, disbelieving journalists from all over the world swooped on Sicily to film the shack near Corleone where Cosa Nostra's great strategist, a man who had been a fugitive from justice for no less than forty-three years, was finally captured. Could a man as powerful as Provenzano really have lived in such humble surroundings, living off ricotta cheese and chicory like some peasant of days gone by? The truth was that he was no peasant: he was a professional criminal. And his home town of Corleone was a last redoubt, a place he had been forced to retreat to when every other operational base had been denied him by the authorities.

The mafia hunters did not let up even after the capture of Riina's heir. Just over two months later, they arrested another forty-five *mafiosi* in the course of an operation that provided a new understanding of political fissures that had brought Cosa Nostra to the brink of civil war, even while the state closed in on its leaders. The fissures had their roots in the most savage conflict in Cosa Nostra's history: Shorty's war of extermination against the leading mafia drug barons in 1981–3. At the time of that war, *mafiosi* from some of the losing Families, notably the members of the Inzerillo clan (who were closely related by blood to the Gambino Family in the American Cosa Nostra), had fled into exile in the United States. Now there was a move afoot to allow the exiles back to fill out the organisation's thinning ranks and rebuild the transatlantic narcotics pipeline.

The proposal to bring the exiles home had been in the air since Shorty Riina's capture, and it was bound to be inflammatory. No less than twenty-one members of the vast Inzerillo clan had been killed by the *corleonesi*. Others had been forced to buy their own lives by betraying their closest relatives to Riina. An entire *borgata*, Ciaculli, had been ethnically cleansed by the victors in the war. Only a deal brokered by powerful American bosses had stopped the *corleonesi* pursuing their surviving enemies after they escaped to the United States. With the *corleonesi* now weakened, the exiles' return was bound to bring a settling of old scores. 'Tractor' Provenzano lacked the authority to impose a solution. So the issue festered, and Cosa Nostra divided into two armed camps: one in favour of the exiles' return, and one against. Once the Tractor was hunted down, the last obstacle to civil war was removed.

The most fervent proponent of the exiles' return was Salvatore Lo Piccolo, who was initiated into the same Partanna-Mondello *cosca* of Cosa Nostra as Gaspare 'Mr Champagne' Mutolo, and who had close links with the Gambino Family in the United States.

Lo Piccolo's plan was opposed by Antonino Rotolo, who was one of the older generation of bosses to whom the Tractor had entrusted leadership roles as part of the submersion strategy. Rotolo viewed the return of the exiles with undisguised dread: as a loyal supporter of Shorty Riina, he had personally taken part in the butchery of the exiles, and knew that his life would be forfeit if they were given permission to return. In 2006 Rotolo was serving a life sentence. Or at least he was in theory: for he had faked a heart condition and thereby won the right to serve out his time in the rather more comfortable surroundings of his own house in Villagrazia. Whenever he wanted to meet his men, he would call them to a humble garage that lay just over his garden wall. The garage, however, was bugged by the police, who listened in as Rotolo set out his plans to kill Lo Piccolo. He was arrested before the plan could be put into effect.

Lo Piccolo was left as the most powerful boss in the province. But not for long: in November 2007, he too was arrested. Investigators found a wealth of evidence in the leather bag he had with him at the time. There was a directory of businesses paying protection money: the monthly sums extorted ranged from €500 for a shop, to €10,000 for a construction firm. There were notes discussing murders and political friendships. There was an up-to-date map of the Families of the Palermo area. There was a sacred image inscribed with the oath that affiliates take when they are admitted to the organisation: 'I swear to be faithful to Cosa Nostra. If I should ever betray it, may my flesh burn as this image now burns.'

Last but not least, Lo Piccolo had with him a badly typed piece of paper headed 'Rights and Duties', which was a kind of 'ten commandments' of Cosa Nostra. Rule One, for example, stipulated that, 'You are not allowed to introduce yourself [as a *mafioso*] either on your own or to another friend unless there is a third party [i.e. a Man of Honour known to both] there to do it.' Several other rules proscribe 'immoral' behaviour: no *mafioso* is allowed to look at the wives of 'our friends', or to disrespect his own wife; and no one is allowed to be initiated into Cosa Nostra if they have 'sentimental betrayals' in their immediate family. As ever, the Sicilian mafia was concerned to make sure that affairs of the heart do not interfere with affairs of the gun. Although we are now pretty certain that similar rules have been in force for as long as the Sicilian mafia has existed, to my knowledge no written version of them had ever been captured before. It seemed yet another symptom of the unprecedented trouble that Cosa Nostra was in.

That trouble became even more profound in February 2008, when a joint operation by the FBI and the Italian police led to the arrest of ninety *mafiosi* on either side of the Atlantic. Many of them were from the clans exiled in the 1980s, whom Salvatore Lo Piccolo had hoped to bring back to Sicily. The operation, codenamed 'Old Bridge', prevented the American Cosa Nostra from crossing the ocean to come to the rescue of its Sicilian sister association as it had done so many times in the past. Even in its name, the operation showed that the lessons of history had been learned: close transatlantic collaboration in the fight against organised crime brings big rewards for justice.

The assault on Cosa Nostra was now remorseless. In the spring of 2008, *Carabinieri* tailing mafia boss Giuseppe Scaduto saw him go to a mob meeting in a garage in the city centre. With the surveillance skills they had by now honed to perfection, officers placed listening devices and even cameras in the garage. They then proceeded to watch live as, between 6 May and 27 June, Cosa Nostra's bosses schemed. It emerged that, with Provenzano in prison, the time had come for the bosses still at large to reorganise themselves – to impose the kind of coordinating structure that Cosa Nostra always has when it is working best: 'a Commission to deal with the serious things, with situations, and that way we all stay friends', as one *capo* explained.

> If we all do our own thing, like the Neapolitans do . . . if we do things like they do we'll never get anywhere . . . Instead, everyone takes his precinct and then we sort things out nicely. And in the end we all sit down and try and create a kind of Commission like in the old days.

A kind of Commission: the hesitancy of this formulation is striking. The men embarking on this new constitutional initiative were without doubt the most powerful *mafiosi* in Palermo. Yet even now, even fifteen years on from Riina's arrest, they did not feel they had the political authority to reconstitute the *official*

Commission. Shorty he may have been, but Riina still cast a long, long shadow over the internal affairs of Cosa Nostra.

The *kind of* Commission never met. On 16 December 2008, after nearly nine months of painstaking investigation, some 1,200 *Carabinieri* made coordinated dawn raids on dozens of addresses in Palermo and across western Sicily. They called it Operation Perseus, after the hero of Greek mythology who beheaded the snake-haired monster Medusa, because the aim was nothing less than to decapitate Cosa Nostra. Among the ninety-nine men arrested were the bosses of nineteen Families, including from mafia territories whose names recur throughout the organisation's long history, such as Santa Maria di Gesù, Monreale, Corleone, Uditore and San Lorenzo. No less than eleven precinct bosses were detained too – the men who presided over three or four Families and took a seat on the Commission to represent their interests. And of course the *capo dei capi* elect was also taken: sixty-four-year-old Benedetto Capizzi. The choice of Capizzi showed that, after 'walking with padded shoes' under Provenzano, Cosa Nostra was ready to don its hobnailed boots again. Capizzi was a former member of Giovanni 'the Pig' Brusca's death squad. Among many other crimes, Capizzi helped plan the kidnap of Giuseppe Di Matteo, the penitent's boy who ended up in an acid bath. Capizzi was a man of action, who could be relied on to deal militarily with anyone who dissented from the new order. One minor drawback was that he was still serving several life sentences. However, he was yet another case of a boss granted house arrest for health reasons, thus giving him the liberty he needed to meet his criminal friends.

Operation Perseus was a stunning blow, which received far less media attention abroad than it deserved – certainly far less than the arrest of Bernardo 'the Tractor' Provenzano two and a half years earlier. It has left Cosa Nostra a fragmented organisation. The *mafiosi* who remain at large do not have the experience or charisma to embark on any major restructuring along the lines of what Benedetto Capizzi was attempting. Their main priority is now survival: finding enough criminal income to support the heavy burden of prisoners and their relatives, and to keep the fabric of the Families together.

The damage inflicted on Cosa Nostra over the last decade has helped create the space for grassroots movements against its protection racket regime. Their goal is to attack mafia power at its base, and their potential is truly revolutionary. Like much that is good in contemporary Sicily, the anti-racket movement has its roots in the tragedies of the 1980s and early 1990s.

Libero Grassi was an entrepreneur who ran a factory in Palermo making pyjamas. When he moved to a new site in the shadow of Monte Pellegrino in 1990, demands for money started to arrive – a contribution 'for the lads shut up in the Ucciardone'. Grassi went to the police, and three of the men who had visited his factory to ask for money were arrested. The demands then became more menacing. Grassi responded with a public letter to the press that began 'Dear extortionist':

> I wanted to tell our unknown extortionist that he can save himself the threatening phone calls and the money to buy fuses, bombs and bullets, because we are not prepared to contribute and we have put ourselves under the protection of the police. I built this factory with my own hands and I have no intention of shutting up shop.

Grassi's cause found painfully little support. The entrepreneurs in the neighbourhood let it be known that he should wash his dirty linen in private like everyone else. He received only one letter from another businessman expressing solidarity. However, in April 1991, Grassi's campaign took him onto national TV screens, where the millions of viewers of a popular politics talk show heard his lucid explanation of how the extortion racket system worked, and the *omertà* that beset him on all sides. He was becoming a threatening symbol of anti-mafia resistance, and an advertisement for the weakness of the boss on whose territory his factory was sited. On 29 August 1991, Libero Grassi was shot five times in the face as he left his house to go to work.

After this appalling murder, many resolved that no one who stood up against the extortionists should ever be left isolated again. The national shopkeepers' association, Confesercenti, founded an anti-racket support group in Palermo called 'SOS Business' in the same year. In 1997, a ruling by the Supreme Court made it clear that paying protection money is a crime. Everyone is obliged turn to the authorities for help against the extortionists, and no one can offer the excuse that they are forced to pay. In 2004, the inheritance of Libero Grassi and other pioneers of the anti-racket movement was picked up by a group of young Palermitans who founded an organisation they called Addiopizzo ('Goodbye Extortion'). Their idea was fresh and beautifully simple: entrepreneurs, shopkeepers, restaurateurs and hoteliers would sign a public pledge not to pay protection money; and consumers would sign a public pledge to patronise businesses that did not pay. The aim was to grow a mutually reinforcing alliance between clean enterprises and honest consumers.

Others followed Addiopizzo's lead. In September 2007, the Sicilian branch of Confindustria (the employers' organisation) announced that it would expel any members found to have been paying protection money or failing to collaborate with the authorities. The days when Sicilian business leaders would grumble that the fight against the mafia was ruining the island's economy were finally gone.

Organising to defy extortion is far from being an empty gesture: it actually works. One mafia penitent from the Family of Santa Maria di Gesù has recently explained why *mafiosi* did not try to extort money from businesses that proclaimed their opposition:

If a shopkeeper is a member of Addiopizzo or an anti-racket association, we just don't go there, we don't ask for anything. It's more because of the trouble it causes than the money. If they report it to the police, you then get investigations, listening devices, and so it's better just to avoid them.

The rebellion against extortion is potentially life-threatening for Cosa Nostra. In late November 2007, *mafiosi* showed how concerned they were about Confindustria's new stance by performing a clamorous act of intimidation: the employers' organisation's offices in the central Sicilian city of Caltanissetta were vandalised, and a number of CDs containing the names and addresses of its members were stolen.

Despite the threats, a virtuous circle has begun to turn in Palermo. As more businesses go to the police when they receive extortion demands, more *mafiosi* are arrested, and the authorities and anti-racket organisations can demonstrate their growing ability to stand shoulder-to-shoulder with people that resist – with the result that more businesses gain the confidence to turn to the police when they receive extortion demands.

Moreover, as so often in our story, Palermo's example has been followed elsewhere. The anti-racket associations that began in Sicily have spread. For example, in January 2010 Confindustria adopted a *national* policy of expelling members who do business with gangsters.

The hunt for fugitives from justice has also achieved crucial results in both Campania and Calabria. Some of the most powerful camorra and 'ndrangheta bosses have taken to building underground bunkers in the hope of avoiding the ever more determined and expert mafia hunters. Some of these bunkers are just secret compartments in a house: hidey-holes into which a fugitive can dash when the doorbell rings unexpectedly. Others are extraordinarily ingenious and elaborate – miniature apartments, complete with plumbing, air pumps and security cameras. Most are hidden among ordinary houses and farm buildings or on industrial estates, and involve secret passages and moveable walls. The 'ndrangheta are bunker specialists. The Bellocco clan from Rosarno took to burying entire shipping containers, perfectly furnished inside, and disguised by vegetation above. The ground underneath the town of Platì, in Calabria, is criss-crossed by hundreds and hundreds of metres of tunnels connecting bosses' houses to a complex of bunkers and escape routes. Here the 'ndrangheta even opened the street up in the process of building its secret bunker network; nobody in town said a word.

Whatever form they take, today's mafia bunkers are not just refuges: they are command centres. Invariably they are built on a boss's own territory, where he can count on a close network of family and friends to provide for his daily needs and, crucially, to shuttle in and out with orders and requests. Territorial control remains crucial for bosses of all three major criminal organisations. As one mafia hunter from the *Carabinieri* explains:

> The first rule for a boss is to never abandon his ground. Going off to evade justice somewhere else is a sign of weakness. If the throne is left vacant, a boss's competitors go into overdrive, manoeuvring and plotting to take his place.

La presenza è potenza, as *mafiosi* say: presence is power.

The bunkers where some bosses now try to maintain their territorial presence are not unprecedented in the history of the mafias: in Sicily, under Fascism, police chasing down *mafiosi* discovered a range of ingenious secret compartments and sunken shelters. But the bunkers are nonetheless an important sign of the pressure the mafias are now under. Until the 1980s, the dreaded Piromallis of Gioia Tauro could still be spotted presiding over the town square, making their authority visible. Those days are gone. The state has become more serious than ever about fighting organised crime, and so the underworld has gone underground.

Sicily remains the place where the anti-mafia fight is most

advanced. And the drop in the number of homicides is only the most obvious indicator of that fact. There were nineteen mafia-related murders in 2009 on the island, eight in 2010 and only three in 2011. These are historical lows. The staggering body-count of the 1980s now seems an aeon away.

Camorra: **A geography of the underworld**

In September 2011, journalists from the news magazine *L'Espresso* secretly filmed an exhibition of underworld power in the Barra suburb of Naples. For anyone with a sense of camorra history, the film provides depressing evidence of continuity over time.

The backdrop was the Festival of the Lilies, one of several similar religious festivals in the region. The 'lilies' in question are actually twenty-five-metre-high obelisks made from wood and decorated with papier-mâché sculptures. They are built and then shouldered by proud teams of volunteers, known as 'crews', who are sponsored by a local grandee known as a 'Godfather'. The crews compete to attract crowds to their lily with an MC, music and dancing. The film published on the *L'Espresso* website showed activities around one particular lily built by the crew that called itself *Insuperabile*. First the local camorra boss's father arrived in an open-top white vintage sports car to the sound of a saxophone playing *The Godfather* theme. As the crowd cheered, the MC hailed the boss Angelo Cuccaro (recently released from prison), then sang him a song called 'You're great', and finally called for a round of applause 'For all our dead'. Meanwhile the boss himself, dressed in the *Insuperabile* crew's blue T-shirt and white baseball cap, was kissed by enthusiastic supporters.

Investigations by the *Carabinieri* subsequently discovered that the Festival of the Lilies had been a platform for the Barra clan for a long time: they extorted money from businesses under the pretext of spending it on their obelisk; the *Insuperabile* crew's 'Godfathers' were chosen from among entrepreneurs close to the bosses; the festival was used to publicly celebrate new camorra pacts. When the neighbouring town of Cercola came under the Barra clan's control, shopkeepers there were forced to display the *Insuperabile* crew's blue and red colours in their windows.

In September 2012 the *Insuperabile* crew had their obelisk confiscated and destroyed because, according to the judge who authorised the confiscation,

> The messages it sends, the hidden meaning of that wood and papier mâché, is worth more than a whole arsenal to the clan. Deploying it on the day of the festival means much more than a victory in battle, than the physical annihilation of a rival: it is a sign of authority.

Using community religious celebrations as a chance to parade criminal might is traditional in the Naples underworld. In the nineteenth century, *camorristi* used to take control of the spring-time pilgrimage to the sanctuary of Montevergine. Each boss, with his woman next to him decked out in silk, gold and pearls, would drive his pony and trap into the mountains at the head of his followers. The pilgrims' progress would be punctuated by drinking bouts, races, more or less stylised knife fights, and camorra summits with the clans of the hinterland.

(Similar things characterised mafia life in Calabria and Sicily. In towns and villages controlled by the 'ndrangheta and Cosa Nostra, criminal territorial control was advertised by taking over the day set aside to celebrate the local patron saint. Barra is far from being the only place where the tradition continues to this day. In Sant'Onofrio in 2010, the 'ndrangheta reacted angrily when the local priest tried to enforce the Bishop's order to ban mobsters from taking a leading role in an Easter parade of statues of the Madonna: the head of the confraternity that presided over the festival received a warning when two shots were fired at his front door. The festival was suspended for a week, and when it eventually took place, the *Carabinieri* were out in force.)

So has nothing changed in Campania? Is the camorra still the force it once was? Certainly, a 'murder map' of underworld deaths over the last few decades would have its dots concentrated in the same broad area that has been blighted by the camorra since the nineteenth century: the city of Naples and a semicircle of roughly forty-kilometre radius extending out into the towns and villages of the hinterland. An enduring pattern is unmistakable. Yet once we zoom in on the detail of our map of camorra power, it becomes clear that the continuities are less prevalent than they first appeared. Less prevalent, certainly, than in Sicily and Calabria, where the micro-territories demarcated by mafia *cosche* have remained all but identical. Places like Rosarno and Platì ('ndrangheta), or Villabate and Uditore (Cosa Nostra) have been notorious for well over a century. In Campania, by contrast, the geography of the underworld has seen some important trans-formations recently.

The camorra fragmented following the war in the early 1980s between Raffaele 'the Professor' Cutolo and the allied clans of the Nuova Famiglia. There were an estimated thirty-two camorra organisations in 1988; that number had increased to 108 by 1992. The years of the Second Republic have seen no reversal of the fragmentation. The most recent estimates suggest that there are still around a hundred sizeable criminal organisations in Campania, where gangland has assumed a lasting but instable pattern. Camorra clans come and go, merge and break apart, go to war and make alliances. Thus most of these camorras have a very short lifespan compared to the extraordinarily persis-tent criminal Freemasonries, Cosa Nostra and the 'ndrangheta. In Campania, the lines on the map of camorra power move constantly as the police make arrests, turf wars break out and clans fissure and merge. Increased violence is the inevitable conse-quence of this fundamental instability: the camorra continues to kill more people than either the Sicilian mafia or the 'ndrang-heta. There have been several major peaks in the murder rate in recent years: there were over a hundred camorra killings each year from 1994 to 1998; and then again in 2004, and again in 2007.

Naples is a port city. That simple fact has shaped the camorra's history ever since the 1850s and 1860s, when Salvatore De Crescenzo's camorra smuggled imported clothes past customs and extorted money from the boatmen ferrying passengers from ship to shore. The port of Naples was where vast quantities of Allied materiel vanished onto the black market during the Second World War. In the 1950s, the travelling cloth-salesmen known as *magliari*, who were often little more than swindlers, would set sail to bring the sharp practices of the Neapolitan rag trade to the housewives of northern Europe. Thereafter, Naples was a point of entry for contraband cigarettes and narcotics. These days, the port is a mechanised container terminal on the model of Felixstowe or Rotterdam. It has assumed new importance as a gateway to Italy for the Far Eastern manufactures that are shipped into the Mediterranean through the Suez Canal. Some of those manufactures – shoes, clothes and handbags, electrical tools, mobile phones, cameras and games consoles – are forged versions of market-leading brands. The Neapolitan tradition of manufacturing counterfeits has gone global. Sometimes, the label 'Made in Italy' or 'Made in Germany' hides a different reality: 'Faked in China'. And in place of the *magliari*, there are international brokers, permanently stationed abroad to find markets for bootleg products. Quite how large this sector is, and quite what proportions of it are run by *camorristi* as opposed to common-or-garden shady entrepreneurs, is still subject to investigation.

Naples is a remarkable place for many reasons. One of them is the fact that, where historic poor neighbourhoods in many other European cities have long ago been demolished or yuppified, the centre of Naples still has many of the same concentrations of poverty that characterised it back in the eighteenth century. Forcella, the 'kasbah' quarter we have visited occasionally through this story, is a case in point. The camorra rose from its fetid and overcrowded alleys in the early nineteenth century. Although much is now different in Forcella, not least the sanitation, eking out a living here is still precarious, often illegal, and occasionally dangerous. No visitor can enter without the distinct sensation of being watched. In this and other neighbourhoods, the camorra's territorial purview is still made manifest by the kids who extort money for parking places, and the cocksure teenagers perched atop their scooters who act as lookouts for drug dealers.

Despite the wholesale economic transformation of the last century and a half, in places like Forcella the camorra continues to recruit among a population made vulnerable by hardship and a widespread disregard for the law, just as it did in the nineteenth century. In 2006, it was estimated that 22 per cent of people with any kind of job in Campania worked in the so-called 'black economy' – paid in cash, untaxed and unprotected by labour and safety laws. It seems likely that a sizeable majority of jobs in small- and medium-sized companies are off the books.

Recent economic change seems to have made the situation worse. In Campania, as in much of the South, the new economic mantra of flexible employment has often meant just a bigger black economy. Since 2008, Europe's dire economic difficulties have increased the power of the camorra (and, for that matter, of Cosa Nostra and the 'ndrangheta) to penetrate businesses, and lock the region into a vicious circle of economic failure. In the summer of 2009, Mario Draghi, then the governor of the Bank of Italy, argued as follows:

Companies are seeing their cash flow dry up, and their assets fall in market value. Both of these developments make them easier for organised crime to attack . . . In economies where there is a strong criminal presence businesses pay higher borrowing costs, and the pollution of local politics makes for a ruinous destruction of social capital: young people emigrate more, and nearly a third of those young people are graduates moving north in search of better opportunities.

In hard times, it is not just fly-by-night businesses that are easy prey for loan sharks and extortionists, for gangsters seeking an outlet for stolen goods or a way to launder drug profits. By the nature of the narcotics business, gangsters are cash rich – and just at the moment southern Italy's entrepreneurs are struggling even more than everyone else to get their hands on credit. When times are hard, cash is *capo*.

The camorra's undiminished power to feed off the weaknesses of the Neapolitan economy has helped remould the landscape of criminal influence. Once upon a time, when Naples was an industrial city, factory workers had a tradition of labour organisation and socialist ideals that gave them an inbuilt resistance to the camorra infection. Nowadays, with the factories largely gone, the camorra has spread to quarters like Bagnoli, where the steelworks shut down in the 1990s.

Today, moreover, the urban camorra economy no longer revolves around the old slums of the city centre. The major concentrations of poverty and illegality have moved away from the Naples that tourists know. Even the camorra in Forcella has felt the force of the new. The Giuliano clan (beloved of Diego Maradona) has been broken by murder, repentance and arrest. More importantly, the most powerful and dangerous clans now emerge from the sprawling periphery of the city, from neighbourhoods that grew anarchically in the 1970s and after the earthquake of 1980. The artisan studios of the city-centre maze cannot compete with the sweatshop factories of the suburbs when it comes to churning out bootleg DVDs and counterfeit branded fashions. With the modernisation of Naples's road network and public transport, addicts now find it cheaper to source their hit from the great narcotics supermarkets operating in the brutalist apartment blocks of Secondigliano or Ponticelli, than to visit the small-time dealers of the Spanish Quarters.

The first fragment of cityscape that springs into the public mind when the word 'camorra' is mentioned is no longer the alleys of Forcella. Rather it is a catastrophically failed housing project in the suburb of Scampia. Known as 'Le Vele' (The Sails), it consists of a row of massive, triangular apartment blocks built in the sixties and seventies, and designed to reproduce the tight-knit community life of the city-centre alleyways in multiple storeys. The outcome, with its ugly, dark and insecure interior spaces, feels more like a high-security prison without guards. The blocks were very badly built: lifts did not work, concrete crumbled, roofs leaked, and neighbours could hear everything that went on three doors down. These problems had already tipped Le Vele towards slum status when desperate refugees from the 1980 earthquake illegally occupied vacant apartments – some of them before they were even finished. Before long, residents felt besieged by a minority of drug-dealing *camorristi*. The police presence consisted of sporadic and largely symbolic tours. Residents say that some cops took bribes to leave the drug dealers unmolested. A long-running campaign to have Le Vele emptied and demolished met with a sluggish political response. At the time of writing, of the seven original apartment blocks, four are condemned but still standing – and still partially occupied.

In the 1990s and 2000s, drug distribution in Le Vele was under the control of the Di Lauro clan. Its founding boss was Paolo Di Lauro, known as 'Ciruzzo the Millionaire'. His base was in Secondigliano, a neighbourhood next to Scampia on the northern outskirts of Naples that was originally a row of large, elegant nineteenth-century houses ranged along the road out of town, but which hosted huge new developments in the 1970s and 1980s. The Millionaire led a centralised organisation moulded around the demands of the drug business. His closest lieutenants included two of his sons and his brother-in-law. Under them were the so-called 'delegates', who handled the purchase and cutting of the wholesale narcotics. Everything below this top level of the clan was run on a kind of franchising system that kept the risky and messy day-to-day business of dealing at a safe distance. Twenty 'zone chiefs' were granted authorisation to manage sales in various areas of the Millionaire's territory, and handle the salaried pushers, lookouts and enforcers who occupied the lowest tier of the organisation. A pusher would earn €2,000 per month, killers a mere €2,500 per hit. Around 200 people counted as formally recognised members of the clan, but many, many more were employed. At the peak of the Millionaire's power, unverifiable estimates put the organisation's narcotics income at €1 billion per year.

In 2002 the Millionaire was forced to go into hiding from the law, and day-to-day control passed to his sons, who struggled to control the ambitions of the organisation's 'delegates'. The result, during the winter of 2004–5, was the most violent of recent camorra wars, known as the 'Scampia Blood Feud'.

The Di Lauro clan was one of the more hierarchically structured camorra organisations of the most recent generation. In the 1970s, *camorristi* learned the advantages of organising themselves as a criminal Freemasonry from members of Cosa Nostra and the 'ndrangheta who were keen to find business partners in Campania. Following the break-up of the Nuova Camorra Organizzata and the Nuova Famiglia in the 1980s, practices such as initiation rituals fell out of favour across Campania. Since then, camorra clans have invented their own structures according to need. Yet, despite the fading of the influence of Sicilian and Calabrian organised crime in Campania, the two fundamental principles of camorra organisation are the same as those that apply to the more formalised Families of Cosa Nostra or the *'ndrine* and Locals of the 'ndrangheta. On the one hand, a camorra clan needs a tight command structure, particularly at the core, and particularly for fighting wars and defending territory. On the other hand, a clan must also be loose enough to allow its bosses to network widely, taking advantage of any criminal opportunity that presents itself at home or abroad. Within the limits set by these two principles, a variety of structures is possible. The term 'camorra' has come to embrace anything from the kind of street drug-dealing gangs that can be found in rundown areas of many Western cities, to major syndicates with iron bonds to the political system and the legal economy.

As was the case with the Di Lauro clan, blood ties often help bind the core members of any camorra organisation together. Camorra bosses are often brought up in a family tradition of violence and 'criminal *savoir-faire*' (to use the words of one Italian expert). Intermarriage between camorra bloodlines on adjacent territories helps consolidate authority and pass this *savoir-faire* down through the generations. One example is the Mazzarella clan, based around three nephews of Michele 'Mad Mike' Zaza, the cigarette smuggler and member of Cosa Nostra who helped turn contraband tobacco into the 'FIAT of the South' in the 1960s and 1970s In 1996, one of the Mazzarella brothers, Vincenzo, saw his family's prestige augmented when his teenage son married the daughter of Lovigino 'Ice Eyes' Giuliano, the boss of Forcella.

The importance that kinship ties have within the camorra clans helps explain why women closely related to a clan's core group can sometimes take on frontline roles. The cases of Pupetta Maresca and the Professor's big sister Rosetta Cutolo tell us that, even before the 1990s, some camorra women were more prominent than was the case with women in the orbit of the Sicilian mafia or the 'ndrangheta. But in the last two decades women in the camorra have become enormously more visible. There are two reasons for this. The first is that the authorities have shaken off old prejudices that made them blind to women's criminal talents. The second is that, because of increased police pressure, the clans have delegated greater power to women when their menfolk go on the run or get arrested. These trends have also made their effects felt in Sicily and Calabria, where the male-centred Masonic structure of the criminal brotherhoods tends to place more limits on women's power. In 1998, Giusy Vitale took over day-to-day management of the Partinico Family of Cosa Nostra when her brother, the boss, was locked up. She has since turned penitent.

But it is no coincidence that it was a female *camorrista*, Teresa De Luca Bossa, who became the first woman in Italy to be subjected to the tough new prison regime set up in the wake of the Falcone and Borsellino murders in 1992. De Luca Bossa was both the mother and the lover of clan leaders, and showed notable military, managerial and diplomatic skill in keeping the organisation together when her menfolk were arrested.

Nor have Sicily or Calabria seen anything to compare with the vicious battle fought out between the women of the Graziano and Cava clans in 2002. On 26 May of that year, a Graziano firing party including three women chased down and rammed a car containing five women from the Cavas. In the ensuing blood-bath, four Cava women were shot dead and a fifth left paralysed. On both the victims' and the perpetrators' side, several generations of women were involved. The Graziano boss's wife, Chiara Manzi, aged sixty-two, coordinated the attack by mobile phone; the shooters included her daughter-in-law (aged forty) and two of her nieces (nineteen and twenty respectively). In tapes of their phone conversations in the run-up to the assault, these women can be heard spitting insults at their intended victims: 'gypsies', 'sows'.

Uniquely among the mafias, the camorra has also allowed affiliates from minority sexualities to reach leading positions. Anna Terracciano is one of twelve sisters and brothers from the Spanish Quarters of Naples – eleven of them active in organised crime. Known as *'o Masculone* (something like 'Big Bloke'), Anna was a male-identified lesbian who went around armed and took part in military actions on behalf of her clan. She was imprisoned in 2006. Three years later, the police arrested Ugo Gabriele, whom the authorities claim is the first transsexual *camorrista* on record. Known as 'Ketty', Gabriele is the younger sibling of one of the clan that broke off from the Millionaire's organisation during the Scampia Blood Feud of 2004–5. According to the police, when her brother was promoted, Ketty graduated from pushing cocaine to her clients (she was a transsexual prostitute) to a more managerial role in the drug ring. As well as the camorra's reliance on family ties, Ketty's promotion may also owe something to Neapolitan popular culture's traditional tolerance towards male transsexuals – the so-called *femminielli*.

No tour of the geography of contemporary Campanian organised crime would be complete without a visit to the vast fertile plain to the north of the city, which is sometimes called the Terra di Lavoro (the Land of Work). In a poem from 1956, writer and film director Pier Paolo Pasolini evoked its eerie beauties as seen from a train:

> Now the Terra di Lavoro is near:
> A few herds of buffalo, a few houses
> Heaped between rows of tomato plants,
>
> Twists of ivy, and lowly palings.
> Every so often, close to the terrain,
> Black as a drainpipe,
>
> A stream escapes the clutches
> Of the elms loaded with vines.

This distinctive landscape has been the backdrop to some of the most important developments in the history of Campanian organised crime over the past century and a half. In the nineteenth century, when much of the area was a marshy wilderness known as the Mazzoni, production of mozzarella cheese from buffalo milk was notorious for being controlled by violent entrepreneurs.

In the drained agricultural land to the south and south-east of the marshes, gangs ran protection rackets on the farms, exploited the labourers, taxed the wholesale fruit, vegetable and meat markets, and controlled the routes by which produce made its way into the city.

If Pasolini were alive and able to journey through Terra di Lavoro today, he would see a landscape radically transformed by the arrival of factories in the 1960s, and by industrial decline and the post-earthquake building boom in the 1980s. But perhaps more than these visible changes, Pasolini would be struck by a new smell. In many parts of the land north of Naples, the stench of rubbish fills the air – rubbish that has become the contemporary camorra's most important new source of wealth.

Camorra: **An Italian Chernobyl**

When the Second Republic was born, Naples and the Campania region were in the midst of a garbage crisis. No scheme to recycle the waste from homes and shops had yet got off the ground. Dumps were full to overflowing. Worrying signs of health problems among the population near the dumps were beginning to emerge.

Early in 1994, the government declared an emergency and appointed a Commissar to manage the day-to-day collection and disposal while the regional government prepared a long-term solution. But no long-term solution emerged: it was the usual story of political stasis and confusion. At that point, in 1996, the Commissariat was given the task of planning Campania's way out of the emergency, and the power to override normal planning restrictions and local government controls in order to put the plan into place.

The resulting scheme seemed sleek. Municipal trash was to be sorted and disposed of in stages. First, recyclables would be creamed off at the point of collection. Then there was to be a further, centralised sifting to extract both biodegradable matter and any dangerous substances. The next stage involved mashing and compacting what was left into so-called 'ecobales' that could be used as fuel. And finally those ecobales would be burned to generate clean electricity. Seven plants to produce ecobales would need to be built, and two new incinerator-generators. Once they were up and running, it was claimed, Campania would have a perfect cycle of environmentally friendly refuse collection and reuse. No one heeded the waste-management experts who said that the scheme was unrealistic and based on principles that had already failed elsewhere.

The solution to Campania's rubbish emergency rapidly turned into an environmental disaster. The rubbish-collection cycle was dysfunctional at every stage.

Eighteen consortia were set up in the 1990s to manage collection and recycling in different parts of the region. But for a variety of reasons they did not do their job: trash entered the waste-management system in an undifferentiated state.

At that point in the cycle the most serious problems started. An alliance of four companies, known as FIBE, won the contract to build the ecobale plants and the incinerator-generators. The main reasons FIBE won were the low cost and high speed of their proposals: this was an emergency, after all. FIBE was offered a contract with the Campania regional government that contained inadequate penalty clauses.

FIBE companies promised they would have the incinerator-generators up and running by the end of 2000. But by that date, they had not even obtained planning permission. Only one of the incinerator-generators had been completed by the end of 2007. Plans for the second incinerator-generator were finally cancelled in 2012.

FIBE companies were also given pretty much a free rein in choosing where to build their plants. The first incinerator-generator was built in Acerra, in northern Campania, just a few hundred metres away from a large children's hospital. The second was originally to be sited only twenty kilometres away from the first. This was a part of the country famous for being the centre of buffalo-milk mozzarella production. But even before the first incinerator-generator was built, the area already hosted more than its fair share of legal and illegal dumps, and dioxin poisoning had been discovered in farm animals and crops. The incinerator-generator that was actually built was quickly shown to be working badly, spreading gases over a ten-kilometre radius.

The seven ecobale plants were even worse: a parliamentary report found that the ecobales they produced were just large plastic-wrapped cubes of unsifted rubbish that were too damp and too filled with poisons to incinerate, even if the incinerators had been working. Nothing could be done except stockpile them. Across Campania, grey and white ziggurats of ecobales began to climb skywards. The regional rubbish Commissar told parliament in 2004 that *every month* 40,000 square metres of land was being used up to store ecobales.

Periodically, throughout the early years of the twenty-first century, Campania's broken-down garbage-disposal system seized up entirely. At the worst point in 2007–8, hundreds of thousands of tonnes of waste from homes and shops accumulated in the streets. The authorities responded by forcibly reopening rubbish dumps that had already been deemed to be full. Local people, justifiably worried about the impact on their quality of life, staged angry protests. News cameras from around the world relayed the pictures of both the trash-mountains and the protests, causing untold damage to the reputation of Naples, Campania and Italy. Only in the last couple of years have the authorities begun to get a grip on the situation, it seems, although many piles of ecobales remain to scar the landscape.

The *monnezza* scandal (named after the Neapolitan for garbage) is still subject to legal proceedings: a number of politicians, entrepreneurs and administrators have been charged with fraud or negligence. Irrespective of the precise criminal blame, the story is one of shambolic politics, irresponsible business (including northern business), bad planning, mismanagement, and inadequate monitoring. The problems started at the top: the Commissariat supposed to keep tabs on the whole system stands accused of cronyism and inflated expenses as well as a manifest failure to make sure that the rubbish cycle actually worked.

The *monnezza* affair bears many similarities to the chaos of reconstruction following the 1980 earthquake. For one thing, both of them created opportunities for organised crime. The camorra was late to enter the construction industry when compared to Cosa Nostra and the 'ndrangheta. While Sicilian gangsters were heavily involved in the building boom of the 1950s and 1960s, and the Calabrians followed suit in the 1960s and 1970s, only following the 1980 earthquake did *camorristi* start earning serious money from concrete. But when it came to rubbish, the camorra clans became pioneers and protagonists. 'Eco-mafia' is a term coined by Italian environmentalists to refer to the damage the underworld inflicts on Italy's natural and other resources – from illegal building to the traffic in architectural treasures. The waste sector is the most lucrative eco-mafia activity, and one of the biggest growth areas in criminal enterprise in the last two decades.

As with construction, the camorra infiltrated the rubbish system in a variety of ways, starting with the eighteen consortia set up to manage recycling in different parts of the region. Many of the people employed in these consortia were drawn from militant lobby groups of unemployed people. Some of those lobby groups, which date back to the 1970s, have been linked to the camorra: their leaders have been shown to have extracted bribes from members in return for the promise of a job; quite a few of the members have criminal records. In 2004, the regional rubbish Commissar told a parliamentary inquiry that: 'It's a miracle even if 200 of the 2,316 people [employed by the recycling consortia] actually do any work.' It is estimated that, by the end of 2007, more than forty of the lorries bought to transport recycled rubbish had been stolen.

The camorra also moved in on the subcontracts and sub-subcontracts handed out for moving the ecobales around. Since the days of the post-earthquake construction boom, the camorra has had a near-monopoly on earth-moving. There is evidence of camorra profiteering on the deals that were rushed through to buy land where ecobales could be stored.

In some places, notably around Chiaiano, young *camorristi* took control of the protests against reopening old garbage dumps.

Inevitably, the demonstrations turned violent. There were probably two reasons why the camorra became involved. First, because their bosses had an economic interest in perpetuating the emergency. And second, because they wanted to pose as community leaders, champions of NIMBYism. Much of the trouble was concentrated at a dump not far from Marano, the base of the Nuvoletta clan. A banner was hoisted above the entrance to the town: 'The state is absent, but we are here'. Nobody needed to be told who this 'we' was.

Mondragone, the buffalo-milk mozzarella capital on the northern coast of Campania, was the base for a waste-management company called Eco4 that was at the centre of a thoroughgoing infiltration of the rubbish cycle by the clans: an illicit circuit of votes, jobs, inflated invoices, rigged contracts and bribes tied together politicians, administrators, entrepreneurs and *camorristi*. In the summer of 2007, one of the Eco4 directors implicated in the case, Michele Orsi, started to give evidence to magistrates. The following May he went out with his young daughter to buy a bottle of Coca-Cola and was shot eighteen times. Other witnesses in the Eco4 case implicated a senior politician close to Silvio Berlusconi. In 2009, Nicola Cosentino was both Junior Minister for Finance and the coordinator of Berlusconi's party in the Campania region when magistrates asked parliament for authorisation to proceed against him for working with the camorra. Berlusconi's governing majority turned down the request. The following year parliament refused to give investigators permission to use phone-tap evidence against Cosentino, although he did resign from his government job later that year when he was involved in another scandal. In January 2012 parliament again sheltered him from arrest under camorra-related charges. Cosentino claimed that he was the victim of 'media, political and judicial aggression'.

However, by far the most worrying aspect of eco-mafia crime in Campania is not directly related to the rubbish emergency and the ecobales affair. In the early 1990s, evidence began to emerge that *camorristi* were illegally dumping millions of tonnes of toxic waste from hospitals and a variety of industries such as steel, paint, fertiliser, leather and plastics. The poisons found to be involved included asbestos, arsenic, lead and cadmium. The picture was confirmed by the investigation known as Operation Cassiopea between 1999 and 2003. Although the camorra's trucks transported and dumped the waste in Campania, they were only the end point of a national system. Agents for camorra-backed waste-management firms toured the north and centre of the country, offering to make companies' dangerous by-products vanish for as little as a tenth of the cost of legal disposal. Obliging politicians and bureaucrats along the toxic-waste route made sure that the paperwork was in order. The *camorristi* tipped the waste anywhere and everywhere in the territory they controlled, ranging from ordinary municipal dumps to roadside ditches. Some of the toxic waste was blended with other substances to make 'compost'. In many cases the waste was placed on top of a layer of car tyres and burned to destroy the evidence, thus poisoning the air as well as the soil and the water table. The camorra also dumped toxic waste into the quarries situated in the hillier parts of the Terra di Lavoro, from which they extracted the sand and gravel for their concrete plants. Many of these quarries were also illegal. In 2005, a judge described the disappearance of whole mountains in what he called a 'meteorite effect'. Hence the harm from one eco-mafia crime was multiplied by that from another.

The profits of this trade were enormous. One toxic-waste dealer who turned state's evidence handed over a property portfolio that included forty-five apartments and a hotel, to a total value of €50 million.

Many of those charged in the trial that resulted from the Cassiopea investigation confessed. Despite that, in September 2011, a judge decided not to carry on with the case because inordinate delays in procedure meant that the crimes would inevitably have fallen under Italy's statute of limitations: according to Italian law, it all happened too long ago for guilty verdicts to be reached. The toxic waste strewn across the Terra di Lavoro recognises no such time restrictions. Generations of citizens living on this sullied land will pay the price for what the magistrate in charge of the Cassiopea investigation called an 'Italian Chernobyl'.

Gomorrah

The peak of the Naples rubbish crisis in 2007–8 coincided with the startling success of a book that has made the camorra better known around the world than it has been since before the First World War. *Gomorrah* (the title is a pun) was published in 2006 by a little-known twenty-six-year-old writer and journalist called Roberto Saviano.

Before *Gomorrah*, the fragmented camorra had once more become the subject of bewildered indifference outside Campania. Reporters who tried to keep the public informed about outbreaks of savagery like the Scampia Blood Feud found that the faces, names and underworld connections proliferated far beyond the tolerance of even the most dogged lay reader.

Gomorrah is, at first glance, an unlikely book to have reawoken public concern about the apparent chaos in Campania. It is a hybrid: a series of unsettling essays that are part autobiography, part undercover reportage, part political polemic, part history. Compelling as they are, none of these ingredients holds *Gomorrah* together. The secret of its remorseless grip on Italian readers resides in the way Saviano puts his own sensibility at the centre of the story. His is a kaleidoscopic and immediate personal testimony rooted in a visceral rage and revulsion. He is not content to observe the holes punched in bulletproof glass by an AK-47; he is morbidly drawn to rub his finger against the edges until it bleeds. He feels the salty swill of nausea rise in his throat as yet another teenage hoodlum is scooped into a body bag from a pool of gore in the street during the Scampia Blood Feud. Anger clutches at his chest like asthma when the umpteenth building worker dies on an illegal construction site. The ground seethes beneath him as he explores a landscape contaminated for decades by fly-tipped carcinogens.

Saviano had every right to make his own feelings so important to his account of the camorra (or 'the System', as he taught Italians to call it). For he hails from Casal di Principe, in the heart of the most notorious part of the Terra di Lavoro. After the eclipse of Carmine 'Mr Angry' Alfieri in 1992, the local clan, the *casalesi*, became the dominant force in the camorra. The core group of *casalesi* were a highly proficient team of killers deployed against the Nuova Camorra Organizzata in the 1980s – the 'Israelis' to the Professor's 'Arabs'. The group evolved into a federation of four criminal families. In 1988, the *casalesi* did away with their own boss, Antonio Bardellino. After a bloody civil war, they were able to take over his concrete and cocaine interests. They also branched into agricultural fraud and buffalo-milk mozzarella. The *casalesi* established a local monopoly on the distribution of some major food brands. Moreover, the Eco4 waste-management business was one of their front companies. The *casalesi* were also the clan responsible for creating the 'Italian Chernobyl' on their own territory with their traffic in toxic refuse. According to a penitent from the *casalesi*, when one of the clan's affiliates expressed doubts to his boss, he received a dismissive reply: 'Who gives a toss if we pollute the water table? We drink mineral water anyway.'

By September 2006, *Gomorrah* had already won prizes as well as tens of thousands of readers, particularly among the young. At that point Saviano returned to his home town to take part in a demonstration in favour of the rule of law. Speaking in the piazza from a raised table in front of an azure backcloth, he was moved to call out to the bosses by name: 'Iovine, Schiavone, Zagaria – you aren't worth a thing!' He then addressed the crowd: 'Their power rests on your fear! They must leave this land!' No one should underestimate the bravery of these words: as Saviano knew, relatives of *casalesi* bosses were watching him from the piazza.

Within days, the authorities received intimations of what was to be the first of several credible threats against Saviano's life. Ever since then, he has lived under armed escort. Gratifyingly, his predicament boosted sales: the latest estimates are that *Gomorrah* has sold well over two million copies in Italy, and has been translated into fifty-two languages. In 2008, a film drama-tisation of *Gomorrah* – which in my view is even better than the book – won the Grand Prize at the Cannes Film Festival and went on to bring Saviano's image-making to a bigger audience still. *Gomorrah*'s author is now a major celebrity: millions tune in to watch his televised lectures, and his articles reliably boost the circulation of the newspapers that host them.

Gomorrah, and its author, have attracted criticism and even denunciation. Some of the sceptical voices ('He only did it for the money!') patently come from the camorra's supporters, or from people who resent his success, or from the usual chorus that would prefer a decorous silence about organised crime. Less easy to dismiss out of hand are those who point out that *Gomorrah*'s style is overblown and occasionally pretentious, that it contains exaggerations, and that it merges fact with imagina-tion and unfiltered hearsay. Saviano himself defines his work as a 'no-fiction novel', but most of his readers have read it as the unexpurgated truth. *Gomorrah* undoubtedly draws on investiga-tive documents, like the Cassiopea case on the toxic-waste trade, or the Spartacus trial mounted against the leaders of the *casalesi*. But now and again there are also stories that do not come from reliable sources – like the book's arresting opening scene, which depicts the frozen cadavers of illegal Chinese immigrants spilling out from a container hoisted above the port of Naples. Other critics worry that Saviano's personalised approach has helped turn him into an oracle or a guru. (Saviano is not the unique figure that the media outside Italy sometimes present him as being: in the first nine months of 2012 alone, 262 Italian journal-ists were threatened in the course of their work, many of them by gangsters.)

Nevertheless, there is much that helps tip the balance clearly in favour of Saviano and against his detractors. In the wake of his success, many other anti-mafia voices won the kind of large audience that they would not otherwise have found. One instance is the magistrate Raffaele Cantone, who is from Giugliano in *casalesi* territory. His books distil the insights he gained between 1999 and 2007 when he conducted camorra investigations, and traced the *casalesi*'s business interests in the North. After *Gomorrah*, the *casalesi* gained a notoriety that they deserved, and that certainly damaged a criminal cartel which had previously done its best to remain invisible. In the years after the publication of *Gomorrah*, the authorities scored a number of successes against the *casalesi*, radically reducing their power. In December 2011, the last remaining historic boss of the *casalesi*, Michele Zagaria, was captured after a decade and a half as one of Italy's most wanted. Fittingly, in his bunker, he had a copy of *Gomorrah*.

In short, Saviano's book once more made the camorra into what it should always have been: a national scandal. Quite what future historians of Italy will make of the whole Saviano phenomenon is anyone's guess. My sense is that his unusual form of celebrity is only the most prominent sign that, up and down Italy, a generation of citizens too young to even remember the ideological certainties of Cold War politics are finding new ways to express their civic engagement, their intolerance of corruption and organised crime. Saviano's young readers are Campania's best hope for the future.

'Ndrangheta: **Snowstorm**

Heroin was the mafias' illegal commodity of choice in the 1970s and 1980s, but by the 1990s cocaine had overtaken it.

Since the late nineteenth century, cocaine has followed a similar trajectory to heroin: from medicine, to vice, to valuable criminal business. When it was first successfully extracted from coca leaves in the 1860s, it became a tonic: Pope Leo XIII was a heavy user of a cocaine-based drink called Vin Mariani, and even allowed his image to appear in adverts. In the early twentieth century, the drug was banned in its biggest consumer market, the United States. From then on, it became a source of profit for the underworld. But not until the late twentieth century did a self-reinforcing cycle of increasing supply, falling prices, and more widespread consumption make cocaine more popular than any other narcotic except cannabis. Soon cocaine prices fell enough for it to cease being a niche drug for the rich. In 2005, a pharmacology research institute in Milan developed a technique for measuring cocaine consumption by examining the drug residues left in the city's sewage. The resulting estimates indicated that consumption was twice as high as previously thought: for every 1,000 young people, thirty were taking a hit a day. Builders were even sniffing so they could get through their overtime and then go out on the town. In 2012 it was revealed that the inhabitants of Brescia, a city of just under 200,000 in Lombardy, are sniffing their way through €625,000 worth of white powder every single day. And Brescia is only a microcosm.

Cocaine is a less debilitating narcotic than heroin (at least in the short term); it can be consumed without the unsightly business of injection; it is more socially acceptable, and it even has the false reputation of being non-addictive. Try as they might, the authorities cannot create the same sense of emergency around cocaine as there was with heroin. Cosa Nostra, the camorra and the 'ndrangheta have found an inexhaustible new source of money.

Mafiosi from all the major Italian criminal organisations indulge in trafficking cocaine, and since at least the 1980s they have often formed business partnerships with one another to do so. Giacomo Lauro, a penitent from the 'ndrangheta who was heavily involved in international trafficking throughout the 1980s, has described his dealings with Sicilian *mafiosi* and with *camorristi* of the calibre of Antonio Bardellino. Already at that stage, Italian drug barons made sure that deals went through smoothly by exchanging hostages with the South American producers. A prominent family linked to the Calì cartel were permanently resident in Holland: they acted both as hostages and as business agents for the Colombians.

But in the 1990s, just as the era of mass cocaine consumption really began, the 'ndrangheta became the leading operator in the cocaine sector. Indeed, it is primarily to cocaine that the 'ndrangheta owes its reputation as Italy's richest mafia today. Three police investigations into drug running tell a snapshot story of how the 'ndrangheta overtook Cosa Nostra as Italy's major trafficking power.

On the night of 6–7 January 1988, a Panamanian-registered merchant ship called *Big John* was intercepted off the western coast of Sicily. Hidden in its cargo of fertiliser were 596 kilograms of pure Colombian cocaine – just as an informer within the drug ring responsible had told Giovanni Falcone there would be. Cosa Nostra, it turned out, had paid in the region of twelve million dollars for the drugs, depositing the money with the Medellín cartel's emissary in Milan. The *Big John* investigation showed that Cosa Nostra, now firmly in the fist of Shorty Riina, was trying to turn Sicily into what Spain had been hitherto: the major port of entry for South American drugs bound for the European market. The confiscation of the *Big John*'s cargo was not just a big financial loss for the Sicilians: it was a huge embarrassment too. When the news broke, American Cosa Nostra learned that its Sicilian sister organisation had cut it out of the cocaine trade, and was now dealing direct with the Colombian producers. From now on, mafia cocaine brokers in the New World would be looking for more trustworthy business partners.

The second illustrative case involves the discovery, in March 1994, of 5,500 kilograms of 82 per cent pure cocaine in a container lorry near the northern Italian city of Turin. The man who exported the load from South America had a name that should sound familiar: Alfonso Caruana, of the Cuntrera-Caruana clan, the Sicilian *mafiosi* who had moved to the Americas and become key members of the Transatlantic Syndicate during the 1970s heroin boom. Significantly, however, Caruana's cocaine was not destined for his Sicilian brethren. Cosa Nostra was in turmoil following the murders of Falcone and Borsellino, Shorty's attack on the Italian state, and an unprecedented flood in penitents. Instead the shipment had been paid for and imported by an investment club comprising the biggest crime families in Calabria. With Cosa Nostra looking increasingly untrustworthy to its international narcotics partners, and with most of the larger camorra clans in the process of breaking up, the 'ndrangheta was left in prime position to take advantage of the most important commercial opportunity international organised crime had seen for years.

In 2002 investigators from the Italian tax police, the *Guardia di Finanza*, broke into the coded communications used by an international cocaine-trafficking ring comprising both Sicilian and Calabrian gangsters. The bugged conversations told a tale of two brokers. The first was a Sicilian by the name of Salvatore Miceli: a Man of Honour from the Salemi Family – and Cosa Nostra's agent. The second was a Calabrian by the name of Roberto 'Bebè' Pannunzi; he had been brought up among the long-established Italian criminal networks of Canada, and he was the 'ndrangheta's agent. The names of both men had already cropped up again and again in connection with international cocaine deals. The two were old friends as well as business partners: the Calabrian had acted as godfather to the Sicilian's son. But it emerged from the phone taps that, in the early 2000s, the Sicilian managed to lose three separate cargoes of cocaine on circuitous routes between South America, Greece, Spain, Holland, Namibia and Sicily. Understandably, everyone else involved in the trade was furious. The Sicilian had forfeited his credibility, and risked forfeiting his life. Investigators intercepted a telephone call he made to his son: 'We've lost face here . . . we've lost everything . . . any minute they're going to have a go at me . . . everyone has abandoned me.'

Soon afterwards, the Sicilian was kidnapped and held prisoner on a plantation deep in the South American forest. The Colombians wanted their money back. His life was only saved following reassurances issued by the Calabrian, Roberto 'Bebè' Pannunzi. But henceforth the 'ndrangheta decided to cut Cosa Nostra out of its affairs altogether. In 2002, the Calabrian broker moved to Medellín, to join a number of 'ndranghetisti who were already based there. The twin messages in the story were clear to all. First, that cocaine was being sourced directly in Colombia for the European market. And second, that Cosa Nostra was now, at best, the junior partner in relations with the South American cocaine barons.

Back home in Calabria, the 'ndrangheta received a major boost to its trafficking operations in the early 1990s when work was finally completed on the gargantuan container transhipment port at Gioia Tauro. The port was the only concrete legacy of the 'Colombo package' – the parcel of industrial investment that was promised in the wake of the urban revolt in Reggio Calabria in 1970. Despite intensive security measures, cocaine has been passing through the port of Gioia Tauro ever since it opened: as a result of a stepping up of surveillance, more than 2,000 kilograms were confiscated in 2011. Quite what percentage of the total volume of cocaine imports this figure represents is anyone's guess.

Yet the port of Gioia Tauro is only one of many options for *'ndranghetisti* seeking a route into Europe for their cocaine. The 'ndrangheta has men stationed in a number of major European ports, notably in Spain, Belgium and Holland. Circa 2003, when the European authorities tried to crack down on imports from South America, the Calabrians also began to use various African countries as cocaine staging posts. Large consignments would be brought into Senegal, Togo, the Ivory Coast or Ghana by ship, and then divided into smaller packages for importation into Italy by boat, plane or drug mule.

The 'ndrangheta also has more local distribution networks. We have already seen how, since the 1950s, the 'ndrangheta has been the most successful of any of the southern Italian mafias at setting up colonies in northern Italy. Today, there are thought to be as many as fifty 'ndrangheta Locals in northern Italy. Given that, by Calabrian mafia law, it takes at least forty-nine Men of Honour to form a Local, that figure suggests there are at least 2,450 members in the North. From gangmastering, construction and kidnapping, those northern Locals have graduated to wholesale cocaine dealing, while intensifying their penetration of local government and the economy.

Nor is this a problem confined to Italy. Since the 1960s, thousands of Calabrians have also migrated to other countries in Europe in search of work. Concealed among the honest majority there were *'ndranghetisti* who have set up a network of cells that no other mafia can match. The starkest illustration of the 'ndrangheta's European influence is not directly related to cocaine: it is the story of Gaetano Saffioti, a businessman specialising in concrete who, having paid extortion money to the Calabrian mafia for years, rebelled in 2002 and handed video evidence over to investigators that put dozens of *'ndranghetisti* behind bars.

Since that time, Saffioti has lived with an armed escort and has not won a single contract in Calabria. When he tried to trade outside of his home region he was thwarted. Seven of his lorries were burned in Carrara, Tuscany. Even more insidiously, he faced a silent boycott everywhere he went in Italy: potential clients would be 'advised' that it was not a good idea to be seen with the Calabrian whistleblower. Saffioti went further afield in search of business. In 2002–3 his machinery was also burned in France and Spain, and in other European countries the same whispering campaign against him was in force. He now does most of his trade with the Arab world where, he says, there is greater commercial freedom for someone like him.

The 'ndrangheta's reach is not limited to the old continent. Calabrian *mafiosi* have had an uninterrupted presence in Canada since before the First World War. In 1911, Joe Musolino – the cousin of Giuseppe Musolino, the 'King of Aspromonte' – was arrested for leading a gang of extortionists in Ontario. Australia is another example: the 'ndrangheta has been down under since before the Second World War. Back in the early 1930s, Calabrian gangsters who infiltrated the booming sugar-cane plantations of North Queensland were able to order up a killer from Sydney, some 2,500 kilometres away. This was the equivalent of sending someone from Reggio Calabria to London to commit a murder. Needless to say, longstanding international contacts such as these also afford today's *'ndranghetisti* unrivalled opportunities for laundering and investing their cocaine profits.

Given the 'ndrangheta's global network of cells, it is hardly surprising that journalists in Italy often refer to it as a 'cocaine multinational' or an 'international holding company'. But this is an oversimplification. Just as was the case with Cosa Nostra in the golden era of heroin trafficking in the 1970s and 1980s, the 'ndrangheta's cocaine business is not a single economic venture. There is no one centre from which the drug trade is run, and no overall cocaine kingpin. Indeed, if there were, the world's police forces would find it a great deal easier to clamp down. Narcotics traders need to keep their business as secret as possible; they constantly change their routes and routines as the authorities close in, or as rivals emerge. Recent investigations indicate that the 'ndrangheta's trafficking operations are even more flexible and wide-ranging than were Cosa Nostra's in the days of the Pizza Connection. Calabrian *mafiosi* have created an intricate and constantly changing pattern of cells and networks, of more-or-less-temporary consortia and partnerships. In the early 1980s, Shorty Riina's men fought the bloodiest mafia civil war in history for control of the heroin route to the United States. To date, there has been no comparable conflict in Calabria. One of the reasons for that is that the cocaine business is just too diversified for any Calabrian boss, however powerful, to even dream of monopolising it.

Yet the 'ndrangheta in Calabria, in the rest of Italy, throughout the world, is by no means confused or centreless. Of that, we have recently become much more certain, because of one of the most important investigations in 'ndrangheta history. In 2010, the *Carabinieri* succeeded in secretly filming the Great Crime . . .

'Ndrangheta: **The Great Crime**

Italy has never been short of information on the Sicilian mafia. The noise of public debate – sometimes loud, and often unproductive – has been a constant accompaniment to every phase of organised crime history on the island. There has only ever been one period when absolute silence was the rule: the last decade of Fascism, when Mussolini muted all coverage of mafia stories in the press. The post-war period has seen the quantity of information increase exponentially. Already, between 1963 and 1976, the first parliamentary inquiry into the Sicilian mafia generated a final report comprising three fat books, plus a further thirty-four volumes of supporting evidence. These days, I would be surprised if the various local and national anti-mafia bodies set up by Giovanni Falcone did not generate more material than that every single year. Today, in mafia affairs, as in every other facet of society, we are in an era of information abundance. It took six years, between 1986 and 1992, for Italy's historic refusal to contemplate the existence of the Sicilian mafia to be destroyed in the courts by Giovanni Falcone and Paolo Borsellino's maxitrial. These days, the police and *Carabinieri* nonchalantly demonstrate its existence every day, in every home in Italy, by posting compelling footage of their operations on YouTube. Everyone can see and hear what the *Carabinieri* of Operation Perseus saw and heard when Palermo's bosses got together to re-establish the *kind of* Commission in 2008.

Nor is there any shortage of news, comment and documentation about the camorra. Once post-war Naples overcame its reluctance to use the 'c' word, the deeds of *camorristi* were widely reported – at least locally, at least for those who cared. For a while in the 2000s, thanks to Roberto Saviano's *Gomorrah*, Neapolitan gangland stories were national headline news.

By no means everything about the camorra that makes it into the public domain deserves to be taken seriously. As has always been the case, camorra dramas are often acted out in public and the culture of the camorra intermingles with some trends in Neapolitan culture. Some of the local newspapers in Campania have been criticised for acting as bulletin boards for the clans. Then there are the 'neo-melodic' singers, whose work is sometimes a scarcely disguised apologia for the camorra. In 2010 neo-melodic musician Tony Marciano recorded 'We Mustn't Surrender', in which he impersonates a fugitive from justice railing against penitents who have 'lost their *omertà*' and 'brought down an empire'. In July 2012 Marciano was arrested on suspicion of drug trafficking. The arrest warrant describes him as being very close to the Gionta clan, 'so much so that he was constantly invited to private celebrations planned by that organisation's supporters and members'. Marciano's only comment when the *Carabinieri* took him away was 'I wouldn't get this many TV cameras if I was putting on a concert.'

For much of its history, the 'ndrangheta has been the odd mafia out: it has failed to capture consistent public attention. Some basic facts help explain why. Calabria is comparatively small: Sicily has a population of 5.05 million, Campania 5.8 million, whereas there are only 2.2 million in the toe of the boot. Calabria is also politically marginal, and its media fragmented: the region's main newspaper, the *Gazzetta del Sud*, is not even based in Calabria, but is instead published across the Straits in Messina, Sicily. For a long time, viewed from Turin or Trieste, the cyclical violence between 'ndrangheta clans in Calabria was all too easily dismissed as something atavistic, incurable and irrelevant. The spate of kidnappings in the 1970s and 1980s only created concern about organised crime in Calabria because many of the victims were northern. Kidnappings apart, what space there was for mafia stories in national news bulletins was taken up by goings-on in Palermo or Naples. Meanwhile, the 'ndrangheta thrived on neglect.

One of the most significant developments of the last few years is that the nation's habitual indifference towards the 'ndrangheta threat has begun to dissipate. The 'ndrangheta's own actions have played a key part in that trend. In October 2005, the Deputy Speaker of the Calabrian Regional Assembly, Francesco Fortugno, was murdered in Locri: the highest-profile politician to be killed by any mafia in the twenty-first century.

Events in the German steel town of Duisburg in 2007 attracted even more attention. In the early hours of 15 August, six men of Calabrian origin, the youngest of them a boy of sixteen, were executed as they sat in a car and a van outside an Italian restaurant. Their deaths were the final act of a sixteen-year-long feud between two branches of the 'ndrangheta, both based in San Luca, up on Aspromonte. The momentum of the feud had spun out of Italy to take in the clans' satellites in Germany. Nowhere outside the United States and Italy had there been a mafia massacre on this scale before.

Grim as it sounds to say it, the Duisburg massacre happened at a good time and in a good place. With Tractor Provenzano's arrest the year before, Cosa Nostra had fallen down the news agenda, leaving space for the 'ndrangheta story to fill. For most Italians, the idea that the 'ndrangheta had spread far beyond the wooded slopes of Aspromonte came as a surprise; to hear that it had strong bases in Germany was a shock.

Important indicators of Italy's newfound concern about the 'ndrangheta soon followed. In 2008, a Calabrian centre-left politician became the author of the parliamentary inquiry's first full-scale report on the 'ndrangheta – roughly one hundred and thirty years after it emerged from the prison system. The Calabrian mob's visibility around the world has grown too: in June of the same year, President Bush included it in the Foreign Narcotics Kingpin Designation Act, a kind of blacklist of traffickers.

457

2010 was an important year both for acts of high-level intimidation by the 'ndrangheta, and for a response from the Italian state. In January, a bomb detonated outside the Prosecutors' Office in Reggio Calabria – no one was hurt. Eighteen days later a car full of weapons and explosives was found on the morning of a visit to Reggio Calabria by the President of the Republic. Other warning messages followed, including a bazooka left near the offices of the Chief Prosecutor. Later in 2010, the text of the Rognoni-La Torre law, the equivalent of the USA's RICO legislation, was finally modified to include the 'ndrangheta explicitly.

At long last, the 'ndrangheta is news. In 1979, only one book was published in Italian with the word 'ndrangheta in the title. In 1980, there were none at all. In both 2010 and 2011, the total was comfortably over twenty. I have even heard people complain that there are *too many* books published on Calabrian organised crime these days. How short some memories are. The pioneering historians, and the brave Calabrian magistrates and journalists who have been trying to document the 'ndrangheta emergency for decades, and who are now finally getting the national readership they deserve, are not among those grumbling.

The investigating magistrates of Reggio Calabria's District Anti-mafia Directorate (the 'pool', in other words) have recently been producing results to match the public's awakened curiosity. Just as in Sicily, the extraordinary surveillance work carried out by the *Carabinieri* can be seen by all on YouTube. The most historically resonant film shows a group of men, mostly middle-aged, and all dressed as if they were just ambling down the road for a game of cards and a glass of wine at their local *circolo*. They are shown stopping in front of a small white statue of the Madonna and Child perched on top of a two-metre stone column. For anyone who has been to Polsi, the site is unmistakable: this is the medieval Sanctuary of the Madonna of the Mountain on Aspromonte. According to prosecutors – and so far the courts have wholly endorsed their case – what happens next is a sacred moment in the life cycle of the 'ndrangheta. Each year, early in

September, chief cudgels from across Calabria mingle with pilgrims at the Sanctuary to ratify the appointment of the Calabrian mafia's senior officers. Once they have all assembled before the Madonna statue, the men on the grainy film slowly form into a circle, and listen intently as the oldest among them sets out his credentials:

> What we have here just wouldn't exist if it wasn't for me . . . I was awarded the Santa four years before anyone. Then they gave me the Vangelo . . . There's a rule: the *offices* can't be given out whenever we want, but only twice a year, and we have to do it together. We need to be all together! The Great Crime doesn't belong to anyone: it belongs to everyone!

The Santa and Vangelo are the 'ndrangheta's senior 'gifts' – permanent badges of status, each marked by a special initiation ritual. (The institution of the Santa, or Mamma Santissima ('Most Holy Mother') triggered the First 'Ndrangheta War in 1974.) These 'gifts' give their bearer access to the higher positions, or *offices*, in the 'ndrangheta's ruling body, the Great Crime, which is also known as the Crime or the Province. The man filmed addressing the ring of *'ndranghetisti* at Polsi in September 2009 was seventy-nine-year-old Domenico Oppedisano, who had just been elected *capocrimine* (boss of the Crime), the most senior post in the 'ndrangheta. (Oppedisano has been convicted and sentenced to ten years. An appeal is under way.)

So what does the Great Crime do, exactly? And how powerful is the *capocrimine*? According to the prosecuting magistrates, and the judges who have ruled on the case so far, comparisons with the Commission of Cosa Nostra, and with a dictatorial super-boss like Shorty Riina, are a long way wide of the mark. Domenico Oppedisano is no Shorty. For one thing, his new job, like all the other positions in the Great Crime, was only due to last for a year, and not for life. Oppedisano was chosen as a wise old head, an expert on tradition and procedure, a settler of disputes. In British terms, his powers combined those of the Speaker of the House of Commons, the Lord Chief Justice, and the Queen. The Great Crime has the power to suspend a Local from the organisation, to recognise a newly established Local, or to decide between two rival candidates for the job of chief cudgel in a Local. As a recent 'ndrangheta penitent explains, the Great Crime has no power to intervene in day-to-day criminal business:

> In Calabria they get together, but not to say, 'What are we going to do?' or 'Shall we bring in that cargo from Colombia?' They get together exclusively to choose the offices . . . But not to set out what we should do, or who we should kill. Those are decisions that are taken by the towns and villages, the Locals.

The 'ndrangheta has an internal political life that is even more procedurally and politically complicated than Cosa Nostra's. The *Carabinieri* were able to record long and involved discussions over which Locals should get positions on the Great Crime. However, everyone involved acknowledged that it was right and proper that the top jobs should circulate between the three precincts into which criminal territory in the province of Reggio Calabria is divided: the plain of Gioia Tauro, the Ionian coast and the city of Reggio Calabria. Domenico Oppedisano, it turns out, was a compromise candidate – chosen because he carried little personal power and would offend no one.

One of the most remarkable features of Operation Crime, and the cluster of other investigations centring on it, is that it shows how the 'ndrangheta's political life embraces affiliates up and down Italy. With one or two exceptions, each of the Locals in northern Italy is the clone of a mother-Local in Calabria. One penitent provided a lively image for the relationship: 'a woman gives birth, but the umbilical cord is never cut'. That 'umbilical cord' consists of the close kinship ties between members of the same clans. But the link is also constitutional. Locals outside Calabria have to refer back to the Great Crime to settle disputes, win approval for the award of senior 'flowers', or have new Locals authorised. (Unauthorised Locals are known as Bastards.)

Locals in Lombardy, Italy's most populous and economically dynamic region, have their own representative assembly, known as 'Lombardia'. In 2008, Carmelo Novella, the chief of the Lombardia, tried to break away from the Great Crime, awarding senior flowers without approval, and setting up new Locals himself. On 14 July 2008, he paid the price for his unilateral declaration of independence when he was shot dead in his favourite bar. The Great Crime then set up a temporary body, known as a Control Chamber, to pilot Lombardy through the crisis. The man put in charge of the Control Chamber, Pino Neri, was a Freemason and convicted drug dealer who was born in Calabria but studied for a law degree at Pavia University near Milan. His final-year dissertation was on, of all things, the 'ndrangheta. On 31 October 2009, the town of Paderno Dugnano near Milan was the venue for a meeting at which Neri put forward a solution to the constitutional issues with the Lombardia. In a cultural centre named in honour of Giovanni Falcone and Paolo Borsellino, the Lombardy bosses all raised their hands to approve the plan. The *Carabinieri* made a film of the whole event which is now, inevitably, on YouTube. At the time of writing, Pino Neri has been convicted and sentenced to eighteen years for his leading role in the 'ndrangheta in Lombardy. It is as yet unclear whether he will appeal.

There is much that still needs to be clarified about the 'ndrangheta's internal political life. Investigators believe, for example, that Locals stationed around the world habitually report back to the Great Crime. The most startling instance is the most distant: in Australia there are reputed to be nine Locals. One of them is based in Stirling, a town of 200,000 people near Perth. In 2009, according to the Italian authorities, the boss of the Stirling Local, a property developer and former mayor called Tony Vallelonga, was bugged when he came back to Calabria to consult a member of the Great Crime. Vallelonga has declared himself angry and baffled by the allegations of his involvement, which were made public in 2011. To date, he has not been extradited.

Recent investigations have not only laid bare some previously puzzling aspects of the organisation's internal political system; they have also revealed new evidence about Calabrian mafia women. Some of the 'ndrangheta's womenfolk can have great influence within the kinship groups – males and females, relatives by blood and by marriage – that cluster around the 'ndrangheta's cells. Women who belong to these core family groups can, as it were, 'borrow' power from their male relatives. Such power goes beyond the usual women's work of inciting their men to vengeance and raising children in the cult of violence, and may even involve more than hiding weapons and ferrying messages to prisoners. A few 'ndrangheta women have even been entrusted with the gang's common fund. There is also evidence that one or two particularly enterprising women have earned a special status in the 'ndrangheta, and with it the title of 'sister of *omertà*'.

Despite the clout that some 'ndrangheta women have, they are entirely *absent* from the command structures identified by Operation Crime: there are no women officers in the Locals, and women are not allowed to be ritually affiliated. Put another way, women may be born or marry into Calabrian gangster bloodlines, but they cannot be part of the 'ndrangheta as an organisation.

Like the other two mafias, the 'ndrangheta weaves together family bonds and organisational ties in a particular way. The 'ndrangheta is as heavily rooted in families as is the camorra; yet like Cosa Nostra, it is also a sworn brotherhood of male criminals, a highly structured freemasonry of delinquency. This specific blend of characteristics seems to make women in the 'ndrangheta's orbit acutely vulnerable: it would appear that they are liable to suffer even more abuse than their peers in Campania or Sicily. Using evidence from women close to the 'ndrangheta who have confided in the law, magistrates in Reggio Calabria have recently begun to look again at some twenty murder investigations concerning women who had either vanished, or whose deaths had previously been dismissed as either inexplicable or as suicide. A submerged history of 'ndrangheta honour killings may be about to surface. One of the victims was Maria Teresa Gallucci. In 1994, in the northern port city of Genoa, gunmen burst into her flat and shot her dead, along with her mother and niece who just happened to be with her at the time. Maria Teresa was the widow of an *'ndranghetista*. Her crime, in the mob's eyes, was to have offended her husband's memory by starting a relationship with another man.

A similarly disturbing case concerns Domenica Legato, who was found dying in the street outside her family home in 2007. She fell from the balcony, her family said. One female 'ndrangheta penitent thinks that this was a disguised murder. Knife wounds found on her hands may suggest that she was resisting an attack just before her death. Domenica too was an 'ndrangheta widow who had found a new love. It should be stressed, however, that the case was treated as suicide at the time, and no new investigation has been ordered as I write.

Perhaps the most chilling case of all is that of Maria Concetta Cacciola, a mother of three whose husband was an *'ndranghetista* serving a long jail sentence. Maria Concetta turned to the *Carabinieri* in Rosarno in May 2011 after being beaten up by her father, who had discovered that she had started a platonic relationship with another man over the internet. Maria Concetta was eventually discovered in appalling agony, having drunk hydrochloric acid. Suicide again, the family claimed. Concetta's father, brother and mother are currently on trial for the abuse that resulted in her death, although *not* for her murder. There has been a great deal of public comment about whether that charge reflects what really happened to Concetta.

Tragedies like these inevitably raise historical questions. For how long, before the awakening of judicial interest in the roles of mafia women in the 1990s, have such horrors been part of the everyday life of the 'ndrangheta? In the early phase of the Calabrian mafia's history, pimping was a key business. Thus when the 'ndrangheta began, a great many of the women closest to the gangs were prostitutes. Beating, disfigurement and murder were the Calabrian gangster's favourite tools for managing his working girls. Between the two world wars, the 'ndrangheta learned that it was in its long-term interests to eschew pimping and use women in different ways: notably as pawns on the chessboard of dynastic marriage. If the cases of Maria Teresa Gallucci, Domenica Legato, and Maria Concetta Cacciola are anything to go by, then this long-term transformation of women's roles in the 'ndrangheta has not liberated them from the threat of being injured, maimed or killed in the cause of masculine honour.

The biggest historical questions of all are raised by Operation Crime. How long have we, and indeed the world, been living in ignorance while the 'ndrangheta existed in this form? It will take years of research to find an answer. All of the documentation gathered about the 'ndrangheta over the last 140 years will have to be re-examined to see if this new diagram of the 'ndrangheta's structure chimes with the recent or more distant past.

My own view, for what it is worth, is that the evidence of Operation Crime is convincing. Moreover I am almost certain that the Great Crime is not an innovation, and that 'ndrangheta has *always* been one brotherhood of crime, with a rich internal political life focused on coordinating institutions (whenever circumstances allowed those institutions to function). Since the 1880s, all 'ndrangheta cells across Calabria have always had roughly the same structure, and have used recognisably similar rituals. By far the most likely explanation for this fact is that the 'ndrangheta has always had a Great Crime, or something like it. It now seems likely, for example, that a body called the *Criminale*, which had very similar responsibilities to the Great Crime, existed between the First and Second World Wars. A generation before that, at the dawn of the twentieth century, police believed that the father of Giuseppe Musolino, the 'King of Aspromonte', had a seat on a 'supreme council' of the Calabrian mafia.

The footage of the Great Crime taken by the *Carabinieri* in 2009 is enough to give a historian goose bumps. There has never been such a direct record of the 'ndrangheta's annual gathering. Over the last century and more, fragmentary evidence about the Polsi summit has recurred, and rumours have proliferated. On one occasion, at Montalto in 1969, the summit was even raided and the 'mushroom-pickers' arrested. The earliest testimony of a meeting of *'ndranghetisti* from across Calabria at Polsi that I have found in the archives dates back to 1894. But until Operation Crime no one had managed to puzzle out the exact constitutional function of whatever body it was that met regularly on the upper reaches of Aspromonte. To this day, there is no legal precedent in Italy that states unequivocally that the 'ndrangheta actually exists, as a single brotherhood, with a single structure and a single coordinating body, rather than as a loose collection of gangs who sometimes form temporary alliances. The underlying aim of Operation Crime is to establish just such a precedent. In other words, the 'ndrangheta still awaits the kind of definitive legal description of its workings that Falcone and Borsellino's maxi-trial produced for Cosa Nostra. As was the case with the Sicilian mafia in the 1980s, Italy has only just begun properly to recognise a criminal conspiracy that has almost certainly existed for more than a century.

The 'ndrangheta is without doubt contemporary Italy's most powerful mafia. The beneficiary of years of disregard by the state and public opinion, it has a remorseless grip on its home territory, an unparalleled capacity to colonise other regions and other countries, and vast reserves of narco-wealth that allow it to penetrate the lawful economy and financial institutions. Yet it remains a largely unexplored frontier for investigators. Calabria has yet to develop the rich anti-mafia culture that now flourishes in Sicily. The number of entrepreneurs who have rebelled against protection rackets is tiny. In all kinds of ways, Calabria is a generation behind Sicily when it comes to the fight against organised crime.

Welcome to the grey zone

There is one member of Cosa Nostra's pro-massacre wing who still remains at large – one boss whose power dates back to the rise of the *corleonesi*. His name is Matteo Messina Denaro. Now fifty years old, he has been on the run for twenty years. According to the Ministry of the Interior, he is wanted for 'mafia association, murder, massacre, devastation, possession of explosives, robbery, and more besides'. Messina Denaro is mafia aristocracy, the son of a great boss. But in some other ways he is less conventional. He has a long-term Austrian girlfriend, and some of his captured communications reveal that he professes no religious faith. His base is in Sicily's westernmost province, Trapani. That fact prevents him taking charge of Cosa Nostra in its capital, Palermo. But he has always had a network of supporters there, particularly in the Brancaccio precinct. And during Operation Perseus it became clear that Messina Denaro was an important influence in the debates within Cosa Nostra over the setting up of the *kind of* Commission in Palermo. Quite whether Messina Denaro is the last of the old bosses of Cosa Nostra, or the first of a new breed, is hard to tell.

Over the last few years, Sicilians have grown used to the scenes when a major mafia fugitive is arrested. Police and *Carabinieri* in ski masks and bulletproof vests punch the air and sound their horns as they bring their captive back to base. Crowds gather outside police HQ to cheer and sing 'We are the real Sicily'. Then there comes the first sight of the captive himself, blinking impassively in the photographers' flashes, as everyone mentally compares his face to the photofit.

It is to be hoped that those scenes will soon be repeated in celebration of Matteo Messina Denaro's capture. For when the Castelvetrano boss is finally caught, it will indeed mark yet another historic victory over an old evil.

Historic, but certainly not definitive. Sicilians will have every right to rejoice at the end of Messina Denaro's career. Yet despite all the good news since the tragedies of 1992, few on the island will have any illusions that the Sicilian mafia is gone for good. The reasons why that is so – like the whole history of organised crime in Sicily – are partly to do with the Sicilian mafia's strength, and partly to do with Italy's weakness.

Every six months, the Anti-mafia Investigative Directorate (the FBI-equivalent set up by Giovanni Falcone) issues a report on the state of the fight against organised crime that is thick with data. Among the least conspicuous but most significant figures it records is the number of acts of 'vandalism followed by arson' – a tell-tale sign that racketeers are at work, a proclamation of Cosa Nostra's ability to make good its threats without resorting to murder. In 2011, there were 2,246 cases of vandalism followed by arson in Sicily: the highest in any Italian region, and an increase on the preceding years.

Of course, this figure is far from reflecting the full extent of Cosa Nostra's protection regime. For one thing, extortion operations lie hidden among the figures for many other kinds of crime: a burglary in a warehouse, for example, is often just an invitation to the owner to find the right person to pay. But it does give an idea of just how difficult Sicily finds it to loosen the racketeers' grip.

The anti-racket movement, Addiopizzo, as its coordinators are only too well aware, remains largely restricted to the better-off quarters of Palermo. Its impact in the suburbs and outlying settlements where the Sicilian mafia originated and is still strongest has been much more limited. The number of businesses that have signed Addiopizzo's pledge has been growing steadily since 2004. But at the time of writing, it stands at 723. There is still a long, long way to go.

Why has the current weakness of Cosa Nostra not triggered a full-scale revolt against extortion? Fear is part of the explanation. Sicilians are only too well aware that any lapse in concentration by the authorities will allow Cosa Nostra to regroup, as it did after two separate waves of Fascist repression, for example, or again in the late 1960s. When one of the last remaining bosses from the pro-massacre wing was arrested in 1998, Guido Lo Forte, a magistrate involved in the hunt, issued a note of caution that is still valid today:

> The experience of the last twenty years has helped us understand that there is never a time for triumphalism. Cosa Nostra is an organisation whose structure was created to dominate territory irrespective of the role of individuals, and it has an enormous power to regenerate and transform itself.

If a mafia boss is captured, his replacement is almost always ready to step up. If thirty bosses are captured, as in Operation Perseus, new leaders emerge from the rank-and-file. Cosa Nostra's soldiers are all generals of crime, as Giovanni Falcone once said. Even when a whole generation of bosses and soldiers ends up behind bars for a while, their sons and nephews – boys brought up by the values of violence and honour – are eager to rise to the challenge. And when old bosses are released from their sentences, they too can step back into leadership roles. No criminal organisation venerates experience more than Cosa Nostra. Among the men identified in Operation Perseus who were due to sit on the re-formed *kind of* Commission was the legendary Gerlando Alberti, aged eighty-one. Alberti has been a constant presence in the crime pages since the 1960s. He was the boss who uttered the brass-necked witticism: 'The mafia? What's that? A brand of cheese?'

One of Cosa Nostra's often invisible sources of strength is its control over ordinary criminals. The mafia governs and taxes crime. *Mafiosi* live by extorting money from burglars and drug peddlers as well as from shopkeepers and construction companies. Control of the underworld begins in prison, and extends out into the streets: the local boss takes a cut of everything, on pain of death. There is a convention in Sicily that anyone who robs a heavy goods vehicle has to wait for twenty-four hours while *mafiosi* run checks on the booty; if it belongs to a firm with the right connections, then it has to be returned. Ordinary crime is no more likely to die out in Sicily than it is in any other part of the world, and Cosa Nostra's authority over street criminals will take a long time to eradicate.

Fear has never been the only resource that Sicily's Honoured Society can call on. Nor has the mafia ever been just a club for cut-throats. In 1876, a pioneering sociologist called *mafiosi* 'middle-class felons' – meaning people who are upwardly mobile, judicious in their use of violence. These middle-class felons were experts at corrupt networking who had their hands on some of the most advanced sectors of the Sicilian economy, and who were able to draw on both passive and active support in the society around them. Cosa Nostra owes its ability to regenerate itself in large part to the fact that its members and allies have always included men who can blend in with the economic, professional and political elite, men who can mould a kind of consensus for their authority. The latest journalistic buzz-word for such people is the 'grey zone': it is an area of society where complicity with the bosses is hard to detect, and where the partnership between the bosses and the businessmen, or between the gun and the laptop, is by no means always tilted in favour of the former. The grey zone is both invisible and pervasive: it cannot be seen on YouTube.

Michele Aiello, a construction entrepreneur who became the leading supplier of hospital facilities in Sicily, came straight out of the grey zone. He was a front for Bernardo 'the Tractor' Provenzano. When he was convicted in 2011, his colossal €800 million fortune was confiscated. (Alarmingly, just a few months into his fifteen-year sentence, he was granted house arrest on the grounds that he was allergic to beans.)

Another middle-class criminal is Aiello's friend Giuseppe Guttadauro, a leading surgeon and boss of the Brancaccio precinct of Cosa Nostra. There is a very long line of mafia doctors – men who have not seen any incompatibility between the Hippocratic Oath and the vows that Men of Honour make when they are initiated into Cosa Nostra. Infiltrating Italy's semi-privatised health system has been one of Sicilian organised crime's major sources of income over the last two decades.

The most recent man from the grey zone was unmasked in 2010. When Salvatore Lo Piccolo was taken in 2007, his soldiers chose one Giuseppe Liga to succeed him as boss of the San Lorenzo precinct of Cosa Nostra. Liga's nickname in mafia circles is 'the Architect' – for the prosaic reason that he is an architect. He has recently begun a twenty-year sentence.

Politics has been part of the Sicilian mafia's grey zone since 1860. It would be naïve to think that the Andreotti faction of the Christian Democrat Party – the 'Young Turks' like Lima and Ciancimino – were the only ones in cahoots with Cosa Nostra. The overwhelming likelihood is that many of the gangsters' political allies from the 'bad old days' of the 1980s got away scot-free. The mafia's politicians have also been inserting their friends and hangers-on into the state machinery for decades.

In recent years, there have been some successful prosecutions of Sicilian politicians with mob ties. The most prominent case is that of Salvatore Cuffaro, another doctor, and the leader of Sicily's regional government between 2001 and 2008. Cuffaro is now serving a seven-year term for 'aggravated aiding and abetting of Cosa Nostra', and he faces other charges too. Among the crimes that earned him his conviction is that of choosing electoral candidates on the say-so of the surgeon-cum-*capo* Giuseppe Guttadauro. Cuffaro was also deemed guilty of leaking information about criminal investigations into Guttadauro's affairs that he derived from a ring of corrupt *Carabinieri* working in the Palermo prosecutors' office. Despite successful investigations like this, colluding with the mafia remains a difficult crime to prove. Quite how many more Cuffaros there are out there is anyone's guess.

Cosa Nostra is also difficult to destroy because of its ability to win supporters in the lawful economy. Over generations, mafia money and influence have dyed much of the island's economic fabric varying shades of grey. No one knows how many companies in business now were set up with mob cash. Or have *mafiosi* as sleeping partners. Or earn from sweetheart contracts and cartel arrangements negotiated under Cosa Nostra's tutelage. Or whose employees owe their jobs to a boss's friendly word.

All of this political and commercial traction gives *mafiosi* enormous power to buy support. It pays to remember the words that the 'devout' boss, Pietro Aglieri, said to the magistrate who masterminded his capture:

> When you come to our schools to talk about justice and the rule of law, our kids listen to you and follow you. But when those same kids grow up, and start looking for a job, a home, a bit of help with health or finance, who do they go looking for? You or us?

At its edges, the grey zone becomes lighter, spreading out into the sections of the economy, politics and society that are not directly under mob control. There are thousands of enterprises that operate on the borders of the law. Labour is cash-in-hand, tax gets fiddled, accounts get falsified, and regulations are dodged. Recourse to offshore banking and tax havens is routine among some sections of the bourgeoisie. A large proportion of Sicily's enduringly sluggish economy depends on the state sector, where favouritism, pork-barrel politics and corruption are deeply entrenched vices. Bosses love to offer their own brand of law to such an ankylotic and lawless wealth-accumulation system. The 'off the books economy', like the politics of patronage, is inherently susceptible to mafia influence.

Even when it is not in league with Cosa Nostra, a great deal of Sicily's business, like much of its political system and state apparatus, is constitutionally averse to transparency. Whatever shade of grey they are, nobody wants the law looking too closely at what they are up to. Ivan Lo Bello is the head of Sicily's Confindustria (the employers' organisation) who introduced the policy of expelling members who paid protection money. He now lives under escort and has sent his children to be educated abroad. Reflecting on his experience late in 2011, he said the following:

> I'm less worried by the response from the criminal organisations than by the response from politicians. In Sicily, we've been met by silent hostility. We have the feeling that we aren't loved by town councillors, aldermen, party leaders and state functionaries who have an interest in maintaining the status quo.

There is a broad section of Sicilian society – from the lowliest shopkeeper to the smartest banker – for whom the fight against organised crime is, at best, extremely inconvenient.

Like Cosa Nostra, the camorra and the 'ndrangheta have a long history that testifies to their ability to adapt to new circumstances and recover from adversity. Like Cosa Nostra, but in subtly distinctive ways, they draw on organisational traditions and family know-how to find their way to the future. Moreover, everything I have said about the grey zone in Sicily applies in Campania and Calabria too. The toxic waste and rubbish scandals demonstrate how bad business and bad politics open the door to the camorra. The 'ndrangheta would not be the 'ndrangheta without its own 'middle-class felons' and its own grey zone. Indeed, in Calabria, where the anti-racket movement is weak, and shady Masonic organisations are notoriously ramified, the grey zone extends even further into society than it does in Sicily. When Confindustria, the employers' organisation, began applying measures against businesses with mafia contacts, other organisations followed its example. One example was the Palermo branch of ANCE, the association of building companies. When the Reggio Calabria branch of the same organisation staged a conference on the rule of law in June 2010, delegates spent their energies *protesting against* a whole range of legislation aimed at prohibiting relationships between *mafiosi* and businessmen.

Historically speaking, the 'ndrangheta, of all the mafias, has also perhaps been the most completely indifferent to ideology. It has always understood that the grey zone has no political colour. The 'ndrangheta's longstanding bases in the North also demonstrate that the grey zone recognises no boundaries between regions. Corrupt politicians and businessmen do deals with *'ndranghetisti* up and down the country.

Even in some areas of the national economy not directly touched by the tentacles of organised crime, sharp practice and corruption are rife – and are found far beyond the South and Sicily. In 2011, the chief of Italy's national anti-mafia prosecutor's office, Pietro Grasso, was talking about the whole of Italy when he said the following:

> The mafia method, which involves promoting illicit privileges and cancelling out competition, has been cloned in some border areas of politics and the economy where predatory cliques of wheeler-dealers have sprung up.

The Italian state is also doing a great deal to alienate those citizens who do still manage to live according to the rules. Italy's criminal justice system is in a lamentable state. The average length of a case is four years and nine months. There are many examples in the story I have told here of mafia-related trials that have dragged on for years, with verdicts being reversed at each successive tier of the system right up to the Supreme Court. These delays are monstrous for the accused, and bring continual discredit down upon the law. The delays can also be made to work in favour of the crooked. Citizens could be forgiven for thinking that the courts offer near-impunity to any white-collar criminal who can afford the lawyers needed to spin out proceedings until the statute of limitations takes effect.

The mafia latch onto the state at its weakest points. Prisons have always been one of the most shambolic parts of the Italian state and for that reason they have always been theatres of mafia activity. Indeed the camorra and the 'ndrangheta were both born behind bars. Since the nineteenth century, detainees in unsafe and overfull conditions have turned to the mafia organisations in the hope of protection, and *mafiosi* have imposed their own arbitrary and brutal rule on their fellow inmates. Italy's penitentiaries are now more overcrowded than those of any European country other than Serbia. The suicide rate is nearly twenty times higher than it is outside. No wonder that today, as in the nineteenth century, serving a first stretch is a rite of passage for aspiring gangsters, and most camorra affiliations still happen in jail.

The state can even help push honest citizens into the grey zone. For example, it is utterly failing to impose fairness and transparency on the national economy. A vital case in point is the civil courts, dealing with disputes between citizens and companies, which are in an even worse state than the criminal courts. In 2011, the World Bank ranked Italy 158th out of 183 countries for the efficiency of its justice system in enforcing contracts, just below Pakistan, Madagascar and Kosovo, and three places above Afghanistan. At the end of June 2011, there was a backlog of 5.5 million cases in the civil courts. The *average* length of a case is seven years and three months. In Germany, when a supplier takes a customer to court for an unpaid delivery, it takes him or her an awfully long time to obtain a ruling from a judge – an average of 394 days. In Italy, the figure is 1,210 days. Which is an *age* in the life of a business: one could go bust six times over. No wonder some entrepreneurs are tempted to find less peaceful ways of recuperating credit. *Mafiosi* welcome such entrepreneurs with open arms and a crocodile smile.

Too much of Italy is dysfunctional. The state apparatus is mired in ineptitude, patronage and corruption. A large slice of the economy is cash-in-hand, and therefore invisible to the law; whole areas of the visible economy are hobbled by inefficiency and sleaze. Italian society seems incurably addicted to the same vices. Nor is there much prospect that Italians will elect a government honest, determined and authoritative enough to implement the reforms their country needs. For as long as Italy remains in this condition, then enduring victory over Cosa Nostra, the camorra and the 'ndrangheta will remain out of reach.

The Cold War gave the mafias a political shield. Behind it, they plundered, prospered, and pushed Italy to the brink of the abyss. But the mafias were around before the Cold War, and they have survived its end. The headline-grabbing violence of the long 1980s may have abated, but organised crime is still a national emergency and a national shame.

However, Italy has more reasons for optimism today than at any point in the past. The anti-mafia magistrates and police forces of Italy are underpaid, underresourced, and understaffed. They operate in very hostile circumstances. Magistrates in mafia-run areas still have constant armed escorts, and live a monastic life for fear that they could be unwittingly photographed in the wrong company. Yet because of the dedication, courage and professionalism that so many of them display, Italy's gangster fraternities are finding life harder than it has ever been. *Mafiosi* have their meetings bugged. They are tracked down when they flee from justice. Even in the wilds of Aspromonte, the 'ndrangheta is no longer having things entirely its own way. A mountain operations unit of the *Carabinieri*, the *Cacciatori* ('hunters') was founded in the early 1990s and equipped with helicopters to combat kidnapping. Since the 'ndrangheta got out of the kidnapping industry, the *Cacciatori* have had notable success in denying Calabrian mobsters full use of their traditional mountain redoubts.

Although the Italian justice system remains extraordinarily lenient and hyper-protective of the rights of the accused, the long history of mafia impunity seems to be over. Gangsters can now expect to be fairly convicted when they go to court. Despite the agonisingly slow workings of the justice system, *mafiosi*, *camorristi* and *'ndranghetisti* are now serving thousands of years of prison. Just as importantly, billions of Euros of their stolen wealth have been confiscated. Inroads are even being made into the grey zone.

Looking back from today over the history of Italy's relationship with the mafias since the Second World War, and indeed since the very origins of the mafias in the nineteenth century, the single biggest and most positive change is that the police and magistracy are, at long, long last, doing their job.

Now it is over to the Italian people to do theirs.

Acknowledgements

Lack of time is a major reason why nobody has ever before tried to write a chronicle of organised crime in Italy from its origins to the present day. *Mafia Republic*, like its prequel *Mafia Brotherhoods*, is the result of a long period of research and writing that it would have been impossible for me to begin, let alone complete, without the support of two institutions. My heartfelt gratitude goes to both the Italian Department, University College London, where my colleagues have created an encouraging and lively environment for teaching and research; and to the Leverhulme Trust, which awarded me a Research Fellowship between 2009 and 2011 – a crucial period in the development of both books.

Thanks must also go to my editors and agents who have waited as my submission deadline receded into the distance, and as the single volume I originally planned grew into two. My fondest hope for this book is that it constitutes some kind of reward for the saintly patience of Rupert Lancaster, Giuseppe Laterza, Peter Sillem, Marc Parent, Haye Koningsfeld, Catherine Clarke and George Lucas. I would also like to thank Kate Miles and Juliet Brightmore at Hodder & Stoughton for their cheerful support.

In *Mafia Republic* I have tried to reach out beyond academia to explain to as broad a readership as possible what we can (and cannot) know about the history of the mafias. From my fellow academics, I can only crave indulgence for sacrificing many conventions of academic writing in this cause. As always, I have called on a team of friends to read drafts of the book in the hope of making it more readable. The following deserve special recognition for their selfless commitment to that arduous

Acknowledgements

endeavour: David Brown, Stephen Cadywold, Caz Carrick, Robert Gordon, John Foot, Prue James, Doug Taylor.

The staff at numerous libraries and archives have been very helpful in making available the sources consulted here. I feel particularly bound to mention the following: Salvatore Maffei at the Emeroteca Vincenzo Tucci in Naples; Maresciallo Capo Salerno and Col. Giancarlo Barbonetti at the Carabinieri Archive; Linda Pantano at the Istituto Gramsci in Palermo; and, yet again, the staff in Humanities 2 at the British Library. A long list of people have helped me with advice, or by locating sources: I would have been lost without Salvo Bottari, Mark Chu, Vittorio Coco, Fabio Cuzzola, Patrick McGauley, David Forgacs, Manuela Patti, Nino Sapone, Diego Scarabelli, Fabio Truzzolillo, Chris Wagstaff, Thomas Watkin, and Francesco Messina. Nick Dines deserves a special mention for his astute and creative research on my behalf.

Pointers from Gabriella Gribaudi were very important in the early stages of my research on the post-war camorra; and my discussions with Enzo Ciconte have also been extremely fruitful. I would also like to express my thanks to Chiara Caprì, one of the founders of *Addiopizzo*, and to the inspirational Gaetano Saffioti for his patience in being interviewed twice. At various points I have relied in various ways on several journalists with a profound understanding of the mafias: Lirio Abbate, Peppe Baldessarro, Attilio Bolzoni, Salvo Palazzolo. A number of people in Campania helped me during a field trip to many of the places mentioned in this book: Alfonso De Vito, Marcello Anselmo, Egidio Giordano, and Vittorio Passeggio.

Cosa Nostra, the camorra and the 'ndrangheta show Italy at its worst. Yet the greatest privilege that comes with studying mafia history is that of meeting some of the extraordinary people who dedicate themselves to fighting the mafias, and thereby show Italy at its uplifting best. I would like to thank them for their precious help and input of all kinds. The list starts with Nicola Gratteri of the *Direzione distrettuale antimafia* in Reggio

Calabria. Capitano Giuseppe Lumia of the *Carabinieri* was endlessly resourceful, and colonnello Jacopo Mannucci-Benincasa, head of the Arma's *Ufficio Criminalità Organizzata*, extremely insightful. My particular gratitude goes to Michele Prestipino of the *Direzione distrettuale antimafia* in Reggio Calabria: conversations with him have been among the most fascinating moments of my quest to understand and explain the 'ndrangheta. In the final stages of writing the book, I was lucky enough to talk at length to Alessandra Cerreti (*Direzione distrettuale antimafia*, Reggio Calabria), Catello Maresca (*Direzione distrettuale antimafia*, Naples), colonnello Claudio Petrozziello and capitano Sergio Gizzi (*Guardia di Finanza*), vice questore Alessandro Tocco and commissario Michele Spina (*Polizia di Stato*), colonnello Pasquale Angelosanto (*Carabinieri*), colonnello Patrizio La Spada, tenente Angelo Zizzi, and the men of the *Squadrone Cacciatori* in Vibo Valentia. My encounters with servants of the rule of law like these were both hugely encouraging as well as extremely useful in confirming or qualifying what I thought about the state of the mafias today. I should stress that they cannot be blamed for any misinterpretation I may have made of their words, and that what I have written in these pages reflects my own views.

Last but not least, my love and gratitude goes to my wife, Sarah Penny, and to my children Elliot and Charlotte for keeping me sane during the journey.

Picture Acknowledgements

©ANSA: 7 above left, 8 above, 9 above right and below, 10 below left. Archivio Carabinieri, Palermo: 13 above left and right, 16 above. Archivio Fotografico Pietro Oliveri, Corleone: 10 above right. Courtesy of Archivio Unità: 2 below left. © AP/Press Association Images: 5 below, 6 above left/ Raul Fornezza, 13 below/Luca Bruno, 14 above/Italian Police, 15 above and 16 below left/Salvatore Laporta, 15 below and 16 below right/ Adriana Sapone. © Bettmann/Corbis: 2 above and centre, 3 below left. © Enzo Brai/ Pubblifoto, Palermo: 4 above right and below. Courtesy of Pasquale Capellupo archive: 5 above. Courtesy of Centro di Studi ed Iniziative Culturali Pio La Torre, Palermo: 10 above left. © Contrasto/eyevine: 9 above left/Angelo Palma, 10 below right/Shobha. © Corbis: 11 above left/ANSA, 12 below/ Antoine Gyori/Sygma. © John Dickie: 14 below. Alessandro Fucarini/ Agenzia Fotografica Labruzzo, Palermo: 7 below, 11 above right. © Eric Gaillard: 7 above right. © Tony Gentile: 12 above. © Getty Images: 3 above/ Mondadori, 4 above left/Gamma-Keystone, 6 above right/Popperfoto, 12 centre/Gamma-Rapho. Lux Films/RGA: 1 above. Private Collections: 1 below left and right, 3 below right. © Rex Features/Contrasto: 11 below. © Alberto Roveri / Rosebud2: 6 below.

I would like to thank the following for their help in sourcing photographs: Chiara Augliera of the Cineteca di Bologna; Maggiore Antonio Coppola of the *Carabinieri*'s Nucleo investigativo – reparto operativo, Palermo; Fabio Cuzzola; Nick Dines; Cecilia Ferretti of the Archivio Unità; Capitano Giuseppe Lumia and the ROS in Gioia Tauro; Vito Lucio Lo Monaco of the Centro Pio La Torre, Palermo; Gabriele Morabito; Nino Sapone; Fabio Truzzolillo.

Notes on sources

In sociology, it has become commonplace to treat Italy's major criminal organisations as different aspects of the same set of problems. Historians have been slow to catch up. All the major historians of organised crime in Italy have made often very precious comparative asides. Yet sustained comparison is very rare indeed. *Mafia Republic*, like its predecessor *Mafia Brotherhoods*, is intended to explore what we can learn by letting the histories of the three mafias run in parallel to one another. It is a task that has presented many challenges, notably at the level of narrative organisation. But the goal is fundamentally a simple one, all the same: a chronicle.

Mafia Republic is also intended for readers beyond Italy, as well as within its borders, for whom the word 'mafia' conjures up visions of Al Pacino before it does the faces of Luciano Liggio, Raffaele Cutolo or the De Stefano brothers. What I hope to do is dissipate some of the confusion generated both by films like *The Godfather* and the catch-all word 'mafia'. In an effort to make *Mafia Republic* as accessible as possible, I have not used footnotes or endnotes. Those of us who are university lecturers and therefore lucky enough to read for a living all too easily forget the huge efforts that many people have to make to find the time to read – and to read non-fiction in particular. Perhaps the least we can do to meet such readers halfway is to produce a narrative unencumbered by references, nods to obscure academic debates, and the name-checking of academic allies and opponents.

That said, footnotes fulfil many duties and afford many pleasures. The following pages can be but a poor substitute for them. My hope is that they will at least serve as a stimulus to further reading, a recognition of my many intellectual debts, an indication of what sources I have used to formulate and substantiate my arguments, and a clue to interesting issues that I did not have time to explore or treat fully.

My particular gratitude and admiration must go to those who, before me, have written narrative syntheses of the history of Italy's individual criminal organisations. These are the books that have been my constant companions while writing *Mafia Republic*. Salvatore Lupo's *Storia della mafia* (Rome, 1993) is one of the books that anyone interested in the mafias must read and re-read. (If you don't know Italian, be warned that an already dense text is badly served by a poor English translation: *History of the Mafia*, New York, 2011.) Lupo's more recent *Quando la mafia trovò l'America. Storia di un intreccio intercontinentale, 1888–2008* (Turin, 2008) provides a unique and perceptive 'transatlantic' history of the mafia in both Sicily and the United States. In several chapters here I have tried to follow Lupo's cues about the many-faceted relationship between the two branches of Cosa Nostra, and have also profited from his insights into the long-lasting dialogue of the deaf between Italy and the United States when it came to mafia matters. The 'Transatlantic Syndicate' is my coinage for what Lupo, drawing on first-hand sources, calls the 'third mafia'. Given that there were already three mafias in my story, I thought it best to choose another moniker in order to avoid confusion.

In its rigour and clarity, Francesco Barbagallo's *Storia della camorra* (Rome-Bari, 2010) stands head and shoulders above all previous attempts to survey the history of organised crime since the nineteenth century in Campania. His earlier books, *Napoli fine Novecento: Politici, camorristi, imprenditori* (Turin, 1997) and *Il potere della camorra (1973–1998)* (Turin, 1999) remain fundamental for the dramatic growth of the camorra in the late twentieth century. I have drawn on them repeatedly. Mention must also be made of Isaia Sales's influential collection of historical essays, *La camorra le camorre* (2nd edn, Rome, 1993), from which I have learned a great deal.

Partly for reasons that I have set out in this book, the 'ndrangheta's history remains much more obscure, in many respects, than does that of the Sicilian mafia or the camorra. Saverio Mannino's essay, 'Criminalità nuova in una società in trasformazione: il Novecento e i tempi attuali', in A. Placanica (ed.), *La Calabria moderna e contemporanea* (Rome, 1997) is rooted in trial documents and remains illuminating. Enzo Ciconte's *'Ndrangheta dall'Unità a oggi* (Rome, 1992) was a pioneering study, and is still the key work of reference today. To his great credit, Ciconte was also the first person to write an avowedly comparative historical account of Italy's three major criminal fraternities: *Storia criminale. La resistibile ascesa di mafia, 'ndrangheta e camorra dall'Ottocento ai giorni nostri* (Soveria Mannelli, 2008). It would be useless to ruminate here on quite why there had never been a parallel history of the mafias before Ciconte. Needless to say, his work has been a rich source of leads while researching *Mafia Republic*, despite the fact that *Storia criminale* takes a thematic approach that is very different to mine. P. Monzini, *Gruppi criminali a Napoli e a Marsiglia. La delinquenza organizzata nella storia di due città (1820–1990)* (Rome, 1999), provided a stimulating precedent for a comparative approach, and insights into various moments of camorra history.

All translations are my own unless stated.

I have used the following abbreviations:

ACS = Archivio Centrale dello Stato

Documentazione antimafia = Senato della Repubblica, Documentazione allegata alla relazione conclusive della Commissione parlamentare d'inchiesta sul fenomeno della mafia in Sicilia

Istruttoria Maxi = Falcone and Borsellino's history making prosecution case for the maxi-trial against Cosa Nostra, Ordinanza-sentenza contro Abbate Giovanni + 706

Istruttoria Stajano = part of the above was published as C. Stajano (ed.), *Mafia: l'atto d'accusa dei giudici di Palermo* (Rome, 1986)

Maxiprocesso = 40,000 pages of other material from the maxi-trial can now be viewed online thanks to the Fondazione Falcone, www.fondazionefalcone.org

Processo Olimpia = Procura della Repubblica di Reggio Calabria, Direzione Distrettuale Antimafia, Procedimento penale n.46/93 r.g.n.r. D.D.A. a carico di CONDELLO PASQUALE ed altri. 'Processo Olimpia' (this vast trial is the fundamental document for reconstructing the history of the 'ndrangheta from the late 1960s onwards).

Sources consulted

Preface

R. Brancato, *Con i tuoi occhi. Storia di Graziella Campagna uccisa dalla mafia*, Palermo, 2010.

E. Ciconte, *'Ndrangheta dall'Unità a oggi*, Rome, 1992. On the word 'ndrangheta's entry into widespread use, p. 254.

G. Fofi (ed.), *Per amore del mio popolo. Don Peppino Diana, vittima della camorra*, Naples, 1994. I found the essay by Conchita Sannino in this volume particularly useful.

S. Lupo, *Quando la mafia trovò l'America. Storia di un intreccio intercontinentale, 1888–2008*, Turin, 2008. On how Cosa Nostra got its name, p. 178.

Graziella Campagna's brother is interviewed in the episode of Carlo Lucarelli's documentary series *Blu notte*, first transmitted in October 2001 and now available on YouTube. The murder, and subsequent judicial saga, were widely covered in the press.

'Così hanno decapitato mio marito', *La Repubblica*, 9/5/1991.

The United States Consul General's 2008 report on Calabria, as made public by Wikileaks, can be found at: http://racconta.repubblica.it/wikileaks-cablegate/dettaglio.php?id=08NAPLES96

1. FUGGEDABOUTIT

Sicily: Threats, terrorism, murder, arson, kidnapping and mayhem

V. Coco and M. Patti, *Relazioni mafiose. La mafia ai tempi del fascismo*, Rome, 2010.

S. Di Matteo, *Anni roventi. La Sicilia dal 1943 al 1947*, Palermo, 1967.

D. Ellwood, *Italy 1943–1945*, Leicester, 1985.

N. Gentile, *Vita di capomafia*, Rome, 1993.

F.M. Guercio, *Sicily. The Garden of the Mediterranean. The Country and its People*, London, 1938. See pp. 64, 88 for the proclamations of the Sicilian canker's demise.

R. Mangiameli, 'La regione in guerra', in M. Aymard and G. Giarrizzo (eds), *La Sicilia, Storia d'Italia. Le regioni dall'Unità a oggi*, Turin, 1987.

P. Pezzino, *Mafia: Industria della violenza*, Florence, 1995. The October 1946 report on the 'occult organisation' is by *Carabinieri* General Amedeo Branca to the Comando Generale dell'Arma, and is reproduced on pp. 190–91.

U. Santino, *Storia del movimento antimafia. Dalla lotta di classe all'impegno civile*, Rome, 2009 (updated edn). On the Santangelo brothers and other aspects of the mafia's political atrocities in this period.

Sources consulted

A. Spanò, *Faccia a faccia con la mafia*, Milan, 1978. 'The mafia has never been as powerful and organised as it is today', p. 130.

The Scotten report on the mafia is in the National Archives, FO 371/37327.

New York Times, 'Mafia chiefs caught by Allies in Sicily', 10/9/1943; 'Mafia in Sicily', 11/9/1943.

Meridiana, 63, 2008. Monographic issue on *Mafia e fascismo*.

Sicily: *In the Name of the Law*

O. Barrese, *I complici. Gli anni dell'antimafia,* Milan, 1978. The quotation from Scelba is on p. 7.

A. Blando, 'L'avvocato del diavolo', *Meridiana*, 63, 2008.

Dizionario biografico dei meridionali, vol. 2, Naples, 1974, 'Lo Schiavo Giuseppe Guido'.

D. Forgacs, *Rome, Open City*, London, 2000. André Bazin's famous 1946 quotation about the 'skin of History peels off as film' is discussed on p. 23.

E. Giacovelli, *Pietro Germi*, Rome, 1991.

L. Sciascia, 'La Sicilia nel cinema' in *La corda pazza*, Turin, 1970.

G.G. Lo Schiavo, *Piccola pretura*, Rome, 1948. The quote comparing the mafia boss to Buddha is on p. 114. The novel would go on to form part of a trilogy of novels with equally questionable visions of the mafia. The trilogy was published together as *Terra amara* (Rome, 1956). The other two episodes in it are *Condotta di paese* (1952) and *Gli inesorabili* (1950). This latter novel was turned into an alarmingly bad film of the same name (dir. Camillo Mastrocinque, 1950) which was issued in the United States as *The Fighting Men* and can be viewed at http://archive.org/details/fighting_men. Charles Vanel reprises his role as a mafia boss – this time as a caped righter of wrongs: 'we protect all honest people'.

G.G. Lo Schiavo, 'La redenzione sociale nelle opere del Regime', *Politica Sociale*, X, August, 1937.

G.G. Lo Schiavo, 'Nel regno della mafia', *Processi*, 5, 1955. Contains Lo Schiavo's fond recollections of Calogero Vizzini.

G.G. Lo Schiavo, 'La mafia della lupara e quella dei colletti bianchi', *Nuovi Quaderni del Meridione*, 4, 1963.

G.G. Lo Schiavo, 'Il cinema alla luce del costume e della libertà', Trieste, 1963 (extract from *L'osservatore economico e sociale*, V, 1). Also contains biographical information.

G.G. Lo Schiavo, *100 anni di mafia*, Rome, 1962. Contains many of Lo Schiavo's writings, including his original 1933 response to Puglia, 'La mafia siciliana', with the addition of some very strange new footnotes in which he tries to wriggle out of his earlier opinions.

M. Sesti (ed.), *Signore e signori: Pietro Germi*, Siena, 2004.

V. Spinazzola, *Cinema e pubblico. Lo spettacolo filmico in Italia 1945–1965*, Rome, 1985.

In nome della legge (dir. Pietro Germi), 1949, is available on DVD from Cristaldi Film and on YouTube.

Calabria: The last romantic bandit

C. Cingari, 'Tra brigantaggio e "picciotteria": Giuseppe Musolino', in *Brigantaggio, proprietari e contadini nel Sud*, Reggio Calabria, 1976.

A. Sapone, *Sant'Alessio in Aspromonte. Uomini e storie dell'antico Casale di Alessi*, Reggio Calabria, 2001.

G.G. Lo Schiavo, *100 anni di mafia*, Rome, 1962. Reproduces 'Requisitoria del Sostituto Procuratore Generale del Re dr. Vittorio Barbera' (Messina, 27/2/1932) in the case against Anile Giuseppantonio + 89: on the Criminale.

F. Truzzolillo, '"Criminale" e "Gran Criminale". La struttura unitaria e verticistica della 'ndrangheta delle origini', unpublished typescript, 2012.

Crescenzo Guarino was the journalist who wrote about the aged Musolino most often, such as in the following articles: 'A colloquio con Musolino', *La Stampa*, 16/1/1950; 'La manìa di grandezza del brigante Musolino', *Stampa Sera*, 18–19/1/1950; 'Una poesia inedita di Pascoli per il brigante dell'Aspromonte', *Il Mattino*, 3/7/1955; 'Arde sempre in Musolino la fiamma della vendetta', *Il Mattino*, 5/7/1955; 'È morto il brigante Musolino', *La Stampa*, 24/1/1956; 'L'ultimo "brigante romantico" viveva tra i fantasmi del passato', *Stampa Sera*, 24/1/1956.

The key archival material on Musolino is in the Archivio di Stato di Reggio Calabria: Gabinetto di Prefettura, n. 1089, Associazione a delinquere in S. Stefano, b. 27, inv. 34; and Gabinetto di Prefettura, Serie prima, affari riservati. Bandito Musolino.

Naples: Puppets and puppeteers

P.A. Allum, *Politics and Society in Post-war Naples*, Cambridge, 1973.

'Camorra', in *Enciclopedia Italiana*, VIII, EUC–CARD, Milan, 1930.

M. Figurato and F. Marolda, *Storia di contrabbando. Napoli 1945–1981*, Naples, 1981.

G. Gribaudi, 'Les rites et les langages de l'échange politique. Deux exemples napolitains', in D. Cefaï (ed.), *Cultures politiques*, Paris, 2001. Very insightful on Navarra.

G. Gribaudi, *Donne, uomini, famiglie. Napoli nel Novecento*, Naples, 1999.

M. Marmo, '"Processi indiziari non se ne dovrebbero mai fare". Le manipolazioni del processo Cuocolo (1906–1930)', in M. Marmo and L. Musella (eds), *La costruzione della verità giudiziaria*, Naples, 2003. On the trial that destroyed the Honoured Society of Naples.

G. Marotta, *San Gennaro non dice mai no*, Milan, 1948, especially 'I "pupanti"' on puppets, 'Re Giuseppe' on Giuseppe Navarra.

G. Marotta, 'L'angelo degli autocarri', *La Stampa*, 13/10/1953, on the *correntisti*.

L. Musella, *Napoli dall'Unità a oggi*, Rome, 2010. A short history of Naples that is rich in ideas for several periods including this one.

'Feroce delitto in Sezione Vicaria. Ucciso un giovane con due coltellate da un camorrista in via A. Poerio', *Il Mattino* 13/7/52. On the murder by 'O Grifone. His story is followed up over the following days in the same newspaper.

'La caccia ai "correntisti". Drammatico inseguimento per i vicoli del Mercato', *Il Mattino*, 1/8/52. For the quotation on the 'fluid' *corrente*.

Sources consulted

Gennaro Abbatemaggio was an intermittent presence in the northern press throughout the 1950s. See for example: 'Lauro sorpreso a Napoli a strappare manifesti', *La Stampa*, 25/5/1952, on Abbatemaggio working for Achille Lauro; 'Il piccolo e feroce uomo dai baffi neri all'insù', *Stampa Sera*, 4/7/1952; 'Gennaro Abbatemaggio fa la prima comunione', *La Stampa*, 4/7/1952; 'Gennaro Abbatemaggio arrestato per le sue false dichiarazioni', *La Stampa*, 24/8/1954; 'Don Gennaro Abbatemaggio derubato da un borsaiolo', *La Stampa*, 24/7/1958; 'Abbatemaggio chiede di esibirsi al Musichiere', *La Stampa*, 9/1/1959; Gennaro Abbatemaggio promette sensazionali rivelazioni sulla camorra', *La Stampa*, 22/4/1959.

'Incontro c'' o rre', Paolo Monelli, *Nuova Stampa Sera*, 30/9/1947, one of many portraits of Navarra in the press; this one includes the quotation about his Bourbon nose.

Navarra was interviewed on 6/3/1952 on the TV programme *La Settimana Incom*, and the interview can be seen via the Istituto Luce archive website: 'Intervista con il Re di Poggio Reale'.

'Il Tesoro di S. Gennaro trasportato a Napoli dal "Re di Poggioreale"', *Roma d'Oggi*, 7/3/1947. 'Il fortunoso viaggio del tesoro di S. Gennaro', *Roma d'Oggi*, 8/3/1947. These are the only press articles I can find on the Navarra San Gennaro story that date from when the event is supposed to have happened.

Gangsterismo

H. Erickson, *Encyclopedia of Television Law Shows: factual and fictional series about judges, lawyers and the courtroom, 1948–2008*, Jefferson, N.C., 2009.

S. Gundle, 'L'americanizzazione del quotidiano. Televisione e consumismo nell'Italia degli anni Cinquanta', *Quaderni Storici*, vol. XXI (1986), p. 62. I could not avoid citing the most cited article in contemporary Italian studies!

E. Kefauver, *Crime in America*, New York, 1968 (original edn 1951). Quotations taken from pp. 14–21. (Published as *Il gangsterismo in America*, Turin, 1953.)

W.H. Moore, *The Kefauver Committee and the Politics of Crime, 1950–1952*, Columbia, 1974. The seagull death rattle quote is on p. 190 from a newspaper source.

G. Prezzolini, *Tutta l'America*, Florence, 1958, for Italy's borrowings from America.

G. Prezzolini, 'La "mafia" nel rapporto del senator Kefauver', in *America con gli stivali*, Florence, 1954.

G. Prezzolini, 'Una catena di delitti nei più ricchi docks del mondo', *Stampa Sera*, 11–12/2/1953.

'Sfilano gli "eroi" della democrazia americana', *L'Unità*, 7/4/1951.

2: 1955

The Monster of Presinaci

S. Castagna, *Tu devi uccidere*, Milan, 1967 (and Vibo Valentia, 2008). The contents of this memoir were widely reported in the press in 1955.

E. Ciconte, *'Ndrangheta dall'Unità a oggi*, Rome, 1992. On the 'Martians' see p. 245.

C. Guarino, 'Sulla intera Calabria l'ombra del 'Aspromonte', *Il Mattino*, 13/7/1955. On the state of law and order in Calabria.

S. Lanaro, *Storia dell'Italia repubblicana: dalla fine della guerra agli anni Novanta*, Venice, 1992. The statistics on poverty are from p. 165.

The physical description of Castagna is from *L'Unità*, 21/4/1955, and the 'problematic' existence of the Calabrian mafia is from *L'Unità*, 26/4/1955. The same paper provides detailed coverage of Castagna's rampage.

Aloi letter dated 16/4/1955 in ACS, Min. Int., Gabinetto, 1953–56, b. 4, fasc. 1066–1.

Prefect's report dated 14/5/1955 in *ibid.*, b. 4, fasc. 1066–1.

Mars attacks!

The archival sources I have consulted on the Marzano operation are the following:

ACS, Min. Int., Gabinetto, 1953–56, b. 4, fasc. 1066–1.

Ibid. (hereafter 'ACS Marzano'), b. 4, fasc. 1066–2.

Ibid., b. 293, fascc. 5160–23.

Ibid., b. 352, fascc. 6995–23.

Ibid., b. 363, fascc. 6995–66.

Report by Marzano to Min. Int. dated 6/9/55 in ACS Marzano, b. 4, fasc. 1066–2 for 'literally in the grip of terror' and further details of Marzano's work.

ACS Marzano: telegram 3/9/54 in b. 4, fasc. 1066–1, aftermath of Polsi pilgrimage the year before; telegram, 2/9/55 in b. 4, fasc. 1066–1, pilgrimage without incident; telegram 26/10/55 b. 4, fasc. 1066–1, arrest of Aloi blackmailers; telegram 25/9/55 in b. 4, fasc. 1066–1, identity card forger; prefect's telegram 19/9/55, b. 4, fasc. 1066–2, Marzano solo operation; letter 30/9/55 from Marzano to Tambroni. b. 4, fasc. 1066–2, Marzano's 'toadying' dispatch.

Capua story: report by prefect dated 4/1/56 in ACS Marzano, b. 363, fascc. 6995–66.

Capua's friendships with gangsters: prefect's report 20/9/55 in b. 4, fasc. 1066–2.

Catalano: see prefect's report to Min. Int. 28/10/55 in b. 4, fasc. 1066–2.

On raiding a house and finding notebook containing the 'ndrangheta's rules, see telegraph dated 29/5/1955, ACS Marzano, b. 4, fasc. 1066–1.

Some indications on the longer term ineffectiveness of the Marzano operation can be gleaned from ACS, Min. Int. Gab. 1957–60, b. 4, fasc. 11001/66, 'Relazioni prefetto Reggio Calabria 1957–60'.

G. Bocca, 'Delianova Paese del West', *L'Europeo*, 11/09/55.

G. Cervigni, 'Antologia della fibbia', *Nord e Sud*, 18, 1956 quotes Tambroni on 'showing no favours', p. 66, and the pastoral letter from the Archbishop of Reggio Calabria, p. 65.

E. Ciconte, *'Ndrangheta dall'Unità a oggi*, Rome, 1992, on the Marzano operation is essential reading for the whole episode. See particularly: sheets to warn of danger, p. 251; 'either you vote DC or I kill you', p. 273.

L. Radi, *Tambroni trent'anni dopo. Il luglio 1960 e la nascita del centrosinistra*, Bologna, 1990.

Sources consulted

Il Mattino provides interesting coverage of the whole Marzano operation, such as 'Nella zona dell'Aspromonte non esistono più "intoccabili"', 7/9/1955, on Romeo.

Sources on Corrado Alvaro:
C. Alvaro, 'La gran cuccagna degli usurai sul cumulo di antiche miserie', *La Stampa*, 30/11/1949: denies existence of Calabrian mafia.
C. Alvaro, 'La Fibbia', *Corriere della Sera*, 17/9/1955.
C. Alvaro, 'I briganti', *Corriere della Sera*, 18/5/1955.
C. Alvaro, *Ultimo Diaro (1948–56)*, Bompiani, Milan, 1959, for his memories of the 'ndrangheta including, intriguingly, the failure to elect the 'capo della provincia' in 1948. The same episode is treated in the fictional (?) short story 'Angelino' from *Parole di notte*, in C. Alvaro, *Opere, Romanzi brevi e racconti, Settantacinque racconti* (1955), Milan, 1994.
A. Balduino, *Corrado Alvaro*, Milan, 1965.
G. Carteri, *Corrado Alvaro e la Madonna di Polsi*, Soveria Mannelli, 1995.
G. Cingari, *La 'politica' di Corrado Alvaro*, Rome, 1978, especially S. Staiti, 'Un incontro con Alvaro' which reports Alvaro as saying during the Marzano operation that the Calabrian mafia, unlike the Sicilian, was 'un'autentica forma di cavalleria', p. 108.
A.M. Morace and A. Zappia (eds), *Corrado Alvaro*, Reggio Calabria, 2002.
L. Vento, *La personalità e l'opera di Corrado Alvaro*, Chiaravalle Centrale, 1979.

Sources on Nicola D'Agostino, the left-wing mayor of Canolo associated with organised crime (D'Agostino's son took part in the Montalto summit and was shot dead in 1976):
ACS, Min. Int., Direzione Generale Pubblica Sicurezza, Divisione Polizia Giudiziaria, Confino di Polizia e Confino Speciale per mafiosi (sez. II) 1945–56, D'Agostino Nicola, b. 4.
E. Ciconte, *'Ndrangheta dall'Unità a oggi*, Rome, 1992, pp. 265–
U. D'Errico, *Criminalità organizzata e politica in Calabria fra XIX e XX secolo*, Università degli Studi di Roma 'La Sapienza', Facoltà di Lettere e Filosofia – Corso di Laurea in Lettere, Cattedra di Storia Contemporanea (degree thesis), 2009.
A. Fiumanò and R. Villari, 'Politica e malavita ("L'operazione Marzano")', *Cronache meridionali*, II, 10, 1955.
N. Gratteri and A. Nicaso, *Fratelli di sangue*, Milan, 2010, on the D'Agostino clan.
E.J. Hobsbawm, *Primitive Rebels. Studies in Archaic Forms of Social Movement in the 19th and 20th Centuries*, London, 1965 (original edn 1959).
R. Longone, 'Il ministro Tambroni e il sottosegretario Capua in disaccordo nel valutare la situazione esistente nelle province calabresi', *L'Unità*, 10/9/1955.
G. Manfredi, 'Mafia e società nella fascia ionica della provincia di Reggio Calabria: il "caso" di Nicola D'Agostino', in S. Di Bella (ed.), *Mafia e potere: società civile, organizzazione mafiosa ed esercizio dei poteri nel Mezzogiorno contemporaneo*, 3 vols, Soveria Mannelli, 1983–4.

On another left-wing mayor associated with the Calabrian mafia, see the famous case of Pasquale Cavallaro from Caulonia in the following sources:

ACS, Min. Int., Dir. Gen. Pubblica Sicurezza, Divisione polizia giudiziaria, Confino per comuni e mafiosi, b. 47. Contains Fascist reports on Cavallaro's 'subversive' activities that led to his period of internal exile.

I. Ammendolia and N. Frammartino, *La repubblica rossa di Caulonia*, Reggio Calabria, 1975.

A. Cavallaro, *La rivoluzione di Caulonia*, Milan, 1987.

A. Cavallaro, *Operazione 'armi ai partigiani'. I segreti del Pci e la Repubblica di Caulonia*, Soveria Mannelli, 2009.

E. Ciconte, *All'assalto delle terre del latifondo. Comunisti e movimento contadino in Calabria (1943–1949)*, Milan, 1981.

P. Cinanni, *Lotte per la terra e comunisti in Calabria (1943–1953): 'Terre pubbliche' e Mezzogiorno*, Milan, 1977.

P. Crupi, *La repubblica rossa di Caulonia. Una rivoluzione tradita?*, Reggio Calabria, 1977.

G. De Stefano, 'La "repubblica di Caulonia"', *Il Ponte*, 1950.

O.R. Di Landro, *Caulonia. Dal fascismo alla repubblica*, Reggio Calabria, 1983.

A. Fiumanò and R. Villari 'Politica e malavita ("L'operazione Marzano")', *Cronache meridionali*, II, 10, 1955.

S. Gambino, *In fitte schiere*, Chiaravalle, 1981.

G. Mercuri, *Cavallaro e la repubblica di Caulonia*, Catanzaro, 1982.

S. Misiani, *La Repubblica di Caulonia*, Soveria Mannelli, 1994.

A. Paparazzo, 'Lotte contadine e comportamenti culturali delle classi subalterne. Il caso della rivolta di Caulonia' in M. Alcaro and A. Paparazzo (eds), *Lotte contadine in Calabria (1943–1952)*, Lerici, 1976.

V. Teti, 'La "banda" di Cavallaro', *Quaderni del Mezzogiorno e le Isole*, November, 1977.

Other documentation from the Fascist era on Cavallaro is in ACS, Min. Int., Dir. gen. amministrazione civile, Podestà e consulte municipali, Reggio Calabria, Caulonia, b. 241.

The President of Potato Prices (and his widow)

Il Mattino is the main contemporary source for my narrative from the time of both the murder and the trial. Like Marmo, I found Etta Comito's articles very perceptive. Federico Frascani wrote two articles that are important for understanding the role of the President of Prices: 'Due testimoni importanti', 14/4/1959; and 'Svelato il retroscena del mercato ortofrutticolo', 15/4/1959. For the trial more generally, see: E. Marcucc, 'Le lettere di Pupetta al fidanzato "Pascalone"', 14/4/1959, 'My nice Tarzan'; 'Drammatico confronto tra Pupetta e l'autista "Sansone"', 10/4/1959, 'You are all lying here'; E. Comito, 'Due mani nervose ed un fazzoletto', 9/4/1959; 'Pascalone confidò anche allo zio i nomi dei presunti mandanti', 22/4/1959, on 'Yul Brynner'; for the other figures of the trial and Gaetano Orlando, see various articles on 1/4/1959.

I supplemented *Il Mattino* with articles from other dailies from the period, such as 'Pupetta maresca piange e svela i segreti di spietate rivalità', *La Stampa*, 5/4/1959, 'I killed for love'.

S. Gambino, *La mafia in Calabria*, Reggio Calabria, 1975. On the wholesale markets in Calabrian towns.

C. Guarino, 'Dai mafiosi ai camorristi', *Nord e Sud*, 13, 1955, provides figures for the trade in fruit and vegetables through the market.

S. Lanaro, *Storia dell'Italia repubblicana: dalla fine della guerra agli anni Novanta*, Venice, 1992, on the recovering economy.

M. Marmo, 'La rima amore/onore di Pupetta Maresca. Una primadonna nella camorra degli anni cinquanta', *Meridiana*, 67, 2010. By far the most insightful source on Pupetta.

P. Ricci, 'La gran mamma. 150 anni di malavita napoletana', *Vie Nuove*, 1959, nos. 16–23.

I. Sales, 'La sfida: il mercato ortofrutticolo', in *Le strade della violenza. Malviventi e bande di camorra a Napoli*, Naples, 2006.

R. Trionfera, 'Sparava con due pistole per vendicare il marito', *L'Europeo*, 16/10/55.

G. Tutino, 'Camorra 1957', *Nord e Sud*, 37, 1957. Including on the cattle market in Nola.

The Pupetta affair also seems to have coincided with an increased interest in the so-called *magliari*: 'Più di cento corone da ieri in via Baldacchini', *Il Mattino*, 21/7/1955; 'Un carro a dieci cavalli per il "magliaro" Pasquale Balsello', *Il Mattino*, 22/7/55; 'Rivalità, rancori e vendette alla base del nuovo delitto dei "magliari"', *Il Mattino*, 8/7/1955; I. Montanelli, 'Le sorprendenti risorse dei famigerati "magliari"', *Corriere della Sera*, 8/10/1959.

3: THE MAFIAS' ECONOMIC MIRACLE

King Concrete

J. Chubb, *Patronage, Power and Poverty in Southern Italy*, Cambridge, 1982. On Naples and Palermo, the Young Turks and Ciccio Vassallo. 'State parasitism and organized waste', quoted by Chubb, p. 32 from A. Statera, 'Chi semina miliardi raccoglie onorevoli', *L'Espresso*, 23/6/1974.

V. Coco and M. Patti, *Relazioni mafiose. La mafia ai tempi del fascismo*, Rome, 2010. On Salvo Lima's father, p. 35.

L. D'Antone, *Senza pedaggio. Storia dell'autostrada Salerno–Reggio Calabria*, Rome, 2008.

P. Ginsborg, *A History of Contemporary Italy. Society and Politics, 1943–1988*, London, 1990. On the miracle.

Mafia e potere politico. Relazione di minoranza e proposte unitarie della commissione parlamentare d'inchiesta sulla mafia, Rome, 1976. On Ciccio Vassallo pp. 62–.

F. Rosso, 'Gli spietati clan di Sicilia', *La Stampa*, 14/3/1976. On Vassallo's life and the Riccobono family.

U. Santino and G. La Fiura, *L'impresa mafiosa*, Milan, 1990. On Ciccio Vassallo, pp. 128–.

J. Walston, *The Mafia and Clientelism: Roads to Rome in post-war Calabria*, London/New York, 1988.

A. Zagari, *Ammazzare stanca*, Rome, 2008. On his father near Varese.

'Relazione sulle risultanze acquisite nel corso dell'ispezione straordinaria svolto presso il comune di Palermo dal dottor Tommaso Bevivino', in Documentazione antimafia, vol. IV, tomo VI.

'Don Ciccio Vassallo impassibile attende "un colpo di telefono"', *Stampa Sera*, 10/6/1971 for the view from Monte Pellegrino.

'Cade colpito da due rivoltellate mentre torna dal brindisi di capodanno', *Stampa Sera*, 2/1/1956. On Calabrian flower-pickers.

'Avrebbe movente politico l'aggressione al segretario della dc di Bardonecchia', *Stampa Sera*, 3/9/1963. This and other articles in September 1963 from *La* Stampa describe the Corino attack.

'Ora c'è la mafia delle autostrade', *La Stampa*, 3/3/1970. 'When northern entrepreneurs come down to Calabria'.

Bardonecchia has become something of a classic case of mafia expansion, thanks to two excellent accounts that I have drawn on here:

R. Sciarrone, *Mafie nuove, mafie vecchie. Radicamento ed espansione*, Rome, 1998. 'We are the root of everything here', quoted p. 267.

F. Varese, *Mafias on the Move: How Organized Crime Conquers New Territories*, Princeton, NJ, 2011.

Gangsters and blondes

G. Dagel Caponi, *Paul Bowles. Romantic Savage*, Carbondale, Ill., 1994. 'I think all Europe's black-market profiteers are here', p. 146.

V. De Sica, *Lettere dal set*, Milan, 1987.

G. Diana, 'La storia del tabacco in Italia', *il Tabacco*, from issue 7(2), 1999. Five articles downloadable from the website of the Istituto Nazionale di Economia Agraria, http://www1.inea.it/ist/lista.htm

M. Figurato and F. Marolda, *Storia di contrabbando. Napoli 1945–1981*, Naples, 1981.

M. Gershovich, *French Military Rule in Morocco. Colonialism and its Consequences*, London, 2000.

N. Guarino, 'Sigarette di contrabbando: il traffico illecito di tabacchi a Napoli dal dopoguerra agli anni novanta', in G. Gribaudi (ed.), *Traffici criminali. Camorra, mafie e reti internazionali dell'illegalità*, Turin, 2009.

S. Gundle, *Bellissima: feminine beauty and the idea of Italy*, New Haven, Conn./London, 2007.

V. Paliotti, *Forcella, la kasbah di Napoli*, Naples, 1970.

C.R. Pennell, *Morocco since 1830. A History*, London, 2000.

L. Vaidon, *Tangier. A Different Way*, Metuchen, NJ, 1977.

'Graziata la donna che ogni anno diventava madre per evitare il carcere', *La Stampa*, 23/01/1958.

Sources consulted

Cosa Nostra: Untouchables no more

P. Arlacchi, *Addio Cosa Nostra. La vita di Tommaso Buscetta*, Milan, 1994. 'Realm of incomplete speech', pp. 84–5.

L. Bernstein, *The Greatest Menace. Organized Crime in Cold War America*, Boston, 2002. 'The intermarriages are significant', Federal Bureau of Narcotics agent Martin Pera, quoted p. 138; figures for organised crime indictments, p. 171.

R.F. Kennedy, *The Enemy Within*, New York, 1960.

S. Lupo, *Quando la mafia trovò l'America. Storia di un intreccio intercontinentale, 1888–2008*, Turin, 2008.

Mafia diaspora

A. Calderone with P. Arlacchi, *Gli uomini del disonore*, Milan, 1992. 'After 1963 Cosa Nostra in the Palermo area didn't exist any more', p. 72.

L. Gay, 'L'atteggiarsi delle associazioni mafiose sulla base delle esperienze processuali acquisite: la camorra', *Quaderni del Consiglio Superiore della Magistratura*, 99, 1996.

P. La Torre, *Comunisti e movimento contadino in Sicilia*, Rome, 1980.

S. Lodato, *Venti anni di mafia*, Milan, 1999. 'What's that? A brand of cheese?', p. 48.

S. Lupo, *Storia della mafia,* Rome, 1993.

P. Pezzino, *Mafia: Industria della violenza*, Florence, 1995.

F. Renda, *Storia della mafia*, Palermo, 1997.

W. Semeraro, 'Lo scandalo di Agrigento impallidisce dinanzi ai fatti che abbiamo in archivio', *Giornale di Sicilia*, 6/8/1966. 'The mafia in Sicily is a mental state'.

N. Tranfaglia, *Mafia, politica, affari*, Rome–Bari, 1992. Extracts from the final reports of the Parliamentary Commission of Inquiry quoted p. 55, p. 154.

'Dichiarazione del compagno La Torre', *L'Unità*, 1/7/1963. 'The truth is that there is no sector of the economy . . .'.

The mafia-isation of the camorra

P. Arlacchi, *Addio Cosa Nostra. La vita di Tommaso Buscetta*, Milan, 1994. 'Now we'd reached as many as 35–40,000 cases', p. 183; 'fraudster mentality' 'to play it sly', p. 185.

F. Barbagallo, *Il potere della camorra (1973–1998)*, Turin, 1999. On Zaza's turnover, p. 7.

A. Calderone with P. Arlacchi, *Gli uomini del disonore*, Milan, 1992.

P. Monzini, *Gruppi criminali a Napoli e a Marsiglia. La delinquenza organizzata nella storia di due città (1820–1990)*, Rome, 1999. Arlacchi quote, p. 127 provides the statistics for the turnover of tobacco smuggling.

Istruttoria Stajano.

I. Sales, *La camorra le camorre*, Rome, 2nd edn, 1993.

'Ritorna in prigione la contrabbandiera', *Corriere della Sera*, 28/6/1992. On the arrest of Concetta Muccardo on heroin-dealing charges.

The mushroom-pickers of Montalto

P. Arlacchi, *La mafia imprenditrice. Dalla Calabria al centro dell'inferno*, Milan, 2007 (original edn 1982). On 55% of the earthmoving and transport sub-contracts going to Piromalli, p. 104.

S. Boemi, 'L'atteggiarsi delle associazioni mafiose sulla base delle esperienze processuali acquisite: la 'ndrangheta', *Quaderni del Consiglio Superiore della Magistratura*, 99, 1996.

E. Ciconte, *'Ndrangheta dall'Unità a oggi*, Rome, 1992.

D. Gambetta, *The Sicilian Mafia*, London, 1993.

S. Gambino, *La mafia in Calabria*, Reggio Calabria, 1975.

La mafia a Montalto. Sentenza 2 ottobre del Tribunale di Locri, Reggio Calabria, 1971. 'There's no Mico Tripodo's 'ndrangheta here!' p. 27; 'superficial' and 'desultory', p. 128; 'restorative vaccine in the bodies of these criminal societies', p. 207; 'living symbol of organized crime's omnipotence and invincibility', p. 258; 'This is an argument that might seem like a travesty', p. 258.

S. Lupo, *Storia della mafia*, Rome, 1993. 'Repress what? An idea? A mentality?', p. 181.

F. Pierini, 'I mafiosi si difendono sull'Aspromonte. Non abbiamo sparato', *L'Europeo*, 13/11/69.

Processo Olimpia. 'This man was the overall boss', from 'Parte II°: Anni Settanta: 'Da Montalto al convegno di contrada Acqua del Gallo', p. 288, words of 'ndrangheta defector Giacomo Lauro.

F. Silvestri, 'Dinasty della Piara', *Narcomafie*, February, 1999.

'Sentenza, emessa il 22 dicembre 1968 dalla Corte di Assise di Catanzaro, nei confronti di Angelo La Barbera ed altri, imputati di vari omicidi, sequestri di persone, violenza privata ed altri reati', in Documentazione antimafia, vol. 4, tomo 17.

'Ora c'è la mafia delle autostrade', *La Stampa*, 3/3/1970. 'There is always someone who rebels against the monopoly held by some *cosche*'.

Mafiosi on the barricades

E. Ciconte, *Processo alla 'ndrangheta*, Rome–Bari, 1996.

F. Cuzzola, *Reggio 1970. Storie e memorie della rivolta*, Donzelli, Rome, 2007.

P. Ginsborg, *A History of Contemporary Italy. Society and Politics, 1943–1988*, London, 1990.

Processo Olimpia.

Sources consulted

The kidnapping industry

L. Ballinari and C. Castellacci, *Carceriere fuorilegge: la storia del sequestro di Cristina Mazzotti (Fatti e misfatti)*, Milan, 1978. 'Our conversations always came back to the crime of the moment', p. 39.

A. Calderone with P. Arlacchi, *Gli uomini del disonore*, Milan, 1992. 'The mafia doesn't run prostitution', p. 5; 'the mafia didn't have any money', pp. 85–6; Corleo kidnapping 'an extremely serious matter that created a huge shock in Cosa Nostra', p. 130.

O. Cancila, *Palermo*, Bari, 2000.

E. Deaglio, *Raccolto rosso: la mafia, l'Italia e poi venne giù tutto*, Milan, 1995.

B. Fontana and P. Serarcageli, *L'Italia dei sequestri*, Rome, 1991. On 650 citizens kidnapped by criminals, p. 214.

D. Gambetta, *The Sicilian Mafia*, London, 1993. '. . . this bloke must die', p. 178.

S. Gambino, *La mafia in Calabria*, Reggio Calabria, 1975.

N. Machiavelli, *The Prince*, translated by N.H. Thomson, New York, 1914.

G. Moroni, *Cronista in Calabria. Storie di 'ndrangheta, sequestri di persona, delitti eccellenti nel racconto di un giornalista-testimone*, Cosenza, 1993. 'I asked, I begged my jailers to cut my ear off. I was totally destroyed, I had lost all hope', p. 120; between 1969 and 1988, seventy-one people vanished and were never seen alive again, Pier Luigi Vigna cited p. 220.

J. Pearson, *Painfully Rich. J. Paul Getty and His Heirs*, London, 1995. 'I have fourteen grandchildren', p. 176.

Istruttoria Stajano.

O. Rossani, *L'industria dei sequestri*, Milan, 1978.

Berlusconi's views on Mangano ('[Mangano] was a person who behaved extremely well with us') were given during the radio programme *28 minuti*, *RadioDue*, 9/4/2008. Consulted via YouTube: http://www.youtube.com/watch?hl=it&gl=IT&v=PD4ixdKJzOE

'Rapito il figlio di Vassallo', *L'Unità*, 9/6/1971.

Tribunale di Palermo Il Sezione Penale, Sentenza nei confronti di Dell'Utri Marcello e Cinà Gaetano, 11 dicembre 2004. '. . . complex strategy destined to make an approach to the entrepreneur Berlusconi', p. 171.

The Most Holy Mother and the First 'Ndrangheta War

P. Arlacchi, *La mafia imprenditrice. Dalla Calabria al centro dell'inferno*, Milan, 2007 (original edn 1982). 'Paolo and Giorgio De Stefano attended university for a few years', quoted on p. 129; 3% cut of profits from construction of the Gioia Tauro steel works, p. 115.

L. Barone, 'L'ascesa della 'ndrangheta negli ultimi due decenni', *Meridiana*, 7–8, 1989–90.

S. Boemi, 'L'atteggiarsi delle associazioni mafiose sulla base delle esperienze processuali acquisite: la 'ndrangheta', *Quaderni del Consiglio Superiore della Magistratura*, 99, 1996. The quotation from Leonardo Messina, p. 13.

E. Ciconte, *Processo alla 'ndrangheta*, Rome–Bari, 1996. On 233 murders in three years, p. 108.

S. Gambino, 'Calabria: i nuovi "malavitosi"', *Il Ponte*, 11–12, 1976.

P. Ginsborg, *Italy and its Discontents*, Penguin. London, 2001. 'All the heads of the secret services, 195 officers of the various armed corps of the Republic', pp. 144–5.

Processo Olimpia. 'Bastardisation' of the Honoured Society's rules: the expression is from 'ndrangheta defector Gaetano Costa, p. 319.

R. Sciarrone, *Mafie nuove, mafie vecchie. Radicamento ed espansione*, Rome, 1998. For the comparative statistics on membership of Cosa Nostra and 'ndrangheta, pp. 53–4.

F. Silvestri, 'Dinasty nella Piana', *Narcomafie*, February, 1999. '. . . only his thigh bones were left over', p. 19.

'Caccia ai due killer del night di Reggio C.', *L'Unità*, 26/11/1974. For the Roof Garden attack.

A brief history of junk

Homer, *The Odyssey. Rendered into English Prose by Samuel Butler*, London, 1900. Book IV, verses 220–21.

C. Lamour and M.R. Lamberti, *The Second Opium War*, London, 1972. On 200,000 heroin addicts in USA by end of First World War, p. 7.

A.W. McCoy, *Drug Traffic. Narcotics and Organized Crime in Australia*, Sydney, 1980. In 1971, 10–15% of all US troops were using heroin, p. 23.

A.W. McCoy, *The Politics of Heroin: CIA complicity in the global drug trade*, New York, 1991.

P. Pezzino, *Mafia: Industria della violenza*, Florence, 1995. Reproduces important passages on narcotics from the Commissione Parlamentare d'Inchiesta.

C. Sterling, *The Mafia*, London, 1990. 'Narcotics track star', quoted p. 71.

D. Twitchett and J.K. Fairbank (eds), *The Cambridge History of China*, vol. 10, *Late Ch'ing, 1800–1911*, Part 1, edited by J.K. Fairbank. F. Wakeman Jr, 'The Canton trade and the Opium War'; J.K. Fairbank, 'The creation of the treaty system'. 'The most long-continued and systematic international crime of modern times', p. 213.

W.W. Willoughby, *Opium as an International Problem. The Geneva Conferences*, Baltimore, 1925. 'By 1924 no more than 110,000 addicts in the United States, p. 6.

Mr Champagne: Heroin broker

P. Arlacchi, *La mafia imprenditrice. Dalla Calabria al centro dell'inferno*, Milan, 2007 (original edn 1982). By 1980, Italy had more heroin addicts per head of population than did the United States, p. 187.

O. Barrese (ed.), *Mafia, politica, pentiti: la relazione del presidente Luciano Violante e le deposizioni di Antonio Calderone, Tommaso Buscetta, Leonardo Messina,*

Sources consulted

    Gaspare Mutolo: atti della Commissione parlamentare d'inchiesta sulla mafia, Soveria Mannelli, 1993. 'When it comes to drug trafficking, if deals are small then they can be managed by a Family', p. 420; 'God bless these prisons!', p. 497.

E. Deaglio, *Raccolto rosso: la mafia, l'Italia e poi venne giù tutto*, Milan, 1995.

L. Galluzzo, F. La Licata, S. Lodato (eds), *Rapporto sulla mafia degli anni '80*, Palermo, 1986. Suite in the five-star Michelangelo Hotel as his office, p. 322.

Istruttoria maxiprocesso, vol. 9. Ferrari Dino and Alfa Romeo GTV 2000, p. 1763.

L. Paoli, *Mafia Brotherhoods: organized crime, Italian style*, Oxford, 2003.

V. Scafetta, *U Baruni di Partanna Mondello. Storia di Mutolo Gaspare mafioso, pentito*, Rome, 2003. I've never felt fear the evening before a murder', p. 55; 'All you have to do is set up good relationships with a few local administrators', p. 61; 'Gentlemen, we have the chance to earn ten times as much with drugs', p. 63; 'if there are any rascals in the story, it's the Swiss', p. 62; 'Gaspare, promise me: as soon as you get out, call me', p. 65.

A. Stille, *Excellent Cadavers*, London, 1995. A fine journalistic reconstruction of the dramatic events in Sicily in the 1980s which I have drawn on for this chapter and several following.

The Transatlantic Syndicate

T. Blickman, 'The Rothschilds of the Mafia on Aruba', *Transnational Organized Crime*, Vol. 3, No. 2, 1997.

Corte Suprema di Cassazione, Seconda parte penale, Sentenza Andreotti, 15/10/2004. 'An authentic stable and friendly availability', p. 83.

Istruttoria maxiprocesso, vol. 5, p. 847. Reproduces the conversation in the ice-cream bar in Saint-Léonard, Montreal's Little Italy.

A. Jamieson, 'Cooperation Between Organized Crime Groups Around The World', *Jahrbuch für internationale Sicherheitspolitik*, December, 1999. For the international traces of the Transatlantic Syndicate, and the marriage of Pasquale Cuntrera's son, p. 68.

S. Lupo, *Quando la mafia trovò l'America. Storia di un intreccio intercontinentale, 1888–2008*, Turin, 2008. For an astute analysis of this episode, and (what Lupo calls) the 'third mafia'.

J.D. Pistone, *Donnie Brasco*, New York, 1989.

The Professor

F. Barbagallo, *Il potere della camorra (1973–1998)*, Turin, 1999. 7,000 NCO affiliates, p. 13.

E. Ciconte, *Processo alla 'ndrangheta*, Rome–Bari, 1996. Cutolo's initiation into the 'ndrangheta, pp. 108–10.

R. Cutolo, *Poesie e pensieri*, Naples, 1980.

S. De Gregorio, *Camorra*, Naples, 1981. Quotes the extracts from the psychiatric analyses of Cutolo, p. 34.

M. Jacquemet, *Credibility in Court. Communicative Practices in Camorra Trials*, Cambridge, 1996. Juvenile inmates in Campania, p. 29; Cutolo's living expenses in prison, p. 43.

M. Jouakim, *'O Malommo*, Naples, 1979.

A. Lamberti, '"Imposture" letterarie e "simulacra" poetici. Il ruolo di Ferdinando Russo nella costruzione dell'immaginario di massa sulla "camorra"', in P. Bianchi and P. Sabbatino (eds), *Le rappresentazioni della camorra*, Naples, 2009.

L. Rossi, *Camorra. Un mese a Ottaviano il paese in cui la vita di un uomo non vale nulla*, Milan, 1983. Contains the harrowing interviews with young *camorristi* I have quoted here, and has a very useful introduction on the 'South Bronxes' of Campania by Pino Arlacchi.

M. Savio (with F. Venditti), *La mala vita. Lettera di un boss della camorra al figlio*, Milan, 2006. This camorrista close to Cutolo is the source for Cutolo's challenge to 'o Malommo and his aptitudes as a 'talent scout', pp. 35–7.

La Stampa: on Cutolo's first murder, 'Sfiora una ragazza con l'auto, provoca un litigio e uccide il paciere', 25/2/1963 and 'Ergastolo all'automobilista che uccise a rivoltellate un passante dopo un incidente', 29/12/1965; on Cutolo as drug-dealer, 'Dirigevano dal manicomio il traffico di stupefacenti', 13/10/1974.

4: THE SLAUGHTER

Blood orgy

P. Allum and F. Allum, 'The resistible rise of the new Neapolitan Camorra', in S. Gundle and S. Parker (eds), *The New Italian Republic*, London, 1996. More than 900 died in the camorra wars of 1979–83, p. 238.

L. Brancaccio, 'Guerre di camorra: i clan napoletani tra faide e scissioni', in G. Gribaudi (ed.), *Traffici criminali. Camorra, mafie e reti internazionali dell'illegalità*, Turin, 2009. For deeper analysis of numbers.

Commissione parlamentare antimafia, Camorra e politica: relazione approvata dalla Commissione il 21 dicembre 1993, Rome, 1994. For the estimate of murders between 1981 and 1990, p. 3.

E. Deaglio, *Raccolto rosso: la mafia, l'Italia e poi venne giù tutto*, Milan, 1995. Estimate of total deaths in mafia wars and comparison with N. Ireland, p. 9.

P. Hofmann, 'Italy gets tough with the mafia', *New York Times*, 13/11/1983. For the opinions of Alberto Moravia.

F. Messina, 'Cosa Nostra trapanese: gli anni del dominio corleonese', unpublished PhD chapter, 2011.

Sutton Index of Deaths. Online resource for calculating number of victims in the Northern Ireland Troubles: http://cain.ulst.ac.uk/sutton/

'Palermo capitale mondiale dell'eroina', *La Stampa*, 10/10/1981. 'Blood orgy'.
'Altro omicidio ieri a Palermo', *La Stampa*, 31/12/1982. 'Don't die!'
The figures for the number of dead are from various dates in *La Stampa*.

Sources consulted

The new family: A group portrait

Corte di Assise di Santa Maria Capua Vetere, Sentenza contro Abbate Antonio, + 129, 'Sentenza Spartacus', 15/9/2005.

S. De Gregorio, *I nemici di Cutolo*, Naples, 1983. '. . . many of the crimes carried out by Umberto Ammaturo were, in reality, dreamed up in her head', p. 38; 'If Cutolo was here instead of me, you wouldn't be making such a racket', p. 33.

L. Gay, 'L'atteggiarsi delle associazioni mafiose sulla base delle esperienze processuali acquisite: la camorra', *Quaderni del Consiglio Superiore della Magistratura*, 99, 1996.

C. Longrigg, *Mafia women*, London, 1997.

D.A. Maradona, *El Diego*, London, 2004 (original edn 2000). 'I admit it was a seductive world', pp. 98–9.

M. Marmo, 'La rima amore/onore di Pupetta Maresca. Una primadonna nella camorra degli anni cinquanta', *Meridiana*, 67, 2010.

I. Sales, *Le strade della violenza: malviventi e bande di camorra a Napoli*, Naples, 2006. 'One day the people of Campania will understand that a crust of bread eaten in freedom' and 'In my eyes they were half *mafiosi*', p. 154; 'In Forcella it isn't possible to live without breaking the state's laws', p. 173.

'Ucciso e mutilato un uomo di Cutolo', *La Stampa*, 22/1/1982. 'Demented, diabetic fanatic'.

'Pupetta Maresca sfida il "boss" Cutolo', *La Stampa*, 14/2/1982.

'Il boss replica alla Maresca', *L'Unita*, 20/2/1982. 'Maybe Pupetta said those things to attract attention.'

'Morti ammazzati 515 e 130 desaparacidos di lupara', *Stampa Sera*, 7/1/1983. On 364 killed; Annamaria Esposito murder.

'Maradona alle nozze del boss', *L'Unità*, 14/3/1989.

'"Bambulella", il camorrista decapitato. Dopo 27 anni trovati i suoi assassini', *Corriere del Mezzogiorno*, 13/2/2009.

Catastrophe economy

F. Barbagallo, *Napoli fine Novecento: politici, camorristi, imprenditori*, Turin, 1997.

F. Barbagallo, *Il potere della camorra (1973–1998)*, Turin, 1999.

J. Chubb, 'Three earthquakes: political response, reconstruction and the institutions: Belice (1968), Friuli (1976), Campania (1980)', in J. Dickie, J. Foot, and F.M. Snowden (eds), *Disastro! Disasters in Italy Since 1860: culture, politics, society*, Palgrave, 2002.

Commissione parlamentare antimafia, Camorra e politica: relazione approvata dalla Commissione il 21 dicembre 1993, Rome, 1994. On Cirillo and patronage, p. 135; 'to demonstrate to Cutolo that he was finished', p. 165.

I. Sales, *La camorra le camorre*, (2nd edn), Rome, 1993. 'I'm not ruling out the fact that bumping him off would have been a pleasure for me', p. 80.

R. Saviano, *Gomorra: viaggio nell'impero economico e nel sogno di dominio della camorra*, Milano, 2006. On the lasting resonance of *Il camorrista*, p. 275.

M. Travaglio, 'Un altro martire', blog from www.voglioscendere.ilcannocchiale.it, 10/8/2008. For the extracts from judge's ruling on Gava.

La Storia Siamo Noi: Il caso Cirillo. TV documentary containing many interviews with protagonists at www.lastoriasiamonoi.rai.it/puntate/il-caso-cirillo/798/default.aspx. 'At number 275, Riviera di Chiaia, under a rubbish bin, you will find Communiqué number one.'

'Il Pci si chiede "Chi ha pagato?"', *La Stampa*, 25/7/1981. 'Without any negotiation and without any concession on the part of organs of the state faced with blackmail from an armed band'.

The Magliana Band and the Sacred United Crown

E. Ciconte, *Storia criminale. La resistibile ascesa di mafia, 'ndrangheta e camorra dall'Ottocento ai giorni nostri*, Soveria Mannelli, 2008. For very interesting observations on the increasing ties between the mafias, and on the Mala Vita.

'Commissione parlamentare d'inchiesta sul fenomeno della mafia e sulle altre associazioni criminali simiari', *Mafia, politica, pentiti: la relazione del presidente Luciano Violante e le deposizioni di Antonio Calderone, Tommaso Buscetta, Leonardo Messina, Gaspare Mutolo*, Soveria Mannelli, 1993. 'In Piedmont, the Calabrians have taken over the region', testimony of Leonardo Messina, pp. 321–2.

G. Di Fiore, *Io, Pasquale Galasso, da studente in medicina a capocamorra*, Naples, 1994. 'But what a race there was to suck up to Cosa Nostra', p. 141.

P. Ginsborg, *Silvio Berlusconi: television, power and patrimony*, London, 2005. The first was 'semi-clean', quoted from F. Tamburini, *Misteri d'Italia*, Milan, 1996.

M. Massari, *La Sacra Corona Unita: potere e segreto*, Rome, 1998. 'Never to allow any family from other regions to lord it over our territory', p. 15; 'At the time, Cutolo's men felt like they were Lord God Almighty', p. 17; 'He wanted me to draw a triangle, the sign of the Holy Trinity', pp. 18–19; 'eight unknown, invisible and well-armed men', p. 32.

'Rapporto del Questore di Bari al Procuratore del Re rivelante l'esistenza in Bari della Mala Vita', 22/8/1890. Reproduced in C. D'Addosio, *Il duello dei camorristi*, Napoli, 1893, pp. 141–. The Mala Vita was also widely covered in the press, even in the UK. Its emergence bears many similarities to that of the 'ndrangheta at the same time. The Mala Vita, however, does not seem to have put down roots.

R. Sciarrone, *Mafie nuove, mafie vecchie. Radicamento ed espansione*, Rome, 1998. 'In 1982 I took part in a meeting of all the Locals in Piedmont. About 700 people were there', p. 235.

Tribunale Penale di Roma, Ufficio Istruzione, Ordinanza-Sentenza contro Abbatino Maurizio + 237 (Banda della Magliana). 'We decided to try and carry out the same operation in Rome that Raffaele Cutolo was carrying out in Naples', p. 65.

'Così fu ucciso il duca Graziali', *Corriere della Sera*, 5/10/1993. 'Go home and wait. Your father will be freed in a few hours'.

5: MARTYRS AND PENITENTS

Mafia terror, 1979–81

A. Dino (ed.), *Pentiti. I collaboratori di giustizia, le istituzioni, l'opinione pubblica*, Rome, 2006.

Gruppo Abele (ed.), *Dalla mafia allo Stato. I pentiti: analisi e storie*, Turin, 2005.

H. Hess, *Mafia and Mafiosi. Origin, Power and Myth*, London, 1998. 'Sensation-hungry journalists, confused northern Italian jurists, and foreign authors', p. 3.

F. La Licata, *Storia di Giovanni Falcone*, Milan, 2002. A fine biography that I have used repeatedly in the following chapters. 'Ruining the Palermo economy', p. 61; 'Well I never. I was absolutely sure it was your turn', p. 54.

U. Lucentini, *Paolo Borsellino*, Cinisello Balsamo, 2003. Another fine biography that I have used repeatedly in the following chapters. 'I had married a man carved out of rock', p. 59.

S. Palazzolo, *I pezzi mancanti. Viaggio nei misteri della mafia*, Rome–Bari, 2010. 'Palermo's mafia organizations have now become pivotal in heroin trafficking, the clearing house for the United States', p. 39.

'Giornalista assassinato a Palermo', *L'Unità*, 27/1/1979.

'Noi politici siamo indifendibili', *L'Ora*, 10/3/1979. 'No longer live for the construction industry and off the construction industry'.

'S'intese col PCI e gli sparì l'auto', *Giornale di Sicilia*, 11/3/1979.

The fatal combination

G. Anremi, *La strategia vincente del Generale Dalla Chiesa contro le Brigate Rosse . . . e la mafia*, Rome, 2004.

P. Arlacchi *et al.*, *Morte di un generale. L'assassinio di Carlo Alberto Dalla Chiesa, la mafia, la droga, il potere politico*, Milan, 1982.

G. Bascietto and C. Camarca, *Pio La Torre. Una storia italiana*, Rome, 2008. 'In a couple of years, La Torre and I should be able to get the most important things done', pp. 26–7.

G. Bocca, 'Quell'uomo solo contro la mafia', *Repubblica*, 10/8/1982.

G. Burgio, *Pio La Torre. Palermo, la Sicilia, il PCI, la mafia*, Palermo, 2010. 'You're an intelligent lad. You'll go far', p. 47; 'We just can't stomach this party. Over there in Russia maybe. . .' p. 47.

C.A. Dalla Chiesa, *Michele Navarra e la mafia del corleonese*, ed. F. Petruzzella, Palermo, 1990.

C.A. Dalla Chiesa, *In nome del popolo italiano*, ed. N. Dalla Chiesa, Milan, 1997.

N. Dalla Chiesa, *Delitto imperfetto. Il generale, la mafia, la società italiana*, Milan, 1984. 'Get lost, *mafioso*!', p. 45; 'I've been to see Andreotti; and when I told him everything I know about his people in Sicily, he blanched', p. 34; 'What we were afraid of has happened', p. 122.

N. Dalla Chiesa, *Album di famiglia*, Turin, 2009.

C. De Simone, *Pio La Torre. Un comunista romantico*, Rome, 2002.

G. Frasca Polara, 'Una vita contro la mafia', *L'Unità*, 1/5/1982.

P. La Torre, *Comunisti e movimento contadino in Sicilia*, Rome, 1980.

P. La Torre, *Le ragioni di una vita*, Palermo, 1982.

M. Nese and E. Serio, *Il Generale Dalla Chiesa*, Rome, 1982. The anecdote about Dalla Chiesa's father's return to Italy, p. 9.

S. Palazzolo, *I pezzi mancanti. Viaggio nei misteri della mafia*, Rome–Bari, 2010.

D. Paternostro, *A pugni nudi: Placido Rizzotto e le lotte contadine a Corleone nel secondo dopoguerra*, Palermo, 2000.

P. Peci, *Io, l'infame*, Milan, 1983. 'His manner was severe but gentle, authoritative but kind', p. 189.

Pio La Torre. 30 aprile 1982. Ricordi di una vita pubblica e privata, Palermo, 2007.

D. Rizzo, *Pio La Torre. Una vita per la politica attraverso i documenti*, Soveria Mannelli, 2003.

Repubblica, 29/3/1982. 'There should be no political difficulties'.

Doilies and drugs

G. Ascheri, *Tortora. Storia di un'accusa*, Milan, 1984. 'Aggressive personality strongly influenced by delusions of grandeur', p. 46; 'My current status as a detainee who is still bound to the healthy principles of Honour', p. 39.

F. Coppola, 'Ecco perché Tortora è innocente', *Repubblica*, 18/12/1986.

M.V. Foschini and S. Montone, 'Il processo Tortora', in L. Violante (ed.), *Storia d'Italia. Annali 12. La criminalità*, Turin, 1997.

L. Galluzzo, F. La Licata, S. Lodato (eds), *Rapporto sulla mafia degli anni '80*, Palermo, 1986. On Buscetta's treatment in Brazil, see the interview with Falcone, p. 35.

M. Jacquemet, *Credibility in Court. Communicative practices in the Camorra trials*, Cambridge, 1996.

R. Lumley, 'The Tortora Case: The Scandal of the Television Presenter as Media Event', *The Italianist*, 6, 1986.

R. Lumley, 'The Tortora Case: Restoring the Image and Putting the System of Justice on Trial', *The Italianist*, 7, 1987.

Maxiprocesso: Tribunale Penale di Palermo, Ufficio Istruzione Processi Penali, Processo verbale di interrogatorio dell'imputato Tommaso Buscetta, 16/7/1984

'C'era una volta Portobello', episode of TV series *La storia siamo noi*: available at www.lastoriasiamonoi.rai.it

'Tra Tortora e il boss Cutolo stretta di mano all'Asinara', *Repubblica*, 3/12/1985. 'No, look, you're the boss'.

Walking cadavers

D. Dolci, *Banditi a Partinico*, Bari, 1955. On the *cassetta*, p. 282.

G. Falcone and M. Padovani, *Cose di Cosa Nostra*, Milan, 1991. 'Was like a language

Sources consulted

professor who allows you to go to Turkey without having to communicate with your hands'.

L. Forte, '20 anni fa', *Repubblica*, 28/7/2005. 'In Palermo there are about ten of us who are a real danger for the mafia'.

S. Lodato, *Trent'anni di mafia*, Milan, 2008. 'Everything conspires to individualize the struggle against the mafia', p. 120; 'Sooner or later all the investigators who really take their job seriously end up getting killed', pp. 166–7; 'We keep a very close eye on the worrying events surrounding both the build-up to the Palermo maxi-trial, and the maxi-trial against the camorra', pp. 166–7.

U. Lucentini, *Paolo Borsellino*, Cinisello Balsamo, 2003. 'We'd better resign ourselves to being walking cadavers', p 122.

S. Lupo, 'Alle origini del pentitismo', in A. Dino (ed.), *Pentiti. I collaboratori di giustizia, le istituzioni, l'opinione pubblica*, Rome, 2006.

V. Vasile, 'La normalità a Palermo', *L'Unità*, 8/8/1985. 'You knew Cassarà. And you understood.'

Antonino Caponnetto interview with Gianni Minà from 1992 available in various versions on YouTube. (Buscetta changed everything 'by opening the door for us from the inside'.)

'Gian Giacomo Ciaccio Montalto', episode of TV series *Blu notte*. Episode first transmitted in 2008. The street where he lay bleeding to death was a narrow one. Interview with Procuratore della Repubblica Bernardo Petralia.

The capital of the anti-mafia

N. Alongi, *Palermo. Gli anni dell'utopia*, Soveria Mannelli, 1997. 'Why are we [i.e. Communists] the only ones who talk about the mafia?', p. 95; 'Street crime, operating in the open, is almost inextricably tied in a complex web with occult manipulators', p. 16; 'For almost an hour the Cardinal waited in vain for the prisoners to leave their cells', p. 29.

P. Catalanotto, 'Dal carcere della Vicaria all'Ucciardone. Una riforma europea nella Palermo borbonica', *Nuovi Quaderni del Meridione*, 79, 1982.

L. Galluzzo, F. La Licata, S. Lodato (eds), *Rapporto sulla mafia degli anni '80*, Palermo, 1986. 'They have shown that, in the struggle against the mafia, party political labels are irrelevant', and the rest of the interview with Falcone, pp. 39–40.

A. Jamieson, *The Antimafia: Italy's Fight against Organized Crime*, London, 2000.

S. Lodato, *Trent'anni di mafia*, Milan, 2008. 'Palermo has always been the mafia's capital city. But I want to express my pride in its ability to be the capital of the antimafia too', p. 212; 'the Church is worried that holding such a big trial might attract too much concentrated attention on Sicily', p. 179; 'Today the mafia is fundamentally unconnected to power', p. 182.

Maxiprocesso: Tribunale Penale di Palermo, Ufficio Istruzione Processi Penali, Processo verbale di interrogatorio dell'imputato Tommaso Buscetta, 16/7/1984– 'The presence of so many Men of Honour in the Ucciardone at the same time further reinforces the links between them', p. 376.

U. Santino, *Storia del movimento antimafia*, Rome, 2009 (updated edn).

J.C. Schneider and P.T. Schneider, *Reversible Destiny: mafia, antimafia, and the struggle for Palermo*, Berkeley, CA, 2003.

F.M. Stabile, *I consoli di Dio*, Caltanissetta, 1999.

The rule of non-law

F. Barbagallo, *Napoli fine Novecento: politici, camorristi, imprenditori*, Turin, 1997.

F. Barbagallo, *Il potere della camorra (1973-1998)*, Turin, 1999.

F. Barbagallo, *Storia della camorra*, Rome-Bari, 2010. 'In the 1980s we realised that we had to "industrialise mafia activities"', p. 154.

Commissione parlamentare antimafia, Camorra e politica: relazione approvata dalla Commissione il 21 dicembre 1993, Rome, 1994. Estimate of number of camorra clans, p. 10; 'The camorra's activities create a generalized "rule of non-law"', p. 55; construction of Pianura without a single building licence, p. 61; 'a conurbation that can only be compared to some of the metropolises that have grown up rapidly and chaotically in South America or South-East Asia', p. 62; arrest of a former mayor, a chief of a local health authority and three bank managers, p. 47.

Corte di Assise di Santa Maria Capua Vetere, Sentenza contro Abbate Antonio, + 129, 'Sentenza Spartacus', 15/9/2005.

S. De Gregorio, *I nemici di Cutolo*, Naples, 1983.

D. Della Porta, *Lo scambio occulto: casi di corruzione politica in Italia*, Bologna, 1992.

G. Di Fiore, *Io, Pasquale Galasso, da studente in medicina a capocamorra*, Naples, 1994. 'Everyone remained autonomous. We weren't like the Sicilian mafia', p. 148.

L. Gay, 'L'atteggiarsi delle associazioni mafiose sulla base delle esperienze processuali acquisite: la camorra', *Quaderni del Consiglio Superiore della Magistratura*, 99, 1996. 'We felt like the Israelis facing up to the Arabs', said by Pasquale Galasso; Sicilian construction companies operating in Campania immediately abandoned the region.

Processo Olimpia. 'He lived to do justice because he was the armed emissary of the Madonna of Polsi', p. 517; 'Great fluctuations in power. Marriages to seal pacts. Secret alliances', p. 558; 'the war's protagonists, who had by now been decimated, were irrationally hitting victims chosen at random', p. 653.

I. Sales, *La camorra le camorre*, Rome, 1993. Figures on numbers of camorra clans, p. 7.

'Assalto alla villa del boss camorrista: tre morti e 2 feriti'. *L'Unità*, 11/6/1984.

'U maxi

G. Ayala, *Chi ha paura muore ogni giorno. I miei anni con Falcone e Borsellino*, Milan, 2008.

Istruttoria Stajano. 'For many a long year the state was practically absent from the struggle against the mafia', p. 328.

F. La Licata, 'La "finta giustizia" di Cosa Nostra', *La Stampa*, 4/10/1994.

G. Lo Forte, 'L'atteggiarsi delle associazioni mafiose sulla base delle esperienze processuali acquisite: la mafia siciliana', *Quaderni del Consiglio Superiore della Magistratura*, 99, 1996.

Sources consulted

Maxiprocesso: Tribunale Penale di Palermo, Ufficio Istruzione Processi Penali, Processo verbale di interrogatorio dell'imputato Tommaso Buscetta, 16/7/1984– 'The Salvos' role in Cosa Nostra is modest. Yet their political importance is huge, p. 465.

F. Viviano, *Michele Greco il memoriale*, Roma, 2008.

'Anti-mafia trial to open in Sicily', *New York Times*, 9/2/1986. 'The prosecution will try to prove how individual acts were part of a vast criminal conspiracy born centuries ago'.

'The Mafia is not dead', *Economist*, 15/2/1986. The Commission as 'semi-mythical', p. 55.

'Cast assembles for Mafia show trial', *Observer* 9/2/1986.

'Trial a challenge to might of mafia', *Guardian*, 10/2/1986. 'Overtones of a Barnum and Bailey production'.

'Anche Salvo non sa nulla', *La Stampa*, 21/6/1986. 'The Salvos paid all the political parties. Money to all of them: no exceptions'; 'You seem bored'.

'Sgomento a Palermo', *La Stampa*, 10/10/1986. 'And they call themselves Men of Honour!' 'We join the Domino family in their grief.'

'Maxiprocesso alla mafia', RAI documentary available on YouTube. Includes Michele Greco's infamous 'peace' wishes.

One step forward, three steps back

C. Duggan, *Fascism and the Mafia*, New Haven, London, 1989.

G. Falcone and M. Padovani, *Cose di Cosa Nostra*, Milan, 1991. 'I warn you, judge. After this interrogation, you will become a celebrity', p. 44.

L. Galluzzo, F. Nicastro, V. Vasile, *Obiettivo Falcone. Magistrati e mafia nel Palazzo dei veleni*, Naples, 1989. '. . . distorted protagonism' and 'personality culture', p. 205; 'no one is irreplaceable . . . there is no such thing as a demi-god', p. 267; 'Has he resigned? Things in Palermo are still trouble', p. 280.

F. La Licata, *Storia di Giovanni Falcone*, Milan, 2002. 'I am a walking corpse', p. 113; 'One step forward, three steps back: that's how the fight against the mafia goes', p. 120.

L. Sciascia, *A Futura memoria (se la memoria ha un futuro)*, Milan, 1989.

Falcone goes to Rome

Corte d'Assise di Caltanissetta, Sentenza nel procedimento penale contro Aglieri Pietro +40 (the trial for the murder of Falcone, his wife and bodyguards). 'Wage war on the state first, so as to mould the peace afterwards', p. 1242; 'destroy Giulio Andreotti's political faction led by Salvo Lima', p. 825.

P. Ginsborg, *Italy and its Discontents. Family, Civil Society and the State 1980–2001*, London, 2001.

A. Jamieson, *The Antimafia: Italy's Fight against Organized Crime*, London, 2000.

F. La Licata, *Storia di Giovanni Falcone*, Milan, 2002. 'Yes, I am Sicilian. And for me, life is worth less than this button', p. 14; 'My country has not yet grasped what has happened. This is something historic: this result has shattered the myth that the mafia cannot be punished', p. 163; 'Don't you understand? You must realise that an equilibrium has been broken, and the entire building could collapse', p. 166.

6: THE FALL OF THE FIRST REPUBLIC

Sacrifice

Corte d'Assise di Caltanissetta, Sentenza nel procedimento penale contro Aglieri Pietro +40 (for the details of the Capaci bomb). 'Giovanni, Giovanni', p. 146.

S. Lodato, *Venti anni di mafia*, Milan, 1999. 'The state seemed like a punch-drunk boxer', p. 305.

U. Lucentini, *Paolo Borsellino*, Cinisello Balsamo, 2003. 'While he carried out his work, Giovanni Falcone was perfectly well aware that one day the power of evil, the mafia, would kill him', pp. 260–62; 'It will be him first, then they will kill me', p. 243.

The collapse of the old order

R. Alajmo, *Un lenzuolo contro la mafia*, Palermo, 1993.

F. Barbagallo, *Storia della camorra*, Rome-Bari, 2010.

B. De Stefano, *I boss della camorra*, Rome, 2007.

G. Di Fiore, *Io, Pasquale Galasso, da studente in medicina a capocamorra*, Naples, 1994.

N. Gratteri and A. Nicaso, *La malapianta*, Milan, 2010. On invitation from Riina for 'ndrangheta to join massacre campaign, p. 63.

Gruppo Abele, *Dalla mafia alla Stato*, Turin, 2005. 'Everyone saw me, and I immediately thought: now they're going to arrest me', p. 461; 'Today I feel as if I am completely one of them, because when it comes down to it we're all running the same risks and fighting for the same cause', p. 469.

D. Parrini, 'Collaboratori e testimoni di giustizia. Aspetti giuridici e sociologici', in *L'altro diritto. Centro di documentazione su carcere, devianza e marginalità*, available at: www.altrodiritto.unifi.it/ricerche/law-ways/parrini/cap1.htm#60

Some of the sheets of protest hung up in Palermo in the summer of 1992 can be viewed here: http://www.rainews24.rai.it/it/foto-gallery.php?galleryid=165442&photoid=392267

'La mafia dichiara guerra allo Stato. Dopo Falcone, uccisi Borsellino e cinque agenti', *La Stampa*, 20/7/1992.

Negotiating by bomb: Birth of the Second Republic

S. Ardita, *Ricatto allo Stato*, Milan, 2011. 'After the second bomb we were genuinely all ready to be killed', p. 7.

Sources consulted

S. Colarizi and M. Gervasoni, *La tela di Penelope. Storia della Seconda Repubblica*, Rome, 2012. 'No agreement with the mafioso', p. 103.

Corte d'appello di Palermo, 29/6/2010. Sentenza d'appello nei confronti di Dell'Utri Marcello.

N. Farrell and B. Johnson, 'Forza Berlusconi', *The Spectator*, 6/9/2003. 'To do that job you need to be mentally disturbed, you need psychic disturbances,' p. 16.

P. Ginsborg, *Silvio Berlusconi: television, power and patrimony*, London, 2005.

Procura della Repubblica presso il Tribunale di Palermo, Memoria a sostegno della richiesta di rinvio a giudizio, 5/11/2012. 'The new pact of co-habitation between the state and the mafia was finally sealed', p. 20.

N. Tranfaglia, *La mafia come metodo*, Milan, 2012. 'The on-going negotiations were the main reason why the plan to eliminate Borsellino was accelerated', p. 129.

Tribunale di Palermo. II Sezione penale presieduta da Leonardo Guarnotta. Sentenza nei confronti di Dell'Utri Marcello e Cinà Gaetano, 11/12/2004.

I have also drawn on the newspaper coverage of the negotiations between the state and Cosa Nostra; the articles are too numerous to be cited here.

M. Fuccillo, 'Vogliono colpirmi a tutti i costi ...', *Repubblica*, 20/3/1994. We'll all vote for Berlusconi'.

7: THE SECOND REPUBLIC AND THE MAFIAS

Cosa Nostra: The head of the Medusa

E. Bellavia and M. De Lucia, *Il cappio*, Milan, 2009. 'Now you tell me that you've got a good level political contact', p. 244.

C. Caprì with P. Maisano Grassi, *Libero. L'imprenditore che non si piegò al pizzo*, Rome, 2011. 'For the lads shut up in the Ucciardone', p. 77.

A. Dino, *Gli ultimi padrini: indagine sul governo di Cosa Nostra*, Rome, 2012.

A. Dino, *La mafia devota: Chiesa, religione, Cosa Nostra*, Rome, 2008.

Direzione Investigativa Antimafia, Relazione secondo semestre 2011.

G. Falcone and M. Padovani, *Cose di Cosa Nostra*, Milan, 1991. 'Getting to know *mafiosi* has profoundly influenced my way of relating to other people', p. 70.

A. Galli, *Cacciatori di mafiosi*, Milan, 2012. 'The first rule for a boss is to never abandon his ground', p. 12.

P. Grassi, 'La svolta: ora Confindustria può cacciare le mele marce', *Corriere del Mezzogiorno*, 29/1/2010.

Procura della Repubblica presso il Tribunale di Palermo, Direzione Distrettuale Antimafia, N. 18038/08 R. mod. 21 D.D.A. Fermo di indiziati di delitto, art. 384 segg. c.p.p. Adelfio Giovanni + 98 ('Operazione Perseo'). 'If we all do our own thing, like the Neapolitans do', p. 1139; 'Provenzano never underwent a formal investiture by the other precinct bosses. So he exercised his supremacy in substance, but not officially', p. 26; 'a Commission to deal with the serious things, with situations, and that way we all stay friends', p. 1139.

Procura della Repubblica presso il Tribunale di Palermo, Direzione Distrettuale

Sources consulted

Antimafia, Fermo di indiziati di delitto, Casamento Filippo + 29, 2/2008 (Operazione 'Old Bridge').

A. Sabella, *Cacciatore di mafiosi: le indagini, i pedinamenti, gli arresti di un magistrato in prima linea*, Milan, 2008.

U. Santino, *Storia del movimento antimafia. Dalla lotta di classe all'impegno civile*, Rome, 2009 (updated edn).

United States District Court, Eastern District of New York, Indictment against Joseph Agate and others, 6/2/2008 (Operation 'Old Bridge').

My thanks to Chiara Caprì for passing on the quotation about Addiopizzo from the Cosa Nostra penitent.

Camorra: A geography of the underworld

F. Barbagallo, *Storia della camorra*, Rome-Bari, 2010. This source is used for the following chapters too.

R. Cantone, *Solo per giustizia*, Milan, 2008.

R. Cantone, *I gattopardi: uomini d'onore e colletti bianchi: la metamorfosi delle mafie nell'Italia di oggi*, Milan, 2010.

G. Gribaudi (ed.), *Traffici criminali. Camorra, mafie e reti internazionali dell'illegalità*, Turin, 2009. Especially the following essays: G. Gribaudi, 'Introduzione', 'criminal *savoir-faire*', p. 13; L. Brancaccio, 'Guerre di camorra: i clan napoletani tra faide e scissioni' for statistics on the murder rate, and the market in fake goods; G. Gribaudi, 'Clan camorristici a Napoli: radicamento locale e traffici internazionali'; A.M. Zaccaria, 'Donne di camorra'; R. Sommella, 'Le trasformazioni dello spazio napoletano: poteri illegali e territoriali', 22% in Campania in the 'black economy', p. 367; L. Mascellaro, 'Territorialità e camorra: una proposta di lettura geografica dell'attività criminale'; L. D'Alessandro, 'Città e criminalità: il commercio come chiave interpretativa', on magliari and today's international commerce; F. Beatrice, 'La camorra imprenditrice'; A. Lamberti, 'Camorra come "metodo" e "sistema"'; M. Arselmo, 'L'impero del calcestruzzo in Terra di Lavoro: le trame dell'economia criminale del clan dei casalesi', cites the Pasolini poem.

G. Marino, 'L' ordine di morte arrivò dal telefonino', *Repubblica*, 29/5/2002. Mentions 'gypsies', 'sows'.

M. Marmo, *Il coltello e il mercato. la camorra prima e dopo l'unità d'Italia*, Naples, 2011.

P.P. Pasolini, *Le Ceneri di Gramsci. Poemetti*, Milan, 1957.

C. Tucci, 'Draghi: la crisi ha reso le aziende più aggredibili dalla criminalità. Le mafie avanzano in Lombardia', *Il Sole 24 Ore*, 11/3/2011. 'Companies are seeing their cash-flow dry up, and their assets fall in market value', also quoted in Barbagallo, *Storia della camorra*, p. 270.

The video of Festival of Lilies can be viewed at: http://espresso.repubblica.it/multimedia/home/30547536

'Ketty, una trans capeggiava gli Scissionisti', *Corriere del Mezzogiorno*, 12/2/2009.

'Festa gigli: distrutto l'Insuperabile. Ma i fan sfilano comunque con i loro colori', *Corriere del Mezzogiorno*, 29/9/2012. 'The messages it sends, the hidden meaning of that wood and *papier mâché*'.

Sources consulted

Camorra: An Italian Chernobyl

F. Barbagallo, *Storia della camorra*, Rome-Bari, 2010.

R. Capacchione, *L'oro della camorra*, Milan, 2008. For the property portfolio that included forty-five apartments and a hotel, to a total value of £50 million, p. 167.

G. Corona and D. Fortini, *Rifiuti. Una questione non risolta*, Rome, 2010.

G. Gribaudi, 'Il ciclo vizioso dei rifiuti campani', *Il Mulino*, 1, 2008.

Meridiana, 64, 2009, *Napoli emergenza rifiuti*. Especially the following essays: G. Corona e M. Franzini, 'Capire l'emergenza rifiuti a Napoli. Un'introduzione'; D. Fortini (G. Corona, ed.), 'Ormai sono venti anni che il Paese è in emergenza rifiuti'; A. Di Gennaro, 'Crisi dei rifiuti e governo del territorio in Campania'; M. Andretta, 'Da *Campania Felix* a discarica. Le trasformazioni in Terra di Lavoro dal dopoguerra ad oggi'; D. Ceglie, 'Il disastro ambientale in Campania: il ruolo delle istituzioni, gli interessi delle organizzazioni criminali, le risposte giudiziarie', 'meteorite effect', p. 129; E. Giaccio, 'Chiaiano 2.0', 'The state is absent, but we are here', p. 152.

P. Rabitti, *Eco balle*, Rome, 2008.

The regional rubbish commissar's testimony to parliamentary inquiry: http://www.camera.it/_dati/leg14/lavori/stenbic/39/2004/0727/s020.htm 'It's a miracle even if 200 of the 2,316 people actually do any work'.

'Camera nega arresto a Cosentino. Il deputato: "Ringrazio Parlamento, non Lega"', *Repubblica*, 1/12/2012.

Biùtiful cauntri (2007), documentary film. 'Italian Chernobyl', stated by magistrate Donato Ceglie.

Gomorrah

A. Dal Lago, *Eroi di carta. Il caso Gomorra e altre epopee*, Rome, 2010.

D. Del Porto, 'Minacce camorriste a Roberto Saviano. Finisce sotto scorta l'autore di Gomorra', *Repubblica*, 13/10/2006. 'Iovine, Schiavone, Zagaria – you aren't worth a thing!'

J. Dickie, 'Gang rule', *The Guardian*, 12/1/2008. Some of the phrases in this chapter are borrowed from my own review of Saviano's book.

V. Faenza, 'Casalesi e l'affare rifiuti: "Inquinamento? Che ce ne frega, noi beviamo la minerale"', *Corriere del Mezzogiorno*, 4/2/2011.

M. Marmo, 'Camorra come Gomorra. La città maledetta di Roberto Saviano', *Meridiana*, 57, 2006.

U. Santino, *Don Vito a Gomorra. Mafia e antimafia, tra papelli, pizzini e bestseller*, Rome, 2011.

R. Saviano, *Gomorra: viaggio nell'impero economico e nel sogno di dominio della camorra*, Milano, 2006.

http://www.ossigenoinformazione.it/ for up-to-date information on threats to journalists.

'Ndrangheta: Snowstorm

T. Bendinelli, 'Cocaina, Brescia "sniffa" 625 mila euro al giorno', *Corriere della Sera*, 11/12/2012.

A. Bolzoni, 'Palermo chiama Medellin', *Repubblica*, 23/2/1990. On *Big John*.

D. Brown, unpublished research paper on Calabrian *mafiosi* in Queensland in the 1930s.

E. Ciconte and V. Macrì, *Australian 'ndrangheta: i codici d'affiliazione e la missione di Nicola Calipari*, Soveria Mannelli, 2009.

F. Forgione, *Mafia Export. Politici, manager e spioni nella Repubblica della 'ndrangheta*, Milan, 2012. 'We've lost face here . . . we've lost everything', p. 64.

N. Gratteri and A. Nicaso, *Fratelli di sangue*, Milan, 2009. On Joe Musolino, p. 237.

A. Nicaso, *'Ndrangheta. Le radici dell'odio*, Rome, 2007.

G. Pignatone and M. Prestipino, *Il contagio. Come la 'ndrangheta ha infettato l'Italia*, Rome-Bari, 2012. On 2,000 kg cocaine confiscated in 2011, p. 91.

Processo Olimpia. For Giacomo Lauro testimony, esp. Chapter 7.

A. Sabella, *Cacciatore di mafiosi: le indagini, i pedinamenti, gli arresti di un magistrato in prima linea*, Milan, 2008.

R. Sciarrone, *Mafie nuove, mafie vecchie. Radicamento ed espansione*, Rome, 1998. On 5,500 kg of 82% pure cocaine in a container lorry near Turin, p. 245.

Istituto di ricerche farmacologiche 'Mario Negri', Milan. A report on the research on cocaine in the Po is available at: http://www.marionegri.it/mn/it/pressRoom/comStampa/archivioComunicat05/cocainaPo.html

'Ndrangheta: The Great Crime

L. Abbate, 'Calabria: la strage delle donne', *Espresso*, 24/7/2012.

F. Forgione, *'Ndrangheta. Boss, luoghi e affari della mafia più potente al mondo. La relazione della Commissione Parlamentare Antimafia*, Milan, 2008.

Meridiana, 67, 2010, *Donne di mafia*. A series of essays with the most up-to-date research on women and all the mafias. For the 'ndrangheta see especially: O. Ingrascì, 'Donne, . . . 'ndrangheta, 'ndrine. Gli spazi femminili nelle fonti giudiziarie'.

G. Pignatone and M. Prestipino, *Il contagio. Come la 'ndrangheta ha infettato l'Italia*, Rome-Bari, 2012.

Procura della Repubblica presso il Tribunale di Reggio Calabria, Direzione Distrettuale Antimafia, Decreto di Fermo di indiziato di delitto, Agostino Anna Maria + 155 (Operazione Crimine).

Tribunale di Reggio Calabria, Sezione Gip - Gup. Sentenza resa nell'Operazione Crimine contro Agnelli Giovanni + 126, 8/3/2012. 'In Calabria they get together, but not to say, "What are we going to do?"', p. 101; 'a woman gives birth, but the umbilical cord is never cut', p. 101; on Tony Vallelonga, pp. 819–20.

Sources consulted

'Arrestato Tony Marciano, il "re dei neomelodici" cantava per il clan', *Corriere del Mezzogiorno*, 4/7/2012.

The video of the Polsi meeting in 2009 can be watched at: http://www.youtube.com/watch?v=A790XiOt5WI

The video of the 2009 meeting in Paderno Dugnano can be watched at: http://www.youtube.com/watch?v=aR7WQhq7TTI

Welcome to the grey zone

E. Bellavia and M. De Lucia, *Il cappio*, Milan, 2009. On truck thefts, p. 103.

G. Bianconi, 'Così si mimetizzano le mafie. Silenzi, complicità, omissioni: perché il contagio si allarga', *Corriere della Sera*, 12/11/2011. 'I'm less worried by the response from the criminal organizations than by the response from politicians'; 'the mafia method, which involves promoting illicit privileges and cancelling out competition'.

P. Davigo and L. Sisti, *Processo all'italiana*, Rome-Bari, 2012.

N. Delgrande and M.F. Aebi, 'Too much or not enough? Overcrowding in European prisons. An analysis based on SPACE statistics', Université de Lausanne, Institut de criminologie e de droit pénal, downloadable from http://ebookbrowse.com/overcrowding-cdap-rome-delgrande-121020-3-pdf-d432188927

G. Di Girolamo, *Matteo Messina Denaro. L'invisibile*, Rome, 2010.

A. Dino, *Gli ultimi padrini: indagine sul governo di Cosa Nostra*, Rome, 2012.

L. Franchetti, *Condizioni politiche e amministrative della Sicilia*, vol. 1 of L. Franchetti and S. Sonnino, *Inchiesta in Sicilia*, 2 vols, Florence, 1974.

C. Macrì, '"Rapporti sospetti con le cosche". Sciolto il Comune di Reggio Calabria', *Corriere della Sera*, 9/10/2012.

G. Pignatone and M. Prestipino, *Il contagio. Come la 'ndrangheta ha infettato l'Italia*, Rome-Bari, 2012. On Calabrian delegates of ANCE, p. 87.

A. Sabella, *Cacciatore di mafiosi: le indagini, i pedinamenti, gli arresti di un magistrato in prima linea*, Milan, 2008. 'When you come to our schools to talk about justice and the rule of law', p. 246.

A. Ziniti, 'Processo Talpe alla Dda, 7 anni a Cuffaro, riconosciuto il favoreggiamento alla mafia', *Repubblica*, 23/1/2010.

'Cosa Nostra, in manette l'erede di Riina', *Repubblica*, 14/4/1998. 'The experience of the last twenty years has helped us understand that there is never a time for triumphalism'.

Ministero dell'Interno, Approfondimento. Direzione Centrale della Poliza Criminale – Programma Speciale di Ricerca – MESSINA DENARO MATTEO: www.interno.gov.it/mininterno/export/sites/default/it/sezioni/sala_stampa/notizie/polizia/latitante matteo_messina_denaro.html 'mafia association, murder, massacre, devastation . . .'

Direzione Investigativa Antimafia, Relazione secondo semestre 2011. On 2,246 cases of vandalism followed by arson in Sicily, p. 24.

World Bank, *Doing Business 2012*. Report downloadable from http://www.doingbusiness.org/ For statistics on Italian legal system.

www.addiopizzo.org/ For updates on subscriptions.

Index

Index

Index

Index

Index

Index

John Dickie

Cosa Nostra

'Monumental and gripping.'
Andrew Marr

'I couldn't put it down. His archival sleuthing is yoked
to his powerful, often coruscating storytelling to create a
chilling account of the mafia's sinister, horrific reality.'
Sunday Times

'COSA NOSTRA is the best book ever written
on the mafia.'
Il Manifesto

Hodder & Stoughton paperback and Ebook
www.hodder.co.uk

John Dickie
Delizia!

'Mouthwatering . . . like lunch in the green hills above
Lake Como, or dinner at the horseshoe bays of Sardinia,
Dickie's book is sheer pleasure.'
Financial Times

'Full of fascinating detail.'
Independent

'Informs as well as enlightens . . . a clever and provoking
account of Italy's history.'
Guardian

Hodder & Stoughton paperback and Ebook
www.hodder.co.uk

John Dickie
Mafia Brotherhoods

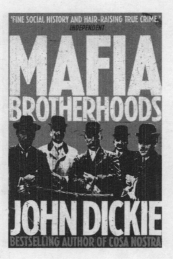

'Fine social history and hair-raising true crime.'
Independent

'His narrative bowls along, powered by the sort of
muscular prose one associated with great detective
fiction. An exhilarating history.'
Financial Times

Hodder & Stoughton paperback and Ebook
www.hodder.co.uk